FROM TRAUMA TO FREEDOM

FROM TRAUMA TO FREEDOM

ONE WOMAN'S JOURNEY
AND A HOLISTIC GUIDE TO HEALING

Kristina Lea & Heather Ensworth, PhD

Copyright © 2020 Kristina Lea and Heather Ensworth, Ph.D.

All rights reserved. No part of this publication may be reproduced, distributed, or transmitted in any form or by any means, including photocopying, recording, or other electronic or mechanical methods, without the prior written permission of the publisher, except in the case of brief quotations embodied in critical reviews and certain other noncommercial uses permitted by copyright law. For permission requests, write to the publisher at the address below.

ISBN: 978-1-7346532-3-6 (paperback)
ISBN: 978-1-7346532-8-1 (ebook)

Front cover image and book design by Lance Buckley

Printed by Rising Moon Healing Center in the United States of America

First printing edition March 2020

Publisher:
Rising Moon Healing Center
PO Box 2116
South Hamilton, MA 01982

www.risingmoonhealingcenter.com
www.open2truefreedom.com

*For those wanting to heal and
for those seeking to be a healing presence on this planet*

Acknowledgements

Kristina: To my children, who from the time of their births have deepened and expanded my life and love more than I ever believed possible. They give me hope for the world, knowing the potential of the next generation. My deepest gratitude for Heather Ensworth, for her wisdom, years of experience, and passion for the well being of the planet, who holds an unwavering faith in the capacity of humanity to make positive change. Without her this book in its fullness would not have been made possible. To Mark for the many years of steadfast support in my healing, especially in the darkest hours, and for always believing in my writing and ability to help others. To Greta and Kimberly whose wise and compassionate support guided me in navigating the stormy waters of healing my childhood trauma. To those that held sacred space for me to feel seen, heard, and validated in my experience, this in and of itself was crucial to my healing and ability to let go of the past. And to those that pointed the way to true freedom, that went beyond healing, eventually being able to let go of everything that kept me in suffering.

Heather: It has been a profound process to write this book. I am deeply grateful to Kristina, for her courage and commitment to healing herself and then birthing this book and bringing her healing gifts and wisdom to others. It has been a life-changing experience to know her and to co-author this book with her.

Across the years, my life has been deeply transformed by the many people that I have been with in my therapy practice. They have taught me so much about the journey of healing and living consciously. I am also grateful for the healers and teachers from around the world who have helped me to deepen my understanding of the healing process. Kristina and I are very grateful to Stephen and Hayden for their support and creative contributions and are also thankful for Emily Han and Edith Griffin for their invaluable help and support with the copy editing. We are also thankful for Lance Buckley for all of his excellent work with the cover design and formatting of the book.

Finally, I am profoundly grateful for the love and wisdom of the Earth, the sky and the Spirit in all of life, and for how they hold us and guide us in our journeys of healing and evolution, individually and collectively.

Table of Contents

CHAPTER 1   **The Healing Journey**   15

  Our Stories   21
      Kristina's story   21
      Heather's story   29
  How this book came into being   31
  Understanding Trauma and Healing   33
      Trauma   33
      Healing   38
      Healing vs. comfort   41
      Pain vs. suffering   43
      There are many ways to heal   45
      The notion that the healing path should progress in a clear linear way   45

CHAPTER 2   **The ARCH Model**   46

  A - Alignment   47
  R - Relationship   49
  C - Consciousness   49
  H - Healing   50
  Coming to center   51
  How to use this book   53
  Embarking on the journey   54

Chapter 3 A - Alignment 57
Deepening your alignment with pure consciousness and being centered *61*
Working with Alignment in the ARCH medicine wheel *68*

Chapter 4 R - Relationship 69
Spectrum of how trauma in relationship may manifest *70*
Forms of healing relationships *74*
   Professional relationships with a therapist or healing practitioner *74*
   Personal relationships with a friend, family member, partner, or lover *81*
   Groups: therapy groups, sacred circles *83*
   Mentors or spiritual teachers *84*
   Relationship with animals, plants, and Mother Earth *87*
Characteristics of a healing relationship *91*
   Trust *91*
   Safe and clear boundaries *92*
   The importance of the witness self *95*
   Respect and avoiding re-enactment of the trauma *96*
   Taking responsibility for your own process and healing journey *96*
   Listening *99*
   Mirroring and empathic attunement *101*
   Avoiding projections *104*
   Having appropriate expectations *107*
   Allowing mistakes, holding yourself with compassion, and repairing the relationship *109*
   Having healthy relationships modeled *110*

Chapter 5 C - Consciousness 112
Topography of the Self *112*
   Levels of consciousness *114*
   Levels of reality *115*
   The nature of trauma and its impact on memory *120*
   Ways to bring what has been lost or buried into consciousness *124*

Ways to listen to your deeper self and recover buried thoughts, memories, and emotions   *127*
Working with parts to heal   *136*
Gathering information and creating a coherent narrative   *156*
Strengthening the witness self as you do the deep inner work   *167*

CHAPTER 6 H - Healing   208

Preparation: Creating a healing environment   *209*
   De-stress your current life   *209*
   Create a support team   *211*
   Build safety in your life   *212*
   Returning again and again to Alignment to support your healing process   *214*
Working with challenges to healing   *218*
   Dealing with triggers, dissociation, depression, anger, dreams, nightmares, and flashbacks   *218*
Some common blocks or obstacles to the healing process   *258*
   Denial   *259*
   Confusion   *261*
   Fear   *262*
   Blame   *262*
   Shame   *264*
   Acting out   *266*
Other challenges in the healing process   *267*
   Hitting times of crisis   *267*
   Suicidal thoughts or feelings   *270*
   Working with addictions   *272*
   Sexual intimacy   *273*
Honoring the process   *281*
Opening more fully to heal   *281*
   Healing is an act of courage   *281*
   The importance of being seen, heard, and having a voice   *286*
   Managing the stormy times in the healing journey   *290*
   The ebb and flow of the healing journey   *298*

Healing on all levels: emotional, physical, mental, and spiritual   *301*
   Healing at the emotional level   *301*
   Healing at the physical level   *301*
   Healing at the mental level   *312*
   Healing at the archetypal and spiritual levels   *319*

CHAPTER 7 Integration - Coming to Center 340

Integrating the parts work   *341*
Developing new beliefs and healthy patterns   *341*
Developing new coping mechanisms   *342*
Integrating feelings and memories   *348*
Grief and letting go   *348*
The issue of forgiveness   *350*
Developing more consciousness and a stronger sense of Self   *356*
Living with gratitude   *356*
Measuring progress   *358*
Living in the mystery   *361*
Gifts of the healing journey   *364*
Opening to joy   *370*

CHAPTER 8 Conclusion 371

Moving beyond the individual Self:
   Healing the collective and the Earth   *371*

Appendix   376

Meditation practices   *376*
   Meditation to align with your center, the Earth and Sky and Source   *376*
   Meditation to de-stress and align with stillness   *377*
   Meditations for moving through depression   *379*
Working with Sacred Circles   *381*
   Being in a Sacred Circle   *381*

About the Authors   385

The Prophecy of the Rainbow Warriors

"This is the way I've heard the legend pass down through the ages. A time will come when the Earth and all of life will need our help. At this time, a tribe will gather from all cultures of the world. They will be recognized by their spirit connection and life-giving actions towards the finned, the winged, the creeping crawling, the standing green growing, the four legged, the two nations and all that is. They will awaken humankind to find a star inside themselves. This star will guide them to overcome the mountains of ignorance, prejudice, hatred and fear through compassion, harmony and honor. They will find a new song and a new dream. The beautiful bow that hangs in the sky after a storm is a monument to these ones. I believe we are living in this time now. All of us with this vision are the tribe, we are the rainbow warriors, we will heal the world. We are the cherished dream and the vision of the ancient ones of long ago."

—Silver Song Cree Blackfoot

The wound is the place where the Light enters you. —Rumi

CHAPTER 1

The Healing Journey

The rainbow is a symbol of healing and the peace that comes after a storm. It gives the promise that the sun will return to bring light into the darkness, and that there will be calm after the powerful forces of wind and rain. In a similar way, this book is meant for those who have experienced the emotional turbulence of trauma. Like the rainbow, it is a message of hope and a reminder that it is possible to heal from the wounds of the past. It is only when we each heal from our wounds that we can support the healing of our world and our planet. Otherwise, we reenact our unresolved trauma with and on each other. To choose to heal is to honor your deepest self and is also an act of compassion for the world. To heal and move into wholeness is to become a member of the "rainbow tribe" spoken of by the Native American prophets who knew that only those who have come through the storm and carry the energy of the "rainbow" can bring hope, healing, and enlightenment to a wounded world.

This book is the story of a woman who has walked through the dark underworld of trauma and knows the storms that can shatter the self and bring relentless waves of pain, confusion, despair, and fear. She has come through the turmoil and now lives with a sense of peace and openness to life and joy. She has courageously chosen to bare her soul and share her experience of her years of healing in order to hold that rainbow light for others to follow. This is both Kristina Lea's story of her healing journey and the distillation of what was most helpful to her in her process as well as what she has learned from her work as an energy practitioner helping to support others in their recovery from trauma. This book is also Kristina's collaboration with Heather Ensworth, a clinical psychologist who has been on her own healing path and has spent the last thirty years guiding and holding others in their healing journeys. Heather shares her professional expertise and years of experience listening deeply to others as she witnessed those who have courageously navigated the tumultuous aftermath of trauma.

Each one of us has experienced pain and some level of trauma. All of us are wounded, and yet we are also whole. Deep within, we have a part of us that remains pure and untouched by the traumas of life. This book is a holistic guide for how to work through the layers of trauma and heal on all levels—physically, emotionally, cognitively, relationally, and spiritually. It is also a reminder that we all hold an inner light, a consciousness, that cannot be diminished by the darkness of life. To come into the fullness of who we are, we need to honor the pain and trauma that we have felt and experienced, and open to healing on all levels. At the same time, we need to remember our inner stillness, the calm center in the eye of the storm that holds the light of love, peace, and connection, even in the darkest night of the soul. Through healing, we become more integrated with this centeredness and with the wholeness of who we are. Through remembering our wholeness, we have the courage and ability to face the winds and challenges of the healing process and be set free from fear and suffering.

HEATHER: In this book, Kristina and I have combined our backgrounds and experiences to share our ever-deepening understanding of the process of healing and returning to wholeness. We discuss what we have learned from our own inner work as well as what we have discovered through the profound experiences of supporting others to heal and be centered in the truth of their unique being. We present an approach that we call the ARCH model that consists of four primary components for the recovery from trauma:

Alignment: Remembering the inner stillness and centered wholeness of who you are beneath and beyond your personality and wounds

Relationship: The importance of having healing relationships to support you

Consciousness: Bringing into awareness the wounds that are buried within and reclaiming the lost parts of yourself

Healing: Having the specific tools and approaches that you need for your healing and integration process

This book, like each of us, is unique and does not fit into any neat box or category. It is not a traditional psychology book on the treatment of trauma. However, it does incorporate many of the stages and techniques of other trauma therapy models, such as the understanding of the stages of working through trauma (as described in models by Herman, Brier and others), including the importance of first establishing safety and stabilization, then working through the emotions and memories of the trauma, and finally moving into integration and healing. This model also includes many techniques and approaches used in cognitive-behavioral, psychodynamic, and holistic approaches. For example, it includes practical behavioral steps and ways to work at the cognitive level to shift false beliefs and negative thoughts. It also includes recent neurological and neuropsychological research on the polyvagal and limbic systems and the importance of ways to calm the physiological and neurological effects of trauma. An understanding of the effects of early trauma on attachment and early development are also an important part of this model. It also incorporates many aspects of psychodynamic, self-psychology, and self-in-relation theories and approaches to trauma therapy, such as the importance of a healing therapeutic relationship, as well as how to increase emotional self-regulation and how to work on the developmental impacts of trauma, such as regaining a strong sense of self and healing relational patterns.

At the same time, this book reflects Kristina and Heather's personal and professional experiences of the limitations of traditional psychology and psychiatry. These can be helpful and necessary methods to recover from trauma but are not always sufficient. Too often, those seeking to work through their trauma in more traditional therapy (especially cognitive-behavioral therapy) find little support in how to understand the meaning of their trauma or how to disidentify from the experience of being a "victim." Also, certain levels of healing may occur in the body and in the psyche, while the soul might still feel tethered to the wounds, leaving one feeling unable to regain a sense of wholeness and oneness with life.

The ARCH model is holistic in nature and includes many elements of spiritual healing approaches as well as energy healing modalities. There is a growing trend toward integrative models for therapy—for example, mindfulness meditation combined with psychotherapy, or models such as psychosynthesis and Internal Family Systems— focused on bringing the parts of the self into consciousness. These are valuable integrative approaches, and the ARCH model incorporates a conceptual and energetic framework that can accommodate all of these theories and approaches in a simple and flexible way that is accessible to those who are in therapy as well as those who are seeking to do healing work on their own.

Therefore, just as this book is not a traditional clinical or academic book on trauma therapy, it is also not a typical self-help book or a spiritual guide to healing. We do not believe that applying certain self-help practices or being on a spiritual path is enough to heal the trauma from the past. Self-help books often fall short of being able to help people access the unconscious or split-off parts of themselves. Kristina and I have also witnessed many times how people in spiritual or meditation groups may learn to move into altered states and into spiritual levels of consciousness yet become increasingly more detached from the layers of pain and trauma within, which leads to becoming disconnected from the self, others, and not being grounded in reality. We have also observed how people in meditation may unexpectedly become flooded and overwhelmed when buried trauma and intense emotions begin to surface, and then not have the tools or emotional support to process the memories and feelings. Without adequate guidance in working with these deeper emotional layers, people often engage in a process of "spiritual bypass" and intentionally or unconsciously try to transcend the trauma, ending up in a state of dissociation or lacking an integrated sense of self.

While this book incorporates the spiritual aspect of healing, it is not advocating any religion or any particular approach to spirituality. Rather, it is an effort to guide you to understand the fullness of who you are and how to integrate all of the layers of healing in your own unique way. This book can be used and modified no matter what religion or spiritual practices you follow.

The ARCH model is also a modern version of the ancient wisdom of the medicine wheel. The medicine wheel is still honored as a healing path in many indigenous cultures and is used as a process of moving into wholeness. It involves reconnecting with all of the parts of yourself as well as remembering your place in connection with the Earth and the cosmos. It is a path of healing, reconnection and integration. This model therefore combines all the understanding of modern forms of healing as well as ancient wisdom and healing traditions that have been with us for thousands of years.

The model that we are presenting includes all aspects of the self—spiritual, emotional, mental, physical, and relational. At the deepest level, this model is a guide to support the compassionate acceptance of all of who we are by embracing the many aspects of ourselves, honoring and loving all that is within us, and by denying no experience or feeling. It is also about finding ways to expand our consciousness and spiritual awareness as we heal, allowing us to regain a sense of meaning and purpose in our lives and the remembrance that we are not alone in this journey but are held by light and energies larger than ourselves.

What is trauma? The root of the word comes from the Greek word for "wound." Trauma is literally a wound to the self and may be physical, emotional, mental or spiritual. All of us carry some level of trauma. Being human means experiencing both the joys and the wounds of embodiment and life on this planet. Often trauma is layered and complex and leads to ruptures or fragmentation in the sense of self. When we experience physical trauma and the pain is too overwhelming to bear, we go unconscious. In a similar way, when we experience emotional trauma that is overwhelming, we disconnect, dissociate, or push the feelings and memories into the unconscious. This allows us to cope, but the trauma then becomes embedded in our psyche or held in the body. It gets stored as images, flashbacks, body sensations, and even cellular memories. We create defenses to keep the pain at bay and often live our lives in more and more restricted ways to avoid letting the memories or feelings rise into awareness. We may use alcohol, drugs, or other addictions to keep numbing out what we don't want to feel or remember.

How do we heal? What is the protocol for effectively healing trauma and for finding a way to hold the process safely through alignment with our inner knowing and the stillness within? How do we go deep inside to unearth the buried wounds in order to heal physically and emotionally while not getting mired in our trauma or caught in an over-identification with our pain and experience of being a victim? How do we hold all of this in the right balance, so that we do not disconnect from any aspect of who we are?

This book demonstrates a simple yet profound model for how you can align with inner stillness and do deep emotional work in order to heal from trauma in a way that is safe, nurturing, and lasting. It also gives tools and techniques to help you heal issues around trust and attachment and move into a deep relationship with yourself, with others, and with the Earth, the Cosmos, and all that is. Through being aligned with your true self and with inner stillness, you remember your interconnectedness with all of life and are able to feel supported, nurtured, and loved throughout the healing journey. This model is a guide for moving into the fullness and uniqueness of who you are, into deep relationship with others and with life, while expanding in love and joy.

The ARCH model includes the awareness that to fully heal from trauma, our process needs to be held in a larger spiritual understanding and context. We are spiritual beings having a human experience. This model describes how, beneath the impact of trauma on the personality, there is the soul self that is infinite, conscious, and available to be present in the experience of the personality, navigating the pain and suffering as well as the joys of this lifetime. The ARCH model also offers a spiritual perspective that does not see trauma as random or senseless but rather as having meaning and being an essential part of the soul's journey of evolution. It also holds the awareness that we need relationship in order to heal and to remember that we are not separate but are a part of the web of all that is. Then we can seek support and comfort not only from other people but also from our relationship with the Earth and our oneness with the cosmos and with all of life.

This ARCH model also holds the understanding that true healing is not merely about reducing problematic symptoms or behaviors or of transcending the trauma. Instead, by diving into the depths of the healing process and doing the deep inner work, we are able to transmute the trauma into deeper awareness and a more integrated sense of self and transform the wounds into healing gifts for ourselves and others. The path of healing then becomes a road to compassion and higher consciousness, and the trauma becomes a portal for emotional and spiritual transformation. When we heal ourselves, we are then able to truly support the healing of others and our planet. It is through our own healing and integration of our wholeness that we are able to become rainbow warriors, bringing light, hope, and healing to the world.

Our Stories

Kristina's story

Each of us has a story, a lifetime of experiences, that have sculpted and molded who we are. The good and bad, and everything in between, influences us, and what we do with our experiences defines who we are and who we will become. I have been asked to share my story to offer hope and guidance to others on a healing path. I have often come to realize that we are more similar than we are different. Even though the content of our stories, backgrounds, color, gender, and beliefs may vary, we tend to share similar ambitions, desires, and dreams. We are all human and experience the same basic feelings of anger, sadness, shame, grief, loss, joy, peace, gratitude, and hope. Although the intensity of emotions may be different, our experience of this spectrum of feelings is the same.

All the people involved in my life have taught me and given me the opportunity to grow in love and wisdom and to stretch and expand my soul beyond what I knew of my own capacities. The pain and suffering of my past ultimately became the gift that led me back to my true Self, back home again to my heart, returning much wiser and spiritually mature. I have received many forms of training and have assisted others in healing from trauma over the past fifteen years, but it is through grace and my efforts to transmute the deep layers of my inner pain that enabled me to transform my heart to truly help others heal. My life's journey included early-childhood ritualistic abuse, incest, rape, and neglect. And yet this part of my journey leads me to you—you are now a part of my story, and mine is a part of yours. In honoring my experiences, I honor yours as well. The words that make up my story will be different from yours, but you will feel how much we are the same. I hope to offer you something in these pages, but if nothing else, I want to honor you and your path, where you have walked and all you have gone through. As we each give voice to what has been ignored, tucked away, and forgotten, we come back to the oneness of the heart. As we bring what has been hidden into the light to heal, we do so as a whole, not in separation. One heart healing at a time, we are one in the unity of love. Here is my story, just one drop in the ocean of us all.

Kristina, age 8

Ironically, after having completed the book, I have come back to the beginning to write my story. Having come full circle, the fear is still waiting to meet me. The fear in telling my story isn't about rejection or the criticism of others. The fear is not that I won't be believed or that my writing will be picked apart. Those things may happen, but the fear I'm speaking about has roots that go much deeper within. This primal fear lives inside my bones and sends a message back to me that if I tell my story, "I will be annihilated." This fear makes my bones shake, freeze up, and my mouth shut tight. And in the past, that is how it has gone. But today, I hold my bones steady, as I rise to my feet and speak my truth. Raw, open, vulnerable, I let the waves of truth flow freely from my heart. As they flow out, I claim my voice, my right to speak my truth.

I was born two months early by a planned cesarean section. There were no physical complications to make this necessary, and no explanation was ever given as to how this decision was made. But the error brought me into this world struggling for survival, and I was taken to another hospital in efforts to save my life. I was incubated until my lungs developed, and I weighed enough to go home. I went home to a mother whose own mother had committed suicide just a year before. My mother felt abandoned and alone. Even after her efforts to ask others to help, no one came. She was anxious and depressed, while trying to raise a three-year-old, a fifteen-month old, and me, a four-pound preemie. Both of my parents came from families with a history of abuse, alcoholism, and emotional neglect. They were victims, just like me. The trauma was multi-generational, and its effects spread extensively through both lines of my lineage.

During my early childhood, my parents were involved in a satanic cult. My father, having been born himself into the cult, was dependent on his father to make a living, which left us all victims to the power of the cult leaders. The year that I turned four was when we finally escaped the terror. This was after a brutal attack and rape that my older sister and I endured. I believe my parents came to the realization that staying in the cult was worse than the danger of leaving. Finding the courage, my parents fled with us to my mother's sister's home. From there, we crossed two state lines and found a place to live for the next three years. We then inexplicably moved back to the state where the cult activity began. For the first few months, we stayed in the same small town of my birth, where relatives on my father's side resided. Our next move was two-and-a-half hours away, and my memories of the cult activity faded, but new experiences of abuse filled the spaces. I was now seven, and my mother who had up to that time sexually abused me, finally made the choice to stop. She rarely touched me again after the abuse, not to brush my hair, tuck me in, or hold me when I was scared. The neglect now became the most pervasive abuse throughout the rest of my childhood. This was also the age that my Sunday school teacher began to come by the apartment. With my mother both physically and emotionally absent, he had full access to me and my sisters. What started out as molestation, eventually ended in rape.

My father was not around much, and like my mother, he was also emotionally checked out. I had experiences of a man coming into my bed at night. This was not the Sunday school teacher that would come during the day. These nighttime visitations also started with molestation and again ended in episodes of rape. Through the many vivid flashbacks that I had as an adult, I was able to physically sense this man on top of me, even to the extent of being able to recall his breath and texture of his shirt, but I have not been able to clearly make out his face. I will never know for sure if the man that came in at night was my father.

This is the part of my childhood that I had to break down into pieces and dissociate from, so that I could gain enough distance from its devastating effects to survive. The more severe the abuse, the more it had to be split off. All of it had to be hidden, deep down in the farthest parts of my being, which allowed me to function and move through life with some sense of normalcy. Even now, some forty plus years away from my childhood, I sometimes drift back to the ordinary memories of when I was a kid, like time collapsing all at once as my life folds into one single moment. Hearing faint hypnotic tones, I can instantly recall similar melodies that came emanating out from the ice-cream truck that methodically made its way through the neighborhood streets luring kids out on hot summer days. The feel of sticky summer nights brings me back to pick-up soccer games that went on until the sun no longer gave light. And the coolness of fall brings back the anticipation and excitement of a new school year. All of these memories remind me of the efforts I made as a child to connect any threads of consistency with those of friends and peers which gave me a sense of regularity and safety that seemed to counteract the utter chaos and secrecy that went on behind the closed doors of my childhood home.

From the outside, my family seemed pretty typical of the time. Growing up in what I always thought to be a normal family of the seventies and eighties, a lot of us were "latchkey kids," left alone and unmonitored for most of the day. My dad was often away, and my mom, although being around more physically, was emotionally absent. It wasn't a loving or emotionally connected childhood, but for the most part, from my perspective as a child, nothing seemed too out of place. However, as my siblings and I began to get older and entered adolescence, things on the outside began to look pretty messed up. By the time my siblings had reached high school, they were acting out with destructive drinking, drug use, physical fighting, sexually promiscuity, and eating disorders. Being the middle child, I could somehow feel I was looking back into the past and into the future at the same time. As I watched my siblings lives chaotically unwind and collapse in heaps of painful crises, I didn't want anything to do with it. Instead of drugs and alcohol, I turned to a conservative

God, where the rules were clear and structured, which somehow gave me a sense of being able to control my environment and my own fate. If I obeyed the rules, I would be kept safe. I created a path to try and navigate my way out of external chaos and deep inner loneliness.

I went to a religious school for my first two years of college, during which time my younger sister, then sixteen, got pregnant while she was in an inpatient psychiatric hospital and later had the baby. My older sister was also in an inpatient program for extreme anorexia and starting to have memories of childhood sexual abuse. About the same time, my brother's new wife decided she no longer liked men. More and more confusion and turmoil began to surround me and encroach on what I later realized was a false sense of safety that had been constructed from an external, religious, moral compass.

As the years have now long passed by, I have come to a deeper understanding of what my relationship with God at that time was really about. I wasn't following God because I loved "Him" and what I was being taught. I was obeying the rules because I was afraid of what would happen if I didn't. What I was really feeling was obligation, not adoration. But at the time, I didn't know another way out of the fear, and my mind was constantly at odds with what my heart was telling me to do. I began to move deeper into a false way of being by acting life out, instead of letting life live through me. I set goals and worked hard for accomplishment. Through marriage, college, being a perfect wife and mother, on the outside, I appeared to be a success. On the inside, something was terribly off, and I felt myself losing the feeling of having real flesh and bones and felt that I was transforming more and more into a "Tin Man" (like in *The Wizard of Oz* and in the song by Tracy Chapman, "Remember the Tin Man"), without feeling and without a heart. Still, I was determined not to let anything disrupt my perfectly safe world.

In order to keep a sense of structure to my world, I had to "stuff" certain painful experiences I was continually having. One of these was the fallout of negative emotions and sensations that I would have after having sex with my husband. I didn't become sexually active until after I was married, and then I became pregnant three months after our wedding day. Within the first few years of marriage, I began to experience deep sadness and depression after being intimate on any level. I had no framework for understanding why, since I loved my husband, so the only way out of the confusion was to bury what I was experiencing. I also had recurring dreams that had started in childhood that left me feeling in disarray with conflicting emotions. Many of these dreams involved violation, levitating objects, dark shadows, and red lights. Again, with no context, I brushed them off as merely bad dreams with no validity in reality, even though they would leave me disturbed for days.

By this time in my life, I had mostly lost contact with my older sister. None of us siblings were close, but I occasionally heard things through the family grapevine. It was during one of these conversations, I learned that my older sister had come out with memories from childhood of abuse and of satanic cult activity. When I heard this, my body froze, and my heart sank. I confronted my parents, who denied any involvement, claiming my sister's psychiatrist and therapist had suggested these things and created these "memories." I desperately wanted to believe that these abuses did not happen. My safe and "perfect" world depended on it. But I was left struggling and in extreme conflict. I had always held bits of memories, like something out of a horror film, but I could never make sense of them. And I didn't think my memories, nightmares, and vaginal scar tissue were enough evidence to give 100 percent proof that such severe abuse had happened to me. I used the lack of infallible evidence as a tool for denial to keep me protected from the unknown trauma that I sensed, on some level, was hidden deep in my being. And my fear of even remotely opening up to that possibility kept me running from myself. I shut my sister out, convinced she had been deceived, and kept moving on with the goal-oriented rules of my life. My husband and I relocated to the East Coast, so that he could start graduate school. This took us far away from my family of origin who were all living in the South. I was a busy mom with a baby and a toddler, deeply absorbed in keeping the house of cards from falling in around me, as I devoted myself to raising my little family. But even with the foreshadowing of my sister's experience, nothing could have prepared me for what lay ahead.

The first full flashback came when I was modeling in New York City with my five-year-old son. He had signed with an agency in the city, and I was modeling on the side. I was very low in weight, under a lot of stress, and was constantly running on fumes. On a typical hot humid day in the city, I had come back from a photo shoot with my son, having caught a cold. It was a particularly long day, and I decided to lie down and rest for a moment before starting dinner, when, just after I closed my eyes, an image flashed in my mind of a scene that I had no reference for. Not being one to watch frightening movies, I could not imagine how I could have created the snapshot so instantaneously. This was the picture: There was a dark, medium-sized room lit only by candles; there were no windows that I could see or any other form of light. The candles were on stands that were surrounding a circle of people that were gathered around an altar, all cloaked in black robes. The most jarring part about this image was that I saw a young girl lying on the altar in the middle of the circle. In that moment, every cell of my being knew that the child in the middle of the circle of people was me. I had neither feeling nor connection to what I was viewing. I began to feel a deep dropping sensation move down from the picture in my mind, slowly penetrating through my entire being, like something ripping through the fabric of my soul. This was the moment my life changed forever.

What followed in the weeks and years to come was an outpouring of flashbacks, nightmares, body memories, and sensations. My world not only crumbled, but so did my sense of identity and almost everything inside and outside of what I knew to be my reality. In the early phases, it seemed like my body and psyche were trying to purge the mental content. I would have horrific memories without any emotion; in fact, overall, I felt emotionally flat and empty. I actually felt like a shell of a being. The only emotion that seemed to play out at large was when I was having a flashback at night, and then the terror and fear of reliving the abuse felt incredibly real and horrendous. This then moved into major depression and years of not being able to access the deeper rage, sadness, and grief. These feelings stayed stuck and hidden inside me, drawing me deeper and deeper into a dark abyss. For a long time, I felt that I could rarely connect to the pain, but then I gradually entered a phase of actually feeling the emotions. This often came unexpectedly, and at times, it was difficult to control and manage in a way that wasn't destructive to myself or to those around me. I knew that I needed to enter this phase to finally integrate the trauma despite how difficult it was to feel the raw, heavy pain that was constantly in my heart.

Mostly, through these years, I felt that this nightmare and the process of trying to heal would never end. I was seeking all forms of western therapy, psychiatry, inpatient hospitals, alternative healing, and medicines—some helpful, some not. I began to feel that my entire life would be consumed with trying to heal what was broken, never really being able to live to my full capacity or even have hope that I could thrive in life. The extreme neglect, incest, satanic ritual abuse, sexual abuse, and multiple childhood rapes that I had experienced seemed like too much damage for me to ever have the capacity to move beyond the brokenness. At this point, I was led to live in the East, moving first to the Philippines and then to India. Through mindfulness and meditation, I learned how to find distance and allow the memories and feelings to just move through me. I began to practice a non-attached approach that allowed a flow to what I was experiencing without it taking me over and consuming my life in full-time suffering. I had more moments of peace and greater ability to be in the present moment.

However, as I spent more hours in meditation, I felt that less and less of my conscious awareness was on this planet. I began to not only bypass my trauma but also my experience of being embodied in a physical way. I started to lose weight and not be able to keep it on. After two years and many medical lab tests, it was discovered that my body would no longer take in fats or nutrients. As my weight continued to drop, I knew that if I didn't find an answer soon, I wouldn't survive. Coming from desperation and what felt like endless searching for how to be in my life in a way that didn't escape the human experience and was not full of pain and suffering, I sent a message out from my heart into the Universe, asking for help to find greater wisdom and insight. The next day, in a quite miraculous and unexpected way, Heather came into my life. Through her understanding of embodied spirituality, I was able to gain a deeper connection with the physical aspects of myself and with how to be in this realm in a more whole way.

Through the healing that has happened in my life and with the choice to align to inner peace and stillness, I can allow emotions to flow through me, to honor and be with myself in a way that feels whole and complete. I am able to hold the full spectrum of emotions and live more and more in the present moment, with a sense of deep gratitude and awe for the experience of being alive.

Heather's story

My life has been a quest to understand the deeper meaning of life and of healing and wholeness, and of what it means to be a spiritual being having a human experience on this planet. Since early childhood, I have sought to comprehend how love, fear, joy, pain, trauma, healing, violence, and compassion can co-exist in our human experience. This quest led me to immerse myself in the religion of Christianity that I grew up in as well as exploring other cultures and religious traditions through a study of cultural anthropology in college. I avidly pursued my efforts to understand healing from both an emotional and spiritual perspective by gaining a graduate degree in theology and a PhD in clinical psychology. Later, following a time of spiritual crisis in my late twenties, I came to understand that there is no one path to a connection with Spirit or to the Divine. There are many paths to the light of love and Source, just as the sunlight moving through a prism manifests in all of the colors of the rainbow.

After completing my graduate training, I focused my practice as a psychologist on in-depth work with trauma. I sought to deepen my own self-understanding and healing through years of personal therapy, and I worked to increase my ability to facilitate healing for others through years of training, including post-graduate training in a psychoanalytic institute as well as in the treatment of trauma (including MPD or DID), neuropsychology, attachment theory, self-psychology, and the self-in-relation model. As I sat with clients, I knew that together we were on a journey of discovery and healing. As I sought to bring my attention, knowledge, compassion, and the capacity to listen and be there to support them in their healing process, I also knew that their experiences, insights, and relationships with me were transforming me as well. We had different roles to play with each other—but I firmly believe that the therapeutic relationship needs to not be a hierarchical or pathologizing dynamic. We all carry pain and sorrow; we all are both whole and broken. All of us are in our own journeys of healing and growth on this planet.

After working as a therapist for sixteen years, I became increasingly discontent with the limitations of traditional therapy. It felt too focused on a cognitive or conscious understanding of the origins or dynamics of pain and trauma and was limited in how to support people in healing at a deeper level. I came to realize that healing does not come through using the proper psychological techniques. Ultimately, what is most healing is to find the path—whatever that may be—to wholeness, awareness, and loving relationship. Healing ultimately comes through feeling seen and heard and held in loving compassion and through eventually coming to see ourselves and each other in a more whole and clear way. It is through knowing and loving ourselves that we are able to be in our wholeness and no longer in identification with our wounds or with our stories about our lives. We then are able to more fully love and be loved by others.

About this time in my life, I had a profound mystical experience in which I inwardly heard a voice telling me that if I did not leave my life as I knew it, I would die. I could feel in every fiber of my being that this was true. Holding my own journey and being there for others in their healing process in this way of working was depleting me, and I was feeling the inadequacy of this multifaceted psychological approach to trauma. Acting in faith, I stepped into uncertainty and dismantled my practice, sold my home, and moved across the country. I felt as if I had walked off a cliff into an abyss. This transition led me into a "wilderness" experience in which my sense of identity as I had known it was stripped away. I went through periods of anxiety, confusion, and depression. But this liminal time was also a profound time of exploration, inner healing, and spiritual initiation. During the next seven years, I deepened my own inner work and also explored healing from other perspectives. I studied with indigenous healers and shamans from all over the world. I learned about herbalism, shamanism, and energy healing. I studied ancient wisdom traditions such as astrology, Earth-based spirituality, and the understanding of the Sacred Feminine. I learned about different spiritual approaches and about the power of sacred circles for healing. I came to realize that there are many paths to spirituality, healing, and wholeness.

As I began to emerge from this time of inner and outer exploration, I created a holistic healing center that allowed me to integrate and practice in a new way. I developed and facilitated sacred healing circles for women in which we used mythology, ceremony, and shamanic practices to support each other in healing individually and together. I incorporated shamanic and energy healing practices in my therapy work. I also started doing psychological and spiritual astrology readings that provided guidance about the soul's purpose, the meaning of the themes in our lives, and the aspects of the self. This is the integrative healing work that I continue to do.

Then another powerful mystical experience several years ago brought me into connection with Kristina and into our process of supporting each other in our own journeys and deepening our understanding of healing and being in wholeness. It meant another radical reshaping of my life on many levels to open to this next phase of self-expansion. As a psychologist specializing in in-depth trauma therapy, I have worked with many people with early childhood sexual, physical, or emotional trauma and even with some who had experienced ritual abuse. I have never met anyone with the depth and complexity of trauma that Kristina had experienced. Her healing journey is a testament to how all of us can heal no matter how early or deep or layered the trauma.

Our coming together launched us both into doing deeper healing work with others and the weaving of psychology, energy healing, shamanic practices, astrology, meditation, ceremony, and sacred circle work as part of our integrative approach. This book arises out of our combined experiences using this holistic model to support others in healing.

How this book came into being

HEATHER: I first met Kristina in person when she was living in the Philippines and was here in the States for a few weeks for a spiritual retreat. Shortly after we met, Kristina announced to me that she felt we would be writing a book together. I blurted out, "Oh really? That's interesting." Meanwhile I was thinking, "I barely know you, and I have no clue what book you are talking about!" I knew Kristina was a gifted intuitive and that she seemed to hold a deeper knowing, so I stayed open to the possibilities that might unfold. As we talked during the next few months, Kristina shared with me that she had been working on a book for almost twenty years about her own process of healing from trauma. She had kept years of journaling and meticulous notes of her process throughout her healing experience. From all that Kristina had learned and been through herself, she hoped that she might be of support and help to others who were healing from trauma. However, even with all of her efforts to complete the book, Kristina felt she was unable to because there were still major elements that were missing. She sensed when she met me that I was the one that held the missing pieces.

What Kristina did not know at the time was how trauma was a primary area of focus of my thirty-plus years of clinical practice as a psychologist. As we discussed our experiences, we discovered that our views about trauma and healing were amazingly similar. We both strongly believe that healing is a multi-layered and multi-dimensional process and needs to integrate body, mind, heart, and spirit. We both believe that, as we heal, we come into wholeness, and as we remember our wholeness, we are able to heal. This first encounter with Kristina and her insight about our working together on the book was to be only my first experience of realizing how gifted she is as an intuitive. I also came to see and respect her gifts as an energy practitioner, helping others to heal. At an even deeper level, I have profound respect for her as a person. Her memories of the trauma began to emerge in her early twenties, and she spent the next twenty years on a profound healing journey. She has come through a long process to heal and come into wholeness. Today, she is one of the most conscious, healed, loving, and whole human beings that I know. It is by going through this deep process of personal healing that she offers her profound understanding of healing to others.

Kristina also has experience living in the Philippines and in India and in exploring other cultural, spiritual, and healing traditions as well as being exposed to the trauma of many people in different parts of the world with little access to traditional medical or psychological care. Part of her desire in writing this book is to offer guidance to people who may not have access to traditional therapy to empower them to find a path to healing and wholeness. I have come into this process as a clinical psychologist with a passion for understanding healing and for being of support to others in their healing journeys. In terms of my background in psychology, I have worked as a psychologist in inpatient psychiatric hospitals and outpatient clinical settings as well as in private practice. I have been the clinical director of two outpatient mental health clinics focused on offering therapy underserved populations. I have worked with people from across ethnic and socio-economic backgrounds. While my primary focus has been on therapy with adults, I also have extensive experience doing therapy with children and adolescents. I have over thirty years of clinical practice and also have several years of experience in neuropsychological evaluation. In addition, I have taught psychology at the graduate level, been a training psychologist at St. John's Hospital in Santa Monica, California, and have decades of experience supervising other psychologists and therapists.

As shared earlier, I have also done training in energy healing and shamanic practices with healers, shamans, and teachers from around the world. I use an integrative approach to healing that includes psychology, spirituality, shamanism, and astrology in both individual and group work. These are the experiences that Kristina and I bring together to write this book. We believe that all people are both wounded and whole. We all have some degree of trauma and are shaped by the pain from our past experiences. We are all here on this Earth to heal and to grow in love and wisdom. As we heal, we evolve and grow in consciousness and then are able to bring that healing energy to others and to the Earth. This is our vision and our hope.

Understanding Trauma and Healing

Trauma

Trauma relates to the ruptures, wounds, and pain of the past that have become embedded in us physically, emotionally, and energetically in a way that block us from being in our wholeness and in the fullness of who we are. Unresolved trauma can keep us stuck in destructive emotions, behaviors, beliefs and negative thought loops, without the ability to trust or be in healthy committed relationships, and sometimes even undermining our ability to connect with and effectively parent our own children. But not all painful experiences are traumatic. If we experience an event that is stressful and have enough inner resources and external support, we can often work through the event without it traumatizing us. It is important to be able to share the experience with another person and to feel cared for and understood. It is also important to feel a sense of agency, that you can in some way take action to resolve what has occurred.

Then, you are able to heal and move on. This is also the case with children who have been through stressful or painful experiences. The traumatic event doesn't get encoded in the body, mind and psyche if a loving, supportive adult steps in to help the child process, grieve, and release the experience.

We all carry some level of trauma or pain from the past. It can range from mild childhood painful events and ruptures in relationships to severe early experiences of neglect or physical, emotional, and sexual abuse. Or it may be due to exposure to violence, war, natural disasters, or physical accidents. Also, emotional wounding or abuse can be as damaging or even more so than physical abuse. For example, you might have felt shamed or humiliated as a child. Or you might have felt as if you were not good enough or lovable for who you uniquely are and may have believed that you had to hide behind a mask to fit in and make things acceptable for others at your own expense.

What happens in the body, mind, and spirit when we are stressed beyond what we can handle? Where does the experience go if it doesn't have a chance to get worked through? Research has shown that there are common neurological and physiological ways the body and brain instinctively respond to trauma.

When in trauma, in the acute phase, you generally experience a physical response as your body mobilizes to cope. You are likely to experience the stress hormone cortisol surging through your system, triggering a rapid heart rate, shortness of breath, and increased hypervigilance, resulting in a heightened stress response. The heart races as blood is being pumped to major muscle groups. The limbic system is activated, increasing anxiety and fear, which can

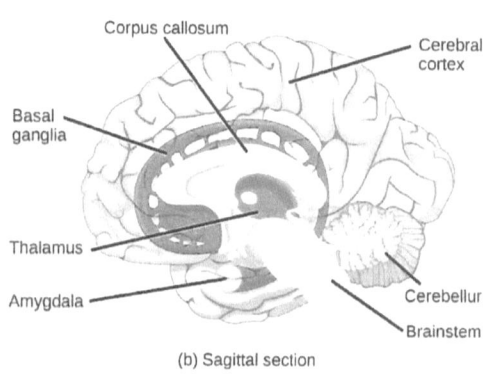

(b) Sagittal section

often turn into anger. This is the body's preparation for flight or fight. Another response that you may experience, if you feel particularly overwhelmed and see no way to act to protect yourself, is going into a freeze state, much like an animal will go limp and seem to be paralyzed or dead in order to avoid being attacked by a predator. Here, your digestion will stop as the blood flow to the digestive organs and brain decreases, causing stomach issues and clouded thinking. The freeze response is due to activation of the dorsal vagus nerve.

If you are able to act in some way to protect yourself or escape the trauma and get support following the event to help you process it, you may be able to release the trauma and not develop more ongoing symptoms of Post-Traumatic Stress Disorder. If not, the trauma becomes encoded in your body and psyche in a more ongoing way and you may develop the symptoms of PTSD such as nightmares, flashbacks, and bouts of anxiety or depression. You may find yourself avoiding situations that trigger memories of the trauma and may become more hypervigilant and cautious in your life.

If the trauma was a single event, you may experience simple PTSD. However, when you undergo more prolonged or chronic trauma such as ongoing childhood physical, sexual, or emotional abuse, or being in a war, you are likely to develop complex PTSD. This results in many of the symptoms described above but also tends to have a deeper impact on you psychologically with other symptoms such as chronic depression, isolation, aggression, dissociation, numbing, addictions, and/or difficulties with trust in relationships. You may experience changeable or volatile moods and be triggered by anything that is a reminder of the trauma. You may experience feelings of helplessness and hopelessness or bouts of rage and acting out. You may find it difficult to focus or to maintain a normal life. If you experienced chronic abuse in childhood, you may have learning disabilities due to the effect of cortisol on your developing brain. It is important to understand that all of these symptoms and feelings are expressions of your psyche's effort to cope with what has happened.

Fight, flight, freeze, and fawning — With complex PTSD, the effects of the trauma result in lasting neurological changes which interact with changes in mood, behavior, and cognitive functioning. Often, the activation of the limbic system and neurological arousal do not return to a normal baseline. In particular, the amygdala and prefrontal cortex are negatively affected. With ongoing trauma, the amygdala, which is responsible for detecting threats and activating the fight-or-flight response, becomes overactive and is unable to return to a normal baseline. This means that you remain in a state of hypervigilance and hyperarousal and may perceive even a minor incident as a major threat.

The prefrontal cortex, which is deactivated by cortisol, the "stress hormone," and is now consistently at higher levels in your system, is less able to function. This is the part of the brain that helps you reason, problem-solve, focus, and effectively make decisions. This can lead you to being in an ongoing heightened state of hypervigilance and reactivity, as if you are constantly in fight-or-flight mode. If predominantly in fight mode, this may result in irritability, anger, impulsivity, and in difficulty making rational decisions. If you are primarily in a flight mode, you may engage in avoidance, feel chronically anxious, and have difficulty focusing and following through with tasks. If in freeze mode, there are often difficulties with motivation and taking action accompanied by feelings of hopelessness and helplessness. Most people tend to experience a complex interplay of these different ways of coping—shifting from fight to flight to freeze at different times and in relation to different triggers. Being in an ongoing physiological stress response can also result in physical symptoms such as digestive issues (for example, either difficulties with assimilating nutrients or with elimination, as with irritable bowel syndrome or colitis). The ongoing toll of stress can exacerbate many other physical and emotional conditions as well.

Trauma, especially early childhood trauma or complex PTSD, also affects our ability to trust others and to form healthy relationships. In addition to fight, flight, and freeze as coping responses to trauma, another relational pattern that can develop has been called "fawning." This involves an effort on the part of the child (and later as an adult) to avoid conflict, to attempt to please or accommodate others, and often to become a caretaker. These patterns often originated as a protective measure in the hopes of appeasing the abuser to avoid further physical or emotional abuse. This pattern is also a frequent result of having had a narcissistic parent who was unable to tolerate assertion or individuation on the part of the child and who punished the child for speaking up or for being independent. The child learned to read the parent's emotional cues and to strive to be the "good child." At times, the child may have become the caretaker to the parent in the hope that this would gain the parent's love or acceptance, or in the longing to heal the parent so that finally the parent will stop the abuse and be more loving and giving. Sadly, instead, the child becomes blocked in developing a healthy sense of self and in feeling valued for who they are and only feels worthwhile in being there for others. It also can lead to the internalization of a sense of worthlessness or never "being enough." Fight, flight, freeze, and fawning are all protective measures and ways of coping with trauma. However, they all too often become lifelong patterns of dealing with stress and may manifest in long-term physical, emotional, and relational problems.

Here are some other possible indicators of having experienced trauma in the past:

- A general feeling that there is something wrong with you
- Deep feelings of shame
- Feeling powerless to assert oneself
- Feeling that if people really knew you, they would reject you
- Suicidal thoughts or attempts
- Self-hatred or self-destructive behavior
- Difficulty with self-care
- Difficulties with trusting your feelings or intuition
- Conflicted feelings about emotional and/or sexual intimacy
- Recurring bouts of depression unrelated to current stressors
- Sleep difficulties
- Flashbacks or recurring nightmares
- At times, feeling out of your body or spacing out (dissociating)
- Having a distorted body image
- Not being aware of body signals such as being tired, hungry, or in pain
- Learning disabilities
- Addictive behaviors
- Having intense, unexplainable, negative reactions to certain places, times of year, objects, colors, or foods

If you are experiencing more than a few of these indicators, it could mean that you have had early trauma that you have repressed or dissociated from. Trauma has a profound effect on every aspect of a person's life. It affects the person's body, emotions, sense of self, behaviors, beliefs, and relationships. Abuse or neglect in early relationships leads to attachment difficulties and problems with trust. Trauma may result in a fragmented sense of self or a negative self-image. Often when dissociated or fragmented trauma starts to come up in the body or psyche, the memories, body sensations, and emotions are not blended together. Initially, you might just get pieces of memories coming up without any feelings attached. Or you may get flooded with emotion with no clear memory connected to it. In the beginning, when past painful memories are coming up to heal, the experience can be confusing, jarring, invasive, and frightening, and it may feel daunting and out of control. Remember that as these feelings and memories surface, it is as if the split-off part that experienced the trauma is still in the midst of the event. This can leave you feeling overwhelmed with the emotions related to the trauma, and disoriented, as this part of you is pulling you back into the past.

If trauma is not worked through, it does not disappear or heal with time. It becomes imprinted in the body and may emerge as physical symptoms. It is stored in the psyche and may manifest in flashbacks, invasive images or memories, sudden overwhelming feelings, or experiences of dissociation. Over time, unresolved trauma may manifest in physical illness, long-standing emotional problems, or difficulties in relationships. Whatever the nature of the trauma, no matter how mild or severe, it is important to face your wounds and to allow yourself to heal. Why? Because only then can the repressed or split off parts of yourself that have been buried in your unconscious mind integrate into the wholeness of your being. And only then are you able to learn and grow from the experience instead of feeling limited, blocked, or constricted in some way in your life. This allows you to reclaim all of who you are—your strengths and gifts as well as vulnerabilities and deep emotions. It is only when you let yourself heal that you can release yourself from living in fear and stop constructing a life based on defending yourself from danger. And only in healing can you move beyond coping and survival into living with courage from the heart and thriving in the present moment. Healing is the path to freedom, and it gives you the ability to open fully to joy.

Healing

Healing is more than the recovery from trauma. It is about regaining the wholeness of who you are. It involves accepting and honoring all of the aspects of yourself including all of the wounds of the past. Treatment is about the reduction of symptoms and the relieving of pain, but healing is also about moving beyond suffering. To heal, you need to be willing to feel pain and to recover the full range of your emotions. Healing is not about feeling better, it is about getting better. In healing, you are no longer mired in the stories or suffering of the past or an identification of yourself as a victim. Healing is about regaining your true self and sense of balance and wholeness. It is about becoming free to chart your own path consciously rather than being unconsciously controlled by the patterns of the past. It involves the healing and integration of the body, heart, mind, and spirit.

Physically
It is important to address the ways that trauma has been encoded in the body in physical symptoms, illness, or in the cellular memory.

Mentally
We need to understand the resulting thoughts, distorted beliefs, learning difficulties, attentional problems, and long-term effects of stress on the brain.

Emotionally
It is necessary to identify the feelings related to the trauma and release old patterns of coping such as repression, dissociation, denial, and fragmentation, as well as to move into healthy patterns in relationships.

Spiritually
It is critical to regain a connection with your soul self, and to find a connection with Spirit or the Divine and with a larger context of meaning for what has been experienced.

Also, as you work all of the layers of the healing process, remember that it will go in stages, and you will move in and out of the different aspects of yourself and of the healing journey. The path of healing is not linear. It is a spiral journey with lots of detours, stops, and starts, and with many highs and lows. It is important to honor the uniqueness of your own process and not to expect your experience to be the same as anyone else's journey or to match up to some external standard. Also, there is no single path to healing. It is important to find the path and ways of healing that work best for you.

Some further clarifications and explanations to help you better understand the model and the book:

1. We are spiritual beings having a human experience. What this means is that we each existed as consciousness and as a soul self before we came to this planet and incarnated here. Our physical bodies decay with time and die, but our spirit or soul self lives on.
2. We come to the Earth as our soul self to be embodied and to experience this realm of time and space, so that we can have experiences that will allow our souls to grow in love and wisdom. We have a choice as to how we live our lives, and what we want to gain from this existence.
3. No matter what our level of trauma has been, we are all complex beings, with different aspects or parts of ourselves that make up the whole of who we are. This multiplicity is not a problem but a gift. The more conscious that we are of the different aspects of ourselves and our complexity, the more integrated and healthy we can be, as we are then more capable of making conscious decisions.
4. Wholeness is when we are able to be aligned and centered in the soul self or in pure consciousness, which allows inner calm and stillness and gives us space to observe and experience aspects of who we are, including our personalities, feelings, wounds, behaviors, and thoughts. This enables us to develop the "witness self." Being in the witness self is like living as if you are watching a movie. You can observe what is happening in the movie, even feel the emotions the movie provokes without identifying with the characters of the movie. You are able to connect to and feel the plot, message, and characters with a level of non-attachment, remaining grounded in your own conscious awareness at the same time.
5. As we come into alignment and integrate this spiritual aspect of who we are with our embodied self, we are able to hold the wholeness of who we are, our individuality as well as our oneness with pure consciousness. Pure consciousness, which can be referred to as the

Divine, God, Spirit, or Cosmic Consciousness, is the original Source of all creation and all of the cosmos. It exists throughout all time and space and yet is beyond time and space. This pure consciousness runs through all sentient beings, including each one of us. Everything is interconnected, because all flows out of and is created by this Source consciousness. We all emerge from this Source and return to it at the time of death.

6. When we refer to the soul self, we are talking about that part of your being that has been with you across lifetimes and is always connected with Source, like a drop of the ocean that emerges and separates, to move through the air or to become part of a wave but is still always connected with the greater ocean, with Source consciousness.

7. When we talk about parts of the self, we are describing those aspects of ourselves that hold different memories or experiences and may relate to different ages or developmental experiences. Some are distinct and well formed, while others may hold only a memory fragment, emotion, or personality trait. With more severe or complex trauma, these internal aspects of the self or parts may not have knowledge of the others. As we heal, we become more conscious of these different parts or facets of ourselves and are able to integrate them and weave them into a more coherent and whole sense of self.

Healing vs. comfort

KRISTINA: For most of my life, I waited on someone else to give me love, acceptance, and a sense of safety, and to take care of my needs and feelings of discomfort. When the person that I had been waiting for showed up to love me in just the right way or to soothe my wounds in a way that I had longed for, it was like water being poured onto dry, brittle ground. I just soaked it in, and as the feeling of being cared for infused my being, it felt like a drug, as it temporarily took all my pain away. However, as I stayed waiting for this healing other to show up, it was always in angst, like a heroin addict, looking for the next hit. I waited in pain as the open wounds oozed, feeling a sense of powerlessness and dependency on the other to arrive. I guess in a way, I was really wanting the people who had hurt me most to come and make things right and to finally love me in a way that I always needed and wanted. This waiting and longing for healing from another is a hard addiction to break, and for me, getting to the place of wanting to let it go didn't come easily. It has taken a number of years for me to finally understand that true and ultimate healing is my responsibility. This does not mean that loving and supportive people are not necessary, they are, and at certain points in my journey, they have been crucial. But the time came when I had to step up and show up for myself like I had been wanting others to do before.

When I became 100 percent responsible for my own healing and stopped looking just for comfort, I took my power back and brought safety and love back to my own being. In a powerful way, the message was given to my whole system: "I am here now. I take full responsibility for me. I am here to love me with an open heart and without conditions. I am here to create safety for myself. It is okay to have needs, and I can take care of my needs. I will show myself love. I will cherish myself. I will see and hear me. I will show myself my divine potential." There are times when I find myself still reaching for the "drug" as feelings of pain and neediness creep in. I ask myself, "Could I really have all the capability inside to love and take care of myself in a way that would feel just as good, if not more complete, than if someone else was there to do it for me?" Then, I go inside, slow and steady, and show up in the exact way that I need. I am always available. I have the most wisdom for myself about what needs to be said and done. I can locate the wound inside my body, because I can feel it, sense it, and have come to know it. I can form a deep relationship with myself, more than I can with anyone else. I can have complete control over the safety of my soul. I can offer security, healing, and love as often as I want and in a way that is most needed. I am my own perfect ally. I have been with me from the beginning of my existence. People have come and gone and have hurt me and loved me. They have stayed true and have abandoned me. But, I have the capacity to always be there for myself.

As I grow and heal, I am getting better at understanding how much power I have to create wholeness within myself. And there is deep peace and comfort in knowing I don't have to wait and rely on someone else to bring me what I am looking for. When I have pulled in my power and taken care of my needs, the gravity of my soul pulls me towards healing and wholeness, and I am left no longer wanting, just being. At some point, I decided to grow up in this way and stop waiting for someone else to make me feel whole. And then, an effortless flow began to happen. My relationships became more balanced and less complicated, and I found and experienced a pure love for myself and others at a depth that I had never known before.

Pain vs. suffering

KRISTINA: We must come to the place, again and again, of surrendering and opening to the pain of life. Whether it is caused by our past or something happening in our present, as long as we are human, we will experience pain. As a species, we have developed all kinds of ways to distract, numb, bypass, and suppress the experience of pain. But, if we are to truly heal and be in our wholeness, we must be willing to surrender to the experience and feel the pain. When we are unwilling to do this, we create our own suffering. Addictions, crisis, depression, and even avoiding not being in the present experience creates more wounds and fragmentation and less possibility for healing and being able to be in the flow of life. As we hold the experience of pain with love, compassion, and understanding, we allow it to wash over us, like a wave peaking and then releasing as it moves through us. We then return to stillness and peace and rediscover joy.

Throughout this book, I will share some of the notes from my journals across the twenty years of my healing process to provide insight into the steps and stages of recovery and coming into wholeness. Here is an example of my learning to be there for and with myself in love and compassion.

Kristina
2013

The hardest part of being miserable at the age of forty-three is the realization that somehow, despite all efforts, I still find myself back in this wretched state of pain. It is low grade at first, moving slowly and steadily, until it often ramps itself up to full-blown hurting. I have done self-care with meditation, exercise, talked to a friend, journaling, accepting all parts and places of myself ... and still, I feel agony.

Gently, I guide my breath to where the pain is being felt and stored. With intention I move the energy of love with my breath, right into the pain. I can visualize the pain lifting and moving out of my body. And yet, the pain is still growing. I briefly feel anger before it turns to hopelessness and despair. How long will I have to be like this? Will I ever heal and be free of the pain? I pray, "Dear Divine, take this from me. I've done all that I can do, and now I surrender it to you ... fully. Merging my will with yours, I ask your grace to flow through me and heal me."

I feel the pain move ... and begin to lift. This time, grace is helping to heal another layer. I take a deep breath. I am starting to be free from it. What is the purpose of the pain? What if I had a knowing that it had importance? What if it arises to teach me something?

Turning in, I listen. I wait. I am patient. I welcome what is there to come closer to me. I speak to all that is within me, "If you are connected to this pain, I welcome you here. I am sending you love and wrapping you in warm acceptance, because you are a part of me. Come. Sit with me, tell me what you know. I feel you are lonely. I am here. Tell me about your sadness. If you cannot tell me, just express your sadness to me in feelings. I will hold you and allow space for your experience. You are valid. Your story deserves to be told." Holding my hands over my heart, I hold the pain, and I tell myself, "You are being heard. Your story is valued. I love you."

I continue to send the inner pain healing, comfort, and love, NOT in an effort to get rid of it, but only for the purpose of loving it and being present with it. Accepting, completely accepting it all, I give myself unconditional love. Being fully present with my suffering, I gently nurture and love the wounds. And because the end goal is not to heal it to get rid of it, that is precisely what happens. I feel the pain begin to trust me and soften as it is heard and accepted. I feel the intensity and sharpness start to diminish and slow down. It is finally being seen. The pain begins to believe that it is not alone, the sadness when expressed is being greeted, respected, and met with love. There is no longer the need to shout for the attention it has been trying to get for so long. It is being understood and embraced. I feel the heaviness of the pain begin to release and let go into the love. It is healing. It is moving on.

There are many ways to heal

One of the purposes of this book is to help you better appreciate that there are many avenues to healing. Sometimes, one modality is most helpful, and other times, you need something else. There is not just one effective way to heal. Just as we are all unique individuals, so are our paths to healing and wholeness. This book offers suggestions, but you are the one who will find your own way with these possibilities. Be creative, allow yourself to explore and find the best people, tools, and ideas that fit for you.

The notion that the healing path should progress in a clear linear way

HEATHER: It is also important to remember that the process of healing is not a linear path. You may circle through the same feelings or memories many times as you work through the layers of healing. So when you go through these cycles, it is not a sign of failure or that you are not healing but is rather an indication that you are working other phases and layers of the healing process. This is different than cycling endlessly and futilely through your old stories, unhealthy patterns, and outdated ideas of your identity.

Healing is a spiral process in which you continue to deepen and expand your awareness of the parts of yourself and the layers of who you are as you work through your experiences, emotions, and memories from the past and increase your range of understanding and capacity to hold the wholeness of your being in the present. As your consciousness and inner strength grow, you will often cycle back through issues that you have already dealt with in order to integrate these feelings or experiences in a more thorough and complete way.

CHAPTER 2

The ARCH Model

Just as the rainbow is an arch of multi-colored light across the stormy sky, so the ARCH model is a bridge for healing and for hope in times of trauma and darkness. This model is also a circle or sphere much like the ancient medicine wheel. The medicine wheel has been used by Native Americans and other indigenous cultures for thousands of years as a way of healing and coming into wholeness. The medicine wheel symbolizes the way to be in balance and wholeness. The medicine wheel is a sphere in which, when you are in the center, you are in right connection with the Earth and sky and the four directions: North, South, East, West.

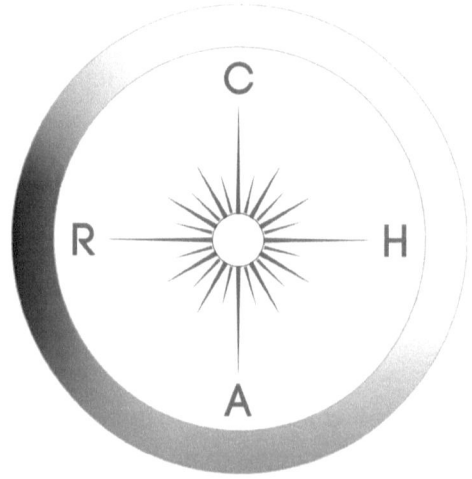

The directions not only relate to finding your place in the world and in connection with the cosmos but with all aspects of life. The alignment of the Earth and sky represent the vertical axis of the medicine wheel and the way in which we honor both the spiritual and embodied aspects of ourselves. The four directions also symbolize our connection with all of the parts of ourselves, our relationships with others, the energies around us, as well as with the stages of life. To walk the medicine wheel or to work with it in a healing way is to move around the wheel, deepening your understanding of yourself and your connectedness with all of life. It is a process of meditation and integration as you work with the healing energy and wisdom of the medicine wheel in an ever-deepening process. The path of healing with the medicine wheel is actually not a circular process but a spiral one. As you heal and evolve, you move more and more into integration and wholeness and deepen your understanding of yourself, your place in the cosmos, and all of life. At the heart of the medicine wheel is the center. This is the place of stillness and of all possibilities. This is where all aspects of the self and all of the directions come into unity and wholeness. It is here that we remember and experience our integration and our oneness with all that is. The center is always there in the medicine wheel and within us as we move through the phases of the healing journey.

The ARCH model is a form of the medicine wheel and is a spiral path to healing and integration. We move through the phases of the healing process and continually come back to the center to remember our essence and wholeness. We cycle through all of the aspects of the process as we heal and grow in consciousness and wholeness. Each phase of the process of healing is interconnected and does not need to be done in any particular order. We weave in and out of different phases and often cycle back through the process many times as we work on different layers. This model is about the integration of healing on all levels—physically, emotionally, mentally, relationally, and spiritually.

ARCH is the acronym for the four directions of this healing medicine wheel and stands for **A**lignment, **R**elationship, **C**onsciousness and **H**ealing. Here are descriptions of these core aspects of the healing journey:

A - Alignment

Alignment is the process of connecting with the vertical axis and the center of the medicine wheel. It is about remembering our place in the cosmos and our connection with the Earth and the sky. As we hold this deeper knowing—that we are never separate or alone but are always part of the oneness of all that is—we hold the awareness that we are both mortal and eternal. We are both finitely vulnerable and infinitely invincible.

Alignment is also about remembering your connection with the center within yourself as you learn how to go deep within to find the place of stillness and calm at the center of your being. The center holds the pure essence of who you are. This is also where you can connect to your soul self that is the aspect of you that is never wounded and is always whole, that never dies and is with you across your journey through many lifetimes. It is always aware of what you are experiencing in this incarnation but is not defined by that story.

Across cultures and across time, in every spiritual tradition, there is the understanding that we are part of the unity of all that is. We are a part of the sea of consciousness that is in all that is and beyond all that is. This is becoming increasingly more evident in the discoveries of modern quantum physics. The soul self is at one with this Source consciousness. We incarnate on Earth to grow in love and wisdom and to experience the range of manifestations of creativity of the cosmos. We may experience our personality selves as separate, but we are always part of the oneness of all that is. As we remember this, we can hold our stories and our experiences more lightly and with less identification, and then explore and work with the deeper meaning of our experiences here, knowing that everything has a purpose, and we are never separate from the unity and love of Source.

This book will guide you in learning how to align your connection with the Earth and the cosmos and with this center, this place of stillness within. Your center is always pure and is often experienced as joy, peace, and empty space. It stays the same, despite what your personality feels and what your mind thinks. It is constant and permanent, without being swayed by attachments, ideas, and beliefs. When you align to your center and to this awareness, you come home to the place that is whole and at rest. Even though you are also your personality including your mind and body, which are having a full range of experiences, when you can align more to the soul self and to this pure state of consciousness at your core, you are able to find peace and a sense of stability and calm, even when under stress or when your personality is in distress.

R - Relationship

We grow and develop in the context of relationship. And our trauma usually occurs in the context of wounding or abusive relationships. To heal, we need to experience being in relationships in which we feel seen, heard, and loved. When we are in alignment with our true self and are at one with the pure consciousness of all that is, we more easily move into being in right relationship with ourselves, others, the Earth, the cosmos, and all that surrounds us. We then are able to tap into rich reserves of wisdom, strength, nourishment, and stability. When we are in right relationship, we are in balance, and there naturally develops a deep, respectful, loving, and nurturing connection within our relationships with others. This connection brings healing and a greater sense of unity. We are able to give and receive love and to feel met, understood, seen, heard, and supported. We also grow and expand in our capacity to love and choose to be fully present in healthy relationships with others.

C - Consciousness

All of us have conscious memories, feelings, and thoughts that are a part of the story of our lives. Yet, we also have unconscious aspects of ourselves—those memories, feelings, and experiences which are buried within us because they were too painful to endure or to hold in our awareness. In order to heal, we have to bring these buried aspects of ourselves into the light. Otherwise, we develop unhealthy patterns to cope with these hidden wounds and are controlled by the painful events that we no longer consciously remember.

Painful wounds are part but not all of who we are, so we can open to the different aspects of ourselves without the fear that we will be taken over by the trauma of the past. This allows us to tune in to the different facets of who we are. We all have various aspects of the self. Different parts of ourselves carry memories, feelings, and experiences, often of different ages, as well as holding different functions or gifts of the self. If we have experienced trauma, we have parts that tend to be frozen at the age that the trauma occurred. By opening to all of the memories and parts of the self, we are able to heal and integrate into a sense of wholeness.

We are then able to move beyond polarity and dualities and be in the wholeness and complexity of our lives. We no longer see things as polarized, such as good or bad, right or wrong, healthy or diseased, whole or broken. We are also then able to see our past and childhood in its complexity—not as all good or all bad, but as both challenging and positive in different ways. We move past fear and are able to hold all of our experiences and feelings in compassion and are better able to maintain co-consciousness with all aspects of our being. Living consciously means bringing into the light what has been hidden and allowing ourselves to see and know the memories and feelings that were too painful to experience in the past. We also are able to discover the hidden gifts, strengths, and uniqueness of who we are that lie beneath the protective armor and defenses. As we bring all of these aspects of ourselves to awareness and open to this unfolding, we are able to hold all of who we are in love and acceptance.

H - Healing

To heal, we need to move beyond symptom relief and get to the roots of the wounds, to honor the hidden messages held there. Healing comes as we weave together all of who we are by folding the trauma, the full range of our emotions, the shadow and light parts of the self into our essence, the core of our being, our soul self, that is and has always been pure, untainted, and complete. Using simple, effective, powerful tools, we can heal our emotional wounds of the past. This does not always mean that we will no longer feel pain, forget our past experiences, or never get triggered again. But we will have the increasing capacity to hold with love all the feelings and parts of the self, along with an ability to act more and more from a place of centeredness. We become able to disidentify from the stories and the wounds in order to live more and more from a place of calm even in the storm. We no longer feel tossed about by the winds of our emotions and unconscious processes, but instead live from a witness self aligned with Source.

Coming to center

As we work all of these facets of the ARCH model or medicine wheel, we move ever more fully into integration, wholeness, joy, and our deep connection to the oneness of all that is. We live more fully from a place of centeredness and true consciousness.

While other forms of therapy and healing engage in aspects of the ARCH model, they can often focus on one part, while neglecting the others. This can be useful and helpful but does not lead to complete healing. Most forms of therapy emphasize behavior or cognitive changes. Some focus on bringing aspects of the self into consciousness and on healing through the dynamic of the therapeutic relationship. But traditional therapy does not integrate an understanding of the importance of alignment and connecting with the deeper spiritual nature of who we are. Mindfulness meditation supports alignment with the spiritual self and ways to calm the emotions and body, but it does not always include the healing nature of relationships with others or the practices necessary to integrate what is emerging emotionally in the meditation process. Medications are often prescribed by psychiatrists to help with anxiety, depression, mood instability, or other symptoms. However, even though medications may calm emotions, help with sleep disturbance, and bring about more physiological balance, they cannot heal the root wounds of the trauma. This may result in a sense of emotional "numbing" or a feeling of being cut off from aspects of the self. Some people go to therapy with the hope that the healing relationship with the therapist will rescue them from suffering, fill the unmet needs from the past, and be the complete healing balm for their emotional pain. But without learning alignment with your deeper self, actively engaging in and taking responsibility for your own healing process, therapy may become an addiction rather than a path to healing.

The ARCH model is an effort to integrate all of these aspects and layers of healing. It also holds the awareness that we are not separate or alone but are interconnected with each other and with all of life. When we integrate deeply held feelings, memories, sensations, and wounds from the past, we are able to find and be in profound inner stillness and centeredness more easily and frequently. And the more we stay aligned with this deep inner peace, the more our bodies, minds, and psyches naturally heal.

Kristina
2015

Sitting with my back against the cool wall on the firm white bed that fills most of this tiny room, I take in my surroundings of the flat in New Delhi, India. As I look out of the large French windows that I have closed in efforts to create some form of separation between me and the street noise and pollution, there is a silence that feels surreal, and I seem to be drifting between worlds. I study the tree branches just outside the window where the evening light softly dissipates across the leaves, revealing beautiful hues of various greens and yellows. I feel surrounded in mystical energies. The air has a certain vibration to it that keeps me questioning life as I've known it and compels me to go deeper. Despite the inconveniences and complexities of living here, I feel I am home, and it is easy to fall into my soul self and to allow my inner self to be revealed in all of its horror, splendor, and beauty. My defenses seem to naturally fall away, and I am left with my naked vulnerability. Here I am. This is me—the uncensored, uncut version, with all of my faults, limitations, weaknesses ... power, beauty, perfection. It is in the wholeness of my being that I feel complete.

I have days where I feel alive and centered. Life seems to move effortlessly with a flow of grace and intelligence that makes being alive easy, light, and pure joy. And there are still times where I feel heavy, spent, unmotivated, confused, and questioning why I feel so different, so dark. How instinctively I want to hold tight to what feels good and run from what doesn't. But I have learned to not judge the feelings or what I am experiencing as good or bad, but allow all to just be, to come and go and wash right through me. I take this focus inward and feel the wholeness of being and of life. To feel the sweetness of finding the place inside that is pure peace and love, no matter what is happening outside of me is exquisite. And knowing that aligning to this peace can be used to greatly help heal wounds and trauma from the past is a miracle.

How to use this book

As you move through this book, you will learn how to become centered and to align with the inner peace that surpasses the limited understanding of your mind. You will learn how to do this even when you are facing great external distress. Using this alignment, you can also heal emotions that are stored in your body. Beyond knowing how to connect with your center and with inner stillness, you will also learn other practices to heal the body, heart, and mind, where trauma and wounds are held. You will be able to use all these techniques interchangeably, applying what works best in the present moment. The methods here will give you a range of options and provide ideas to help inspire you to create your own way of healing that best fits with your pace, comfort level, beliefs, and preferences. We include a variety of spiritual and healing practices such as meditations, healing ceremonies, journaling, inner dialoguing, affirmations, and more. These practices are designed to help you heal on all levels—physically, emotionally, mentally, and spiritually. We encourage you to be open and to do what works for you and let go of what doesn't. You will become your own healer, although this does not mean you need to do it alone. It means that you are in control of your process and outcome. Discover what feels right and fits for you.

We offer tools gathered from over fifty years of combined personal experience as well as from helping others heal and live in a state of increased wholeness. One of the main reasons for writing this book is to give back to others who are walking similar paths of conscious healing. Our hope is that this book will give you light in times of darkness, a sense that you are not alone in your process, and a reminder that you are deeply held and supported in unconditional love as you heal and grow through your deep and expansive time of transformation. May we all more fully heal and move into wholeness and compassion for ourselves and each other and together help heal the world and the planet.

A note of caution: The words in italics are Kristina's journaling about the unfolding of her trauma memories and healing process. If you find these unsettling or that they trigger your trauma memories in a way that does not feel safe to you, we encourage you to skip these italicized journal entries and continue on with the text.

Embarking on the journey

Setting up a medicine wheel to support your process of healing and integration

As you work with the meditations and healing practices in this book, you may want to create an actual medicine wheel as a way to incorporate, strengthen, and integrate your process. We will discuss ways you can develop a deeper understanding of the directions and energies of the medicine wheel, but the beauty of using the medicine wheel is that you can engage in its healing energy at any level of understanding. Making and using a medicine wheel is a profound form of walking meditation (somewhat like walking a labyrinth).

You can make a medicine wheel as simple or as elaborate as you want it to be. We recommend building it outside if at all possible. One simple way to do this is to make a circle (and it does not need to be exact) and place large stones at each of the four directions. Use a compass to put the stones in the proper places on the wheel. Also place a large stone in the center of the circle. The circle can be any size as long as you can easily move around it. A ten-to-twelve-foot diameter circle is a good size if you have space for this. If you want, you can add to the medicine wheel at any time by putting more stones or crystals in the directions or around the circumference of the wheel. You will use this framework of the circle and directions to walk the medicine wheel.

Once you have built the structure of the medicine wheel, you may want to smudge it with sage, burn incense, or in some way honor this as a healing and sacred space for yourself. Before you enter the circle to walk around the medicine wheel, give thanks to the Earth and sky and your spirit guides or others who are supporting you in your process. When following indigenous traditions, you enter the wheel from the south. Enter silently and remember that this is a sacred circle.

Once you enter the wheel, you may want to walk around the circumference counter-clockwise first. When going in this direction, you are releasing stress, negative thoughts, or any heavy energies that may be weighing you down. Once you return to the place where you started, you now turn and walk clockwise around the wheel. Moving in this direction is energizing, and if walked with intention, can help build up energy to support the healing you want to manifest. Pause at the stone for each of the directions (south, west, north, east). Allow yourself to begin to tune into the energies of each direction. Look out and see what is there in your line of vision at each direction. Remember how the Sun rises in the east and sets in the west. Pay attention to how you feel as you stand facing each direction.

You may continue to circle around the wheel as many times as you want. Then, when you are ready, after completing a final circuit, walk from the stone in the south into the center. As you stand there, feel the quiet and stillness of this place of centeredness. Allow yourself to open to the energies of the Earth beneath you and the sky above you. Remember that you are connected to the Earth and sky and to each of the directions. You are part of the web of life and are held by these larger energies of the cosmos. Give thanks for the wheel and these healing energies. When you are ready, walk back to the south where you entered and step out of the wheel.

Walking meditation with the ARCH medicine wheel: As you work with the medicine wheel in relation to the ARCH model, you can work with the aspects of the model as they are associated with the four directions. Here is a brief overview, and we will describe ways to deepen this practice as we explore each segment of the ARCH model as you move through the book.

South: Alignment is associated with the direction of the south. As you enter the wheel, you pause and tune into your connections with the Earth and sky and with the center of the cosmos and the inner stillness (the center) within you. Take time to stand here and begin to breathe in and out deeply, allowing your mind to quiet and release any distracting thoughts or tension in your body. Tune into your heart and feel how your soul self is connected to the consciousness of the cosmos and all that is.

West: Then, as you walk clockwise, you come to the direction of the west which is associated with **Relationship**. As you stand by the stone in the west, take time to meditate about how you are in relationship with yourself. Are you relating to yourself with love and compassion or are you critical and judgmental with yourself or even self-destructive? Contemplate the relationships in your life that are healing for you. These may be relationships with family, friends, a therapist, mentor, or others. Take in how those who are supportive of you see you, and feel their love and care for you. Tune into other relationships that are healing and helpful to you. These may be relationships with pets, other animals, plants, or with spirit animals or guides. Feel how you are held in these healing and loving connections.

North: Now, continue on in the wheel to the direction of north. This is associated with **Consciousness** in the ARCH model. Pause here and look around you and be aware of your surroundings. Then, allow yourself to tune into your inner world and hold an openness and acceptance for all that is within you and all that is in your awareness, and honor the aspects of yourself or memories and feelings that lie buried in your unconscious. Let yourself hold all of these facets and parts of yourself with compassion.

East: Then, continue clockwise to the east. This direction is associated with **Healing**. Take time to meditate here on the ways that you are working to allow yourself to heal and evolve and become more whole. You may want to say a prayer or set an intention about the wounds or issues in your life that you want to heal. Allow yourself to absorb the healing energy that is surrounding you. Then, when you are ready, continue on the wheel and complete the full circle by returning to the direction of the south.

Center: Now, slowly turn and walk into the center. This is the place of integration and of wholeness. Allow yourself to quiet your mind and open your heart. Honor this profound place of stillness at the heart of the medicine wheel and feel how it holds the interconnectedness of all that is and the alignment with the Earth and the sky and with the directions and all of life. Take time to meditate here, then when you are ready, give thanks for this experience and slowly walk back to the stone in the south and out of the medicine wheel.

Remember that when you do this process, it is a sacred and ceremonial meditation. Allow yourself to open to the images and feelings that come to you as you walk in silence. If you want, you can also set an intention for your walk or ask a question and then tune into the guidance that may come to you when you step into the center of the wheel. As you continue to work with the medicine wheel, the process will deepen and expand as you develop a relationship with each of the directions and begin to explore the ways in which they represent aspects of yourself. This is a process of bringing your whole self into healing, integration, and fullness.

CHAPTER 3

A - Alignment

As we begin our work with the ARCH medicine wheel, we start in the south with Alignment. As we work with each aspect or direction of the healing medicine wheel, remember that they all interact with each other, and all are connected to the center. Alignment is about remembering that we are not separate but are part of the connectedness of all that is and that at the center of yourself is a place of pure consciousness and peace. Here you can connect to your soul self and remember your place in the cosmos and that your connection with Source is not outside you but within you. You come back into that realization that you are a spiritual being having an earthly experience. Awareness—this remembrance of our true nature as beings of energy and of pure consciousness—is our true home and essential nature. As we come into alignment with this, we are better able to experience with love and compassion our journey here on Earth, in physical embodiment.

A crucial aspect of healing and coming into wholeness is to be able to hold our lives and our experiences, including trauma, in a larger context. This gives us a sense of meaning and purpose as we are able to accept the full range of ourselves within a larger universal unfolding. We can then begin to see that the events of our lives are not random. We are on a path of evolution and growth, and in connection with the infinite wisdom and love of the cosmos. We come to this deeper knowing not through our minds but through the eyes of our hearts and souls. As we open to this remembering, we realize that we are never separate or truly alone but are always held in the embrace of that cosmic consciousness and divine love that is in all.

Kristina
2015
At Home in Oneness

Standing at the edge of the universe ... I wonder.
With outstretched arms I jump ... free falling into ... the openness of space.
She envelopes me into the deepest places of Her womb.
We dance as lovers. Create like Gods. Explode into stardust ... in and out of galaxies we move like gentle waves that stroke the sand.

Warm and safe, I am home.

Looking down, I see the tiny form we call a baby. I wonder. I jump.
Shrinking my expansive being ... smaller, smaller, smaller, down into this physical body ... we attempt to merge. Tight, constricted, heavy ... I feel awkward in these clothes. I gasp for air. In and out, I breathe and move ... the mantra of the soul.

As the body grows, my spirit settles in. Separate. Alone. Confined ... I am lost to this world of ideas.

I look up and see the vastness of the dark night sky. I feel a pull to remember.
I am each breath of air that fills my lungs. I am the stars and moon and depths of the deepest ocean. I am love and hate. I am me, and I am you. Aligned with Oneness, I am home.

KRISTINA: I had never heard of meditation until I was well into my adult years. Looking back, there were ways I naturally found my way back to the stillness inside. As a child I was often outside collecting grasshoppers, digging in the dirt, or laying in the sunlight. But without a conscious way of knowing how to align with the calm center inside myself, I didn't know how to accept and allow experiences to pass through me rather than getting stuck in them. Without this skill, I was not prepared for how to handle the trauma memories in a stable and transformative way when they came flying out, up front and center, permeating every aspect of my life.

When the intense memories and feelings eventually came to the surface in my late twenties, they carried with them a great force that demanded to be seen, as they were no longer tolerant of being ignored, like a terrible nightmare making its way into daily life. I quickly became taken over with the symptoms of PTSD, depression, anxiety, and flashbacks. Feeling that I had little control as to how to navigate the experiences I was having, I tried hard to stuff it all back down and pack it away. When that failed, I tried distraction and running, because the idea of allowing it to just be scared the hell out of me. I was afraid that it would completely take me over, as often it did. I tried everything I could to avoid the mayhem inside.

In the initial years, I turned to many different forms of avoidance. I created endless suffering for myself as well as inner confusion and a pattern of cycling through the wounds that kept them alive within me and had me continually reliving the trauma. Finally, after I had had enough suffering, living in chaos and pain without real progress, I reached a point where I was willing to do something different. With a great deal of grace and just enough openness to see the truth, I was given insight to realize I could potentially end up spending the rest of my life avoiding authentic living through distraction and suffering, or I could choose to face the pain and have a chance for deep healing, growth, and change.

Directly meeting the pain took me into feeling immense amounts of raw vulnerability. Being stripped of my defenses, I finally began to hold my feelings of worthlessness, betrayal, abuse, and brokenness in a way I never had before. I began to own my process, and though I had support from others, I no longer looked for my therapist, partner, or friends to be responsible for my healing. It was only inside of me that I would find the never-ending source of all peace, love, joy, and healing, even in the midst of the wounds. I was the one I had been waiting for.

What became a crucial component in my ability to finally meet myself in this direct way was learning how to find the stillness inside of me, even in the midst of the intense inner noise. I had to allow the pain to be, even if at times

I felt that I was going to be consumed by it. I found a way to hold the pain, connect and integrate it, instead of seeking temporary relief and comfort from something outside of myself. I gathered all of me in, denying nothing that came. I let it flow through me and tried not to attach to what I was experiencing, no matter how overwhelming and long-lasting it felt. I let go of the idea that I was ultimately in control of my process and began to grow in faith that there was a greater force in charge, one that was much more loving and wiser than I was. And I started to turn more and more of my pain over to this benevolent presence. My suffering began to lift, as I lowered my expectations of how things should be. Aligning myself instead to a deep inner peace, I could allow the pain to surface, flow, and release. Pulling in the essential wholeness of my being, I was able to be truly connected to myself and others, which brought me out of just surviving in a shell of a being into thriving in my authentic self.

More than ever before, at least in the West, we are learning the benefits of meditation and mindfulness, two closely related practices. There are many definitions and protocols for meditation, but for me, it simply means to dis-identify with thoughts and the conditioning of the mind. By doing so, we align and open to awareness, presence, or a pure state of consciousness. Mindfulness, at its root, means being aware of all that we are experiencing both internally and externally, and allowing one's self to experience all that is in the present moment. Whether that is focusing on your breath, drinking a cup of tea, or watching the sunset, your thoughts about the past and future fade and lose their grip when you are absorbed in what is happening in the present moment.

Meditation, through mindful living or other more formal practices, helps us to hold the wholeness of ourselves in a balanced and centered way. The act of surrendering to the present moment by aligning to the stillness within is not only an important key to the foundation of this book but is also a way out of the endless suffering that happens when we get hooked in our past or perseverate on our future. Some think meditation is being without thoughts, but really it is more about not attaching to our thoughts, just allowing them to come, and letting them go. Thoughts on their own have no power, but when we believe our thoughts to be true, they can have tremendous energy.

We do not have control over how or when our thoughts come, or even how they are constructed when they initially rise into our consciousness. Most of the thoughts that we have are cyclical in nature, which means they are not organic or new. They are thoughts about the past or future and tend to make us feel depressed or anxious. Over time, we become conditioned to these thoughts, and they become habitual. We then forget that we have the ability to create our own experiences through how we engage with our minds and our thoughts. Often thoughts about the past can come up and be extremely charged or become stronger over time as we give energy to them, so it might be difficult at first to find any space between the thought and the emotion that becomes connected with it. We have a thought, and by habit, we instantly believe it to be true. And soon, one thought leads to another, and a story is formed. From this process, our perceptions about reality become altered. This can quickly lead to a sense of feeling depressed, blocked, fearful, or in a state of suffering.

What we pay attention to grows. We feed our thoughts as we give them energy and focus on them. As we entertain and cultivate our thoughts, they stay around and create life forms of their own. We can lose touch with the deeper knowing that we are much more than our thoughts and feelings. When we lose the sense of a witness self or the awareness of the space between our thoughts, we are less able to work with ourselves in a way that is healing. However, we have the ultimate power in working with our thoughts, and by doing so, our minds can be in service to our hearts and deeper wisdom. We can choose to not believe and not attach to our thoughts. We can gain distance from them through quieting our minds, and then we can begin to question whether the thoughts we are having are true or real. From here, we have a greater capacity to work with them in a healing process and to let go of what is no longer serving us.

Deepening your alignment with pure consciousness and being centered

HEATHER: Imagine being in a boat on the surface of the sea. Each day, the weather and waves are different. Some days are calm, and other days are stormy, with the winds and waves buffeting your small vessel. As you live on the surface of the sea, you are impacted by all of these changes in the weather, waves, and in the currents of the sea. But imagine now diving deep below the surface of the sea. As you go deeper and deeper, you eventually come to a place of quiet and calm below the wind and waves. Stillness is here. You are no longer controlled by the weather and waves but are now a part of the vastness of the sea. This is what it means to live in stillness and to remember the consciousness that exists beneath the surface and storminess of our lives.

KRISTINA: As we choose to align to inner calm or stillness through the power of our attention, it grows stronger within us. We gain more stability and more inner peace as well as a spaciousness to allow everything to just be—to come and go, without needing to change ourselves and what we are experiencing. That means that we can also let our memories and negative beliefs about ourselves just be, without identifying with them or letting them define who we are. In this connecting to Source, stillness, or awareness, there is nothing to do, fix, take care of, accomplish, or create. It is a space of pure consciousness that has no agenda, and there is no need to do anything or to work anything out when we are here. In this state, we allow life to live through us, instead of us living life. It is the effortless effort in which a greater intelligence is flowing freely. In the presence of this pure consciousness there is nothing broken or wounded. Like empty pure space, there are no states of personality, but personality can be there. There are no feelings or thoughts, but they can be there too. Awareness or pure consciousness has no structure, rules, institutions, disease, or illness. It does not arrive or leave; it is timeless, limitless. It can neither be created or destroyed. It cannot be touched or manipulated by anything or anyone. This is the essence of your being. This is your soul's true self.

Our thoughts and beliefs are transitory; they come and go and change over time. They move over the surface of our underlying awareness, which is a constant state of pure consciousness. This deeper awareness is what perceives or is a witness to our mind and states of personality. In the pure space of inner consciousness, there is no sense of identity. This inner state has not been polluted, because you cannot touch it. There is no birth or death, gender, or age. This unaltered state of consciousness is our truest nature. All sensations, thoughts, and feelings appear in this presence, which is a vacuum or space in which all things transient come and go. All forms of our personality, thoughts, beliefs, and feelings come out of this state of consciousness. And when our form passes, this pure state of consciousness, this awareness, your soul self will remain. Presence, or pure consciousness, is like the sky. Thoughts, feelings, experiences, personality, all things that are transient, are like the clouds, which come and go, yet the sky remains the same—consistent, immoveable, and untouched.

HEATHER: Imagine that you are like the astronauts who gazed at the "beautiful, blue-green Earth" from their spaceship. While the astronauts viewed their planetary home, wars were waging on the surface of the Earth, and people were experiencing their lives in a diversity of ways, but the astronauts were in the stillness of outer space. Our Earth is a tiny speck in the vast expanse of the universe. All visible matter comprises only four percent of our universe. The rest is invisible. This is the consciousness that moves through the Cosmos. This is the fertile void. When we remember that we come from this Source, we remember that we are part of all that is. Then, we can come back to that deeper awareness and align with that consciousness within us that always is and never dies and is untouched by the surface events of our lives.

KRISTINA: Nothing can obliterate or take away this inner presence, but often we must intentionally choose to connect to it. When we lose our alignment to this purest form of consciousness, we begin to perceive ourselves as separate from peace, joy, and love. We form more of an association or identification with the turbulence of our emotions, negative thoughts, and past trauma. Our truest nature can be forgotten when we have invested too much in our personality, stories, thoughts, and feelings. We come to believe that this is all of who we are, and that we are made up of the experiences of our past and the effects it has had on us. We begin to lose touch with the reality that we are so much more than what we appear to be.

No matter how much we try to heal, healing alone will never be enough to stop our suffering. It is crucial to the process of being whole to unwind the conditioning of our mind, that when left unchecked, creates the illusion that we are separate from the true nature of our being, which is pure love. Each of us is able to break out of this conditioning by choosing not to attach to our thoughts, which gives us space to align with inner stillness. When thoughts, images, feelings, or body sensations arise, it is fine to let them come, but you must also let them pass through you. It is important to build the energy of that deeper awareness inside our bodily form. The more our attention can rest in stillness, at the center of our being, the more we will be able to feel this as our truest nature. From here, we can bring all our thoughts, feelings, emotions, and wounds into this pure state of inner calm.

If we are aligned mainly to our personality, feelings, thoughts, and wounds, peace will be fleeting and dependent on what we are experiencing in the moment, which leaves us on shaky ground. There will always be a sense that something is wrong with us, that we are not enough, and that something needs to change, which leads to endless suffering. When we step into awareness, it is not that we ignore our pain or the feelings we are experiencing. It simply means we are not rooted there. We hold more of the truth and wholeness of ourselves when we are able to fold the woundedness into stillness. This allows us to be at peace and to experience gratitude for what is, even in the midst of the healing process. We do not lose ourselves to what we feel is broken; instead, we are able to be in balance and integrate what is fragmented in the personality. When we hold more of this complete way of being, we are capable of working our past trauma in a way that is healing and not re-traumatizing.

As we align with our soul self, this inner spaciousness expands, and our feelings and thoughts can be there, but they become background instead of foreground. Through the healing process and beyond, the more consistent state that we experience is this inner peace, and all pain, from the past and present, can have its movement without becoming our identity. This allows for there to be a more constant and open flow of emotions, thoughts, sensations, and memories to bubble up from stuck and stored places inside of us, that are then able to be released in a natural way, as our psyche and body come back into balance.

Some people feel that there is a particular way to meditate correctly or align with stillness, but in reality, we naturally do it all the time, although we might not recognize it as meditation. It can be helpful to realize the times we enter inner stillness without effort, even if it is just fleeting moments. Then, it becomes a matter of stretching out these moments. The mind may tell us these few seconds or minutes don't matter, but they do. As we are able to stretch these quiet moments, little by little, peace grows within us. Have you ever watched the sun rise and felt yourself open to its rays? Or in seeing light reflecting off of water, sensed a pull that held your gaze and kept your thoughts more at bay? Have you experienced walking in the woods and hearing the birds or a stream nearby, and felt a peace wash over you, or a sense that everything is being held in a larger perspective? Maybe you have looked into the innocence of your baby's eyes, and this connection brings your own sense of awareness back to you. Many activities can quiet the mind and bring you into alignment with stillness, if you are present to it and give it your full attention.

Using mindfulness as a way to meditate or find stillness allows us to focus on the present moment through our senses. One easy way to do this is by paying attention to your breath, because it is always there and with you. Gently counting the breath, paying close attention to how the air feels in your nose and chest and the rise and fall of the abdomen, can bring you back into the knowledge of how perfectly your body functions on its own, without needing you to do anything. You can also place your attention on what you see or hear that is around you. When you do this, pay attention to the details, to the subtle differences in the shades of color or the tones in the melody of music.

Tuning into the sensations in our bodies, both internal and external, is another way to focus our attention on the present moment. Taking a warm bath and feeling the water on your skin, recognizing and thanking each part of your body as it is washed over, connects you not only to your own physical body but also moves you much deeper into sensing the awareness that runs through you. Even in the simplicity of watching water boil or the flame of a candle, you can gain space away from your thoughts as you become more aware of the nuances and subtle movements. There are countless ways through using your senses to focus on the present moment to give less attention to the thoughts that arise. Another way to align to stillness is to spend time with animals who have not lost their connection to presence. As we tune into their energy, we are reminded of our true birthright, and the wisdom to allow ourselves to just be.

Sometimes motion provides an easier way to stillness. While walking or running, we can observe and feel more aware of the details of our surroundings, or we can zone out from what is around us and drop deeper into the quiet space inside. Yoga, qigong, swimming, and martial arts are also forms of meditation in movement and are potential paths to inner stillness. Another way to meditate is to block out all forms of body sensations and anything coming in through our five senses. Dropping directly into the silence or gap between sounds, words, or music, we align to awareness. This is the practice of being in stillness, even when there is activity around us.

Mantras can be used as a powerful tool to break the constant stream of thoughts. A mantra is a word or sound that when repeated carries a powerful energy of peace and truth. From ancient Sanskrit or other ancient wisdom traditions, these mantras have the power to expand awareness and diffuse the control of our thoughts and mind. One powerful mantra is the syllable "Om" from the Vedic text, which is pronounced "ohm" as in "home." Om is the sound for God, Source, pure consciousness, and when repeated it increases your life force and connects you to the oneness of all that is. Another possible Sanskrit mantra is "Namah Shivaya," which means "I bow to Shiva." Shiva means your true nature, which is your pure state of consciousness.

Many spiritual teachers feel the only mantra needed is to say, "Thank you." To me, it encompasses the energy of gratitude with an understanding that everything is flowing in its perfect state of being. Gratitude can be a powerful path into alignment. This can begin with focusing on all that you are grateful for in your life. If you go beyond the attitude of gratitude and move more into the feeling of being grateful, you will move into a higher vibrational state and begin to open more to peace and even joy. As you work with this form of meditation, it can eventually lead you into a deeper state of gratitude that is less about what you are grateful for in your life in an external way and more about your gratitude for your awareness that you are eternal. You are a soul self having a human experience and are held in the love of the infinite, and ultimately you will return to this Source.

As you strive to align with Source and inner awareness, if your mind is very active, it might be helpful to use a guided meditation, particularly one that is given by someone who more consistently stays in a state of presence. You can find numerous meditations or guidance into awareness or higher consciousness in the companion workbook. Just by listening to the voice of someone who is speaking from a place of centeredness will often be enough to align you there. It is an energetic field that you open to and become a part of, and it can be a direct way to bring you home to your innermost being.

Another way to drop deeper or expand more into alignment is to step out of your thoughts and focus your mind. You might imagine yourself in peaceful surroundings, like sitting on the sand watching the gentle waves rolling in and out on the shore or standing in a meadow surrounded by wildflowers and sunlight. When we meditate, either through a formal practice, or with focused attention, we are aligning to the purest form of consciousness that is our natural, most organic state of being. We can align to stillness anywhere, anytime, and under any circumstance; all it takes is to focus our attention on the awareness that is always there, never changing. The more attention that we give to this inner stillness, the less we feed the mind, and the more our sense of inner calm will grow.

Aligning to pure consciousness changes our relationship to pain and our woundedness. As we merge with stillness, we gain greater tolerance and acceptance and an ability to embrace what is, in a way that is not attached yet is deeply connected. As long as we are in human form living on this planet, we will experience pain. But pain passes, if we can form a healthy relationship with it. It does not linger as ongoing suffering. We *allow* instead of deny by recognizing and welcoming the experience, keeping it all in fluid motion. This way, we naturally create a balanced, stable, and safe way to facilitate being in right relationship with ourselves. Our bodies are able to feel most present and integrated when we allow all to be and flow, while staying in this state of consciousness. From this place, we are centered and clear about how to be in right relationship with others and about how to work with the more complex aspects of our personalities.

When you are aligned to stillness, you are centered in your heart and attuned to the deepest wisdom of your being. This is the everlasting spring from which all organic, creative, and divine forces originate within us. When this is your foundation, your mind is in service to your heart instead of your heart being in service to your mind. The premise of the ARCH model is to have at your base a strong alignment to your soul self and to stillness. This gives you a solid ground to be in right relationship with yourself so that you can bring all aspects of your being into pure consciousness and ultimately heal. We are all here as consciousness in embodied forms to experience separation and duality so that we can have the opportunity to grow in wisdom and compassion. When we are wounded, we feel the pain of separation. As we choose how to hold the pain and heal the wounds within this inner stillness, we feel connected again and our souls evolve as our consciousness expands.

Working with Alignment in the ARCH medicine wheel

Smudge with sage or say a prayer of gratitude for the medicine wheel and then walk silently into the wheel from the south. Stand beside the stone in the south and connect with the meaning and energy of Alignment. Tune into your heart. Remember that you are a spiritual being having a human experience. Connect with your deeper soul self and, at the same time, tune into your body and emotions and honor all of who you are. Place your hands on your heart and breathe in and out slowly, releasing any stress or tension with the out breath, and when breathing in, focus on your heart.

Now, walk silently and slowly into the center of the medicine wheel. Connect with the energy of the center of the wheel and with the place of centeredness and stillness within you. If you are feeling a lot of intense emotions, visualize yourself as in the eye of a hurricane. Picture in your mind's eye the winds and rain swirling around you, but feel yourself in that place of calm in the center. Now, breathe in and out slowly and allow yourself to feel your connection with the Earth. Feel how the Earth grounds you, supports you, and nurtures you. Take in that grounding, loving energy. Now, shift your focus to the sky and feel the light of the Sun and the energy of the stars and planets above you. Look up at the blue expanse of the sky and gaze at the clouds. Allow yourself to feel that expansive energy and see yourself from that higher perspective. Breathe in the wisdom and boundless energy of the sky while still feeling your grounding connection with the Earth. Now, draw all of those energies into your heart. When you are ready, walk back to the stone in the south. Giving thanks for this experience of alignment, walk slowly out of the circle.

(Refer to the appendix for more meditations on how to come into alignment.)

CHAPTER 4

R - Relationship

HEATHER: As we continue around the healing medicine wheel, we come to the direction of the west and to the Relationship aspect of the ARCH model. As you walk the medicine wheel, enter from the south and take a moment to feel aligned with your inner stillness and to the Earth and sky and center of all that is. Then, walk slowly clockwise around the circle to the stone in the west. Pause here to meditate on the relationships in your life. Hold with gratitude the relationships in the past and in your current life that are supportive of you. Also, allow yourself to honor what you have learned from those relationships that have been painful for you. Tune into how you are in relationship with yourself and whether you are being compassionate and loving with yourself or ways you may be critical, hurtful, or neglectful. Allow yourself to hold with gratitude the relationships in your life and how coming into right relationship with yourself and being in healthy relationships with others are a profound part of your healing process.

Feeling loved, held, and supported in your life is fundamental to the formation of your sense of self, your healing and moving into wholeness. We are relational beings and are meant to be in loving relationships with each other and also to have a sense of being in relationship with the Divine or with our understanding of cosmic consciousness. We develop our sense of self, evolve, and heal in relationship. If you have grown up in a loving environment, you internalize a healthy sense of self and have the capacity to give and receive love in your relationships as well as relate to yourself in a caring way. Having a sense of connection with or relationship to Spirit, to cosmic or pure consciousness or your understanding of the Divine, is also an important part of your identity. Without this, you are likely to experience at some deep level a sense of separation or alienation from Source and lack a deeper sense of meaning in your life and understanding of your path and purpose.

Our deepest wounds occur in relationship and involve some sense of rupture or separation (usually through experiencing abuse, neglect, or abandonment). These traumatic experiences may then lead to a fragmentation of the sense of self, difficulties in relationships, and a sense of separation from the Divine or from our connectedness with the oneness of all that is. To be whole, it is important to have a good relationship with yourself, with others, and with your understanding of the Divine or Spirit or cosmic consciousness. Disruption or trauma, at any one of these levels, leads to imbalances or difficulties in the others. When you experience rupture or a sense of separation in relationships, this can manifest in a wide range of behaviors and emotional difficulties. The spectrum ranges from the extreme of feeling that you are a victim of events or the actions of others, to the other end of the spectrum of becoming a perpetrator. This range extends from a sense of powerlessness to a compulsive need for control as a way of protection. There are many other variations and manifestations of imbalances in the sense of self and relationship along that spectrum.

Below are some common ways that the effects of trauma may manifest at the extreme ends of the spectrum in different levels of relationship. At core, trauma leads to a sense of separation—from self, others, and from Spirit.

Spectrum of how trauma in relationship may manifest

From extreme victimization to becoming an abuser:

Victim	*Abuser*
Identification with victimization	Abusive or violent behavior
Helplessness, powerlessness	Need to dominate, be in control
Difficulties with trust	Treating others as objects
Fear or avoidance of relationships	Pattern of exploitation

Separation from a healthy sense of self:

Loss of a clear sense of self

Fragmentation of identity (Dissociative Identity Disorder)

Dissociation

Lack of self-esteem or self-worth

Self-destructive behavior

Grandiose sense of self

Living a facade, false sense of self (Narcissistic Personality)

Denial; inner emptiness

Grandiosity, underlying feelings of inadequacy

Need for control or affirmation from others

Separation or rupture from a sense of Spirit or the Divine:

Separation from Source

Existential despair, meaninglessness

Atheism

Sense of life and the universe as random

Lack of trust in life

Identification of ego with the infinite

Hubris, ego as god

Rigid religiosity

Assertion of dominance

Need for control, fear of death

If you have experienced severe trauma, this can have a profound effect, not only on your sense of identity but on your trust and ability to engage in healthy relationships and with connecting with the Divine. If you lose trust in your relationships, you are likely to also feel abandoned by God or Spirit. You will tend to have a diminished sense of self and may suffer from chronic anxiety and depression. Or you may overcompensate and develop a grandiose or exaggerated sense of self to cover underlying feelings of inadequacy and emptiness and have an obsessive need for power and control, and you may become rigid or dogmatic in your religious beliefs.

For most of us, the source of our trauma is in our close relationships. Early childhood trauma has an especially damaging effect, since the first few years of life are crucial in the development of our personalities and in learning to trust and to feel safe with being vulnerable, open, and connected with others. Early trauma can lead to significant difficulties with attachment issues and often results in a tendency to be anxious, avoidant, or ambivalent in interactions with others. Trauma can also lead to confusion about boundaries in relationships and a susceptibility to getting into relationships that repeat the neglect, abuse, or trauma of the past. To heal from your past trauma, you need to experience what it means to be in a safe, supportive, and loving relationship. This allows you to internalize this as a model for how your adult self can relate to the young, wounded parts of yourself. Otherwise, you may tend to treat yourself and your young child aspects with the same neglect or destructive patterns that you experienced in the past.

A healing relationship can come in many forms. You may experience this in a relationship with a therapist, healer, partner, friend, family member, or another significant other. You can also experience healing relationships in group contexts such as in therapy groups, sacred circles, or in a supportive community. At times, for those who have had severe early trauma, there may be a pervasive distrust of human relationships, and a loving connection may be sought through a relationship with a pet or with nature. Some children experience a primary safe relationship with a stuffed animal or imaginary friend. You also may seek relationship through connecting with the Divine and with those in other realms (such as with ancestors who have died or spirit guides). As humans, we need relationship. At whatever level we begin to reconnect and feel a sense of being loved, we are able to move towards healing and wholeness.

HEATHER: Early in my career, I worked with many people who had severe early trauma, who were abused, neglected, or experienced active hatred from their parents and were diagnosed with schizophrenia. As adults, these people tended to be socially avoidant and spent most of their time alone. However, they would hunger for relationship and seek it with imaginary friends or lovers, through a relationship with a pet, or even through connecting with characters in movies or in books. One young schizophrenic adolescent client that I worked with showed no interest in connecting with peers or other people and could not even make eye contact with me. We would sit side by side on the couch in my office (since even sitting face to face was too difficult for him). I would listen as he talked in a detached and often obsessive way about his fascination with science and with black holes in particular and about their capacity to destroy matter. His description of these black holes was a profound metaphor for the destructive and invasive dynamics that he experienced at home with his parents. His only sense of a safe connection in the world was with his dog.

The earlier the trauma and lack of safety, the greater the difficulties there will be with trust and with forming healthy relationships with others. Early trauma also results in a stunted, distorted, or destructive relationship with the self. It is difficult to relate to yourself with care and compassion if you have not experienced this from another. Not only does trauma often result in difficulty forming relationships, but it can lead to a tendency to relive the traumatic patterns experienced in your childhood in later adult relationships. You may tend to re-enact the abusive patterns that you experienced in the past in your current relationships. This may be due to not having internalized a model for a loving relationship in your childhood. It also can be a way that the young wounded parts that have been repressed or split off from your adult self are trying to show what they experienced (by re-enacting it for your adult self). Acting out or self-destructive behaviors may also be due to the beliefs that you internalized through your traumatic experiences, such as "I don't deserve to be loved," "to be loved means being hurt or abused," "I deserve to be punished because I am bad," or "it is my fault that the abuse happened to me." You might replay your past painful experiences in an effort to change and heal them, but instead end up re-enacting the very patterns that were so traumatizing for you.

How then do you heal from trauma if relationships don't feel safe or if you tend to confuse intimacy and abuse? And how do you know if the relationship you are in is a healing relationship? If you have never experienced a safe relationship and are unable to trust others, it is important to seek out a therapist or healing practitioner who understands attachment issues and who can gently be a support in building a sense of trust and of what it means to be in a healthy relationship.

The qualities of a healing relationship are:

- having a sense of being seen and heard (empathic attunement)
- feeling that the other person holds you in respect and compassion
- feeling that the connection is not based on your being used, abused, or exploited, but is based on what supports you in being who you are
- experiencing clear boundaries in the relationship, so that you don't feel neglected, invaded, or violated emotionally or physically

Our journey here on Earth is a process of growing in love and in wisdom, of moving towards healing and wholeness. We do that in the context of relationship—relationship with the Source of all that is, with ourselves, and with each other.

Forms of healing relationships

There are many forms and types of healing relationships. The healing relationship may be professional (such as with a therapist or healing practitioner) or personal (such as with a partner or spouse, a close friend, or a family member). We also may have healing relationships with spiritual guides, mentors, supportive circles or groups, or with nature.

Here are some of the possibilities of healing relationships:

Professional relationships with a therapist or healing practitioner

It is often an important and necessary part of the healing process to have the support of a therapist or healing practitioner who is experienced in working with trauma to guide you as you move through the more intense parts of your healing journey. This can help you in pacing the process, in managing the intense emotions and memories that surface, and in knowing how to navigate your current relationships and responsibilities as you heal the wounds from the past. If you are dealing with early trauma, it is important to seek out a therapist who is willing to engage in a more in-depth ongoing process with you that will incorporate different therapeutic modalities but that also fosters a chance to experience a genuine healing relationship. Find a therapist who has experience working with different aspects or parts of the self, so that you can begin to connect with the dissociated and wounded parts of you that still hold the trauma. This book discusses a way of working with these aspects of the self. Other models of therapy such as Internal Family Systems, psychosynthesis, or psychodynamic models also incorporate an approach to working with the parts of the self.

It is also important to work with a therapist who is committed to getting at the root of your issues and who seeks to understand you as a unique individual. If you feel labelled and diagnosed and treated in a programmed way rather than heard and understood in the uniqueness of who you are and your history, find another therapist. Also, if you are looking to find healing through a relationship with a therapist, make sure that the therapist not only has training in working with trauma but also understands attachment issues (and problems with trust and safety in relationships). It is also important to work with a therapist who has done work on their own issues in therapy so that they stay clear about their own wounds and past trauma and don't in any way project that onto you or re-enact that with you. Ask the therapist if they are in therapy or have done therapy in the past. If the therapist has not done any personal therapy or becomes defensive when you ask about this, it is likely that this is not a safe person for you to do in-depth work with. It is important to work with someone who is conscious of their own wounds and issues, so they will not unconsciously try to work out their unresolved issues in relationship with you.

HEATHER: I was in my own therapy for almost twenty years, during my training and then throughout the years that I was doing intensive trauma work with others. I felt that it was crucial to engage in my own therapy to work on my past wounds, to become more and more conscious of my patterns and issues, and to work through the profound emotions evoked by sharing in the trauma of others. I also engaged in ongoing supervision and training across many years to refine my clinical skills and understanding of trauma. I realized how not doing ongoing personal work can lead to blind spots or limitations in being an effective therapist. For example, I remember a period of time in my personal therapy when I was confronting my fear of conflict and of expressing my anger. As I began to work this through and was more able to face my own feelings of anger, several of my clients spontaneously began to talk about their anger for the first time in their sessions with me. I realized that at some unconscious level, they had sensed my discomfort with this emotion, and so they had avoided bringing up their own feelings of anger.

It is also important to work with a therapist who engages with you in a respectful manner. Too often, there is a hierarchical dynamic in the therapy relationship, with the therapist and client joining together to perceive the therapist as the healthy, wise, and knowing one and the client as the dependent, unhealthy, or "mentally ill" one in the relationship. This is a dangerous dynamic and can lead to ways that the therapy relationship re-enacts past painful patterns rather than being healing. While the therapist has been professionally trained to be of help to others and has, hopefully, done personal therapy to be aware of their own issues and to heal their past wounds, both people in the therapy relationship have gifts and weaknesses. Both are to varying degrees healthy and wounded, and both are a complex union of diverse parts of the self. It is important to be in relationship with a therapist who sees you with respect and holds the complexity of the therapeutic process with humility.

Pay attention to whether you feel heard and respected for who you are by your therapist. I remember working with a number of people in an inpatient psychiatric hospital who were there after an acute psychotic episode. They had been diagnosed as delusional and were on heavy antipsychotic medications. While the medication was often needed and helpful in supporting them in becoming stabilized in order to resume their lives, it saddened me to hear how many said that the hospital staff rarely listened to them or took their stories seriously. Even people who are in acute psychosis or "delusional" are relaying what has happened to them and what is at the root of their pain, and if listened to, can be understood in what they are trying to say about their trauma through their feelings, images, dreams, and metaphors.

It is also important to have a therapist who believes in your capacity to heal and who trusts that you are more than your wounds. Work with a therapist who sees you in your wholeness and supports you in believing in yourself.

Kristina
2005

I had been hospitalized in a psychiatric ward just a few blocks from my house in Washington DC. I couldn't stop wanting to die, and prolonged anorexia, misuse of prescription drugs, and self-destructive behavior were just enough to get me admitted. Either way, I didn't care, I was just too scared to directly kill myself. And the only thing keeping me on the planet were my two sons, and I was growing stronger in my conviction that they would be better off without me. Looking back, if I knew how bad an inpatient experience would be, it might have been enough motivation for me to keep myself out of it. It was not a place to heal; it was a holding place until I figured out how to get out.

Shuffling myself into a bare, sterile room, with my only belongings being the clothes on my back, I was met with an aggressive roommate, who immediately said, "Don't touch any of my stuff." I curled up on my bed in the fetal position and cried. I was not prepared for the stark reality that the place that was supposed to help me would reinforce my trauma. I was a shell of a being, and it felt like there was nothing left of me. I had given up that I would ever get better.

I was called into a room where there was a psychiatrist with a group of medical students, probably eight to ten of them, all sitting in a group with notepads. He asked me a few basic questions, and then began to dictate to the students as he read through my chart. They didn't look up as they took notes on me, the "subject." He read from my file: "She has an extensive trauma history, incest, attachment disorder, she is diagnosed with PTSD, an eating disorder, and DSM ... blah, blah, blah." I could see his mouth moving, but the words sounded like they were under water along with my head. The only utterance that seemed to come together with such clarity, to the extent that I could feel the words vibrate and echo through the shell of my being, was when he said, "She will never get better or be able to contribute to society. There's no treatment for her to recover." And I watched as the students, along with the doctor, closed their notebooks in a definitive way, and left me sitting in the empty room ... in my empty vessel.

I guess in the end, there was something in me that refused to believe it.

HEATHER: Another pitfall that many therapists might have is in trying to unconsciously work a past wound around having had a depressed or troubled parent by being a therapist to others. A primary unconscious motivation for me to become a therapist was that I had been trying since early childhood to heal my mother of her depression and emotional reactivity. As a child, I felt that if I was able to heal her, then she would be more safe in relationship with me and better able to love me and see me in the ways that I longed for. So I developed a compulsive pattern with her and then later in my other relationships of being the caretaker. This is a dynamic that is true for many of us who become therapists, and this often leads to the therapist's need to be needed and can foster an unhealthy dependency in clients. The therapist may also unconsciously base their own sense of worth on how the client responds to their efforts to be helpful.

The foundation of the therapy or healing relationship needs to be based on compassion and respect, not on need—neither the neediness of the young parts of the client longing for a parent or the wounded parts of the therapist longing to be a healer. The more there is a conscious fostering of an adult-adult connection in the relationship and a strengthening of the witness self in both people, the more healing the relationship will be as, together, both can witness and hold the healing process. We are each on our own journey. Therapy can be helpful and healing, but it is ultimately the responsibility of each one of us to take charge of our own life and healing. It is dangerous when the client seeks the therapist to be the miracle healer who will transform and "save" them whether or not they fully participate in the process, or who seeks the therapist to be the rescuer or the loving parent they never had. It is also dangerous for the therapist to collude with the client's idealization or longing for them to be the perfect, loving other. This can often lead to the therapist becoming angry or punitive with the client when, inevitably, this idealization shatters, and the therapist is then seen by the client as disappointing if not harmful.

One further note about finding a therapist: A term that you will often hear is that therapy should be "evidence-based," meaning that the approach is based on empirical research. While there is value in the emphasis on "evidence-based" approaches to therapy, it often leads to short-term treatment with forms of therapy (such as Dialectic Behavioral Therapy or Cognitive Behavioral Therapy) focused on symptom management and is often used in collaboration with psychotropic medications. These approaches can be helpful, but it is important to differentiate between treatment and healing within a therapeutic context. The notion of therapy as "treatment for mental health issues" comes from a more allopathic understanding of therapy. In other words, it is modeled after the current western medical model, with a heavy emphasis on the belief that there are physiological or neurological origins of "illness" and on methods of treatment through medication and behavioral or cognitive interventions. This can help a person to stabilize and to manage symptoms, but this type of approach does not engage in getting at the root of the difficulties or in deeper healing that results in an integrated and whole sense of self.

It is very helpful to meet with a therapist for an initial consultation. Take time after the session to tune into all of the parts of yourself to sense whether this person feels like a good fit for you. Honor your own feelings and intuition, and do not override your perceptions by focusing on external credentials or any other factors. Ask yourself if you feel safe with this person and whether you feel seen and understood.

If you are working with a healing practitioner other than a therapist, set up a consultation or initial session and tune in to how the process feels. Does the modality feel like a good fit for you? Is there a resonance on some level that you can trust the work and practitioner? What is their training and experience? What will the focus be for the healing—is it energy work, bodywork, or some form of emotional or physical healing? Also, it is important to be clear in your expectations. It is good to have a discussion about the healing process, what you can realistically expect, and how to assess indications of progress and healing.

Here are some questions to ask a potential therapist (and issues to be aware of):

- What is the therapist's level of training and have they done their own personal healing work?
- Does the therapist have experience working with trauma? Do they understand how to work with the different aspects or parts of the self (such as the young parts still caught in the trauma)?
- When you consult with the therapist, do you feel respected, and do you feel truly seen and heard?
- Is the therapist focused on helping you get to the root of your issues or is the therapist concerned primarily with managing your symptoms and behaviors?

A note to therapists: Engaging in deep therapeutic trauma work is not easy. It is important to allow yourself to be supported in the process—through supervision and peer consultation. Doing your own therapy is also critical in that we cannot take any of our clients deeper than we have been able to go ourselves. Hold yourself and your clients with compassion as you are on this journey together. Remember that there is no right or perfect way to do this process. It is inevitably messy and imperfect, like parenting. What is most important is to be present, to care, and to be open to hearing and seeing your clients to the best of your ability. When you hit a rough spot in the process, take time to look at your own part in it and explore what may be playing out in the dynamics between you. Do not get caught in blaming the client for your own mistakes or limitations. But also, do not blame yourself when the therapy does not meet your hopes or the expectations of the client. Sometimes, it is not the right time to do the work, or the right fit between you and the client, or the client may be ambivalent about going more deeply into the process. Or, you may have hit the limitations of your own training and experience. Honor that, if you have done your best and been respectful and fully present, whatever has transpired has the potential to seed further healing in the future.

Ongoing training and understanding the current research on effective approaches are valuable. When doing trauma work, it is particularly important to know the manifestations and complexity of PTSD and different therapeutic modalities. With clients who have childhood abuse, it is vital to have knowledge of early developmental stages in order to fully understand and support the parts of the client that may be mired in these early phases. But also remember that all of our modalities and theories are helpful templates but are ultimately limited. Learn as much as you can and then, when with your client, let go of the filters of your theories and listen to your client as a unique person. Let yourself open to your intuition as well as your intellect, and listen with your heart more than your brain. Allow yourself to be in the not-knowing rather than trying to label or diagnose your client and then fit them into a pre-packaged treatment plan. Do what is healing and not what is based on research or insurance companies' expectations. Empathic attunement, deep listening, and compassion are more healing than prescriptions, directives, or interpretations.

Honor that the therapy process is at its root a relationship. You are not neutral in the process. If you do this work deeply, you will be impacted and your own issues or unresolved conflicts will be triggered. This can be mutually healing if you maintain responsibility for your own conscious and unconscious process and do your own work. The therapy process is a synthesis of both individuals and the energy of the relationship that arises from your interactions with each other. Hold yourself and your client with respect and, together, honor that intersubjective field. Be willing to admit mistakes, to be vulnerable yet also respectful of your own boundaries, feelings, and limitations. Therapy is an improvisational dance with no predetermined script or choreographed plan. Be in the mystery of the process and the profound transformation that can result for you both, and hold yourself and your client with love, respect, and acceptance. And trust that you both are held by universal energies larger than yourselves.

Personal relationships with a friend, family member, partner, or lover

HEATHER: Often deep healing may occur for you in the context of a close personal relationship, such as with your partner or spouse, a close friend, or a family member. It is important to remember that in your closest relationships, your deepest vulnerabilities and wounds will tend to be triggered at some point. If you have a history of significant early trauma, your painful memories will get activated in many different experiences in your intimate relationships. It is important to hold this process with compassion and tenderness as you continue to become more conscious of what precipitates the wound or pain of the past that gets activated.

If one or both of you in the relationship gets triggered, and you are in a reactive interaction, take a time-out. It is important for you both to individually take time to calm down, reflect on what you are feeling, what younger wounded parts of you may be getting triggered and acting out in the moment. Create time and space for this inner dialogue or reflection, so that you can bring what is happening internally into consciousness. Once worked through individually, and when you are feeling centered again, return to the relationship in a clear, balanced place. It is also helpful for this to be part of an ongoing dialogue in your relationship, so that you are both able to hold these moments with tolerance, to be better able to work through ways in which you activate each other's deeper wounds. Remember also to avoid the false polarization and projection that one of you is "normal" and the other "damaged." We are all both wounded and whole; we may just be in different places on that spectrum, with different past experiences and current vulnerabilities.

Sibling relationships

Kristina: Sometimes, siblings who have grown up in the same abusive home environment can provide each other with a common understanding and be mutually supportive. If you have siblings that have done their own healing, or at least are actively working on it, they can then empathize with your process, and be a true support. This relationship can be a catalyst for healing the past. At other times, siblings may play out their own anger and pain in their relationships with each other. If this is the case, it is often more helpful to work out the healing of your past within a neutral setting with someone who can be supportive and hold space for you without reacting personally to your experiences. This can be a therapist, healing practitioner, spiritual teacher, or mentor. This can also be done with a friend or partner who did not have similar trauma experiences, as long as the person is able to be non-reactive and nonjudgmental. That way, your feelings and memories can be heard without triggering the other person or activating their denial or need to discount what you are sharing as a way to protect themselves from their own wounds. It is also essential to remember that, if you have an early trauma history, your memories and feelings may not always match up with those of your siblings who might have had a different experience within the family system or who may have responded to the abusive environment in a very different way. Honor and trust your own truth and be careful not to question or discount your feelings and perceptions if they are different from those of a sibling.

Parent relationships

Heather: It has been profound for me across the years to see how people with early trauma are often able to help heal young aspects of themselves as they strive to be a good and loving parent for their own children. If you had early abuse and did not feel safe with your parents, the young parts of you will be witnessing the difference in how you are relating to your own children and will be internalizing that difference. In this way, you will be better able to gain the trust of your young parts and also increase your capacity to hold them in love and compassion.

However, it is critical that you stay observant about any ways that you might be relating towards your child that is the same or similar to what you experienced in your childhood with an abusive or neglectful parent. Allow yourself to bring these into conscious awareness and to seek out your own healing so that you can shift these patterns and develop a more whole and healing relationship with yourself and with your child. Remember that it is a process, and that no parent is perfect—ever. Your child does not need you to be perfect but to be open, self-aware, and responsive, and for you to take responsibility for your behavior in relationship to them.

Know that you are likely to have painful memories from the past that may have been long buried or split off that will come to the surface when your child reaches the age of your own trauma. I have known many people who have experienced intense, overwhelming emotions and trauma reactions arising at these times, often without any clear, conscious awareness of where these feelings were coming from. It is vital to allow these feelings to rise up and to find a safe context within yourself or in a healing relationship to begin to explore these feelings and allow the memories to emerge. This can be a profound albeit painful portal for deeper healing.

Groups: therapy groups, sacred circles

HEATHER: Therapy groups are often a helpful context for doing healing work in a supportive way with others who are working on similar issues in their lives. For some people, this form of therapy feels safer than the more intense and intimate context of individual therapy. Groups may offer a way for healing within relationships that feel safe without feeling too threatening or intimidating. This can then allow more readiness for further, more intensive, individual therapeutic work at a later date.

A format for healing which I have found to be particularly profound is being in a sacred circle. A sacred circle is not a therapy group, although it involves sharing and healing at a deep level together. A sacred circle is a group that comes together to engage in sharing, ceremony, and growing in consciousness. These groups are usually spiritual in their focus but not affiliated with any particular religion or belief system. I have facilitated sacred circles, especially for women, for over thirty years and have been profoundly moved by the healing and transformation that can occur as we hold each other's stories and experiences with compassion, honor our uniqueness, and have the understanding that the circle is more than the sum of all of the individuals involved. Part of the power of a sacred circle is consciously calling in the energies of the circle and of Spirit to guide the process and to hold everyone in safe and sacred space. As we share and engage in ceremony together, we learn to see ourselves more clearly and heal. We are able to feel met, accepted, and become more empowered to be in the fullness of who we are.

I will say, however, that whether in a therapy group or a sacred circle, the power of a circle has the potential to be either extremely healing or re-traumatizing. If the group is not facilitated well and if there are undercurrents, projections, or acting out in the group that are not directly addressed, the process can be deeply wounding. If you are choosing to be in a therapy group or in a sacred circle, make sure that you know that the facilitator(s) are well trained and experienced in holding the process in a safe and healing manner.

(Please see the section in the appendix for more information about working in a sacred circle.)

Mentors or spiritual teachers

HEATHER: You may develop a strong healing relationship with a mentor or spiritual teacher. This can provide you with an increased sense of support, guidance, and counsel through your process. With a spiritual teacher, you may gain a greater understanding of the larger context of your trauma and how to deepen in your experience of being held in Divine love. As you connect with the love of the Divine that is within you and beyond you, you often find a source of safety and compassion that can hold you through the dark times as you heal from your wounds and traumatic experiences.

However, you must remember that you may also project the painful dynamics with your parents onto your relationship with your spiritual teacher and even onto your understanding of Spirit or the Divine. If your parents were abusive or neglectful, this may evoke a sense of your teacher and of God as judgmental, punishing, or detached. If you have a spiritual teacher or guide who is experienced, they can help you become conscious of these patterns. Having a healing and loving relationship with a spiritual teacher may then help you to reframe and rebuild your relationship with God or Spirit. As you develop your witness self and learn to align with inner stillness, it is more and more possible to experience true divine healing love, as you feel a sense of oneness with something larger than yourself.

Being in a relationship with a wise and caring religious leader or spiritual teacher can be an incredible source of healing and guidance. Many who are highly sensitive and working through severe early trauma can also inadvertently attach to a spiritual teacher or guru or immerse themselves in a spiritual group as a way to remain dissociated from the pain of the past. The relationship with the spiritual teacher or group may provide guidance, compassion, and solace, but will not necessarily lead to healing in a more integrative way. Your wounded parts may continue to remain split off and unseen. Religion or spirituality can be a source of healing and of growing in consciousness, or it can become a form of addiction or spiritual bypass as a way to avoid facing your pain and doing the deeper healing work. It can be easy to fall into idealizing the spiritual teacher and to look to them to be the perfect loving other you have been longing for. You may then give your power away to this person and lose your sense of self or fall prey to being controlled or manipulated by an unconscious, narcissistic, or unintegrated spiritual teacher. Be clear about your expectations, do not give your power away, and ultimately take responsibility for your own spiritual journey as well as your healing process.

People seek relationships with gurus, guides, or spiritual teachers in the earthly realm, but many also seek to connect with spirit guides, angels, or helpers from other non-physical realms. This can be a powerful form of spiritual relationship that may be profoundly healing. However, individuals with trauma might use connecting to other realms as a way to avoid relating with humans and the pain of this physical reality. This can become a way to avoid facing the fear of being in relationships. In these cases, it becomes important to work on the trauma and trust issues to deepen the capacity to be in healthy relationships in the physical dimension, as well as being in relationships with spiritual guides or helpers in the invisible realms. Any relationship that does not guide you into greater wholeness and integrative healing, with the capacity to feel more empowered to be in the fullness of who you are, is not a healing relationship; instead, it may be a way in which you are becoming dependent on an idealized other, giving away your power and losing a true sense of self.

Kristina
2015

Through the healing process, my soul had to begin searching for God again. I had lost hope and connection through my dark night of the soul. I had to dig deep to find the willingness and courage to no longer let fear control my relationship with God. This meant finally letting go of my religion and every outside source that had defined God for me. I had to go into my heart and begin to listen to the truth that was trying to speak to me from within. I was being told by my inner knowing that God was much bigger than the walls and intellectual constructs that we try to place on "Him." The truth for me was that the Divine was everywhere and in everything, and that included me.

Finding my true connection with the Divine was important for me to come back to my authentic self. It was this piece that was so crucial for me in order to keep returning to wholeness and deeper healing again and again. And it still is. Through a vigilant effort to keep turning in, I began to allow space for God again. I could feel my innate connectedness, because I began to experience that we were never separate. I realized the times that I felt God had left me were actually when I had left the Divine. These were inevitably the darkest times of my life, when I believed my thoughts of separation were true. But the more I tune into Divine consciousness inside of my own being, the more I also recognize it outside of me. And then all boundaries begin to disappear, and I sense the highest truth for me is that everything is love. I feel the Divine in its purer form in nature, animals, and babies. But God runs through everything. The more I observe, the more I find God even in the mundane details of my life.

Connecting to Divine energy naturally opens my heart to trust and to surrendering what I feel I need to control. I then see each encounter in life as grace-filled, and I stay willing to explore what life and God could be showing and teaching me. The message sometimes comes in seemingly random ways; a sentence dropped by a passerby can sink in deeply to help clarify something I have been struggling with. A sudden insight can come when least expected and change the direction of the path I am on. A gentle smile from a stranger, a baby's laugh, watching the kindness of others, all may pull me back to my heart, inner truth, and deeper knowing.

There have been times when I felt so hopeless, because no matter what I did, I could not find relief from the pain. And I had no one in my life that could help take it away or even relate to it. I felt completely alone, and it was very difficult to muster any energy or hope to keep searching for God. Even, at times, trying to connect by going inside, just seemed that I found more pain and darkness. But sometimes I found God's light most intensely in the darkness. Still, I didn't give up my search to know God fully, with my whole being, no matter what my outside or inside circumstances were. Today, I look outside my window as I type these words. I see the gentle rain falling on the surface of the still lake and hear the soft chirp of song birds. Dropping into the stillness inside, I sense everything is in its perfect place and aligned to Oneness, to God. Even if I fall out of this alignment, I know it is always there to return to. This is God's grace, this knowing, washing over me, again and again, bringing me back to my divine Self.

Relationship with animals, plants, and Mother Earth

HEATHER: Indigenous cultures carry the profound awareness that we are held and loved by Mother Earth, not just by our parents and human relationships. Often, these cultures have a rite of passage in adolescence that involves separating from the primary reliance on the parents and community and encouraging a sense of identity and relationship with personal spirit guides and with Mother Earth, the

Great Mother. This ceremony creates a profound opening for deepening healing relationships with Spirit and with the energies of nature. So many of us have experienced some level of trauma, betrayal, or disappointment in our relationships with our parents. Ancient and indigenous cultures realized that it is too much to ask of our human parents, and often the biological mother in particular, to meet all of our physical and emotional needs. Instead, they encouraged a transfer of that dependency and longing for love and for healing on to the "Great Mother," Mother Earth, or to the divine Mother who never leaves us or betrays us. Connecting with Mother Earth, with the divine Mother, and with nature can be profoundly healing for our hearts and for the young wounded parts of us.

For many people who have felt wounded or traumatized in their early development and in their primary relationships, often their safest and most nurturing relationships have been with animals, plants, or with nature. As a young child, I was deeply bonded with a group of willow trees who all had names and individual personalities for me. I would sit for hours in one willow tree, feeling held and loved in its warm and solid branches. Later in adulthood, when I was going through a traumatic time, the most profound healing balm for me was not my therapy but my long walks in the woods. As I walked in the forest, I felt and took in the nurturance and healing energies of the trees and of Mother Earth. At another point in my life, building a relationship with the plant bee balm through meditation and working with the energy of this plant as a flower essence was both healing and transformational for me as I worked through my fears of finding my voice and being visible in the world.

The Heartmath Institute and other researchers have shown that when we open our hearts and connect with trees or plants, a powerful energy field is created that is healing for us and for the natural environment around us. The institute also found that when we are in a coherent or harmonious connection with the Earth, our hearts and brains synchronize with the rhythms of the Earth. This is known as the Schumann effect. "As the Earth naturally pulses at various frequencies, this acts as a kind of master entrainment signal that entrains a whole hierarchy of frequencies, including those of the human heart, brain and mind." [1]

---

[1] "The Schumann Effect Part 1- How the Earth Influences Your Brain Waves," Subtle Energy Sciences, accessed December 7, 2019, https://subtle.energy/the-schumann-effect-how-the-earth-influences-your-brain/

Being with trees can be powerfully healing; physically, emotionally, and spiritually. I also have experienced deep healing through profound encounters with animals and birds who became much-needed guides and helpers. And I have known many people whose relationship with a pet was their primary healing relationship that enabled them to experience unconditional love and safety. We are birthed, nurtured, and sustained by our relationship with Mother Earth. And I believe that plants and trees are profound healers for us, and that animals can be wise and helpful guides and companions to us on our healing journeys if we open to their presence and their gifts.

KRISTINA: When I lived in Manila in the Philippines for five years, I was surrounded by billions of people, dense pollution, and sprawling concrete. There was little nature to be found unless I drove in heavy traffic for hours to get outside of the city. Nature has always been a simple way for me to connect to the silence within. I remember as a child, how natural it was for me to be in the present moment, just through smelling the grass or hearing the birds. But as an adult, finding any form of nature was hard in this overpopulated city. There were a few palms trees that grew around the swimming pool in my apartment complex. I would spend hours, lying beneath them on a patch of island grass. Looking up at the large swaying fronds, I seemed to sense the deeper wisdom that they held.

There was one particular palm tree that became my spiritual teacher. No words were needed; it taught me by example. In the hurricane winds, I noticed it would surrender. In the endless island heat, again, it only surrendered. It would become battered, torn up, and whipped around, but it never complained or tried to run away. It would just be. I learned through observing the peace of the palm tree that, if I surrendered to what was, I would be in the organic flow of life, and when times of pain and difficulty would come, those feelings would also flow through me. I began to trust that I was being held, guided, and watched over, just like the palm tree, by something more expansive than my own efforts. My suffering no longer existed or was real, not because my life was without pain, but because something inside me was beginning to perceive the world and my engagement with it differently. I learned that if I could stay aligned to presence, life just naturally happened. Just like my breath or heartbeat, there was a movement beyond me that was trying to flow, and all

I needed to do was to align to that flow and get out of my own way. It wasn't that I sat around and did nothing, but when I did make choices or used my mind, it also became a part of this movement. The palm tree was crucial in my spiritual transformation as I deepened more and more in this Awareness and into the essence of my being.

HEATHER: Being with nature is profoundly healing and helps us to remember our connections with all of life. I also believe that when we disconnect from nature and act in an abusive and exploitative way with the Earth and the natural environment around us, we not only damage our home planet but are destroying important aspects of ourselves and our awareness that we are only one strand of the interconnected web of life with everything around us.

Kristina
2011

When I think of all the cruelty in this world, the acts of violence and aggression, the many ways we defile each other and ourselves, it seems as if our souls are being stripped of the purity and love we were born with, and everything around us mourns and begins to die.

Where is God in all of this? What does She think? Has He grown tired, given up, and turned away? When does the suffering end? When do we stop hurting each other? What will it take for us to gather in our light, nurture its growth, and share it with others?

When will the walls that divide us fall? When will we see ourselves in another's eyes?

Who will say, "Enough! We can no longer tolerate abuse, torture, arrogance, and the loss of souls." Where is God?

Here. God is here, beneath the pain and illusion of separation. Even in the darkness, God is still here. Turn in. Feel the Divine grow inside of you. Nurture the light and share it with others. This is how the soul mends, and violence stops spreading. This is how the Earth stops mourning. It is how we heal ourselves, each other, and our planet.

Characteristics of a healing relationship

While there are many forms of healing relationships, we will focus in this section on the most important characteristics of a healing relationship with a therapist or close personal relationship (such a friend or partner). These are the characteristics and how to allow yourself to open to this healing process:

Trust

HEATHER: The first step in a healing relationship is to establish a sense of trust. This may be a long process if you have early trauma. You may need to negotiate with the protective parts in yourself who will not want you to open up for fear that this will be dangerous. Pacing is a key part of the healing process. It is important to honor the defenses and protective mechanisms that you have used for coping with the trauma and allow them to melt and be released only as you feel a sense of safety and connection in a healing relationship and are in a place within yourself and in your life in which it is safe to let these emotions and memories come into consciousness for healing.

If you are the therapist or healing other, hold with compassion that it will take time to build this trust. There may be a process of testing or of approach and then retreat until there is a sense of safety in the relationship. If you can see this as a needed phase in the process, you are less apt to take this personally and feel offended that the other person does not immediately trust you. Again, the more that you both foster an adult-adult and conscious connection, the more there can be clear communication about the trust issues of the young wounded parts of the self and a way to heal ruptures or misunderstandings in the relationship.

It is also important to realize that in any relationship, we are actually in a triad: the self, the other, and the energy of the relationship between us. Some therapists describe this as the "intersubjective field" or the energy of the relationship. We co-create an energy field in any relationship that is more than the sum of the two individuals involved. This energy field includes the energy of the dynamics between the two people, their conscious and unconscious processes, and their experiences of the relationship. We are also held by a more expansive, invisible quantum energy field that is within us and beyond us. I think of it as an energy field of consciousness and of compassion and healing to which we can open, that is there for us, and that we can call on and live in as we move into alignment with inner stillness. In many ways, this is analogous to what we now know about the nature of our universe which is four percent visible matter, 96 percent invisible energy. We are all swimming in a sea of energy and consciousness that holds us, informs us, heals us, and sustains us.

When I was closing my practice in Los Angeles, I experienced a tangible expression of this healing energy field that surrounds us as we are in relationship. I didn't fully realize how powerful this energy field was until I was terminating with all of my clients as I was preparing to move across the country. I had had a number of plants in my office that somehow thrived across the years even though I tended to forget to water them or care for them in a consistent way. As I gradually terminated and worked through the leaving process with all of my clients over a period of months, one by one each of the plants began to wilt and die. I realized that the plants had been nurtured by the energy field of compassion and healing that had been there holding me and my clients, and as that energy was being released, they weakened and no longer were able to survive. Perhaps the plants, in their own way, were also experiencing the grief in the room or realized that they had completed their part in the healing work. Everything is conscious, and they too were experiencing the emotions and energies in the room.

Safe and clear boundaries

HEATHER: Whether professional or personal, it is important to have clear boundaries in our relationships. In a therapeutic relationship, it is important for there to be clarity about the time and schedule of sessions, the amount of contact outside of sessions, and about touch. Having this clearly spelled out allows a sense of trust and safety in the relationship. This structure is also important because young traumatized aspects of the self may not have known this clear structure in the past and may pull for ways of relating that mirror the past boundary violations. To have an objective structure allows both the therapist and client to avoid re-enacting these violations and to begin to address the experiences of the young wounded parts of the self.

In personal relationships, it is also important for there to be clear emotional and physical boundaries, which may need to be worked through in an ongoing way. Especially in a relationship with a lover or partner, one person may be very comfortable with certain forms of emotional or sexual interaction that may feel unsafe or traumatizing to the other. It is important in a relationship to be clear and to honor the feelings and needs of both people. Otherwise, even a loving relationship can become re-traumatizing. There might be parts that are in conflict about what feels loving and what feels violating. All parts need to be in communication around how intimacy will be handled before engagement happens. Otherwise, this may manifest as mixed messages to the partner as well as inner conflict with some parts agreeing to certain behaviors, while other parts become traumatized. This results in the person feeling confused, depressed, sad, or angry.

Another challenge in establishing safety in relationships is the issue of self-destructive behavior, reactivity, or acting out. With early or severe trauma, often there is no internal model or template for what a safe and loving relationship looks like or feels like. The young parts are often prone to re-enacting the scenarios of the past and may try to engage in blurring the boundaries of the relationship or relating in ways that ultimately feel re-traumatizing. Also, protective parts of the self have often learned ways of trying to cope or diffuse the trauma that are now no longer helpful or healthy. For example, I worked with many clients who used self-cutting or addictions (such as sex, alcohol, or drugs) to numb or buffer overwhelming pain. While every self-destructive behavior was originally used for some adaptive protective reason, it is important to see, in the present moment, how harmful this is, and how it actually derails the young wounded parts of the self from being seen and having a chance to heal.

As both people in the relationship foster a conscious witness self, these issues can be talked about and addressed. If the traumatized person is caught in a self-destructive or addictive compulsive patterns and unable to hold onto the witness self, it is important for the other person to compassionately confront them and set limits on this behavior. Only when the destructive behavior stops are the feelings related to the trauma able to emerge for healing to take place. (This will be addressed in more detail in the chapter on Healing.)

HEATHER: I once had to go through a very painful termination with a client who had a history of early trauma and neglect. After years of trying to work with her through intensive therapy and be present with her in a compassionate way, her use of self-destructive crises, destructive acting out towards me, and her repeated violation of the clear, agreed-upon boundaries of our relationship led to my need to end the therapy. She rejected my efforts to help her see the destructiveness of these behaviors and did not want to explore her own deeper feelings and emotions or the painful patterns of the past. She was unable to establish a witness self but stayed determined to get the symbiotic merger with me that her young parts sought, and then acted out with intrusive, aggressive, and self-destructive behavior when she didn't get what she wanted. Finally, after many months of trying to address this with her (and after hours of my own personal therapy, consultation and supervision focused on this), I had to terminate the therapy. She then stalked me and sent threatening letters.

She was not seeking a healing relationship or emotionally corrective experience, but actually trying to get me to respond to any request for contact and engagement that her young parts wanted and to do it without any limits or boundaries. For me to collude with that and attempt to be the idealized and all-available parent that she longed for would not only derail the healing process but would usurp that role from the adult part of her that needed to take responsibility for her own healing. This healing could happen only if she could begin to experience the longings of the young child part, without completely identifying with that part, and instead of acting out that child's feelings and needs, she could allow her adult witness self to join with me to help her heal. Then, there would be the possibility of using the therapeutic relationship to help heal and form a healthy, internalized, parent part of herself that could be there for her desperate young parts in a truly conscious and consistent manner. For me to respond to her acting out and engage in only relating to her young traumatized child part without honoring her adult self would also have been a profound lack of respect for her strengths and capacity. The termination was needed both to protect myself and to set limits on her self-destructive behavior, and it also allowed me to respect her choice to heal or not heal.

The importance of the witness self

HEATHER: Sometimes we engage in relationships from the young aspects of ourselves and are unaware of patterns that we are re-enacting from the past. Our present relationships then become the arena for us to replay old wounds and past painful experiences rather than a context for healing. To shift this, it is vital that both people in the relationship consciously foster and strengthen a witness self. The witness self is that aspect of us that can step back from our feelings, reactions, and behaviors and observe what is going on. This is the wise part of us that is not identified with our past or with our story and is able to view our feelings and experiences in a more neutral way. This is why the work of alignment discussed in the previous chapter is critical in fostering healthy relationships with the self and with others. Only if we are able to gain distance from the intensity of our feelings and from the ways that we are compulsively pulled into repeating past traumatic patterns can we begin to break the cycle and heal.

When trauma memories are triggered, it often results in a response of flight, fight, freeze, or fawning. The witness self then goes offline. I had one adolescent client who had a seizure disorder and would have a petit mal seizure in our sessions if I said something unsettling to her or got too close to her feelings about her childhood abuse. This was a rather brilliant way that her body and psyche would take a time out. A few seconds later, she would emerge from the "freeze" with no memory of our discussion. I have had other clients literally walk out of a session or lash out in anger if we got into territory that was too triggering for them. Rather than taking this personally, it was important for me to hold with compassion that the traumatized parts of the self were not feeling safe, and we needed to re-establish safety and a connection with the person's witness self to begin to talk this through in a more conscious way. At such times, the therapist or partner in the relationship needs to stay strongly rooted in the witness self and in inner stillness as much as possible or both people can get pulled into the stormy energies of these moments. For this reason, it is key that the therapist understand the meaning of "transference," which is how the feelings and patterns of the past are likely to get re-enacted in the therapeutic relationship. If the therapist understands this process and can witness what is going on, the therapist can be the guide in how to understand these patterns and bring them into awareness with the client for healing.

Respect and avoiding re-enactment of the trauma

HEATHER: As discussed above, it is important to realize that we all are a complex union of diverse aspects of the self, holding different memories, feelings, and even ages. The earlier and more severe the trauma, the more we may hold unconscious memories or have split-off aspects of ourselves. (We will go into this in more depth in the next chapter.) Different aspects of the self have different agendas in relationship. This can be confusing to both people in the relationship. For example, the adult part of the self may be wanting intimacy and connection, while a younger wounded part may want to flee. Meanwhile, a protector part may want to lash out to keep distance in an effort to protect the traumatized, vulnerable child part. It is only as we bring these parts of ourselves into consciousness that we can navigate this complexity within ourselves and in relationship.

Wounded parts of the self may actually try to re-enact the trauma. This is rarely masochistic but more often is a reflection of the way early trauma gets encoded in the personality such that these patterns were deemed "normal" or the appropriate way to be in relationship with the abusive parent or other person. At such times, it is important for the therapist or healing other to say "no" and refuse to participate in this re-enactment. This is especially important when the abused young parts are engaging in sexualized behavior as a way to connect or re-enact the past or in self-destructive or abusive acting out behavior. It is important for the therapeutic other or intimate partner to stay aligned and in the witness self to help be an anchor of compassion for the person who is struggling with a post-traumatic stress response.

Taking responsibility for your own process and healing journey

HEATHER: It was a profound and painful lesson for me to realize that no matter how much we care about or love someone or are trying as hard as we can to be a healing other in a relationship, if the person is not able to take responsibility for their own behavior and establish a strong enough witness self, healing will not happen. I learned this the hard way with the client I mentioned above and in a subsequent abusive and turbulent personal love relationship. Clearly, I was needing to work with my own young traumatized child part that felt that it was important to endure and tolerate volatility and emotional abuse in a relationship as a way to stay connected and to try to heal the other. After re-enacting this a number of painful times, I began to gain consciousness of this and work it through. I came to realize that a relationship can be a compassionate context and catalyst for inner healing, but we ultimately heal within the self, not through the other. We must want to heal and take on the responsibility for our own healing journey. If we look to another to heal us and to take care of the wounded aspects of ourselves, we will end up feeling even more helpless and overwhelmed and disappointed, because the other person can never be the perfect healer or parent that we are seeking.

If you are in a personal relationship with someone who is actively working through their trauma history, it is not your role to try to be the healer or the rescuer. Be present, be caring, be authentic, and be clear with your own limits and boundaries. Do your best to be in an adult-adult dynamic with the other person while both of you work to strengthen your witness selves. Also, remember that both of you need to be doing your own healing work. Again, as I painfully discovered in my volatile love relationship, I may not have been the one overtly working childhood trauma, but I was unconsciously acting out my own wounds by being in a relationship in a way that was unsafe for myself and by tolerating the abuse. In this way, we were both in a destructive, re-traumatizing feedback loop in the relationship.

Often young parts re-enact the intense primal energy of early trauma that can trigger wounds in the relationship and result in a type of destructive feedback loop in which both people are triggered and may end up re-experiencing their early trauma. If one person is seeking a healing response from another, but instead does not feel safe and understood, it can lead to increased anger, blame, and feelings of being abused, abandoned, and re-traumatized. This can sometimes happen in therapy and not just in personal relationships. Each person in the relationship (whether it is a professional or personal) needs to be committed to doing their inner work and responsible for the part they play within the relationship. We need relationships to heal, but ultimately, we heal through developing a healing relationship within the self. My father, a psychologist himself, used to have a favorite saying: "We need to be responsible to each other, not for each other." We heal with each other, not through the other or by the other.

Kristina: *I had a therapist once, who I knew cared deeply about me. It wasn't so much what she said, but how she engaged with me. The tenderness in her gaze towards me made me feel I was cherished and loved. It did more to heal me, teach me, and change my damaging thoughts about myself than anything else she could have done or told me at the time. I had to first believe that I was worth something, so that I could feel I deserved to be loved and taken care of. And once I understood this on a heart level, I was able to put into action, and use, the tools and skills that would help put me back together again. Because in the end, I had to do the work myself. I am the only one that truly knows my own needs and how that should be carried out and applied to find the peace, love, and healing that I'm seeking. Who would better know the little ones inside than the one that has always been here?*

Kristina: There is a place inside that feels intense healing when someone else loves and takes care of us. We revert back to the child in us that holds a wound and is desperate for a healing balm to be applied. And while another person can help you heal to an extent, ultimately you must choose to be the healer of your own self. Lasting recovery comes when you show up for yourself, to love and nurture your whole being, to listen, be fully present, and gently guide yourself, not just through the healing process, but through life. And you have to keep making this choice, again and again and again.

When we reclaim our power and stop giving it away to others to do our personal work, we stop being the victim, waiting and hoping that love from outside us will come to heal us. Instead, we create the love and kindness for ourselves, knowing exactly how and when it is needed. Often when we feel we can only be healed from an external source, it becomes an addiction. In this way, we wait for the "hit" of someone who will soothe our wounds in just the right way. We begin to believe and feel that we are being healed by their actions. But this will only go so far, if we do not continue to do the work ourselves. If we wait for another person to come and rescue us, we foster a dependency and a sense of powerlessness which makes it hard to be in a healthy committed relationship with another, as well as within oneself.

This does not mean that we do not need others. Instead, we cultivate skills that enable us to ask for what we need in a healthy way. At first, it might feel awkward to be reliant on our own abilities to love and care for ourselves. But through practicing this, we come to learn what actually feels most empowering, mutual, and healing in our relationships. We are able to trust in our own abilities and establish healthy relationships with appropriate boundaries, clear communication, and a balanced sense of give and take. We begin to feel our inner power restored as we reclaim ourselves and no longer look to another to liberate us from our pain. We are able to come back to ourselves with acts of self-care and love, over and over again, knowing on a deep level that what we have been searching for on the outside, is actually within. We are then able to align to our deepest self, our soul self, and come back to the love that we have been searching for, our true essence, which is pure complete love. This homecoming is beyond limits and time, as the inner stillness beckons us, in every moment of each day, to come home.

Listening

HEATHER: A vital component of any healing relationship is the experience of feeling seen and heard. It has amazed me over the years how few people truly hear each other. Sadly, I have even experienced this lack of true listening with a few of my own personal therapists. One of the most profound phrases that has stayed with me across the years is feminist theologian Nelle Morton's description of how we "hear each other into speech." I have experienced how key this is both in the therapy process and in the spiritual healing circles I have facilitated. When we hold compassionate presence with one another in silence, we actually empower the other to open up and share at an honest and vulnerable level. The deep listening that occurs both before and during the verbal expression is as important as understanding what the person is saying.

In my group work with sacred circles, we often used the indigenous practice of the "council" format for sharing with each other. In this model, there is the understanding that we are held by energies larger than ourselves and that, in the group, each person holds a part of the whole needed for the healing of all. In a group context (this can also be done in a one-on-one relationship), you pass a "talking stick" or object with the understanding that, when the person holding that object is speaking, the others are quiet and are actively listening. There is no cross talk or responding aloud to what is said. The key is to listen from the heart and be fully present to the other. As we hold the energy of stillness and actively listen with compassion, this is often able to melt the defenses and fears of the other person, and their deeper truth, feelings, and experiences are able to emerge into speech. I have experienced being in a sacred circle and finding myself sharing something that I hadn't even been aware of prior to that moment, as I felt the group energy of compassion and of deep listening calling me into speech. This can be a profound way to bring our untold stories or previously hidden feelings to the light of consciousness and into healing. This council format is a powerful healing practice to use in a family as well as in a group. I have even used this in organizational contexts with management teams. It provides an effective way to open up with each other at a deeper level and to allow safety for everyone's feelings, concerns, and needs to be heard.

Also, if you are in a difficult dynamic with a friend or lover, you can use this technique. In this context, first take some time to align to stillness and sit in silence together. Then, pass an object such as a stone back and forth. The person holding the stone tunes in and speaks from the heart. Then, the stone or object is passed to the other person, who shares what they are feeling or experiencing. Again, don't react or respond to the words of the other person. When you are not holding the stone, truly open to listening to the other from the heart and not from your head or from emotional reactivity.

This experience can often dissipate patterns of defensiveness in a relationship and allow more space and safety for truth, vulnerability, and deeper feelings to emerge, leading to healing and transformation. If this process does not shift the dynamic from one of defensiveness or reactivity, try taking a break, then come back and slow down the process. Take time for one person to share their feelings. When you feel ready, pass the stone to the other person, who then expresses their sense of hearing the words and reflects back the feelings that were expressed. Then, pass the stone back to the first person who now has an opportunity to clarify what has not been heard or understood or to confirm that the message was accurately heard. Once the first person feels that what was shared was truly heard and understood, pass the stone back to the second person, so they can express their feelings and experience. Continue the process with these same steps and allow it to continue until both feel that they have been listened to and understood. This way, there is a structured process that supports truly hearing each other rather than projecting, making assumptions, or getting caught in reactivity.

Mirroring and empathic attunement

HEATHER: Another important aspect of healthy childhood development is to have had the experience of healthy mirroring with a parent. Beginning in infancy, a mother will often form a loving bond with her child through mirroring the infant's facial expressions; when the baby smiles, the mother smiles back. Later, as the parent verbally reflects back the child's feelings or gifts and strengths, the child then is able to begin to see and internalize these and to develop a healthy internal sense of self and a witness self (a capacity for self-awareness and reflection).

If this has not occurred in childhood, you may need to experience this mirroring (or sense of being accurately seen and reflected) in a healing relationship with another. It is an important step in the healing process to feel seen and understood and to have that actively mirrored back to you. I remember ending a long-term relationship with a man that I had planned to marry because I did not feel truly heard and understood by him even though I knew that he loved me. I explained to him that I often felt in his responses to me like I was seeing myself in a circus mirror. There were elements of the image that I saw reflected back to me from him that I recognized as myself, but too much of the image was distorted through the lens of his projections, misunderstanding, and inability to truly see and hear me.

In a close relationship, whether it is professional or personal, we attune to each other through unconscious communication between the right hemispheres of our brains. The left brain is responsible for verbal communication and expressing what we know consciously. The right brain is where we hold our feelings, unconscious experiences, and our intuition. This is also the part of the brain that processes visual, social, and emotional cues. As a therapist and as an empath, I became aware of how often I was listening to a client visually, intuitively, and emotionally, and how this was often more important than hearing what they were expressing verbally. The American psychologist and researcher in neuropsychology, Allan Schore, PhD, has written extensively on the importance of this right brain to right brain attunement for a positive therapeutic alliance and effective therapy process.

Another interesting scientific study carried out recently assessed the level of seriousness in suicide risk for depressed clients who had had a previous suicide attempt. The reliable predictors were not related to behavior, social support, or other known risk factors but to micro-expressions of movement and facial expressions on the part of the client *and* the psychiatrist interviewing the person. At some level, the right brain of the person and therapist were attuning and realizing what was going on beneath the verbal and conscious level. Both the face and micro-expressions and movements of the client as well as the face of the therapist were each unconsciously mirroring the suicidal feelings and risk level of the client.

When we connect with our left brains, we hear each other's words and experiences and stories. When we empathically attune with our right brains, we are sensing and mirroring each other's feelings and unconscious experiences. Both are vital in healing relationships. Deep listening includes this mirroring and empathic attunement as well as the capacity to truly hear each other's verbal expression. Some of my most profound experiences as a therapist have been in holding this empathic attunement and safe space for someone as the person courageously struggled to bring a painful memory or story to the light of consciousness and share it with me. To witness the protective defenses begin to slowly be dismantled, and to watch the vulnerability of a person's authentic self emerge as they open to being seen and heard in relationship, is a profoundly moving experience. I remember one client talking about how she had lived for years feeling unseen and alone as if isolated in a barricaded castle. Over time, as she felt heard and held in compassion, she gradually grew in trust and spoke of "letting the drawbridge down," allowing me to enter into the sacred space within the castle. These moments of healing in relationship are profound and transformative—for both the client and the therapist. In these moments, we feel the energy and compassion of the cosmos flowing in us and through us, knowing that we are all in this healing journey together.

Empathy is when we attune to others' feelings and felt experience; it is holding the wholeness of another with compassion. Empathy is not sympathy. Caring is not care-taking. A great saying that I learned from one of my clients was the importance in relationship of "caring not carrying." When we relate in an empathic and respectful way with each other, we draw out the best in each other. An intuitive energy healer once said that when he met with someone for a healing session, he would begin the session by saying to the person, "Pray that I might see you whole." When we see each other and ourselves in our wholeness and remember the pure consciousness at the core of who we are, then we align with that in ourselves and respect that in the other in a way that fosters a healing dynamic in the relationship.

Ongoing practice of aligning to the center within and the center of the cosmos (Source or Spirit) is key to moving into right relationship with ourselves, each other, and all the dimensions of life on this Earth. I never begin a therapy or healing session without remembering the medicine wheel, calling in the energies of the four directions, and aligning with the sense of being held by the Earth and sky and centered in Source. In that way, I am attuning myself to the consciousness that is in all and beyond all. This facilitates a deep sense of alignment with the center within me and the center of all that is. The process of calling in the directions involves facing each of the directions and giving thanks to the energies of the four directions and to the Earth and sky and center. This is a simplified version of the walking meditation with the medicine wheel that we have discussed. Again, it is a way of remembering and honoring our place as part of the Earth and the cosmos and that we are on the medicine wheel path of healing and wholeness.

Another powerful technique to strengthen this ability to hear and see each other in a personal relationship is the eye gazing practice. If you are doing this in a relationship, first, set aside time for this process where there will be no interruptions, so that you can do this in a safe and sacred space together. It is often best to keep this practice limited to a short time initially and to agree on the time frame together. It is often helpful to use a timer. Set the timer for five, ten, or up to thirty minutes depending on what feels comfortable and safe for you both. If either of you has difficulties with emotional intimacy, set the timer for an even shorter period such as one to five minutes. The time can be lengthened as this practice feels safer to you both. Align to stillness, call in sacred space with each other, and then sit in silence, gazing into each other's eyes. Do not talk or make facial expressions or movements in an effort to covertly communicate. Sit in silence with the intention to be as present and open as possible and to be open to truly seeing the other. Again, this fosters nonverbal empathic attunement. As the eyes are the window to the soul, this can be a profoundly healing and intimate experience.

Avoiding projections

HEATHER: Unless we have done our deep inner work, we tend to see each other through the lens of our past experiences. We see certain aspects of our past in other people or situations, and then unintentionally fill in the gaps and create a story that fits with those past experiences. We are then actually living in the past and not in the present reality. Our eyes and brains visually see the world around us through pattern recognition. Our eyes gather bits of information about shape, color, and texture, and then our brain configures it into a meaningful pattern and lets us know that what we are seeing is a chair, a tree, or the face of a loved one. When we are in a relationship, we filter our perceptions of the other through the lens of our past experiences and do not see the other person clearly but instead through the similar patterns from our early formative and perhaps traumatizing past relationships. This is the classic understanding of what is called "transference" and "projection" that can occur in the therapy process and within our personal relationships. For example, if you felt abandoned by your mother as a child, you are likely to project this onto your significant relationships by not easily trusting them because you anticipate being abandoned again.

Kristina
2006

I have been trying to avoid myself for days now, running around and staying busy in efforts to escape self-destructive feelings that seem to be looming around, stalking me. Yesterday, I finally got brave and stopped. I put my hand on my heart and felt deep loneliness. I felt it everywhere, all over my body. I tried to connect it to my past, to some experience that I could remember. I was able to recall coming to a point in childhood when I stopped looking for someone to come and help me. I came to some acceptance of what life was for me, and what I could expect, which was not being able to connect to anyone. No one was around physically, and when they were, they were emotionally absent. The most painful thing is when the people you so yearn to connect with are void of feeling themselves. So then there is this sense of moving through the motions of life without ever getting what you need and want. It is so lonely. It is not just that

I didn't connect with my parents, but I didn't with my siblings either. We were all scattered, lost, and hollow inside.

When I saw my therapist on Wednesday, I wanted to feel an intimate connection with her, one I knew was possible based on past experiences held in the sanctuary of her office space. But as I walked away from my appointment, I didn't feel anything. I think it brought up all of this pain and loneliness from the past and how I dealt with it back then, because I'm playing out the same pattern today. I tend to numb out with my therapist in the way my mom would numb out with me. I don't even know I'm in the process until it's over, and I'm left with this vast empty feeling inside. It's like I'm experiencing her as my own mother—empty, numb, hollow, like no one's inside looking back at me.

When I feel connected to my therapist, it is the greatest high, and when I'm not, it is an intense low. When I don't feel connected, it brings up all the painful feelings from the past—the deep disconnect, loneliness, and sadness, and when it goes unrecognized, it leads to depression. When I felt it this morning, I let myself sit with the feelings and was able to understand what was happening, what I was feeling. I remember being seven years old and having intense feelings of loneliness and separation. It all leads me to feeling afraid that I will have unrealistic expectations of my therapist, because I will be looking to get from her what my mom didn't give me. I struggle between wanting to connect to my therapist and pushing her away for fear she will become vacant to me, like my mom. Sometimes there is a strong need to feel close, and then at other times, no feeling at all; I go numb to it all. I don't want to need anything from her. I don't want to get hurt because I'm depending on her for something. And I'm ashamed to even be having these feelings. But at the same time, it feels so incredibly healing to connect, like it's going all the way down to something deep inside that needs the experience. My therapist seems to understand why I do this, going back and forth with her. She seems to just be there, no matter how I'm acting or feeling. She is unmoved, and there is something that makes me really trust her because of it.

HEATHER: In a therapy relationship, it is important for the therapist to hold space for these feelings and projections and to gently clarify what is being projected from the past onto the present relationship together. Therapists need to have done enough inner work so that they can see themselves and their clients as clearly as possible, to not only be aware of their clients' projections but of their own as well. However, in personal relationships, it might be helpful to keep in mind that we are often in the sea of what is conscious and unconscious in the dynamics between us, and we may get caught in the confusion of projections, with both relating to each other from the past rather than being truly present with and for each other. Working on your own self-awareness and maintaining clear and honest communication with each other can help to differentiate these projections from what is real and true in the present moment in the relationship.

Another type of projection is known as "projective identification." This can be particularly confusing and challenging in a relationship. This is when you project feelings that you cannot tolerate in yourself onto another person who then may absorb and identify with the feelings as being their own. An example of this is when you find yourself feeling overwhelming sadness while talking with someone you love, but you can't figure out why you are experiencing this feeling. Your loved one may be talking about a traumatic experience in the past in a detached and neutral manner, because they cannot tolerate feeling the sadness within themselves. You are picking up on the pain and sorrow that has been repressed by your loved one and feeling it or even embodying it yourself. This is actually an unconscious form of communication. If you are self-aware enough to realize that this is not your feeling but is coming from the other person, then you can share this in a way that helps the other person reclaim and work their deeper emotions in a clear and conscious way. Otherwise the emotions and issues are being passed back and forth without being dealt with consciously, and this can create havoc in a relationship.

I once had a client who was dealing with the trauma of being physically and emotionally abused in her childhood. As she struggled with these memories, her feelings of anger and shame were often close to the surface. She was married to a man with a lot of suppressed rage that he was not at all aware of or able to own in himself. He would often do something provocative or demeaning in interaction with her. Then, when she exploded in anger, he blamed her for her reactivity and attributed it to her trauma and "mental illness." She felt ashamed and believed that this was all her fault. I helped her to gradually differentiate her anger and feelings about her past trauma from the ways that her husband was triggering her in the present and provoking her to feel and act out his rage as well as her own. This ongoing pattern was crazy-making for her and was allowing him to continue to disown and detach from his own anger and abusive behavior, enabling him to see himself as the "normal one" and to feel superior in the relationship. Until this was brought into a conscious dialogue between them, it prevented them from healing individually or in relationship with each other.

Those of us with a trauma history are often magnets for these types of confusing or destructive dynamics in a relationship. As you grow in self-awareness, it is essential to be clear about what is yours in a relationship and what belongs to the other person so as not to inadvertently engage in this type of dynamic. It is important to have the courage to be clear and explicit with these emotional boundaries in your relationship and give back to the person what is theirs to feel and heal in themselves. This is why it is so critical that we all do our own healing work and bring into consciousness what needs to be healed within ourselves. It is only when we see ourselves clearly that we can truly see and love another person for who they are rather than for our needs or projections. And it is only then that we can distinguish what feelings and issues are ours as opposed to what we are absorbing and feeling for another.

Having appropriate expectations

HEATHER: It is important for both you and the healing other, especially a therapist, to be clear about expectations. As a therapist, it was important for me not to support unrealistic expectations from a client about the therapy process or about my abilities as a therapist. There are no magic pills or quick fixes in the healing process. It takes time and a committed effort on the part of both the therapist and the client. Also, it is important for the therapist to know the limitations of their own experience and expertise and be willing to get added training or consultation as needed. I was continually in my own therapy, in consultation, and getting added training when I was doing therapeutic work with trauma. For clients, it is important to know when your therapist is "good enough" and to understand that there will be times that the therapist makes mistakes or doesn't fully understand what you are saying or experiencing. If there is enough of a foundation of trust in the relationship, these issues can be addressed and worked through together.

KRISTINA: As you gain more awareness of your own feelings and projections and take more responsibility for your own healing process, you are then able to have more clear and appropriate expectations in your relationships. As the client in a therapy relationship, this means that you look to the therapist to guide you and support you in your process, but you are not looking to that person to be perfect in how they interact with you. Allowances must be made for mistakes and for repairing ruptures in the relationship.

This is also true in personal relationships. It is important to be clear about what you are expecting from the other person and to discern if these expectations are realistic or if you are wanting the other person to be the flawless parent that you never had. It is also important to tune into the expectations of different aspects of yourself. Part of you may hold an appropriate expectation of what is healthy and possible in an intimate adult relationship, while younger parts of you may be looking for that other person to flawlessly understand you and support you. It is helpful to take time and write down what your expectations are in a relationship. That way, you can bring these more into your conscious awareness and begin to see which ones are appropriate to the relationship and which may be coming from younger or wounded parts of yourself. If you are not clear with your expectations, you may give your partner mixed messages or have some expectations that are conscious and some that are operating unconsciously. This can create conflict and confusion and will often lead to difficulties in the relationship. Once you are clear within yourself about the expectations you have of your partner and the relationship, it is important to share these together, so that both sides are heard and a mutual understanding of how to best engage and work through expectations can be achieved. This most often is an ongoing dialogue and process as your relationship goes through changes and different life events.

Allowing mistakes, holding yourself with compassion, and repairing the relationship

HEATHER: It is important to realize that even though we may be committed to our own inner work as well as trying to be clear and present in a relationship, inevitably we will still make mistakes. There will be moments of projection, reactivity, or rupture. This is true in therapy relationships as well as personal relationships. I have been grateful when a client would challenge me and let me know that they felt misunderstood or that something was off between us. This indicated that there was trust and authenticity between us. To have my mistake or misunderstanding pointed out allowed me to take responsibility, to deepen my own understanding of my triggers or blind spots, and to then repair this moment of disruption between us. This process actually deepens and strengthens the relationship.

If a person reacts to this type of communication or confrontation with defensiveness or denial, whether in a therapeutic or personal relationship, it can be crazy-making and toxic. It is especially dangerous in a therapy relationship when any honest perception or challenge by a client may be seen as a threat, and the client is then discounted or even pathologized. In my experience, people with a significant early trauma history often have a heightened level of vigilance and sensitivity to the nuances in a relationship. When these perceptions are accurate but are discounted, then you are re-traumatizing the person rather than helping them to heal. When someone has been abused in childhood, the perpetrator told them to keep this a secret and has disempowered them from trusting their own perceptions and experience. Even psychotic clients that I worked with who were paranoid or delusional and disconnected from reality in the present moment were often mired in the trauma of the past that was metaphorically encoded in the content of their delusions. To be heard, respected, and gradually guided to honor the roots of their stories and eventually to be able to see and feel the truth of their trauma and work it through was deeply healing for them. It enabled them to differentiate the pain and experiences of the past from the present moment.

Learning to communicate in intimate relationships can feel threatening, especially when bringing up something that might lead to conflict. Most of us did not have good mentoring or experiences around conflict as children. We learned that conflict led to fighting, break ups, violent words and actions between people. So many of us have an avoidance to conflict because it brings up painful feelings of the past, and fear about how the conflict could play out. But if disagreements can be heard and worked through, we can learn that communication can be a way to bridge gaps, rather than being divisive.

In a personal relationship, when we get triggered with each other, it is important to step back, take time to assess what old wounds or patterns were reactivated in each of us, and come back and talk things through. We need to hold these moments of reactivity or rupture with understanding and compassion. If there is enough trust in the relationship and a sense of true love and caring, then we can repair these disruptions and actually grow in our understanding and sensitivity to each other. There is no way around conflict and disappointment in relationships. We are only human. It is not about being perfect; it is through our imperfections that deeper healing and an expansion of consciousness can happen. As we hold each other in honesty and love, we work out the rough edges of things that re-trigger or wound each other. We can then become agents of healing with and for each other.

Having healthy relationships modeled

HEATHER: As we engage with each other from an adult witness self and work to be as conscious as possible in our relationships, then we both model and internalize what it means to be in a healthy relationship. If you have severe early trauma, it is important to be in a relationship with a therapist who is able to hold space for what may be a slow and painstaking journey into trust and safety, to show how being held with compassion, empathy, and respect feels, so that gradually your adult self can relate to your young wounded parts in this same loving way.

Kristina
2005

Wow, I feel such incredible healing inside. It was one of those rare times in session when everything went still, and I could listen, really hear what was being said to me, that it wasn't my fault, and I wasn't alone anymore. And you know ... I didn't feel alone. I felt surrounded with compassion, that's what helped my insides to quiet down and feel what it feels like to be loved by another. And once I felt that, I could understand her words and really get them, deep down in my bones, that it wasn't my fault ... and I believed it. I thought that if someone could love me, and it feels this wonderful, then I couldn't possibly be bad. I wanted to shout, "I'm good! I am good and innocent. I came good and stayed good." And me, all of me, felt that—maybe, for the first time.

CHAPTER 5

C - Consciousness

As we continue our walking meditation around the ARCH medicine wheel, we now continue clockwise around the circle from the west and move to the north. Here we honor the importance of Consciousness in our healing journey. As you walk the medicine wheel and move to the north, take time to tune into this aspect of yourself. Honor the importance of self-awareness and living consciously. Also, honor what is held within you that still lies buried in your psyche or held in your body that is not yet in your conscious awareness. Take time to send compassion to all of the parts of yourself—known and unknown. Give thanks for your soul self that knows every aspect of who you are and helps you to stay in alignment with your true self. You might take a moment and say a prayer or set an intention to allow more of yourself to come into the light of consciousness to support you in being fully connected to yourself and on your path of healing and wholeness.

Topography of the Self

This section of the ARCH healing model guides us in opening more fully to all levels of our consciousness. As we explore what it means to live consciously, it is important to remember the layers and facets of who we are as spiritual beings having a human experience. At the core of who you are is your soul self. This is your connection to the realm of spirit and pure consciousness that is within all and holds all that is. When you align with stillness, you remember your essence, the part of your consciousness that is infinite, expansive, whole, and untarnished by the trauma and experiences of your life. This soul self manifests in this lifetime as the person that you are with your physical and emotional traits and the personality that you have developed. In this incarnated self, you are the individual drop of water in the ocean, separate yet still at one with all that is. As you move through life, your experiences continue to shape your feelings, thoughts, and personality. The stories and memories of your life get encoded in your body, emotions, and perceptions, and are also stored in the energy field that surrounds your body.

When you have trauma experiences, this impacts the physical, emotional, cognitive, and spiritual aspects of who you are. Trauma memories are often repressed and embedded in the body as well as in the psyche. If you have experienced ongoing or overwhelming trauma, you may have dissociated and split off parts of yourself that hold memories and feelings about the trauma. We all have different parts of ourselves that hold certain memories, emotions, and experiences from our lives.

The more trauma you have experienced, the more these parts may be disconnected and distant from each other, leaving you feeling unintegrated, as if you have lost parts of who you are. As you heal, it is important to clear the trauma in all of these layers—energetically, emotionally, mentally, and physically. You heal as you bring into conscious awareness the parts of yourself that are stuck in painful memories that have been stored in your subconscious, your body, and your energy field. Otherwise, you remain aware of only a segment of yourself with much of what is controlling your emotions and behaviors buried deep within your unconscious. It is amazing to realize that by the time we are thirty-five years old, on average, 95 percent of our personalities are coming from unconscious thoughts, feelings, and beliefs. We have established certain patterns and ways of acting, reacting, thinking, and feeling which keep us in a feedback loop reinforcing these ways of being (cf. Joe Dispenza, *Becoming Supernatural*). [2]

---

[2] Dispenza, Joe, *Becoming Supernatural: How Common People are Doing the Uncommon.* Carlsbad, California: Hay House, 2017.

To change, you have to be willing to become fully conscious. By bringing your thoughts, feelings, and patterns into awareness, you have the capacity to change them. In changing them, you change your life. Otherwise, you are repeating the patterns and feelings of the past. This is true for all of us but especially so when you have experienced trauma and feelings, thoughts, images, and sensations are encoded in memories that are split off and repressed and thus not easily accessible to our conscious minds. It is critical that you have a plan for how to bring these lost memories, feelings, and beliefs into your awareness so you can work through what blocks you and keeps you in dysfunctional patterns and locked in old wounds. It is vital to become fully conscious of your behavior so that you can thoroughly heal, be able to let go, and be free of your past and live in the present moment.

Levels of consciousness

We have different levels of consciousness or awareness. There is the conscious mind, which holds the thoughts, feelings, and behaviors that we are aware of. There is the subconscious mind that contains our thoughts, feelings, beliefs, and habits that influence us and are just below the surface of our conscious awareness. Then, there is the unconscious mind where our past experiences and trauma memories and feelings are held that we are not able to easily access. We also have a fourth level of consciousness, the superconscious, which is our soul self, the infinite part of us that holds the awareness of all of who we are and is never separated from pure consciousness or the love and wisdom that permeate the cosmos.

Conscious mind (10%)
Subconscious mind (50-60%)
Unconscious mind (30-40%)
Superconscious (Soul Self)

It is profound to realize that, on average, we are truly conscious of only 10 percent of ourselves. The remaining 90 percent is influenced or controlled by what is beneath our conscious awareness.

Levels of reality

HEATHER: As we explore what it means to become more conscious, it is important to realize the layers of reality that also relate to the different aspects of ourselves. One of the most profound things that I learned through my shamanic training[3] and through studying ancient wisdom traditions is that in this modern era we tend to have a very limited view of what reality means. From a shamanic perspective, there are four primary levels of reality:

- The physical level
- The emotional and mental level
- The archetypal level (level of beliefs, myths, archetypes, ceremony, etc.)
- The spiritual or energetic level

Physical level

The physical level includes the experiences that we have with our bodies and the material world around us. Many of us get focused on this level of reality and believe that, "if I can't see it, it is not real." This is actually a harmful way to live in that it severely limits your awareness of reality when you realize that 96 percent of our universe is invisible.[4] Only 4 percent of the universe is visible matter, and we have only explored and come to understand about 1 percent. The remainder of the universe is invisible energy. So if something has to be visible or tangible to be real, you are limiting your sense of reality to 4 percent of the universe.

At the same time, it is important to honor what our bodies and our physical senses and experiences are telling us. Your body does not lie, and your physical symptoms or sensations are often trying to guide you to bring unconscious aspects of yourself into the light of awareness. If you are not allowing yourself to feel certain emotions or aspects of yourself in a direct conscious

---

[3] Alberto Villoldo discusses these levels of reality from a shamanic perspective in The Four Winds Society's Healing the Light Body program, accessed December 7, 2019, https://thefourwinds.com

[4] "Dark Matter and Dark Energy," National Geographic, accessed December 7, 2019, https://www.nationalgeographic.com/science/space/dark-matter/

way, your body will often try to get your attention and guide you to deal with those buried feelings or parts of yourself.

Emotional and mental level
The emotional and mental level is about our thoughts, beliefs, and emotions and our conscious psychological and cognitive processing of our experiences. As we see from the image above, if you live by the concept advocated by Descartes that "I think, therefore I am," and who you are is who you believe yourself to be and all of the thoughts, emotions, and aspects of yourself that you are conscious of, then you are only identifying with 10 percent of who you are. Perhaps this is why our world is in such conflict and chaos. So many of us are interacting with each other unconsciously and yet denying that a large part of ourselves is out of our awareness. In honoring the emotional and mental level of yourself, it is important to realize that you are more than your conscious awareness. Honor that you hold feelings, thoughts, and memories that are held in your unconscious. As you develop your witness self, you will begin to see how these buried emotions, thoughts, and beliefs often emerge indirectly in your actions, reactions, dreams, or "slips of the tongue."

Archetypal level
The archetypal level relates to deeper, more collective or cultural beliefs and archetypes that we hold within us, including the realms of symbols, myths, rituals, and ceremonies. Just as we have a personal unconscious, we also carry within us a collective consciousness and unconscious. The collective consciousness holds the cultural and religious beliefs and practices that we adhere to. It also relates to our cultural conditioning and can include the effects of social programming through education and social media that influence our values and beliefs. At a deeper level, within the collective unconscious, are the universal archetypes, symbols and rituals that are a part of being human and that connect us beneath our surface cultural, ethnic, and religious differences. As we learn to honor these collective energies and archetypes that reside in all of us, we can work with them in ways that allow us to be more in right relationship with ourselves and with each other.

Also, working with ceremony and archetypes is a way to heal and transform ourselves beneath the level of the conscious mind. Symbols, ceremonies, and rituals engage the conscious, unconscious, and superconscious aspects of ourselves and integrate mind, body, and spirit. You might think of this archetypal and ceremonial level as similar to an electro-magnetic field. This binds galaxies together and has a gravitational force. As we honor and work with the level of ceremony and archetypes, we are remembering and reweaving connections with each other and with the energies of the cosmos.

Spiritual level
The spiritual or energetic level is the realm of spirit and is connected with the superconscious part of us. This level relates to what we have known for thousands of years through ancient wisdom traditions and is now emerging in our awareness through quantum physics that everything is energy, and everything is interconnected. This is the realization that we live in a holographic universe and are not just experiencing how life impacts us, but actually have the capacity to co-create our reality through our intentions, thoughts, beliefs, and emotions. When we honor and integrate this level of reality, our consciousness grows and expands, and we are living in and through the soul self, the superconscious within us. We are then, also working with the currents of pure consciousness. This is similar to the way that the vastness of invisible energy flows throughout the universe and causes the universe to expand. It is limiting and dangerous if we confine ourselves to the surface levels of reality and acknowledge as real only that which we can see and touch and hold in our conscious minds. As we allow ourselves to explore what is hidden within us and the energies that connect us with each other and with the universe, then we gain in awareness, consciousness, freedom, and wholeness.

The process of true healing incorporates all of these levels. The more we can work at all levels, the more powerful the healing shifts and transformation can be. We can integrate and strengthen changes made on one level with all the other levels. Aligning with inner stillness allows us to hold all of who we are. As we honor each level, it in turn supports the healing of the other levels. As we heal at the level of spirit, it guides us to be more engaged in ceremony and understand the archetypal energies that bind us all. As we heal at that level, it guides us to expand and heal at the emotional level. As we allow ourselves to become more aware of the experiences and feelings held in our unconscious, we become more whole and able to make choices in a more clear way. This in turn helps our bodies heal as we move out of imbalance and into harmony within ourselves and release the stress and disease that we carry at the physical level.

This section of the book is a guide as to how to work with and integrate your healing process at all levels and how to deepen and expand your consciousness to live in a more clear and full way.

In our modern western culture, we tend to live primarily on the physical, emotional, and mental levels. From this perspective, medical treatment is focused on understanding what is going on physiologically, and intervention is at the physical level, through pharmaceutical drugs or surgical interventions. Too often, therapy is seen through this medical lens, and treatment approaches are based on the belief that "mental illness" is ultimately a biochemical or neurological imbalance in the brain. From this perspective, with the proper psychotropic medications and treatment aimed at changing behavior or thought patterns (such as cognitive-behavioral therapy), the "illness" can be managed. These approaches are helpful in addressing symptoms and providing some measure of stabilization, but this is not a path of true healing. To truly heal, you need to get to the root of the issue; the deeper wounds and trauma. When we split off and deny parts of who we are and bury painful experiences, they don't disappear. They lie in our unconscious minds and emerge in symptoms, behaviors, physical illness, or emotional imbalances.

Physical and emotional imbalances are guiding us to heal at a deeper level. Our bodies and psyches are trying to get our attention to help us heal and come back into balance and wholeness. Often our physical or emotional symptoms are messengers, speaking to us in a symbolic language about what we need to bring into conscious awareness and deal with in order to heal. For example, I (Heather) was diagnosed in 2001 with a thyroid problem. As I explored the deeper meaning of this, it became clear to me how this weakness in my thyroid (in the location of the throat chakra) was symbolic of my karmic and emotional struggle with finding my own voice and expressing my creativity. As I have worked to heal these blocks, my thyroid has come more fully into balance.

Many of our current therapy approaches are not actually about healing but are more about symptom management. While psychotropic medications are sometimes necessary as a supplemental part of the healing process, they are not curative and are rarely helpful on a long-term basis. Often, I have heard my clients complain about the ways in which their medications numbed their capacity to fully feel. At times, these medications are helpful in giving us relief from overwhelming emotional states, but as we come back into balance, we need to have access to our feelings and bring what was repressed into consciousness in order to truly heal. It is important to honor the symptoms and messages of our physical or emotional imbalances and then seek to bring into awareness what needs to be seen and heard to be healed.

To heal means to work with all of the layers of consciousness and to attend to what is going on physically, emotionally, and mentally. We must honor the deeper beliefs and archetypal energies that we carry, the energy of the collective consciousness that we live in, and the energies of cosmic consciousness that are within us and that surround us. This requires listening to the messages of the body and psyche and also diving deeper into the beliefs and perceptions that shape our experiences. It means remembering that we are more than our bodies and our minds, and we can tap into the quantum field of consciousness that is within us and surrounds us to remember our wholeness. This will enable us not only to deal with all of these layers of consciousness in who we are but also to honor what is unconscious within us. As we heal, we come into alignment with what is whole. As we are more and more in this alignment, we are better able to heal.

When we experience pain or trauma that is too much to bear, those memories and feelings get pushed into our unconscious so that we can cope and move on with our lives. To fully heal, we have to excavate what has been buried and bring it into the light. We have to honor what is in the shadows of the underworld and retrieve the lost parts of ourselves. However, what has been buried deep within may not always fully emerge into conscious awareness in the same way that more neutral memories do. Trauma memories rarely rise to the surface as intact, clear memories. More often, these painful experiences surface in body sensations, flashbacks, nightmares, or through experiences that trigger us. Healing involves honoring the truths hidden in the darkness and allowing the feelings and memories to emerge in whatever ways that they can. We need to hold these aspects of ourselves with compassion and not be critical or demand that it all make sense in a logical, linear way. When we remember our wholeness and complexity, we are able to honor what is now in the light and what remains to be discovered in the shadows, and what may continue to stay in the darkness as a mystery.

When we are aligned with inner stillness, if aspects of the unconscious become activated, we are able to work with them in a connected but non-attached way, not denying any part of ourselves but rather welcoming the wholeness of who we are as a way of being fully embodied. Our relationships move from reactivity into being more compassionate, rich, and mutually understanding. Trauma can make aligning to stillness more challenging, but as we quiet the mind, we create an opening for the undercurrents of the subconscious to come forward. Pain, disappointment, rage, sadness, abandonment, and other intense feelings and body sensations that have been concealed and trapped for years, now have a chance to be seen and felt. When we are able to be still and experience these deeper feelings as they emerge, we move into healing and wholeness.

The nature of trauma and its impact on memory

HEATHER: As discussed earlier, ongoing trauma has profound effects on us emotionally and cognitively as well as neurologically and physically. Trauma often results in difficulties such as hypervigilance, hyperarousal, reactivity, mood changes, behavioral and relationship problems as well as physical symptoms. It can also affect our memories. Trauma is not encoded in the brain in ways that normal memories are encoded. Ordinary memories are processed and stored in the hippocampus, which does not fully develop until after age three. Early childhood traumatic memories are encoded in the right brain as sensations, feelings, and body memories. After age three, normal memories get encoded in the hippocampus and can be accessed as explicit memories. We are then able to mark the time and remember details about what we have experienced. With trauma experiences, the left brain goes "offline" and the trauma gets encoded in the amygdala (the deep unconscious part of the brain) or in the right brain (our preconscious mind), rising to the surface later on in the forms of feelings and implicit memories, not as clear or conscious memories. We may remember bits and pieces or have sensations related to the trauma but have difficulty accessing the memory in a more clear or full manner.

KRISTINA: Trauma can also have a profound impact on our sense of identity and connection with our soul self as well as our experience of fragmentation or separation. In normal development, when we are born, we are still in a state of pure consciousness, being one with the Divine and all that is. As a baby, we do not realize that we are separate from the Divine or even from our mother. But as we grow, we learn that we are separate and have an individual identity. We are taught that we have a name, gender, and identity that is separate from other people and life forms. As we grow and begin to explore the world, we learn how to navigate being a separate entity in our environment. This is necessary for our soul's development, to feel and experience the separation from Source, the Divine, and everything that is around us. If we are raised by loving and supportive parents, we develop healthy attachments and relationships with others. We then are better equipped to navigate and handle situations and relationships. But if we come from unhealthy attachments with our parents or experience early wounds or neglect, we will have a heightened sense of separation from ourselves and others.

Trauma has spiritual and energetic effects and causes that sense of separation to become more extreme and destructive. If the trauma is severe enough, we will experience fragmentation, not just within the experience itself, but from our personality and soul self. It is as if our personality becomes fragmented as does the experience and memory of the traumatic event. Images, sensations, and feelings are shattered and separated from being a whole integrated experience. When this happens, we also lose a sense of centeredness and connection to our soul self and the divine consciousness that runs through us. When trauma is complex or repeated, there is a greater divide, not only in our personality, but there is also a further separation from the sense of who we truly are. However, even with trauma, the deepest essence of our being (our soul self) cannot be touched or defiled.

In addition, trauma often triggers dissociation as an effort to cope with the overwhelming stress or pain. The conscious mind will split off and focus on something safe (like an image of playing at the beach) while the trauma gets encoded in the body and the emotions are stored in the right brain. When later confronted by a trigger, we will then be flooded by feelings, fear, or pain without the story or context of what it is connected to. Sensations and feelings around the trauma are also stored in the cells as a way for the body to remember. As the body ages, the cellular memories get buried deeper, becoming more entrenched and stuck. Memories stored in the brain and body can be triggered and can surface at unexpected times. Trauma memories are charged and powerful energies, and when they arise from the subconscious in an unpredictable way, it can feel frightening and disorientating.

The effects of the trauma being activated and causing fragmentation can be visualized as a large gumball machine, which has a round glass container that sits on top of a metal base in the middle of an empty room on a smooth marble floor. Inside the round glass container are hundreds of round colorful gumballs. The metal base represents the centered soul self; it is pure consciousness. The glass container is the personal identity, and the gumballs represent our thoughts, feelings, and experiences. A large steel sledgehammer represents trauma. As a traumatic event impacts us, it is as if a sledgehammer is catapulted across the room, smashing directly into the round glass container of the gumball machine. One moment it stands silent, still, and at ease in the middle of the quiet empty room; in the next moment, upon instant contact with the flying sledgehammer, shards of glass splinter off in all directions, sending loose gumballs bouncing and rolling all over the marble floor in jumbled chaos. Once a unified, whole, and properly functioning machine, it is now broken in pieces, spilling out all over the place. The glass represents the pain and shattering effect of trauma. The gumballs are parts or aspects of the self often felt or experienced through feelings, body sensations, thoughts, beliefs, and images that are now separate, as the gumballs are no longer contained in the wholeness of the glass container.

As we heal from trauma, we navigate through the shards of glass. Barefoot, as we are often vulnerable in the process, we gently and attentively move through the loose gumballs. Sometimes we feel the pain of getting a piece of glass in our finger or foot, as we carefully collect lost parts of ourselves.

When we have gathered enough gumballs or lost parts of the self, we might find it necessary to create a new container, as the round glass one might not be suitable anymore. Maybe the new one will be made of another material, one less rigid or fragile. Maybe it will be more like a boat, more open and less protected and confined, so that it can easily and effortlessly flow downstream with the gentle, natural current that is aligned with the soul self. As we gather the pieces of the trauma, through memories, body sensations, and lost parts of the self, we start to put the puzzle of the self back together again and release what has been stuck, so it can heal, integrate, and finally let go. We link the dots, fill in the missing gaps, and gather the fragmented self. We give voice to what had been held in silence, a sense of safety and knowledge that the trauma is over, and finally set ourselves free from the past. Through the healing process of bringing all aspects or parts of the self into the light, we come to relate to and know ourselves in a more whole and authentic way.

It is often not necessary to go digging into the past looking for trauma. It is right here in the present moment, trying to find healing and showing us that we hold trauma encoded in us through beliefs that don't serve us, as well as in our destructive patterns, depression, anxiety, physical and emotional illness, or over-reactions to certain life events. Even just a gut sense that something isn't quite right within us can indicate that deeper healing is needed. When trauma comes up in the present moment, it is seeking help and restitution. Just as we would not turn a child in need away, neither should we turn away from intrusive emotions, memories, or thoughts. Rather, it is important that we stay in the present moment with them, sitting with the experience in a state of awareness and compassion. In these moments, our past has come to meet us in the present, so that we can open to the fluid movement of our feelings, knowing that as we heal, these feelings and sensations will pass. As we allow this flow, without letting it take us over, we can work with our wounds in a healing way. If we deny what is coming up, we could inadvertently push these memories and feelings back down into our bodies, where they become trapped, motionless, blocked energy. This suppression or repression may then lead to physical and emotional illness and disease.

When a traumatic event happens to us, and we are not helped and supported through it by a safe and supportive person in our lives, the experience becomes fragmented to enable us to live through it. These fragments are then stored in an unconscious way. It is as if the trauma becomes frozen in time, being stored and experienced internally as a constant happening, not as a past memory. When the frozen pieces come into conscious awareness, it feels as if the past trauma is happening in present reality. Again, this is due to how traumatic memories are encoded in our brains. However, when these traumatic memories are activated and the fragmented parts of the self are given proper attention to be helped in a loving way, these aspects are then able to experience healing and can come to trust that the trauma is over. This blocked energy or frozen parts of the self are then able to release from the body-mind and be integrated into the wholeness of our being.

Ways to bring what has been lost or buried into consciousness

Physical level

Often, if your trauma memories are deeply buried in your unconscious, your body becomes the messenger, trying to help you to tune into what needs to be healed. It is important to honor your body's symptoms or imbalances as both real at the physical level but also as a metaphor for what is needing to be addressed. This means that you can both seek to address the physical illness while also listening to the deeper meaning of these symptoms as a clue to what is out of balance or needing healing at a deeper emotional level.

HEATHER: I once had a client who had a sensitive digestive system. She would often have bouts of stomach pain or intestinal distress. This was really stressful for her, and she tried different diets and sought medical help to address these problems, all to no avail. Through our work together, she began to realize that the digestive issues that she had were not a medical problem but a valuable barometer, calling to her attention times when she was in a situation or relationship that was toxic for her. As she learned to trust these symptoms and honor their connection with the deeper intuitive part of herself, she became more discerning about her choices, and the digestive symptoms gradually reduced and then disappeared.

Take time to listen to your body's symptoms and sensations. Also, learn where in your body that you experience certain emotions. Do you feel fear and anxiety in your stomach or intestines? Do you feel depression as a sense of heaviness and physical fatigue? Do you experience grief as pain in your heart or chest? We are each unique in how we experience emotions in different sensations and body symptoms. Allow yourself to track where emotions are held in different parts of your body. If you are feeling angry, where are you experiencing that physically? And if you have a headache or another physical symptom, tune into what feelings may be lying beneath this physical pain. As you learn your system's own unique language, your body becomes an ally to alert you to emotional issues that are needing to be addressed and guides you to heal at a deeper level.

As mentioned earlier, buried trauma is also often held in body memories. If you have a recurring physical issue, allow yourself to hold this part of your body with gentleness and listen to what it may be trying to tell you. For example, I had another client who had recurring stomach aches with no clear physiological basis. As she took time to tune into the timing of these stomach aches and what the triggers were, she started to realize that they occurred when there was a significant rupture or separation in a primary relationship. As she meditated on this, she began to remember a traumatic period when she was four when her mother became depressed and was physically and emotionally unavailable. As she brought these memories and feelings of being abandoned into consciousness, she was more able to let herself feel the sadness, anxiety, and grief related to these memories. When current situations in her life reactivated the feelings of the past, through times of separation or rupture in a significant relationship, she was then able to let herself feel her pain and anxiety in the moment and no longer unconsciously become mired in her childhood trauma. As she brought this more into her awareness, her stomach aches diminished and finally disappeared as she worked in a more proactive way with her emotions around the experiences of separation.

Here are other ways to help bring the messages from the body into your awareness:

Massage, myofascial release, somatic experiencing, therapeutic yoga, or other forms of body work: Allow yourself to have a healing and gentle massage with a massage therapist or with a friend or partner that you fully trust. Or find a body-worker who specializes in trauma and uses myofascial release or other forms of physical healing to allow the body to release the memories of past trauma. Pay attention to where you feel tension or pain in your body. As this area is massaged or treated, tune into what feelings or memories are surfacing for you. Also, working with someone trained in a healing modality such as therapeutic yoga, dance, or movement medicine can help you to tune in more deeply to yourself and to release trauma held in your body.

Emotional and cognitive level

There are many possible ways to begin to connect with the buried memories and pain from your past that are living in the shadows of your current life. Any approach that allows you to take time to safely go into your inner world and tune into your emotions and thoughts will support you being able to heal and release the blocks that are holding you back.

Here are some helpful ways to begin to open more to these hidden memories, thoughts, and feelings to allow what has been in your unconscious to emerge:

- Meditation
- Psychotherapy
- Shamanic journeying
- Eye Movement Desensitization and Reprocessing
- Journaling
- Contemplative art
- Dream work
- Observing triggers
- Inner dialoguing (working with the parts of yourself)

Ways to listen to your deeper self and recover buried thoughts, memories, and emotions

Meditation: Meditating is another way to open to your subconscious mind. Take time to do mindfulness or vipassana meditation, both of which foster greater insight into yourself, and monitor the thoughts and feelings that may be coming up in a repetitive or insistent way. What lies beneath these thoughts and feelings? Allow yourself to dive deeper into this exploration. Notice where resistance or blocks come up or when you feel the impulse to distract yourself. What is it that you are trying to avoid? Explore what is rising up and what the ego mind is striving to be in control of and distance you from. Notice what deeper feelings or truths are trying to emerge.

Psychotherapy: Being in therapy is also a valuable way to explore your feelings, memories, and experiences. Having support and guidance will help you feel deeply seen and heard. It can also be a valuable way to gain insight into behaviors and patterns that you might be unconscious of.

Shamanic journeying: Shamanic journeying is an ancient indigenous practice that helps us to both access what is hidden in our personal subconscious as well as gaining guidance from the spiritual realm. Seek out someone who can help you learn to do shamanic journeying who also has experience working with trauma.

EMDR: Eye Movement Desensitization and Reprocessing therapy is another effective approach for releasing stuck or blocked trauma memories and supporting the healing process.

Journaling: One way to connect to what is in your subconscious that needs to heal is to allow yourself time and space to open up and listen to your deeper self. Keeping a journal can help facilitate this. You might do automatic or free writing each day to see what comes up for you without censoring your thoughts and feelings. Or you may want to journal at the end of the day, reflecting on your experiences of that day and the emotions that were activated for you. Pay attention to those times when your feelings seem to be more intense than the circumstances would warrant, and ask yourself what the event or experience reminded you of from the past. If there are certain smells, sights, or conditions that evoke fear, anger, or sadness for you, write about them and let yourself free associate to other memories that arise for you in relation to those triggers.

Contemplative art: Art is a way to access what is held in the right side of the brain. This is the area that holds emotions and trauma memories. Allow yourself to draw or paint intuitively without controlling the process or censoring it with your left brain or analytical mind. After making the images, allow yourself to meditate on them and journal about any feelings, memories, or other images that arise for you.

Dreamwork: It is also very valuable to keep a dream journal. Dreams are often a way in which the subconscious is trying to bring feelings or memories to the surface for us to more consciously process and heal. If you set the intention to record your dreams every morning, you will begin to remember more of your dreams. Let yourself take time to reflect on the dream images and the feelings that the dreams evoke in you, and journal about this.

Observing triggers: Also, pay attention to how you respond in interaction with different types of people. Are there certain people or particular interpersonal dynamics that set off intense reactions in you? Journal about this and explore any past memories that are at the root of these reactions. If you are in a committed love relationship or deep friendship, these relationships can be an arena in which you can discover unconscious aspects of yourself. In the vulnerability of intimate relationships, you may see or experience feelings or memories that had previously been suppressed. What triggers you in relationship? Where do you experience fear or anxiety? Allow yourself to be mindful in your relationships.

Inner dialoguing and working with parts of the Self: With complex PTSD, it is often more challenging to reclaim the buried memories and thoughts and feelings related to past trauma. Often, different parts split off from the conscious personality in order to manage the intensity of the trauma. Learning to identify these different parts and bringing them into conscious awareness is a critical part of the healing process. Doing inner dialoguing and working with these split-off parts of the self was a critical aspect of Kristina's journey in healing her complex PTSD. We will go into this process in depth in order to guide you through ways that you can begin to connect with these parts of yourself and how to help them tell their stories and release their feelings in order to experience being heard and held. In this way, you reclaim these lost parts of yourself in order to heal and become more integrated, conscious, and whole.

Find the path that feels right to you. Know that the conscious mind is often only 5 to 10 percent of who you are, and to be truly aware and whole, you need to explore the deeper realms of your subconscious mind. If you have not had more severe or chronic trauma, what is needing to come up for healing may arise in a more gradual and less complex manner from your subconscious mind as you commit yourself to this deep listening. However, if you have had more extensive or ongoing trauma, you are more likely to have complex PTSD and have split off parts of yourself that are holding buried memories and wounds from the past. Then, it is important to work more consciously to discover and bring to awareness the different aspects or parts of yourself to heal and be free of the past.

Kristina
2008
Dusty Doll

I found her in a rubbish heap. Although you would not have been able to see it on her face, I knew she was lost, alone, and afraid. She was in a huge pile of junk that was surrounding her, swallowing her up. I think she's been there for years. A crying shame that no one even noticed her before. Her body is naked, covered in dust and spider webs. Did she even have a name? If she could talk, what would she say? What is the story behind her far-off stare? Her lashes covered in grunge ... did they ever hold tears? Are there any feelings left inside her plastic body?

Here, let me take you ... and clear the dirt from your mouth. And now, tender one, what do you say when your mouth is free to speak? Where? Where, do you ask, have all the children gone? Well, they have all grown old and gone away. No longer do they climb from trees or sing their silly rhymes. Too old for dreams and dolls, they do not pay attention to childish things. And most have grown secure in their fears and have little use for make believe and love and sacred memories. They have long forgotten that dusty dolls remain the diligent keepers of their stories. And that underneath all the earth and wreckage ... you still live.

Come, little one. Let me clean the grime from your eyes, so you can see I have come back for you. Let me wipe the dirt from your ears, so you can hear me say that I still love you and have not forsaken you. Let me wash your soiled body and hair, so you will understand that I still care for you. That I have searched through my inner garbage to find you. Your eyes, they are still blue and filled with promise and hope, gentleness, and innocence.

Once you were abandoned. Left in your shame and terror. Waiting for someone to come and find you and take you in again. Safe and warm and protected from all that is bad. You are mine, my little one. Now that I have found you, I will never leave you. Come, take my hand ... and I will lead you to a place inside where love never ends. Where the light is always shining, never to go out. Where dreams are nourished and rhymes are still sung and trees are still climbed. No more wanting. No more fear. I have lifted you out of my wasteland and have placed you where you have longed to be ... right in the center of my heart.

HEATHER: We all have parts of ourselves that make up a whole self. Whether we come from extensive trauma or not, we are still multifaceted beings. The more conscious we are of our parts, the less reactive and more mindful we become of our own behavior. However, the more trauma you go through, the more the different parts of you become defined, developed, and separate from each other. This makes working with and understanding the parts of yourself more challenging and complex.

KRISTINA: For a long time, I never thought about having different parts. I viewed myself as one dimensional, and as a result, I wasn't able to live a very conscious life. I was not tuned into my emotions and body, and I lacked the capacity to observe my own behavior. This made being in relationship very difficult, because I was quick to react and slow to understand my behavior. But once I started to sense into my trauma, my feelings, and my body, I began to experience different aspects of myself, and this complexity deeply resonated with me as being more of who I ultimately was. I observed that I not only had various parts, but everyone around me did as well, even those without an extensive trauma history. I came to understand the complexities of human beings, their behavior, responses, and interactions with each other. At times, I would observe how different environments or situations could bring out certain responses, emotions, and states of being in myself or in others.

As a child I had no way to escape the trauma, so I would splinter myself into pieces to be able to handle the abuse. Part of me would leave my body, so I didn't have to feel it. I would rise up to the ceiling and watch from above. Another part of me would hold just the emotion, while the sensation was held by a different part. I started to develop different aspects that would take on certain roles, so I could continue to survive the impact of the trauma and still function and live. When one part began to hold too much pain, it would divide and distribute the trauma even further. I had parts that held the abuse, and some that packed it away, so others could wake up and go to school. The more intense the abuse became, the more divided and fragmented I became, so that parts began to not know of other parts or the experiences they were holding. As the years went by, my parts went deeper inside, taking with them the feelings they held, which affected my capacity to feel in general. The disconnect I had with myself grew as did my depression. I was losing touch with myself and was left feeling like I was living detached from my own being. When my trauma started to emerge in a way I could no longer ignore, I decided it was time to face my fear of what was buried deep inside. At first, it was slow and awkward, because I was terrified of going into unfamiliar territory with mainly my instinct to guide me. Initially, I had to gain enough space to witness my behavior so that I could become more aware of what was out of balance. I was then able to break out of reactive patterns that were hurtful to myself and others.

Kristina
2000

I am continuing to excavate my soul and find the parts of me that I have often felt and been somewhat familiar with; however, I have never thought of defining them in such a way as being fragments of myself. I am trying to understand that my thoughts, behaviors, and moods are not just coming out of thin air, but that they are all connected to something that is very real and solid inside of me.

Often, it seems as if these aspects of me will fly out at random times, as if something from the outside world triggers a response. Not only am I often not aware of the emotional or behavior changes, I also feel I have no control over them. When my husband points out a sudden mood change, or if I am feeling a sudden surge of anger or sadness, it is as if someone else has taken over my body, and I am left feeling confused and helpless. It seems the only thing that helps to move past the mood change is to let time pass and get some distance from other people, so that I don't do or say anything that will be hurtful. And eventually I will return to feeling "normal" again. I feel so out of control and helpless as to how to stop switching my personality.

At the beginning of my process as I worked to gain more understanding of these disconnected parts of myself, I only had a general sense of a younger aspect of me who always came through as an image of a little girl, who was silent, sitting alone on the floor in a small room. I finally gathered enough courage to take a step towards her and try to gain entrance into her world. What I didn't know at the time was that it was the first real step into healing and reclaiming my lost and broken self.

Kristina
2000
Dialogue between Adult self and my Little One

A: *Adult self*
LO: *Little One*

A: Hello, Little One. I have finally come inside your room. It's pretty cold and grim in here. Why do you keep yourself in a small room?
LO: Because it's safe.

A: *Here you are in this tiny room, back against the wall, legs curled up, head in your arms. You know things, but never talk.*

LO: *There's no one that will listen.*

A: *I'm trying to figure this all out, so that I can hear you. I sense your pain and have felt it at times. I would like to help you, take it from you, so you don't have to live with so much sadness. They did terrible things to you, didn't they? And then they left you alone.*
Would you take my hand and let me help you? You won't take my hand, and yet I know you want help.

LO: *I don't trust you.*

A: *Why?*

LO: *You will leave me, everyone does.*

A: *How can I leave you when you are a part of me?*

LO: *We are not one. You are you, with your own reasons to be here, I am me with my own feelings and memories in my room. You have felt and remembered our past at times, but you and I are not one.*

A: *You are right. Will you ever be able to trust me?*

LO: *I do want to, and I do think about trusting you as I see you change.*

A: *Change how?*

LO: *Getting help.*

A: *Why do you look away?*

LO: *I don't know.*

A: *I'm so sorry. I am trying, and I am here.*

I continued to try to tune into these young or lost parts of myself whenever I noticed that something had triggered my mood changes and behaviors.

Kristina
2000

I am starting to notice patterns to my behavior. Like when my mood starts to change, or when I am feeling young or defiant. I am learning to put thoughts with feelings and behaviors with moods. As I see these come together, they are taking form. I am identifying these forms as parts of me that have been blocked off or hidden from my conscious self. The more I come to understand them, the more I see myself being able to communicate with them, and hopefully, help them. I realize they were created and exiled because of the abuse, and the only way I can help them is by first getting to know them. I have come to sense into a number of parts that feel distinct and real, that seem to have their own memories and personalities. It feels so strange to be talking this way about myself, but perfectly normal at the same time. I have given them names to make it easier to work with them.

Adult Self:
I call this part my Core, because it seems she is out in the world the most, and she tries to manage what is going on inside of me as well as the outside realities. She is the part that tries to find and work with all of the other parts inside. She is the most adult part. She is good at being responsible, logical, and resourceful.

Little One:
If I let myself find her, I can visualize her in a room. I can tell where she is emotionally by looking at her. She holds a lot of information about the abuse. But there are many other parts that have split off from her. She doesn't talk much. She holds a lot of feelings as well. Other young parts, that seemed to split off from her, send her information as a way to tell their story. I often find her dissociating from her body.

Defiant:
I have a part that feels like a defiant adolescent. She seems to function based on feeling and impulse. She tends to do what she wants, without much regard. It seems like she will be hard to work with. She doesn't seem to understand long-term consequences. Her main job is to protect other parts, especially young ones. She has a need to be in control. She is very defiant with male authority figures. She feels invincible, and her behavior, which blends with other parts at times, shows it.

Creative:
The creative part yearns to express her gifts, step into her life, and not be weighed down with the past. It feels as if her very existence depends on her ability to express herself.

Spiritual:
The spiritual aspect gravitates to all things spiritual in nature, not to religion, but to everything free of structure or of someone telling her how to be with the Divine. She goes inward, away from the harshness of the world. She does not understand the ways of the world and has an especially low tolerance for the cruelty and injustice she sees around her.

Apathetic:
When life gets too hard, the apathetic part comes forward. She shuts everything down inside. She will disconnect me from my feelings. When she is afraid that other parts are at risk of being hurt, she will step in and not allow anyone to access them, not even my core part.

Extrovert:
This part is outgoing, energetic, and fun to be with. She works well with the Adult part and in being out in the world.

Destructive:
The destructive part of me engages in self-destructive behavior. This helps to shut down intense feelings and send other parts into hiding. What she is really trying to do is to protect the young parts by not having them feel any more pain. She doesn't understand that hurting the body is not helpful.

Protector:
This part is always on guard to protect me at all costs. It is extremely hard for her to understand and compromise with others outside my system. She is always alert and on guard with the outside world.

Polly:
This part is easy to please and non-confrontational. She always takes the high road in order to avoid conflict. She will agree and cooperate to help things run smoothly. She is closest to the Little One.

KRISTINA: Although not all wounds are held as distinctive parts with defining characteristics, labeling them in this way can be a helpful way to structure and work with complex trauma. Even if parts do not need names or have not taken on a distinct form, you can still work with parts as feelings, body sensations, and memories, or simply just as energy.

The next chapter will deal with working with trauma as it manifests in distinct aspects of the self. The structure and examples are intended to be a general demonstration on how you might approach the work. Let your own intuition guide you in your healing process.

Working with parts to heal

HEATHER: Remember that the more severe and chronic the trauma was that you experienced, the more likely it is that you will have numerous distinct parts you will need to connect with and help heal. In more severe cases of complex PTSD, you may have parts that are not aware of each other and that function independently. This is known as Dissociative Identity Disorder. If your trauma was a single event, you may have one part that is holding the memories and feelings around that experience. Honor your own process in connecting with the aspects of yourself that need to be heard and allowed to heal. For some, like Kristina, there will be many parts that need to come forward to be reintegrated. For others, it may only be a few. And for some, it is more a process of reclaiming repressed or denied feelings and memories rather than retrieving distinct parts that have split off from the self due to dissociation or fragmentation. Trust your own experience and intuition as you work with allowing whatever needs to come forward to be seen and to heal for you to move more into wholeness.

KRISTINA: For me, it was an ongoing process to find and reconnect with the different parts within me due to the extent of my trauma. I found that one major advantage to working with parts of the self is that it gives you direct access into the wounds that may be hidden from your conscious adult self. Often in therapy, if you are dealing with childhood trauma, you are talking from the adult self about what happened to you in the past as a child. But the adult self is not the one who is holding the thoughts, feelings, and sensations about the wound or the unhealthy core beliefs. The adult is also not the one who is still trapped in the trauma state and living in the past abuse. So if you are in a more cognitive model of therapy, such as the cognitive-behavioral approach, and not doing this deeper work, you may have difficulty being able to fully heal and change. Working with your parts helps you move past the surface level of the cognitive process and more into your heart and into the deeper energetic layers of memories and feelings.

As you work with your parts, you might begin to sense their ages and their characteristics. You may have a young child part that is still yearning for the loving or rescuing parent to show up. Your young parts and those holding the wounds from past trauma need to be acknowledged and pulled out of the abuse, so that they know it is over, and it is now safe to be in the world in a different way. As you explore these aspects of yourself, you will also begin to identify the coping mechanisms developed by different parts. They are typically related to the age and developmental phase that you were in at the time of the trauma. These coping mechanisms were adaptive at the time and were the best means these parts had to protect you and keep you safe. However, in adulthood, these old ways of coping are often disorganized, destructive, or disruptive in current life. As you work with these parts by helping them to heal and feel safe in the present moment, old ways of coping can be released, allowing you to develop more mature, conscious, and effective ways of functioning. You also become more aware of when these parts are activated, so that you can shift and be able to make choices from your centered self rather than reacting out of the patterns from the past.

A major ongoing emotional wound for your parts is when they do not feel seen and heard. For them to be able to tell their stories and relate what happened to them validates their experience and allows them to move out of a frozen state, integrate feelings, and make progress in the grieving and healing process. These parts of yourself were often silenced in and through the abuse, so it is important to allow the truth of their experiences to be expressed and heard. When stories are told in the part's own words and validated by someone who can hold loving safe space, it can heal the wounds. When you don't access these lost parts and allow this truth to emerge, you continue to live in the feelings, thoughts, and behaviors that were forged in the trauma and remain controlled by and mired in the abuse of the past. True healing requires being able to help all aspects of yourself understand how to trust, communicate, be in healthy relationships, work together, tell their stories, and eventually integrate into the whole self.

You are able to reclaim your power as you state what has gone unnoticed and ignored and are able to stand in the truth that you matter, and that what happened to you is important. For those with childhood trauma, that child part of you was a victim, and what was done to you was not your fault and was not okay. As you are able to openly tell your story, you are able to purge what has been held silent in your body and mind. A door is opened, your inner child is reclaimed, and you are then able to more consciously let these memories and feelings in to heal. As you tell your story, you acknowledge and embrace the feelings and beliefs that you hold because of what happened and are better able to understand and connect with the trauma and its effects. Thoughts, beliefs, memories, body sensations, and feelings are all gathered together to form one cohesive story of the trauma and the impact it had on you. You then are able to listen, honor, acknowledge, and hold your experience, with love. You are able to free yourself from the thoughts, beliefs, and emotions tied to the trauma in the past and are free to make new choices, allowing you to create a new way of life. Then the wound heals, the pain releases, and compassion and forgiveness for yourself becomes possible.

The general structure for working with parts of yourself

1. Create an environment that can contain the work and hold your process in a way that feels safe.
2. Align to stillness, your calm inner center, and your witness self.

3. Gain access to your parts, or the feelings, thoughts, and memories related to the trauma.
4. Allow the parts, feelings, thoughts, beliefs, and body sensations related to the trauma to come forward to express and tell their stories.
5. Re-parent the parts in a healing way.
6. Close down the process by making sure all parts are in safe places inside the body, and by having a way to contain what was worked on, so that your adult self can transition back fully into the present moment.

1. Creating a safe environment and a way to contain the work

KRISTINA: Finding a safe way to work with your parts is critical to helping them heal. During the abuse, some parts were literally threatened into silence and informed that if they opened up and told anyone about what happened, they would be punished, hurt or even killed. Others endured abuse that left them trapped in terror and frozen in the experience. These parts need to know and feel that when they are with you or anyone else doing this healing work, that they are safe.

It is helpful to have a particular physical space in which to do the work of connecting with your parts. Once you open up to the deeper work, it is also important that you can do so in privacy, knowing that your process will not be interrupted. Some find it helpful to set a timer for a certain amount of time, and the time frame becomes part of a standard process. When the timer goes off, the work stops and is put away and contained until next time. This supports you in having a safe and protective container for the process with a clear time limit to help you and your parts feel safe.

It can be useful to have an established and consistent practice to create a sense of sacred space when you do this work. The process of opening up to your wounded parts is sacred and needs to feel safe to you and to all of your parts. This is a way of working at the archetypal or ceremonial levels of healing, and it adds more powerful and transformative energy to the work. For example, you might want to say a prayer or call in guides, healers, or helpers from other realms to help hold and support you. Smudging with sage to clear the space, calling in the four directions, and lighting a candle, can all be simple ways to use ceremony to begin and end a session. Consistent patterns and ceremonies help create a powerful healing structure and morphogenic field for your work. Once you have a routine, it is important to stay consistent with the process. Even if the structure needs to be changed or modified, try to stay with a regular routine. In this way, your parts will begin to feel safer as the process is more predictable to them.

Another feature of safety is emotional containment. Having a way to hold the trauma and bring parts back into safety, is crucial in doing the work in a balanced and safe way. Containment is helpful so that your system doesn't get overwhelmed and can stay centered in present life. When memories, feelings, and wounded parts have a safe and structured place to be inside, they settle down into a sense of safety, and you are able to feel more integrated and better able not only to function but also to thrive.

One way to have containment for the work is to keep a box that has a proper lid and maybe even has a lock. All paper, written dialogues, and journaling can be opened up at the beginning of the session time, and put back into the box, locked away, and stored at the end of the session until next time. This creates an environment where your parts can feel safe and tended to, and where you can easily access them again. It is also a ceremonial way of holding the process that increases a sense of containment and safety for all aspects of the self.

Some materials that you might want to have on hand while working with your young parts:

- Markers, crayons, pens, and pencils
- Large white paper
- Finger paint
- Watercolor paint and paper
- A doll
- Children's books
- Soft blanket
- Stuffed animals

You can also use an imaginary safety box that is held inside, as a way to contain emotions, thoughts, and memories that might be too overwhelming for parts.

Here is an example of how Kristina set up this safe internal "box" for her parts:

Kristina
2011

I count down to go deeper inside my system and into my heart, so that I can send a message to all of the parts inside of me. I tell them, "I want to show you something that I have that might help you. It is a box, and it has an automatic lock that opens with your handprint. If you are carrying feelings or sensations in your body that you don't want to hold anymore, you can put them inside this box, and when you shut it, it will lock, and all that you have put inside the box will be kept safe.

"Inside this box are many boxes, so that as many parts that need to can use this safe container. When you need to get access to your stuff, you just put your hand on the container, and it will open to your box of things. This way, anything you put in will stay private and safe. For example, if you are holding a pain in your heart, and you don't want to feel it all the time, you could use the box, by pulling all the pain out of your heart and moving it into the container. When the lid shuts, you will feel a distance between the pain and you. And when we come together to put more pieces together, you can retrieve the pain from the box and help move it up through our system and merge it with the story that it is connected to, so that it can fully release from the body."

It is helpful to have a way to methodically go down inside your system to find and bring the parts of yourself up to the surface, so you can work with them in a conscious way. Afterwards, as you conclude your work with them in the room, you will need a way to bring them back down into your body-mind system until your next session time. If working with parts feels overwhelming or too complex to do on your own, it can be helpful to use a guided meditation to lead you down to access parts and begin to work the trauma consciously. Then you can use a similar method to guide them back down into a safe place inside.

Another option is to count down slowly, starting at ten and ending at one as you open into your heart space. From your heart center, or wherever feels most comfortable for you to open up in, begin the process of connecting with the parts of yourself. Later, you can reverse the numbers, going up from one to ten as you move back up the system, coming fully into the present moment and into your adult self.

Another way to create safety inside is by using certain music or tones or even a message that you repeat to yourself. Here is one example:

Letting my voice go down to all parts everywhere inside of me, so that every part of me can hear my voice with the message: You are safe. The abuse is over. No one can hurt you anymore. I am here, and everything is going to be okay. We are all safe and free. There is no more hurt, and no more reason to fear.

2. Alignment to stillness and your witness self

KRISTINA: Once you have gathered all of the materials that you might want to use and have created a safe place with your containment or safety box nearby, bring your attention to the stillness inside. This will give you space from your parts, which will allow you to maintain a witness self so that your feelings and memories will not overwhelm you. The idea is that you are a character in a movie, and you are also watching the movie. The more you are centered in this witness self, the better able you are to observe your parts and the trauma. It doesn't mean you won't feel the emotions, but you will be able to experience your feelings at the same time that you are also grounded in a sense of peace or calm, deep inside the center of your being. It is as if you are in the stillness in the eye of the storm, witnessing the winds and storminess around you rather than being swept into it. As you work with parts in this way, you are in essence folding the inner wounds into the space of awareness and inner calm. This will allow you to work the trauma in a more neutral way and in a space of unconditional love. If you fall too much out of this inner stillness, you may begin to experience what is happening in your body and mind as your only reality. You then become re-traumatized when you no longer are able to observe the memories and feelings from the witness self. Instead of watching the movie, you merge with the characters, replaying and re-experiencing the painful scenes. This is why it is so crucial to stay, as much as you can, in alignment with your center and inner stillness.

Initially, some find it difficult to align with inner stillness and the witness self. As the outside distractions go away, often deeper undercurrents are felt that relate to the pain of the past. Trauma is heavy, dense energy in the body and psyche, and it is sometimes intense and raw, making it difficult to keep enough space to remain in the witness self. But as you heal the wounds, the body and mind begin to quiet down, making alignment easier and a more natural way of being.

As a reminder, some ways to align to stillness are: observing the breath, gentle movement (like yoga, Qigong, or Tai Chi), focusing on a candle flame, concentrating on certain sounds, or through a meditation that helps you to not attach to your thoughts. Find something that works well for you. Then, deepen into this awareness, so that you feel somewhat distant from all of your thoughts, emotions, pain, and memories that may be trying to surface. In this way, you become a witness to all that you are sensing. It is as if you are behind a glass window, and all that you are feeling is like rain drops hitting the glass. You can experience the rain without being in or becoming the rain. Or you can imagine that you are looking at the scene from a vantage point up in the sky rather than being in the event. Do whatever works for you to support being in the witness self. Then, if you can, continue to drop even deeper or expand further into the stillness, so that you begin to feel that you are a witness to the witness. This allows you to move into a deeper meditative brain wave pattern (such as alpha or theta) and to open your connection to the consciousness that is within you and beyond you, as well as bringing into your awareness your deepest soul self.

As you feel solid and grounded in this alignment, you are then able to open up and invite the emotions, thoughts, and energies from deeper in your body and psyche to come meet you and fully express themselves, while you are also able to hold all of yourself in safe, loving space, without feeling like you will be taken over by what is needing to emerge. This then becomes a fluid dance of staying in inner stillness, as you also connect with hidden aspects from the unconscious. Remember, if at any moment you begin to feel too pulled into the emotion or story or are becoming anxious, agitated, or overwhelmed by the thoughts and emotions, you can take a deep breath and re-align yourself with stillness and the witness self. If you choose to work with your breath, you can do so by counting the breaths, or taking gentle deeper breaths as you feel how your abdomen rises and falls. You can also use the 4-7-8 relaxation technique developed by Dr. Andrew Weil. In this technique, you breathe in slowly for a count of four, then hold your breath for the count of seven, and then release your breath slowly to the count of eight. Do this entire process four times, and it will calm and relax your whole system. Another technique is to breathe in slowly to the count of five and then breathe out slowly to the count of five as long as it takes until you feel your system calm down.

When you feel you are not so overcome with emotion, you can return to working with your parts, thoughts, feelings, and body sensations. Tell them that they are safe. Ask them what they need. Then, when the time is up or you feel enough work has been done, surround them in love and guide them down inside you (perhaps into your heart space or an imagined safe room), so that they are held in a safe place within you. When you are working from a place of stillness, there can be a flow of emotion that can more easily come up and move through you. Even if the experience feels powerful and sharp, you can allow the flow, while at the same time feeling connected with deep inner peace.

Sometimes, the work will be this simple. You will come into your safe place, align to stillness, become the witness, and invite all that needs healing into your heart. The wounded part might need to simply express something or to release a feeling. As you move into the witness self, hold that part, allow the release, and then fold the energy of love around the trauma, weaving both together in your heart. Hold this release and healing until it feels done or until the time is up, then come back into stillness and into your witness self, and gently close down the work. As you allow for deeper feelings, memories, and thoughts to arise and move through you, send compassion and unconditional love into the wound that is coming up to heal. Simple pure intent can heal wounds as they come up and release. You may find it helpful to connect to spiritual or cosmic healing energy, by placing a hand over your heart, and visualizing white light coming through the palm of your hand and into the trauma. Another way to do this is by visualizing the healing, purifying energy of the Sun flowing into your heart and throughout your whole body.

KRISTINA: When I lived in India, I began to work with a woman in her eighties. One day, she confided in me that after a lifetime of deep meditation and yoga practice, she recently had felt that she could no longer do them. Two years previously, her husband had died, and shortly after that, she had surgery done on her heart. After this, her blood pressure became elevated, and she began experiencing sudden anxiety attacks. She tried anti-anxiety and anti-depressant medications, but these did not help and had side effects that were hard to tolerate. She began to feel more and more disconnected from life and hopeless as to how to find inner peace again.

Through a few simple methods of helping her tune into her wounds and grief, the pain that she was carrying in her heart began to melt away. Her body and mind began to lighten, which gave her some space to align more easily to peace. Moving between stillness and anxiety, she continued to work on healing even when the anxiety was intense. By allowing herself to go more and more deeply into the pain, she was able to find stillness. Once there, she went deeper into the wounds beneath the anxiety. She did this with each anxiety attack. She would go into the anxiety as a way to find awareness, and then pull the anxiety into the inner space of stillness. She would work the energy in this way until the anxiety attacks subsided. As the anxiety lessened, she was able to more naturally quiet her mind and body and again was able to do the meditation and yoga practices that she so loved to do.

3. Gaining access to your parts and trauma

KRISTINA: After you have entered your safe place and are aligned to stillness, you are ready to work with your trauma. As we know, when trauma happens (particularly in childhood), it often becomes fragmented in the body, brain, and psyche. Part of the process of healing is gathering information and putting the stories together. This helps to make the healing more integrated. It is not always necessary or needed to work the wounds this way. Pay attention to your own process and how your symptoms of trauma are manifesting and trying to express what is needed. Attune to what is coming up and ask what the trauma or wounded part needs to fully heal so it can release from the body. If the wounded part needs to tell its story, it is helpful to gather as much of that story as possible. The story will probably include body sensations, thoughts, beliefs, memories, and feelings. When working with a part, keep in mind that it might be holding only a fragment of the story, and other parts within the self may hold more information.

Kristina
2011
Opening up to inner parts of the self

After counting down from ten to one, I open up into my heart space and feel into my breath. Feeling solid in inner stillness, I send a message out into my system that we are all safe, and everything is going to be okay. I then ask, "If there is any part inside that wants to come forward and join me, I am here to be with you, to hear your story, and give you love and safety."

(I then wait, holding space for anything that might come. It could be a feeling, an image, a belief, or a thought. There is no expectation; I am here to hold space for any wound that needs healing to come into my heart. Whatever comes forward, I know it is most likely a part of a larger story.)

4. Allowing parts to come forward to express, feel, and tell their story

KRISTINA: *I then continue the process. I see in my mind images of a dream I had with my father in it. I start to feel tense in my heart, and my stomach drops.*

I then ask, "Is there any other part, that has a piece to this story? If so, please come forward." (I wait and sense into the undercurrents of my emotions and body sensations, allowing all to come up. It is important not to edit or judge; this is just a space to allow all to be. I let myself be here as the witness, gathering as many pieces of the story as I can.) I then ask, "Does any part want to tell me their experience, and how it relates to what I am seeing and feeling?" (I get my paper and colors, pens and markers that are nearby.)

I ask, "If you have a story, please share it with me using my non-dominant hand. You do not need to use words; you can draw pictures and even scribble. You can also let your feelings out through the colors onto the paper." The words come slowly from my non-dominant hand in childlike writing on the paper, "I'm sad. I'm lonely. I want someone to hold me."

I respond as the adult witness self, through the dominant hand, "I am here. Please come, and I will hold you. You are safe. Thank you for coming and meeting me. Is there anything more you would like to say or draw?" She responds to me, "No. I am just sad."

I ask, "Does anyone else know why she is sad? Does any other part have a memory, maybe the part that sent the dream?" A new part comes forward, "I know why she is sad. I know what happened to her."

Adult: "Can you tell me through writing it on the paper?" (With my non-dominant hand, this new part draws a picture of a scene inside a truck with the father and a little girl.)

Adult: "Is this you? Did something happen to you inside this truck?"

Part: "Yes, it happened to us."

Adult: "Can you tell me on the paper?"

The scene unfolds with more pictures and frantic scribbling. I begin to feel sadness as tears drop from my eyes to the paper. There are sensations in my body that begin to pulse, as if they are screaming. I breathe back, and find the stillness, as the waves of energy release from my body, through the arm and hand onto the paper. Gradually, I feel the intensity begin to slowly fade.

5. Reparenting parts in a healing way

The process then continues: "I am so sorry. I am so very sorry that the father did this to you. I am sorry you were alone, unprotected, frightened, and confused. It is over now. Our dad is gone. You are all safe. Thank you for coming, for sharing your story, it is important. I love you." I imagine bringing these little ones into my heart, holding them, and sending healing, loving light down into my whole system. I then ask what the parts need.

Adult: "What do you need? How can I help you feel safe and loved?"

Child part: "I need a mom to hold me and a stuffed animal."

Adult: "Come with me, I will hold you for a while, and let's create a safe place inside, a place where you are always safe, and you have everything that you need. Are you ready to come with me?"

Child part: "Yes, thank you for coming and getting me."

Adult: "*You are very welcome. Thank you for all that you have held for me. It is over. All the abuse with the dad is over, he is never coming back. I love you.*"
Child part: "*I love you too.*"

6. Closing down the process

Then, I take these two parts of me and hold them, while we imagine a room inside, just for them. It has everything they need and want, and a loving grandmother figure to keep them safe and tended to. I make sure they are tucked in safely and are okay, and tell them that I will come back later to check on them. They feel safe and are not sad anymore. From one, I count up to ten as I go from my heart space (where the parts are held in safety) back to my safe room in present reality. As I slowly count up, I sense myself separating more and more from the trauma and from my parts. I know that I have done important work today. I pack my materials away in my box, put the lid on, and lock it away until I am ready to do the work again.

Telling the story with the non-dominant hand through drawing, free writing, and art

It is helpful to use your non-dominant hand when writing or drawing as this will support you in bypassing the efforts of your conscious mind to control or block the process. Also, if you are right-handed, your non-dominant hand is your left hand, which is associated with the right hemisphere of the brain, which holds and stores the traumatic memories and emotions. If you are left-handed, explore whether using your non-dominant or dominant hand is the most effective way to access feelings, memories, and split-off parts of yourself. Using drawing and art are also effective ways to engage the right hemisphere and to open to traumatic experiences and visual images. The left hemisphere is more dominant in language and linear thinking.

At first, it may be difficult to open up to the trauma, because you may be blocked by protector parts who are trying to keep the younger parts from being overwhelmed or from feeling more pain. It is important to first work with any parts that developed specifically as a way to protect you or your younger parts from further hurt. What needs to be explained to the protector parts is that their ways of coping were really helpful in the past but may now be blocking you from healing and being free from the pain. As these protector parts learn to trust you and feel that the other parts are now safe to heal, they will come together as more of a team, to help assist in the healing and integration of information and memories. It is also important for the adult who is facilitating and leading the dialogue to make sure all other parts that are not involved with the memory being processed are kept in a safe place, so that only the parts involved in the experience have exposure to the information. All other parts should be secure in their safe places inside of you.

Kristina
2011

I let my voice go down, down, down to all the parts that are needing healing from any abuse from the father: "If you are a part that does not have knowledge or a memory of being sexually touched by him, this time is not meant for you to be out and having access to this knowledge. It will not be helpful to you. So please, all other parts, find your safe places, and go there now. I will let you know when it is safe to come back out and be more in the body with everyone. Now, I am asking all parts that need healing from what happened with the father, from any physical touch from him that felt harmful or hurtful, to come out. I am counting down now to be with you more fully in my heart. Ten, nine, eight, seven, six, five, four, three, two, one ..."

Dialogue between Adult self (A) and Child part (C):

A: Hello, I have come back to check on the parts that are sending me messages about the father and his touch that hurt us. Can you tell me how you are doing?
C: Okay.
A: Are you still sad? You seem to be sad.
C: Yes.

A: It is okay to be sad. Do you want to let the sadness go from your body? Is it time for that?

C: No, not yet.

A: Okay, you can share your own story. It is safe now to do that. How do you feel about that?

C: Not so good.

A: Why?

C: It will make you sad.

A: Yes, it probably will. And sometimes it doesn't feel good to be sad. But I am big now, and I'm going to ask you to trust me, that when I get sad, I will be able to hold it and work with it. And if I need to, I will ask for help. And if you hold onto your memory, I will stay sad, because you and the sadness are inside of me. I need to feel, so I can work with it, and let it move through me, through us. Does that make sense?

C: Yeah.

A: So please, you will be helping all of us if you tell, and we can all feel. You are being brave, so thank you. How old are you?

C: Eight.

A: You are eight?

C: Yes.

A: You seem so sad. Would you be willing to tell your story? That just means anything you want to say. You can even draw it out or just use a color to scribble it out, maybe just picking a color that feels like sadness to you, and letting that color be sadness on the paper.

C: Okay.

A: Thank you for being so brave.

With my non-dominant hand, this part draws a stick figure, head down with a frown and with her arms and hands together in front of her.

C: Here is me. I'm eight. I'm all alone. I don't have anyone to tell. I am so sad inside. I have to shrink up and go inside of myself.

A: Do you remember when your dad would touch you in ways that felt bad?

C: No, I don't remember, I just feel sad.
A: I am sorry you are so sad inside. Would you like to put the sadness on the paper, color and let out all the sadness?
C: Okay.

She colors many pages a solid, light blue.

A: It looks like you have so much sadness inside. Maybe you are holding other parts' sadness too. That is a very big and heavy job. You know you are safe now. You can just let that sadness go, and you can cry, and someone can hold you and help you feel better. Maybe you will feel loved, like you never have before. Can I hold you?
C: Yes.

I picture myself holding her, giving her love and healing light energy. While I continue talking to her, I put my hands on my own heart and stomach, where I feel a dull ache.

A: I am so sorry you were never held, and that no one was there to listen to you. Someone should have been there for you, because you were just a little girl, and little kids need older people to take care of them, to listen, and be able to hear what was so terrible that happened to them, so they can help them. You needed someone to help you, so that you could feel loved when you most needed it. I'm sorry you had to wait this long to get what you needed. Are you feeling better now?
C: Yes, I feel much better.
A: All right, then is it okay if I talk to another part now?
C: Okay.
A: You can go down into your safe and comfy room, while I talk to the others, unless you feel your sadness is about how your dad touched us in a way that hurt us. Do you feel like you might know something more about this but do not remember?
C: Yes. I think I hold the sadness, but I don't remember why.

A: *Do you think it would help if you knew more about why you were so sad, what your sadness is attached to? Maybe if you knew, you could also understand that it is over too, and that you don't have to be sad any more.*

C: *Okay.*

A: *Do you want to try?*

C: *Yes.*

A: *All right, why don't you stay right beside me, stay close to me, and let me know if what you are seeing is too much.*

C: *Okay.*

I now open up my attention in a broader way inside my heart space and ask,

A: *Is there anyone else that has a story about Dad and wants to tell about that experience through words or pictures or coloring? I have a feeling that some of you are scared, because this is a secret that you have held for a long time. But we don't have to keep secrets from each other anymore. We are all here to love and support each other. That is all. Nothing bad will happen to you inside this safe place that we have created for you to express what happened to you. We just want everyone inside to have help and to feel better.*

(I sense a part come forward. It doesn't take form, but I can feel a presence, so I just work with that.)

A: *Hi. You are very brave to come forward. Thank you. I think it would be really helpful to you, and all of us, if you would share what happened with you and Dad. You don't have to use words if you don't want to. Can you write, draw, or color what your experience was with Dad, or anything you want to share, so that you can let these heavy memories out of your body?*

2nd C: *Okay.*

A: *I have some paper here with crayons and markers. So if you can let yourself come more fully into my body, so that your energy just moves through the left hand and into the fingers, you can let everything out that you have kept inside for so long. Thank you.*

2nd C: *He used to come in. (She draws a picture of stick figures, one lying on a bed, the other at the end of the bed, looking down at her.) Lie beside me. Take my clothes off and have sex with me. I didn't resist him. I cooperated. That way, it went faster. I don't remember what happened after he put his penis into me. I only remember when it was over, and I was lying back on my side like before. Frozen like. Numb—especially in my chest. I would fall asleep that way.*

(In present time: It is typical when having sex with my husband that I feel some level of physical pain. There is almost always some type of emotional response during and after. But I have always associated the physical pain with my mother's abuse. In fact, there was a long period of time when I wasn't able to orgasm without there being pain involved. But I never made a connection to my dad, with the physical pain and soreness that would come up the day after having sex. Typically, when having sex with my husband, I just comply, to get it over with. I now realize having sex with him might be triggering for this part, as if the abuse is still happening.)

A: *I am so sorry you went through this so many times. Not just with Dad, but currently as well. I am sorry it was this way, and we did not know. Did you have any feelings when Dad would do this to you?*
2nd C: *A sinking feeling. My chest felt heavy and tight. And I would just sink into this heavy, heavy feeling. I felt depressed, apathetic, hopeless. And I would fall asleep. I didn't cry. I skipped over sadness and became despondent.*
A: *I am very, very sorry. Can I hold you and wrap you in a soft blanket and give you healing light? And if you have tears that need to fall, will you allow them to?*
2nd C: *Okay.*
A: *While holding her, I say, "It's okay, just breathe, just let your breath move through the frozen feeling. Let it move through the numbness, you can let the feelings move slowly if they need to, you are safe now. Nothing can hurt you. No one can hurt you anymore. Your job in*

> *holding this in is done. And you don't have to be involved in having sex any more. It is done. All of it is over. Yes, just like that, you can let the tears come. It's done. You just needed someone to step in and take care of you and love you the right way. You needed someone to protect you from these terrible things. You did nothing wrong; you did not deserve this."*

As the adult self, I was able to hold this part until she was ready to go to a safe place. Following this, in working my father's abuse, I continued to gather all the parts that were involved in the same memories, so I could better put all the pieces of the trauma together. Sometimes, it is helpful to create a space that is specific to those parts that have gone through similar or the same memories, so you more easily know where to find them to help integrate their information.

KRISTINA: It might be the case that younger parts use more sophisticated vocabulary than common for their age. They might be using older parts to help them articulate, or maybe the abuse happened at an older age, and the older part is speaking through the younger part who had a similar experience. Although my mind will, even today at times, question the validity of certain memories that have come up, I remind myself that I am working to heal. And as I trust and work with content, feelings, and sensations as they arise, it is more important to pay attention to how things are shifting internally, rather than focus on whether or not what I am remembering is completely accurate. I often find that denial is used more as a protection from feeling deeper pain than it is as an indicator of the accuracy of a reality. I find it best to let what comes up just *be*, and to hold it with love and compassion as it moves through me to release.

When using any art form to express emotion, memory, or internal experience, it is often valuable to simply let what is inside have its own organic flow without engaging the left-brain or analytical mind. This is not the time to critique the work; it is the process that counts. Some find it helpful to set some limits when using art to express deep, intense feelings. Setting a time limit by using a timer and having a safe place to put the piece you have worked on can help contain the trauma that is coming up. Pay attention to whether having the piece out to be viewed by yourself or others would feel healing or unsafe. If you feel that displaying the piece feels more healing (as a way to honor and stay connected to the work) rather than re-traumatizing, make sure that it is placed in an area that, if viewed by others, would feel supportive to your healing process.

It is important to stay in a natural movement when working with younger parts of the self. Make it a process that works for you. There are no specific rules here, just guidelines to help you get started. For many people, dialoguing through writing and alternating between the dominant and nondominant hand becomes too "heady" and doesn't work well to access various parts. Another approach is to try holding a stone and move it back and forth between your hands. You can also switch hands back and forth as you place them over the heart, as you dialogue out loud or in your head, to do the communication exchanges between the adult and the child part. In this process, we are working with energy, wounds, feelings, memories, and sensations to try and gather as much information as possible to help the trauma come together, so that it will release more as a whole experience and not leave any remnants behind. Allowing parts to express, find safety, and decide how they want to live within you going forward are all important facets of helping the trauma heal. Part of the healing is allowing parts to find their voices and have support in getting what they need.

Sometimes, parts do not want to release from your body after they have come into conscious awareness, but they want to merge with the energy of your whole system. In any case, it is helpful to try and gather as much information about the traumatic event before merging energies or releasing them. This is not always possible, as wounds that are fragmented throughout your system tend to be stored in layers and even in different energy systems or parts of the body. Trying to gather all the pieces around a memory, to bring more cohesiveness and integration to the parts trapped in trauma, will bring deeper understanding to the parts, so they understand that the trauma had a beginning, middle, and that it did, in fact, end. This integration process can help release old patterns and ways of being that no longer serve you.

Gathering information and creating a coherent narrative

HEATHER: Because trauma often leads to repressed or fragmented memories of what happened, the process of gathering the bits and pieces of the story and the associated feelings and sensations is often challenging. You may need to dialogue with different parts in order to gain more insight into what happened and to access the emotions that are connected with the memories. For healing to occur, it is important for all of the parts of the self to realize that the trauma is over. Because traumatic memories are stored in the right brain and in the temporal lobe, connecting with them is often experienced as if you are back in the trauma, as if it is happening right now. As you dialogue with your parts, you are letting them tell their stories and allowing your witness self to encode the memory through language and observation in the left hemisphere of the brain, so the memory can now be seen as being in the past and can be experienced in a more neutral manner without reactivating the trauma. Then, the trauma and story of what occurred can be stored in your memory as having a beginning, a middle, and an end, and can be placed in a context of time in the past. In that way, it will no longer be experienced as still active and alive in the present moment.

Here is a new example of how to allow different parts of the self to share their pieces of the trauma and then weave together a more coherent story as to what happened to allow healing to occur:

KRISTINA: I let my voice go down inside, asking all parts why the system or body is so depressed. "Can anyone help explain why the body feels depressed, and why it feels like no parts want to be here, in my body?" (My body feels vacant to me, like there is no one home inside.) "Can anyone come forward enough to help me understand?"

C: Hi.
A: It's okay, you are safe.
C: It's completely dark inside.
A: Why is it so dark inside? Where are you?
C: I don't know, I'm lost.

A: Can I help you find someone? Can I help you not be lost?
C: Okay.
A: Do you belong with people?
C: I'm not sure.
A: How old are you?
C: Four.
A: Okay, do you know how you got here?
C: No. I was just here.
A: I think something very scary might have happened to you, and it made you kind of zap here into this dark place. Are you safe?
C: I feel alone.
A: Okay, can you try really hard to remember the last thing that was happening to you before you got here? Take your time. I am here for you. I'm not going to leave you. What were you doing before you were here?
C: I was playing at my grandfather's house. It was after breakfast.
A: Then what happened?
C: Then the men gathered together and grabbed me.
A: Did your grandfather know?
C: Yes.
A: Then what happened?
C: I got in here.
A: What probably happened was that you knew something very bad was going to happen to you, so you came in here to be safe. Do you understand that?
C: Not really.
A: Okay, let me try to find the other parts that were also in this body when you left to come in here.

I let my voice go down to all other parts in the body, so that every part can hear me: "There is a little girl that was playing at the grandfather's house. She had breakfast there too. Then, some men came and grabbed her. Is there anybody else that remembers this that can help us understand the story? Please come forward so we can understand what happened." (I sense a part come forward, and I start a dialogue with her.)

A: Hi. Did you come into my body too?

2nd C: Yes.

A: Who are you? *(The child part shrugs.)*

A: Can you tell me what happened to you? Do you know this four-year-old girl?

2nd C: Yes, I came after her.

A: Can you tell us what happened?

2nd C: I shot into the body fast. I don't know how I got here. I was carried into the car. It was hurried. It was daytime.

A: Where did you go?

2nd C: I couldn't see out the window.

A: When you got out of the car, where were you?

2nd C: The ranch. Grassy. Yellow.

A: Did you know something bad was going to happen to you?

2nd C: Yes.

A: Then what happened?

2nd C: They dragged me to the little cabin.

A: It's okay, you are safe now. What happens next?

2nd C: They are chopping meat.

A: Like for dinner?

2nd C: Yes.

A: Then what happens?

2nd C: We are walking. Yellow grass. Dirt.

A: Where do you go? What happens next?

2nd C: He is holding my hand. I want to break free. I want to run and scream.

A: I am so sorry you cannot scream and run. I am so sorry that this is stuck inside of you. Where does the man take you?

2nd C: To a well.

A: What's in the well, water?

2nd C: No.

A: What happens next?

2nd C: He tells me I'm going to go into the well.

A: Do you go into the well?

2nd C: No.

A: What's in the well?

2nd C: People.

A: How do you know that?

2nd C: He told me.

A: What happens next?

2nd C: We walk. I try to get my hand free, but I can't, he has my wrist.

A: Where do you go next?

2nd C: I don't know.

A: Do you go down deep into your body or out of your body?

2nd C: No, I go into a dream.

A: Okay, hmm. Thank you. Can I ask again throughout my system if there is another part that has more information about this experience, so we can put the story together?

3rd C: I came next.

A: Hi.

3rd C: Hi.

A: Can you tell me what happens next, and how you got into my body?

3rd C: I came, because I thought they needed me.

A: What happened next? (I keep getting the image of coming up to water.) I ask, "What is that image?"

3rd C: Her dream. It's not real. It's where she goes (referring to the 2nd C).

A: Is that your safe place?

2nd C: Yes.

A: You can go back there, if you feel safe there.

2nd C: I don't feel safe there anymore.

A: Why, what happened there?

2nd C: Nothing. I just don't feel safe.

A: (Talking now to all child parts that are here with me.) Can we create a place inside that feels safe for you to be, that has everything you need in it, and all the things that will make it safe for you?

2nd and 3rd C: Okay.

(Together we create a safe place that has everything that they need.)

A: You will be safe and taken care of here. I will come back and check on you here. Can you tell me anything else that you remember after the well?

3rd C: I walked around with them on the ranch. The grass was tall. They were telling me things. People that got killed and buried there.

A: Then what happened?

3rd C: There was another girl. And I left.

A: *(I send another message out through my system asking if there is another part that knows the rest of the story.)*

4th C: Yes. I know, but I don't want to talk about it.

A: Can you draw a picture?

4th C: Yes. (She draws a stick figure with a black blob over the stomach and writes the words "Sick to my stomach. Scared. Pain. Excitement. I want to cry but I can't.")

A: Is there anything else?

4th C: No.

A: I am so sorry you went through this. I am sorry you were alone, and no one was there to help you. I am sorry you could not scream and cry when you needed to. You are safe now. I am here. Thank you for sharing your story with me. Thank you for being brave. Thank you for being strong and for holding this heavy story for so long. Will you stay with the others, and I will come back and check on you?

4th C: Yes, okay.

A: I am asking down deep inside of me for the parts that have any knowing about this story to please come forward, to let us know what happens next.

5th C: Hi.

A: Hi. Can you tell us what happened? When did you go deep into the body, what was happening?

5th C: They were putting my clothes on.

A: Then what happened?
5th C: We got into the car. I knew it was over.
A: Where did you go?
5th C: I went to the grandfather's house.
A: And then what?
5th C: I played. It was a dream. I was always playing. Nothing bad happened to me.
A: How does your body feel?
5th C: Numb, but my vagina is very sore, I don't know why.
A: I love you. I am sorry you are sore. You are safe now with me. Can you come up in my body and see through the eyes, and look around? Can you see what it looks like on the outside of this body? What do you see?
5th C: I see trees. Buildings. The sea. I see the sea.
A: Yes, this is where we are now. Far, far away from the grandfather's house. Can you come with me to see the other girls? I think you might want to meet them.
5th C: Yes.

A: Hello girls. I am back to check on you. Can you all come around me, so that we can talk, and you can meet each other? Thank you. Can you all see each other? Yes, that is very good. Do you know each other?
Child parts: Not really.
A: Well, you were each very important in helping one another. When one of you was not doing so good on the outside, another one of you would come in and give the girl on the outside a break. There might be other girls that are in a lot of pain or really scared and either went out of the body, or way down deep into the body, so that they wouldn't know or feel what was going on. You should all be very proud of the help and love you gave to each other. And you also should know what happened, because when you know the full story, you will know there was an end, and that the scary and bad stuff is not happening anymore, and that the bad people all went away. Kristina and this body that you are in is all grown up. I am an adult, and I can help you now. You will also know what your involvement was, and how you helped us all stay alive

and manage on the outside. We are now in a very safe place on the outside, and we are around people that are nice and not mean to us.

I gathered you together, so that we can put all of what you have experienced together and make one big story. If the story that someone else is telling is too scary for you, you can create distance around it by putting it up on a screen high above you, so it is like you are watching a movie. Remember, this isn't happening anymore. It is over, and you are safe. Is everyone okay with this? If it starts to not be okay, please raise your hand, and we will stop and talk about it. Okay, let's start by calling in all the things that help us feel safe, so we feel really held and protected as we tell this story. Remember this story already happened, and now we are able to tell it and be heard, and finally, know deep in our hearts that the bad stuff is over. And we can feel safe and at peace.

The story starts with Kristina playing after breakfast at the grandfather's house. Some men come to the house and take her and put her in a car. She can't really see where she is going. But when she gets there and sees the ground, there is yellow grass and dirt. She is taken into the cabin where someone is chopping meat, maybe for dinner. The men leave, taking her with them, and go for a walk. They come to a well. They tell Kristina that they are going to put her inside the well, but they don't. Kristina wanted to scream and run, but she couldn't. The men took Kristina around the ranch, telling her that people were killed and buried there. Then, the men do mean and hurtful things to Kristina's body. There is a picture that shows hurt to the vagina. Kristina is scared, in pain, wanting to cry, and feels sick to her stomach. After they hurt Kristina, they put her clothes back on and put her in the car. She knew it was over then. They took her back to the grandfather's house. Kristina played. It was like a dream and like nothing bad ever happened. The story ends. The men are gone. Kristina is now safe and alive.

I am sorry this happened to all of you. I am sorry you were not taken care of, and that there was no one there to protect you. I am sorry you have held onto the pain for so many years. No child should ever go through something like this. You did not do anything wrong.

You did not deserve this. Each of you are amazing. Thank you. Without you, I would not be here. You have helped me so much. Thank you. You are safe now. And your stories have been told. They have been written down. You matter. You always did. You are of great value. What happened to you matters. I hear you! I see you! Thank you for coming forward to share and to heal. What do you need now? Do you need anything to find more healing and comfort? Can I send down light and love to you, that will help you further heal and be able to let go of the pain?

C: *Yes.*

A: *Will you come together with me, so that we can hold each other? Can we ask all parts everywhere inside, if they would like to come and join in this healing circle, that we can all feel connected and loved?*

C: *Yes.*

A: *Okay, I will shut my eyes and visualize this wonderful gathering and ask all parts to come together on the count of three. One, two, three. See ... we are one. We are whole. Feel our oneness and love. We can all stay together for a while, and when you are ready, you can merge with the energy of our whole system, or you can release from this body if you want to. If anyone feels they need to stay in the body, because they have more stories to share, that is okay too. And we will find you a safe place to be until your story is told. Please take in the love and healing if you are ready to receive it. And now that you have received love, light, and healing, you can decide if you want to stay in this body, merge with the greater energy of pure love, or release your energy out of the body. Wherever you go, know that you are safe. Know that you are of great worth, that you are this pure light and love. I am here, if you need to come back to talk, I am always here.*

HEATHER: Sometimes, even with dialoguing with young parts, it is challenging to get this level of detail about the trauma and the story of what happened. For me, in my work with clients, there often is an awareness of the nature of the trauma from recurring nightmares or body sensations or triggering events, but it may not always be possible to access more of the details of what occurred. For example, many of my clients have had a strong sense of having been sexually abused in childhood without being able to retrieve specific information about the abuser or the event. It is important to honor the feelings and the young parts that are clearly holding the wounds from the trauma and not allow the mind to critique the lack of detailed information. Again, this relates to the way that trauma is encoded in the brain and the way in which severe trauma often triggers dissociation. This process is not about establishing a legal case with details and corroborating evidence. It is about healing. Allow yourself to honor the deeper sense of the trauma and the trauma signature that you may carry. Then, you can allow the parts to find their voice and share their feelings and fears whether or not you, the adult, ever has the full story.

KRISTINA: One way to work with parts that have been trapped in fear inside the body is by asking the parts to come up through your body and look through your eyes into a mirror to see the body that they are now in. You can also ask the parts to come up close to the surface, so that they are just beneath the skin. This allows them to actually see, feel, and understand how the body has grown, and how they are now in an adult body. This usually helps them feel more secure and safe, and to trust that the adult in you will be able to help them heal their wounds. Then you can have them see the outside world and where your body actually is and be better able to sense into and know their surroundings. This helps them replace the trauma they are experiencing inside with a different situation and awareness.

Parts that have formed out of the trauma believe that the abuse is still happening and usually remain in your system stuck in a freeze, flight, fight, or fawning state. It is helpful to know ways to help the parts move past these states of distress. For example, if you find that parts are frozen in fear, you can energetically help them to thaw and breathe life back into them with the message, "You are safe to feel; you can now come home to the heart space to find rest and healing." It is important for parts in the freeze state to physically move out of it, and you might have to find a way to physically move your body to do this. Shaking (which is how animals release trauma from the body), dancing, or going for a walk are all helpful to release the parts from that frozen state.

If you have a part inside that is angry, agitated, and in full fight mode, you can help that part understand the reality that the abuse has ended, and you are safe now with the people who are around you in the present moment. At times, it might be helpful to let that part release its tension through hitting pillows or a punching bag or by throwing rocks into a pond. If you feel that there is a part that is in constant flight, you can help calm down your sympathetic nervous system. Ways to do this include slow breathing (counting to five as you slowly breathe in, and then to five as you breathe out). It is also helpful to put cold water on your face or hold your hands on your heart and send healing energy to every aspect of yourself. Then, go inside yourself, find the part, and bring that part into your arms to be held and soothed by actually using a weighted blanket, heating pad, or taking a warm bath. (This will also be discussed in the Healing section on how to heal the physical body.)

Here's an example of Kristina's work with a part that was in flight mode:

A: How are you, my little one? Not so good? Why? I know it's hard stuff that you are dealing with.

C: They told us things all the time, most of it I didn't understand.

A: Do you remember any of what they told you?

C: They used to tell us that we could never get away from them, that they would always find us, no matter what, that there was nowhere to hide.

A: Did you believe them?

C: Oh, yes.

A: That must have been very scary.

C: Yes, it was because I could never get away from them. They would always find me.

A: Like the time when I came and found you inside, and you were still running.

C: Yes, I do keep trying to run away from them, because they keep chasing me.

A: You must be tired and want to stop.

C: Yes, I do get tired, very tired, but I never stop running.

A: Can I help you get to safety away from all the bad men, so that you don't have to run anymore?

C: *Can you do that?*

A: *Yes, together we can. If you look around you right now, what do you see?*

C: *I see darkness, and I feel them behind me, coming.*

A: *Okay, I'm going to count up from one to ten, and as I count, I want you to come with me, up, up, up, through the body, so then you can see through my eyes and into the mirror.*

C: *Okay.*

A: *Are you ready?*

C: *Yes.*

A: *One, two, three, four, five, six, seven, eight, nine, and ten. Now, that you are just behind the eyes of this body, close your own eyes, and then, when you open your eyes, you will change your focus and now be looking through the eyes of my body. Yes, that face and body that you see, that is the body that you are now in.*

C: *Oh.*

A: *Look around, this is where you are now. It is not happening any more. The men are not chasing you.*

C: *Inside, are they inside the body?*

A: *No, they are inside your mind, it is what is playing inside your mind, but it isn't happening anymore.*

C: *Oh.*

A: *We are safe now. Look around. See that we are safe, and that you are inside of this adult body, and I keep us safe.*

C: *Oh.*

A: *How does that feel?*

C: *Good, that feels good.*

A: *Now, when we go back inside the body, we can create a place for you that is also safe, that has everything you need and want, and a way to be in contact with me, when you need something. How does that sound?*

C: *I like that. Thank you.*

A: *Do you feel you are safe?*

C: *I am starting to feel safe.*

KRISTINA: The heart space is one way to reference a place for parts to be with you, but some people find there is too much pain there, so they choose to meet their parts in a different place inside. It is important to take these examples just as possible ways to do the work. It is up to you to determine the best way to organize the process and help your parts heal from the trauma. Sometimes, it is helpful to work with the parts inside by actually drawing their safe places on paper, including everything they might feel they need. You might want to have a tangible way to organize what parts you are finding and working with, and where they are inside. Some find it helpful to make a diagram or to draw how the inner system is laid out. As you find your parts and gain access to their trauma, it is important that they feel seen, heard, and fully met by you. You will have a few parts that hold main themes or that do certain tasks. There are many ways that the parts may be organized within you in holding different feelings, memories, coping mechanisms, or aspects of the trauma. There is no wrong way to do this work. Trust your inner guidance and what feels most helpful for you and your parts.

You might start off needing to clearly know your parts' characteristics, how they came to exist, what they are holding, and how they operate within the makeup of your personality. But this could shift into working more with themes, feelings, or beliefs. Another shift might be made if you view your system as energy. As you work with the emotional wounds, which create energy blocks in your system, you can monitor how these blocks release as you heal. You could move in and out of how to heal the wounds in different ways. What is important is to have a range of options to use, so you can choose what is most helpful for you in the moment.

Strengthening the witness self as you do the deep inner work

As you work with your parts, it is important to continue to strengthen your witness self. As explained above, this is the part of you that is able to observe what is going on within you, to hear and see the needs of the wounded parts of you, and to help facilitate the healing process. As you gain more and more co-consciousness—which is the capacity to feel the energies and feelings of a part while also being in the witness self—you gain more of an ability to modulate and regulate your emotions so that you can consciously choose how you will act rather than being triggered and reactive. There are many ways to strengthen your witness self so that you have the capacity to be in a centered, grounded state, rather than feeling as if you are on an emotional rollercoaster as different parts of you get activated and rise up to potentially take over. Here are some possible ways to do this, but it is important for you to explore and find the ways that work best for you.

Here are some additional ways to strengthen the witness self:

- When you meditate or find ways to align to the stillness inside, you will naturally connect more with your witness self.
- Pay attention to where you experience different parts physically in your body and what body sensations indicate that a certain part has been activated.
- Monitor what events or triggers tend to activate a certain part of you. This allows you to more easily sense or see when that part is up and reactive.
- Journal each day about your feelings and thoughts and begin to identify some of the emotions and beliefs that are associated with different parts of you. Often certain parts have different feelings, words, or beliefs that they are most identified with. As you begin to notice these associations, it helps you to recognize when that part is present.
- Try to be aware of when you have been triggered or become reactive, step back and move into the witness self. Practice ways of observing your behavior and be curious about it.

As you practice these activities that strengthen your witness self, you will feel increasingly more centered in your adult, aware self and less and less vulnerable to being overtaken by a part when it is triggered.

General protocol for working with a part, sensation, or feeling that is taking over
KRISTINA: It might feel at times that the wound of an inner child is too strong, and that the trauma is taking over and the feelings or sensations that are coming up are your full reality. When this happens, it is good to have a plan in place, so that

you can more easily breathe back out of the trauma and pain. It might be helpful to have a list of coping strategies that you have prepared in advance for these times. Engaging in one of these activities allows you to shift your attention and no longer be solely identified with the feelings and thoughts of this part and of the past, and it also grounds you in the present moment and gives you another focus. Have this list easily accessible or in a place that will be a clear reminder to you.

This list might include activities that are grounding, calming, and nurturing for you, such as:

- Taking a walk in nature
- Drinking a cup of tea
- Taking a bath
- Dancing
- Doing yoga, tai chi, or qi gong
- Listening to soothing music
- Meditating
- Doing artwork
- Reading a good book
- Calling a friend or therapist

After you feel you have gotten enough distance from the pain or trauma, you can further turn in to your wounded parts and the feelings that are coming up to comfort them and calm them directly. Add as many things as you can to this list, and put it in a place where you can have access to it when needed.

Here are some activities that might help calm the distressed part and reduce the stress response:

- Hold a stuffed animal or favorite blanket.
- Find a quiet and safe place to rest, curl up in the fetal position, and imagine holding those young parts of yourself.
- Imagine white light coming through your arms, out the palms of your hands, and into your heart as you hold your hands over your chest. Also, imagine this white healing light moving through the parts of you or the feelings that need healing. Trust that you are healing yourself.

- Do the Heartmath Institute quick heart coherence meditation: Breathe in and out deeply, focusing on your heart. Imagine that you are breathing in and out through your heart. Now visualize an image that brings you joy or fills you with a feeling of love or of gratitude. Continue to hold this elevated feeling as you breathe in and out of your heart. This creates an energy of coherence that calms both your heart and mind.

Another way of calming your system down is to allow the part to feel heard by you or by someone else who is helping you through the healing process. This could be your witness self, a therapist, or some other person who knows how to hold safe and loving space. Young parts heal through loving relationships. They can learn that they can share their experiences with someone who is safe and can be trusted, and that being in an intimate relationship can exist without abuse. When they learn that the abuse is over, and it is now safe to be in the present moment, they are then able to stop sending messages through triggers, flashbacks, nightmares, and body sensations. Gradually, they become an integrated part of you rather than a split-off vortex of feelings, sensations, and fragmented memories of the trauma.

It helps to maintain co-consciousness with your parts and with your witness self, so that you feel the presence of both within you. Then, the adult witness self can dialogue with the activated part and help the part to understand that their feelings, reactions, and behaviors are in response to the past and are not congruent to the present moment. Through dialoguing, you can begin to understand the reasons that this part was triggered and then be able to address the needs of this part. This will enable the part to calm down and will reduce the stress in your whole body-mind system.

As you strengthen your witness self through alignment with stillness or inner calm and identify and work with your parts, you are able to begin to map out the various feelings, sensations, or thoughts that are associated with those parts. For example, you may have a child part that is frozen in the terror of the abuse. Or you may have an adolescent part that is angry and wants to act out. As you begin to understand the feelings and beliefs of these parts, you can more easily see the warning signals as to when one is becoming increasingly dominant. As you strengthen your witness self, you will have time to name this part, address it, and help it to calm down before it takes over and becomes the dominant force in you. When a part has gotten activated to the point that it is now controlling your whole system, you may then be flooded with feelings and sensations from the time in the past when this part had the traumatic experience. You feel the same fear, pain, and overwhelming sensations, and your body goes into the same stress response that you had at that time, with cortisol (the stress hormone) flooding your system. Your body and mind feel as if you are back in the moment of the trauma. It is important to have strategies in place to help you when the witness self goes offline and a part takes over. It is helpful to keep handy something written or recorded for the times when one part has gotten activated and has become dominant, and the feelings are too intense to separate from. If you feel you cannot get distance from the trauma or if it is hard to work with what is coming up from inside using the witness self, a recording that you have made or a list of calming words that speak directly to the parts may help to comfort those parts. At these times, a message from an outside source (prepared ahead of time) can offer a clear and structured way out of inner chaos by reminding yourself about what might be happening, ways to cope, and tools to use.

Here is an example of a message that might be used to help bring stability and space to the activated part, or emotional state:

"There is a strong feeling, sensation, or part that is activated right now, needing and wanting to be heard and understood. What I am experiencing in this moment might feel like my full reality, but it is not. It is not all of who I am. It is just one aspect of who I am. These feelings are related to the pain of my past, and there have been many more times in my life, especially in my current life, when I did not feel this way. These feelings are important, but I also know that they will pass. I will not always feel this way."

It can also be helpful at these times to connect with your therapist, healer, or a supportive person in your life to gain more clarity about what might be going on, so that you can have support in strengthening the witness self.

You can also gain space from a dominant part or emotion by using the breath. Take a few moments to step away and be with yourself to sense into your breathing. Breathe in and out slowly and deeply and see if you can gently blow this feeling or part away from your chest or body a bit, so you can have some distance to see it more clearly. Also, as you breathe in and out, call on the witness self to come forward. See if you can visualize both your witness self and this part. This allows you to regain co-consciousness with the awareness of both the adult self and this part.

In times when you are highly activated by a part and its feelings, it might also be helpful to visualize yourself pulling back from what you are experiencing, so that you are looking at it from above you. To get even more distance and a feeling of neutrality, you can pull even further out of that perspective and observe the witness self, the one that is witnessing the experience.

Another way to regain a connection to the witness self is to visualize your emotions as being like the currents of the ocean. See this as a time of storminess, when the winds are strong and the waves are turbulent, and as you breathe slowly and deeply, see the winds moving and the currents flowing, allowing the feelings to flow through you. Remember that the more you focus on the feelings and identify with them, the stronger they will become and the more you will be mired in them. As you allow them to just be and to flow, they will continue to move and pass through you. You can imagine that you are treading water in a storm, keeping your head above the water as you allow the waves of emotion to pass through you and then move on.

Working with Young Parts
KRISTINA: Reparenting is an important aspect of the healing process for young parts who have been neglected or who have been through traumatic experiences without parental protection or support. For many who have been through trauma, there is a longing to find the perfect parent in another person who can help give to their young parts what they missed in their developmental process. While being in a healing relationship, particularly with a trained therapist, can help to internalize this loving, caring, and protective adult support, it is vital and necessary to eventually take over this process of reparenting yourself. Then, the young parts within you know that they will never feel abandoned again and that the adult part of you will always be there

for them. When healing inner children or young parts, by reparenting them, we are helping them learn the following:

- How to ask for help
- How to be nurtured by the witness self or adult part
- How to find safety
- How to be loved without abuse
- They are not responsible for the abuse
- They are not bad or defective because of what happened to them
- How to feel seen and heard in a loving and supporting way, so they can gain a more accurate and compassionate sense of their identities and experiences

When you talk about your past from the witness or adult self, you are re-telling the story as a historical account from a more neutral perspective. But when you meet with your young parts through direct interaction, you allow the child part to speak in the first person, and you are then able to work the wound in a more direct and effective way. This allows the child part to be seen and heard and released from being stuck in the trauma. Again, this allows the traumatic memory to be released from the right hemisphere and encoded as a more normal memory in the left hemisphere of the brain.

HEATHER: As adults, we are able to process our experiences with the frontal lobes, which allows us to reflect on and more fully witness our experiences. Reasoning as an adult does not work when dealing with young parts whose memories are encoded in the more emotional and primal parts of the brain. When dialoguing with the young part, it is possible to access these buried feelings and memories in a more direct way and then allow them to be worked through in relationship with the adult/witness self with the use of the processing of the frontal lobes. This opens a way to access the trauma without being consumed by it and allows for more release, healing, and integration of the feelings and memories.

Peter Levine's work and other trauma research indicates that trauma is less likely to get encoded in the brain and body as a traumatic memory if the person either has a chance to take action rather than feeling helpless in the experience, or if afterwards, the person or child is able to tell their story and feel heard, seen, and held. This is what you are doing for your young or wounded parts as you allow them to finally feel heard and to experience their needs being taken care of. Even after years of time, these parts can still release their trauma and move into a healing process.

KRISTINA: As you deal directly with these young parts, they begin to understand and trust the adult part more fully. They are able to see the differences between the care and compassion of your adult part and the therapist or healer working with them and the adult that abused or neglected them. Your young parts that are frozen in trauma are waiting for the loving adult to show up, and when they feel this is happening, they are able to shift core beliefs and feelings and begin to heal their wounds. When abuse happens to us as children, the trauma often results in fragmented, split-off young parts. To work directly with them, they first need to feel safe. Building this trust takes time, as these young parts are often hypervigilant and are acutely aware of whether the environment and relationships around them feel safe. When young parts do not feel safe, they may activate other parts in your system to be defensive or protective. Working through feelings of abandonment and fear, and providing structure and safe containment for the work, all help to develop greater trust.

Parts are often created under different situations and so have different needs as to how to heal. It is helpful to have a loose structure of how to work with the parts either in a therapy session or on your own, so that all of your parts feel seen, and the work is contained safely. It might be helpful to gather all of your parts together when your system is calm and come up with what feels most helpful to all of these parts of you. It is important that the adult or witness self stays present as the observer and main caretaker. How to do this can be worked out with a therapist or healing other, so that it is balanced in a way where you can still fully feel your young parts and their vulnerability and emotions, while also feeling safe and held by both the therapist and your adult witness self.

However, as described above, sometimes when the trauma has been re-activated, it may be difficult to access the adult part of the self, and a younger part may be dominant. Often, at such times, the younger part is seeking reparenting or trying to get its story out. Knowing how to work with that part is crucial. It is important to have someone that you trust, like a therapist, who can help set limits and calm the young part, while also calling out the adult to come back and take charge in order to keep the young parts safe.

As you work directly with young parts, it is important to consider that you will need methods of communicating and comforting the parts that are appropriate to the age of the part that was formed at the time of the abuse. Here are some helpful questions and suggestions as to how to prepare to support these parts:

1. How could you comfort this part? What does this part need or want?
   Be as specific as possible. For example, the part may want:
   - To be held
   - For you to read a comforting story
   - To go for a walk in nature
   - To eat a favorite food

2. What tools can you use to help your young parts to express feelings or work things through?
   For example:
   - Journaling or drawing
   - Using markers on paper
   - Finger painting
   - Dialoguing or telling stories through stuffed animals or puppets
   - Feeling held by your adult self through holding a baby doll or stuffed animal

3. What does the part need in order to feel it is safe to come out and share its story?
   For example:
   - Being in a safe, quiet place with no interruptions
   - Having a trusted person with you
   - Being able to pace the process to share only what can be said without becoming overwhelmed
   - Doing healing work during the day instead of in the evening

Do this deeper dialoguing and healing process with your young parts only when your witness self is strong enough to have distance from the part to be able to work the process in a safe and healing way. Then, you can begin to dialogue with that part to have a way to gain more information about what needs to be seen and healed. Follow the protocol above to open up and work with inner parts of the self. If the steps above feel like too much to do at a given time, then simplify hold the part or visualize the process in your head. The goal here is to get the young parts out of the trauma state they are trapped in and allow them to begin to heal and to feel safe in your body. Working with your parts directly also guides you in how to protect them from exposure to situations in your life that are re-triggering or re-traumatizing to them. This also helps you to not feel overwhelmed by the feelings and the reactivity of these parts, and you are able to make decisions and take action more consciously from your centered adult self.

Kristina
2005

I'm still feeling very raw and depressed and having thoughts of wanting to die. I am barely at a functional level. I'm so raw and have a lot of pain. I went to therapy today with no significant change of feeling or mood. I'm feeling disconnected from my therapist. I went to bed feeling so much emotional pain, that my heart physically hurt. It is hard to breathe. I'm sick to my stomach because of the pain. I couldn't sleep last night, because even the touch of the covers hurt my skin. The pain is making me physically ill. I prayed last night that God would take this pain from me. I prayed so hard for help. I fell asleep in intense pain, and when I woke up, I felt a significant change. I did not feel as raw, and the pain had lifted. I still feel very heavy, and the rawness is uncomfortable, and it's hard to breathe.

(Three days later)

I started the day with some depression and back to barely functioning like three days ago. I started sliding as the day went on, and by 3 p.m., I was in significant pain again. I got home and went to lie down on the couch. The pain started to increase. *I felt raw, and it was hard to breathe. I felt sensitive to everything and very jumpy. My therapist called me and reminded me of being in the present moment and to take care of my needs. But I felt immobilized in my pain like I wasn't able to move to help myself.*

I couldn't physically get off the couch to get help but knew I had to do something. I was desperate to get out of the pain. I sensed it was a young part inside that was hurting really badly. All I could think was that she must be right in my chest, because that's where all my pain was, like she was wrapped around my heart and my lungs. So I visualized myself actually pulling her out of my body and putting her on my lap. And then I started to rock her and talk to her. I just repeated to her over and over again, "You are safe, you are safe. Everything is going to be okay. I am here. You are safe."

This part was stuck in a very horrific scene and needed help getting out. Through dialoguing with her, I was able to gain consciousness of the suppressed memory and the feeling that was now at the surface. I was able to explain that the abuse she was living in was now over.

Here was our dialogue:

A: *Look down at yourself and where you are. You are with me. I am here, rocking you. You are safe and warm. Here is a blanket for you, that will help you feel loved. It is over.*
C: *Really?*
A: *Yes, you are safe now. What do you need to help take the pain out of your heart?*
C: *I need to be held.*
A: *I am here, and I can do that.*

With my eyes closed, resting on the couch, I continued to visualize holding and rocking her. After working with this part, the pain in my chest lifted, and I could breathe easily again. I still felt raw, but I felt much better.

KRISTINA: As you continue to work through the trauma and the memories that you regain, you might feel as though the parts and feelings that are coming up will be endless. But this is not the case. Some parts release as soon as they tell what they have been holding. Others need more time to share and heal. Some parts hold core beliefs and patterns that need to be corrected and changed. In any case, it can be helpful to track the parts that come up, especially if they keep coming up or needing help repeatedly. Keeping a folder or paper large enough to accommodate a diagram or visual structure, and listing the parts, what they have shared, their characteristics and jobs, helps the work to stay organized. Sometimes, depending on the level of trauma, this step might not be as important. But just making the small effort to write down what is coming up in an organized format can help connect the dots later between current behavior and how it relates to the past. Creating a timeline showing events and times when parts were established or split off from the self could also be used to hold an overall perspective of the trauma, as to how and when it impacted you.

Some parts might hold more of a certain energy and tend to come out at specific times. Other parts might be less engaged in behaviors or feelings that are held by others. For example, some parts might be more artistic, creative, spiritual, defiant, young, extroverted, introverted, able to guide or lead, and some might just feel like certain ages or hold certain memories. As you identify and become more familiar with the parts of yourself and chart these, then when one is activated, you have your outline to guide you in how to help that part in feeling seen, heard, and supported in the ways that are needed. As described above, in dialoguing with your parts, they will share ways that their needs can be met. Also, as you work with them from your witness adult self, you can clarify what is needed to reparent them and support them in healing.

An example of the adult self clarifying the needs of a young part:

My inner child needs:

- Good food to eat that is comforting and nutritious
- Treats or special snacks
- To be held and calmed down

- To have a chance to express herself and be heard
- To have a safe and supportive place to cry
- To play and not have responsibilities
- To be protected from what might be potentially harmful or stressful
- To be creative and explore
- Help setting boundaries
- A good night's sleep

Possible ways for the adult self to work with young parts that are frightened:

- Snuggle up in bed with them with a special blanket or stuffed animal.
- Check on them throughout the day, so that they know they have not been abandoned.
- Use coloring and children's books to help stay connected with them and to help them feel supported by you.

It is also important for your witness or adult self to become clear about what may trigger or frighten your young or wounded parts. For example:

- Too much information about the abuse
- Loud noises or arguments
- Confrontation or conflicts
- Transitions
- Night-time or the vulnerability of falling asleep
- Specific places that trigger trauma memories
- New environments
- Frightening movies

As your witness self becomes more aware of the identity and vulnerability of your wounded or young parts, then you are more able to recognize when they are getting activated or re-triggered. This can be a signal that your adult self needs to attend to them, care for them, and reassure them that you, the safe adult, are in charge.

Some examples of signals which might indicate that a young part is re-triggered and is becoming dominant:

- Difficulty with eating or loss of appetite
- Difficulty asserting yourself, feeling helpless and overwhelmed
- Not feeling that you can ask for what you need
- Difficulty in engaging in daily acts of self-care (bathing, grooming, etc.)
- Feeling overwhelmed even by small tasks that normally are not a problem for you
- Abrupt mood shifts or an overwhelming feeling (such as anger) that feels like it is an over-reaction to the event in the moment
- A sudden feeling of panic or an impulse to run out of the room

It is important at such times to remind your young parts that they are safe and can exist now in a different way. You can help them by guiding them down into safety to feel held and taken care of by the adult self. This will help calm down your whole system. Having the adult self back in charge and giving the young parts simple instructions on what they can do to feel safe, nurtured, and loved will continue to build inner trust and bring healing to all aspects of yourself.

Understanding the different nature of parts

As you work with your parts, you will learn their different characteristics and forms. Some may be of different genders (no matter what your actual gender is). Some may appear as animals or take a particular symbolic form as a way to convey what that part experienced and is holding from the past. Others may appear to be ugly or gruesome, or present in a frightening way as an effort of self-protection. Try not to judge what comes forward. Just by holding a safe, non-judgmental space for parts to open up and express themselves is often all that is needed for the protective mask or form to release and the gifts and strengths of each part to emerge.

An example of Kristina working with a young part that appeared as an animal:

(A young part draws a picture that looks like a porcupine.)

Kristina
Dialogue 2010

A: Hmm, that looks like a porcupine? Is that right?
C: Yes.
A: Oh, nice. She looks very pokie.
C: She is.
A: Oh. Is she a friendly porcupine?
C: Mostly, no. Sometimes, she will be nice.
A: Where does she live?
C: In a hole in the ground.
A: Does she live with other people?
C: No, she doesn't like people. She stays by herself.
A: Does she have a name?
C: No.
A: How do you feel about this porcupine?
C: She makes me sad.
A: Oh, why?
C: Because I want to get close to her, but I can't because she'll poke me, and it will hurt badly.
A: Oh, yes, I suppose it will.
C: And ...
A: Yes, it's okay.
C: No. Nothing.
A: Hmm, does this porcupine make your heart hurt?
C: Yes.
A: I'm sorry. It seems like you want to say something?
C: Do porcupine moms and dads have porcupine babies?
A: Yes, yes, they do.
C: And do the babies stay by them?
A: Yes, I believe they do.
C: So even though they have pokies, they don't hurt the babies?

A: *Yes. That is how it works for porcupines.*

C: *What if the mommy and daddy didn't like the baby. Would they poke the baby?*

A: *Maybe. I'm not sure.*

C: *If the mommy and daddy don't like the baby, then I think the baby porcupine is bad. And no one will ever really like her.*

A: *Oh, that is a very sad thought. That would be a very sad porcupine.*

C: *She can't help it. She was just born wrong, and no one can like her.*

A: *And why can no one like her?*

C: *Because she is wrong. She was made wrong.*

A: *How do you know she was made wrong?*

C: *Because the mom and dad don't like her.*

A: *Well, maybe the mom and dad are wrong.*

C: *What?*

A: *Well, maybe there is nothing wrong at all with the baby porcupine. Maybe the mommy and daddy porcupine are wrong, so they can't see how special the baby porcupine is. And even as the baby porcupine grows into a little girl, the mom and dad still can't see her clearly, so they don't know or feel what a beautiful, wonderful, little porcupine is right there with them. So they miss being with the little porcupine, because they are always walking around seeing her wrong. But it doesn't change the little porcupine who came to them, who is beautiful, special, and was already a perfect little porcupine to hold and love. And the little baby porcupine didn't have to do anything different or be anything different to be loved by other porcupines. She just had to grow bigger and find other porcupines in the forest that weren't walking around confused and were able to see right away how this little porcupine was made perfect, and how she was easy to love just because of who she is, and she didn't need to do anything to try to change, so that people would like her. And maybe she needed her quills to poke and keep away anyone who might try to harm her. So they were important for her to have.*

C: *I never thought about it like that before.*

A: *I'm sorry you didn't have a mommy and daddy that liked to be with you. I'm sorry you were not loved or cherished or wanted. I'm sorry for all the times you felt rejected by them and felt you were never good enough to be loved. I'm sorry that you felt it was your fault that your mom and dad didn't love you. I know that makes your heart so sad. I'm sorry that you didn't get a mom and dad that wanted you, and that could take care of you. Can I hold you? You are lovable. You are worthy of love. You are special. You came to parents who were very wrong in their heads and couldn't see you for who you truly are. I am very glad you are here with me, and that you showed me a picture of the porcupine. Your feelings are very important. Can I send some white healing light into your heart? And maybe it will help heal some of your sadness.*

C: *Yes.*

A: *Then let us find a safe place for you to be inside. Do you have a name you go by?*

C: *Little One.*

A: *Thank you for coming, Little One, and telling part of your story to me. It is very important.*

KRISTINA: Getting to know the different parts of the self and their wants and needs leads to having more consciousness of the wholeness of who you are. Often these parts hold trauma and negative core beliefs that need healing and correction. But these parts also hold strengths and gifts, and as the trauma heals, the gems hidden in the depths of the self beneath the trauma are revealed. As you come to know the qualities of each part, you will begin to recognize them for who they distinctly are. This way, you will be able to quickly address and work with them as they come up to share what they are holding. Trust your own sense of the rhythms and pace of the inner dialogue and the ways in which parts are able to integrate as they heal or blend with the whole self or remain distinct aspects of who you are. We all contain a multiplicity of parts of the self. Your personality is a mosaic of these parts and aspects of the self. The key to healing is to allow all of these aspects of who you are to be held in consciousness and compassion.

The more you are able to recognize the different parts of you by understanding their characteristics and knowing when they are activated, and the more you are able to step out of the reactivity, feelings, and patterns of the past, the better you are able to respond to and work with the wounded parts to help them heal. The more consistently your parts are met, understood, cared for, and feel safe, the more this healing takes place. Parts that have only known how to be defensive or destructive in the past start to understand and believe that they do not have to function that way anymore. When parts' needs are taken care of, there is less need to act out, stay frozen in the past, or bury the pain inside. Parts can then work together in a healing way as the blocks or destructive patterns fall away. You then foster more integration of all of these aspects of yourself rather than feeling as if you are fragmented and acting out of different parts at different times.

HEATHER: You might think of it as if you are forming a council with all of your parts present in a circle, seeing and relating to each other, with you as the adult witness self in the center of the circle, guiding the conversation and creating a safe and loving community for all of the parts to come together in a unified and healing way. Your adult witness self is guiding collaborative decisions with all of the parts in order to draw on your strengths and gifts to be utilized so that you can thrive and live in joy.

You might want to envision working with your parts as you walk the medicine wheel. You as the adult witness self are at the center of the wheel. As you connect with the different aspects of yourself, it is as if you pull them in from all directions, right into the center of the wheel to be with you as you are grounded in stillness. Here in the center, you are able to see all of these parts of yourself and honor your wholeness. As you align with the center of the wheel and with the Earth and sky, you are able to rest here and feel held by these energies and divine love and come home to your true self.

Parts working in collaboration together
KRISTINA: It might be necessary to have parts in your system get to know each other or be in dialogue when making decisions about your life, so that

the action to be taken does not elicit conflict but can be made in a supportive, unified collaboration. For instance, when working on breaking long-standing behavior patterns that may have been adaptive in the past but are now unhealthy or destructive, some parts may be ready to change this, while other parts might be terrified by the idea, leaving them feeling vulnerable and unprotected. For example, a stronger part might be ready to take a stand against an abusive partner, but a more sensitive part might feel a lot of fear around confrontation and want to stay in a submissive pattern. So there might be a strong conflict in the psyche. Once a choice has been made to change an old pattern or behavior, one part might feel elated in the moment, while others may feel a lot of fear around the decision. You may then experience an initial sense of accomplishment and excitement only to have the feelings later shift to depression, heightened anxiety, fear, or being agitated and unsettled.

By gathering your parts together and being open with regard to potentially disruptive decisions being made, you give all of your parts a chance to express concerns and wants. Then, there is opportunity for a plan to be made, so that all parts feel they are on the same team, involved in the process, and safe in the system they are in. The adult self can work with the parts that feel uncertain to bring them into safety and the understanding that this way of coping from the past is no longer needed or healthy. Again, think of the process as holding a council meeting, allowing all of the parts of the self to gather in a circle to be heard, with the adult part being the facilitator and ultimately making the decision that is in the best interests of all the aspects of the self. In this way, a younger part is not taking charge of the process, and all parts are heard and seen and feel that the decision is a collaborative process.

If at times you are struggling with parts that are trying to dominate your system, then writing down what has been decided on by the group council helps to keep your adult self in charge and to have a tangible reminder of these decisions. In the midst of intense trauma work, it might be helpful to keep these agreements out in a visible way, so that all parts can see them often. For example, if self-destructive behavior in the past was used as a way of coping with pain, write out a contract, for all of the parts of you, that this behavior will be replaced with other, more healthy ways to cope. If you find at times that a part is resisting the agreement, then tune into that part, read the agreement, and ask what it is feeling or needing, and how you can help meet those needs rather than letting that part act out and engage in the familiar behavior of the past. As another example, if eating healthy foods has been agreed upon, put a post-it on the refrigerator as a reminder of the agreement that has been made. This helps all parts to remember, honor, and work with the process as needed.

When there is internal dialogue and communication, and the adult self is taking charge, then you are able to meet your own needs and not have to seek out other people to do it for you. It can help to visualize a place inside of you that you can create with your parts that helps them to feel there is structure, safety, and a consistent place to collaborate with each other. For example, you might visualize this as:

- Gathering around the medicine wheel with the young parts on the outer ring and the adult self in the center.
- A special place in nature, that feels safe and nurturing as a gathering place.
- A room created inside yourself that is furnished with a round table and enough seats for all of the parts that are meeting each time.
- A healing room with loving healers, ancestors, or guides to surround and support all parts as they meet together.

As you connect with your parts and provide them with a safe place to be inside of you, then you are also able to protect them from being "out" or exposed to experiences in your adult life that could be triggering or re-traumatizing to them. This is especially important for young parts that have experienced early sexual abuse—to not be out or engaged when in an adult sexual experience. Otherwise, it creates confusion and often re-activates the trauma. If you work with these parts with awareness and allow your adult/witness self to be in charge, then you will be able to protect them from getting re-triggered, and you will find yourself being less reactive, less fearful or overwhelmed, and better able to make conscious adult decisions. Working with parts in a collaborative way helps bring a sense of community and cohesiveness within yourself. It also helps to clarify what feelings in the present are related to these younger parts and their past experiences in a way that allows you to be more conscious about what is real in the present moment.

Kristina
Journal entry

A: I let my voice go down, down, down to the part that was angry yesterday and then got really sad. I am trying to find you in your safe place. I am back to check on you, and I see you are still very sad. Maybe it is your sadness that is making me depressed. We should help you with your sadness. You seem old enough to be able to talk about it, but if you want to, you could draw or color the sadness. We could pull some of the sadness out of you with a magic wand. It's okay to cry. It's safe now. I am here with you. I won't leave you. Can you tell me why you are so sad? Can you write through the left hand?

C: I've been alone for a long time.

A: That would make me very sad. I'm sorry. How did you get to be alone?

C: Just because no one was there. And I was alone a lot when I really needed help.

A: Like from an adult? Like a mom or dad?

C: Yeah.

A: Oh. Are you sad about anything else? It's okay, you can cry.

C: No, I just feel stuck here. I need help, and I need someone to help me.

A: Oh. Okay. Maybe I could help you. Where do you come from?

C: Nowhere. I just float around everywhere. I don't belong anywhere.

A: Would you like a place to belong?

C: Yes.

A: How about you and I can create a place that is just perfect for you? It will have everything you need inside to help you feel safe and comforted and taken care of.

C: Okay.

(Through the use of imagination, we set up a room that is mostly created by this young part. She has books and art supplies and access to a yard with a playground. She can also call on a mother figure when needed or other young parts to play with.)

A: You seem to be feeling better. Is it nice to have a place to be?

C: Yes, I've never belonged to something before.

A: Well, you belong here. And I am glad I found you. Why do you get so mad at certain people?

C: I get angry. But it just comes out of me, then you feel angry, and then you get mean.

A: Oh, that makes sense. Because sometimes I don't know why I'm all of a sudden acting that way.

C: I'm glad you found me.

A: Yes, me too. I'm glad I thought to go inside, because we needed to find you. You are very important to all of us.

Most parts have split off from the whole, because they have not had a safe place to belong as part of the self or in expressing themselves in an outer way. By pulling them back into yourself, through dialogue and creating safety, you are healing the inner wound of being alone and neglected.

A continuation of the above dialogue as it relates to this sense of neglect:

Kristina - dialogue (continued)

A: Do you know how you got here inside?

C: I just know I've been lost for a long time.

A: Do you know the outside world?

C: Some things.

A: Like do you know about mom and dad?

C: Yeah. I know I needed them really bad, because I needed someone to belong to. Someone to help me. But I didn't get it, so sometimes the need was so big, I would escape inside. And I guess it happened enough I got stuck in here. Well, anyway, I would rather be inside here then outside where really bad stuff happens.

A: Oh. What do you know about?

C: Well, I know once this strange thing happened to me.

A: What was that?

C: When I was on the outside, I belonged to this group. I wanted to belong so badly to someone that would protect me, and teach me things,

	and care about me. So I wanted to belong to the group, because that's all I had. And so I did. But there was another part of me that didn't want to belong to the group, because they scared me so much. So I split off and went inside, and the other part of me went with the group. (The group this part is referring to is the cult that Kristina was raised in until she was four.)
A:	*Do you know where she is, the part you split off from?*
C:	*No, I haven't seen her since then.*
A:	*I'm really glad you told me all of this, because it is very important information. Can we maybe talk about it again sometime?*
C:	*Yes.*
A:	*Thank you. What do you need? Do you want to spend a little more time creating your room inside?*
C:	*Yes.*
A:	*Would you like to meet some of the other parts sometime?*
C:	*Yes.*

Having space for parts to work through feelings and become aware of each other brings integration to the whole system. Neglect, feeling lost, and not having secure roots as a child can leave one feeling empty and alone as an adult. When working with different aspects, we are working to pull together the fragmented and scattered energies of the self into a more interconnected wholeness of the total being.

Working with parts that internalize the abuse, feeling it was "my fault, and I am the one to blame"

HEATHER: As a young child, you come into this world with certain personality traits, but your sense of self is shaped in relationship with others, predominantly with your parents or primary caretaker. Your core sense of identity is formed by age three. Remember that it is only after age three that you begin to encode memories in the left hemisphere of the brain in a way that allows for conscious recall. So these early experiences with your parents form the core sense of yourself and emotionally imprint in the right hemisphere, and you also carry this sense of identity in your unconscious feelings, thoughts, and beliefs about yourself and the world.

For healthy development, it is crucial for the infant to feel bonded with the mother or primary caretaker and to feel held in love and in safety. It is vital for the parent to be attentive to the child's physical needs and emotional state. Then, as the child develops, it is important to experience a parent's empathic attunement to the child's feelings and mirroring of who they are. In this way, the child is able to internalize an acceptance of their full range of feelings and also to feel seen and heard. The child then develops an internal sense of self that is in alignment with the real self. If the child does not experience this due to neglect, abuse, or ruptures in these early critical relationships, a distorted or fragmented sense of self will develop. Also, if there was abuse or ruptures in these early relationships, the child may develop attachment difficulties and internalize a sense of guilt or shame and of being "bad," "dirty," or "wrong," and feel in some way at fault for the abuse or neglect. Often, as an adult, the person who has been abused or neglected will relate to the younger parts of the self in a similar manner as to the neglectful or abusive patterns that were experienced and internalized in childhood. To heal this, it is critical to bring these early feelings and beliefs into consciousness and to experience a healthy and loving relationship with another person to be able to internalize a new way of relating to the parts of the self.

Kristina
1999

Cognitively, I know that as a child I was innocent. I wasn't capable of being responsible for what happened to me. And yet, I still do not feel I was ever innocent, pure, sacred, or clean. From my earliest memory, I have been involved in dirty, shameful, unclean experiences, and I cannot seem to separate the two: me (my self) from my experiences (what happened to me). I was involved; therefore, it is who I am.

When I was a little girl, my hands and feet were so small. My skin was smooth with no wrinkles or age spots, just perfect skin. My heart was sad and broken. Most of the time, I was looking for someone to love me, because I lived in a house with no love, and I was alone. If I was ever sad or scared, no one was there to help me. And I needed lots of help. I needed someone to take care of me, because I was just a child. It was hard to be lonely and carry so much sadness inside. I wished my parents loved me. I wished my heart would get better, but it was always sad and heavy. I felt I was bad, and that I came that way. Why else would a mother abuse her own child? I'm dirty and ashamed. I feel guilty, but mostly I feel bad. Why do the big people not care about me? Somewhere inside, I am bad, and people cannot love what is ugly and bad.

KRISTINA: Young parts are trapped in the trauma that they experienced and in how they interpreted what happened to them. When we are able to get to the parts that carry these core beliefs of being bad, dirty, ashamed, or feeling that they did something wrong, we can hear what they have been holding, give them a new experience through reparenting, help them heal, and then develop different beliefs about themselves. This releases the energetic hold these old beliefs have had. It might be helpful to explain to the parts that they were trapped in the roles that were defined for them. The "rules," as they were outlined by the adults, need to be looked at, questioned, and better understood. Feeling trapped in a role or in the way that the abusive adult demanded that they behave is never the responsibility or fault of the child. The rules were never the child's rules, and the child's needs and feelings were never part of the equation in the abusive or neglectful situation. It is important to explain to the young parts how much they needed their mom and dad or another significant adult in order to survive, and how crucial is was for them to feel loved and accepted. Parts need to have the space to express how it felt to not be met or loved by the adults that they were so dependent on. Do not edit their words, but let them tell how they experienced feeling trapped in pain, neglect, or trauma, and in behaviors or roles that were confusing and left them feeling bad, guilty, or dirty.

It is also necessary to let the parts know that the abuse is over, and that the old rules and patterns no longer apply. When you break these patterns, you can begin to grieve. You grieve the loss of the love and support and care that you didn't have. It may be frightening to let go of these patterns because, even if they were painful and abusive, they were familiar. Your child parts don't know another way to be in relationship. It is important to be gentle and compassionate with the feelings of fear or resistance that may arise and to gradually guide these parts into knowing that it is safe now to take in love and acceptance in more clear and healthy ways.

Kristina
2005

Feeling the shame, disgust, pain, and dirtiness from the abuse, and not being able to separate from it, I decided to find the young part inside that is carrying these feelings. I bring her close to me and tell her she is now safe inside my heart.

A: *What do you need?*
C: *To be seen and heard.*
A: *Why do you feel ashamed and dirty, like the abuse with your mom is your fault?*
C: *Because I didn't say no.*
A: *No six-year-old chooses to be abused; your mom chose to do that to you. It is her shame, her choice. You are a child; you are good and pure.*

(I look inside at this part, so small and young. I begin to cry as I finally realize it wasn't my fault.)

C: *Why would my mom do that to me? I am so confused. I feel bad, but you are telling me that I am good. In my heart, it was bad what my mom was doing to me, and I felt dirty and ashamed about what we were doing, but it was my mom, and I didn't want her to stop, because I wanted her to touch me, and the only time she did was when she was abusing me. And I wanted the abuse. I wanted her to see me.*
A: *It is natural for your body to have responded this way, and you emotionally needed the connection with your mom. You would have given anything for your mom to pay attention to you and touch you. But it wasn't your fault. It was your mother's fault. She was sick and perverted and wrong, and it was wrong and bad for your mother to have done this to you. You don't have to hold her shame and guilt anymore. You can give that back to her, because it is hers. You are a child. You*

>   *are pure and innocent and separate from what happened to you. Do you want to release these feelings and not hold them anymore?*
>
> C: *Yes.*
> A: *Can you start to feel that this was not your fault?*
> C: *Yes. It makes me sad.*
> A: *It is okay to be sad. I will help you with your sad feelings. And we can also let the other feelings go. Let's give them back to who they belong to.*
> C: *Okay.*

When working with parts, you will also come into direct contact with core beliefs that were formed in childhood. These beliefs can be met, seen, understood, and changed as we reparent our young parts. Finally, destructive patterns can shift, and you can move from survival mode to thriving.

Understanding how wounded parts continue to play out patterns and abuse in the present

HEATHER: When you have not yet fully brought the parts that hold the trauma into conscious awareness, they tend to show themselves in your beliefs, feelings, thoughts, and behaviors. You are then unconsciously re-living and often reenacting the pain of the past in the present. This is why it is such a common pattern for someone who has experienced childhood abuse to gravitate towards abusive relationships in adulthood. This is both an effort to allow the adult self to see what occurred in the past in order to finally heal it, but it is also a reflection of the beliefs about the self that were formed and internalized due to the neglect or abuse. Often, if you have an abuse history, you may feel and believe that you are not lovable or worthy of a healthy relationship. It is also common to reenact both roles in the traumatic situation. At times, you may seek out situations that are re-traumatizing and again feel victimized. At other times, you may act in a manner similar to how your abuser acted or relate to others in a similar traumatizing manner. Both roles are related to unconscious efforts to try to bring the trauma into awareness in order to heal as well as a reenactment of your core distorted beliefs about yourself that were internalized through the trauma.

Kristina
2007

It never mattered what I did. Good or bad, I remained invisible to my parents. I guess my heart broke a little more each time, but I didn't realize then, the effect it was having on my soul—how, all along, I was slowly fading away and diminishing. I was not only invisible to my parents, I started becoming invisible to myself, feeling like my inner light was fading away inside of me, getting smaller as the layers of emptiness began to build. It seems that I did this to keep safe and to protect myself from the next time I would get hurt. I'm just treating me like I was treated then—disregarded, small—I was not worth noticing. Day after day. Year after year. Nothing in return as I reached out to be seen. If my heart could talk, what would it say? "I'm ashamed that I exist. I don't want to be visible in life. It feels safe to blend into the background. Who am I to be noticed? Good at something? No, better to stay small."

Kristina
2005

I talked in therapy today about taking care of my young parts and how I have started to slack off. I am not really sure why I stopped checking in with them. I just stopped working on my healing in general. My young parts are sad tonight, I feel them. I haven't connected with them in a while, and I start to get depressed and withdrawn when I do that. My therapist said that my needs were okay, and that it is good to have needs. And it would be better to respond to them than to ignore them. I am parenting just like my mother did, and that pattern is so hard to break because it's what comes naturally to me. Doing something different has taken someone showing me that I can do something different. Why does making healthier decisions feel so exhausting?

HEATHER: It is important to remember that making these healing changes is an ongoing process, and that the experience of progress often ebbs and flows. So hold yourself with compassion when you slip back into the old patterns that you have been trying so hard to change. Remember that even the awareness that you are getting caught in old destructive patterns is a reflection of the strengthening of your witness self and of the ways that you are no longer acting and reacting unconsciously but are now more tuned into these different parts of yourself.

Working with parts in therapy
KRISTINA: Working directly with the parts of yourself in therapy can be profoundly healing. In the beginning stages of working with trauma, it will be vital that you come to know and recognize your parts and how best to work with them. Your parts kept you alive by acting as a container for the trauma and by adopting ways to cope, so that you could hold yourself together and protect yourself from further abuse. Once the abuse is over, many of these protective coping mechanisms are no longer helpful, but the parts need to come to an understanding of this before letting go of old ways of being.

The more deeply you go into the healing of your trauma, the more you will come into contact with your parts and so will your therapist. This creates a beautiful opportunity to get outside help on patterns of behavior, reactivity, belief systems, and old coping mechanisms used to survive, and to relearn how to love and reparent yourself through allowing you and your parts to come into a healing relationship. This also allows you to internalize a more loving parental part within you that can be a healthier caretaker for the younger parts than what you may have internalized as a child. When working with parts in a therapy session or in your own process of dialoguing with them, you have more conscious and direct access to your parts and your inner process than when those parts communicate indirectly by acting out their feelings with others in an unconscious way. This helps the healing become more effective, as you have a way in to deeper material and to what was previously unconscious.

This is an example of how Kristina became more aware of the divide between her unconscious inner beliefs and how she then gained more conscious awareness of her sense of herself after a therapy session:

Kristina
2005

I had been working on my mother's abuse with my therapist, who had little experience or understanding of parts work. She asked me how I viewed my mom as an adult. And the part that was out in session with her, which was the same part that was usually out in therapy, the insightful, logical adult, answered, "I know my mother is mentally ill, and because of her own childhood and woundedness, she made some bad decisions. But I don't take that personally." The session appeared to go well on the surface.

However, hours after the session, my young parts that actually hold the memories of my mother's abuse came out, and I was flooded with feelings of how terrible a person I am. I felt dirty and bad and began to believe that I must have been born defective because no mother would have acted this way to a good child. I then fell deeper into destructive impulses as a way to punish myself and escape from the emotional pain.

When parts emerge to be seen by a supportive other such as a therapist and are met with a compassionate and understanding connection, then we are able to get to the root of the wound and better learn the underlying cause of cyclical or repetitive behaviors. Finally, we are able to unlock unhealthy patterns that may have played out over and over again for years. Coming from extensive trauma, it is rarely the part presenting first in therapy that needs the most help. The parts that are hidden deeper beneath the surface are those that most need support in coming to the light to be seen and held and healed. If the therapist can help access these parts and bring them forward within a therapeutic context, it provides a safe container for working with the trauma in a healing relationship. This also supports the adult self in building a more caring and conscious internal relationship with the younger parts and becoming more able to manage the whole system in a healthy way.

Kristina
2005

I have been feeling young for a few days, so it was perfect that I had a session today. It gave my young parts a place to feel safe. When I allow my young parts to come into session with me, I really feel myself learning and growing. It's like my therapist could say the same thing to me on other days, and it wouldn't make a difference because those parts that needed to hear it wouldn't be there in session, like the time when she was talking to me about how people could be safe, rather than my just trying to find safe places. It's like when she told me that today, with my young parts there with us, a huge light bulb went on. It felt like this concept was completely new and had never existed in my mind before. Sometimes, I know she has said the same things over and over again, but then, it really hits home because she is actually saying it to the part that holds the distorted belief.

Showing up for yourself—you are the one you have been waiting for

KRISTINA: Wounds are caused by injuries done to us usually through the actions of others. If the wound is not quickly attended to and nurtured back to health, it will settle down into the body and psyche. Deeper it will go, and larger it will grow, until it is finally dealt with. Like a festering infection, it does not go away until the coverings are removed, deep cleaning is done, and healing balm is applied. Healing happens more rapidly and effectively when we are able to meet with those who caused us harm and find reconciliation, forgiveness, understanding, and love. In my case, I waited and hoped for years that my abusers and parents would come and help me in my healing journey. But this never happened, and my life fell apart waiting for it, so I had no choice but to take on my own healing process. Part of this was learning how to reparent myself, since a good portion of my abuse and neglect took place at the hands of my parents. I had to first learn what good parenting was. This was the easiest part, because it mostly involved getting information that my brain could understand and take in. Eventually, however, it involved more than just reading good parenting books. It involved coming to know myself in a more intimate way than ever before. I needed to understand which words and actions felt healing, and when and how to apply these. It involved listening to my psyche and being in touch with my body, so that I could act with love and not push my feelings or younger parts away through distraction and addictions.

The next phase was more difficult, because my heart had to relearn that I was worthy of such parenting and love. This process took many years and involved more than myself. I had a therapist who was instrumental in helping me learn to love myself. And it was through her caring example and interaction that I was able to crack the core belief that I was unlovable. As I internalized that, somehow, I was worth her time, attention, and love, it challenged the belief that I had been taught through the abuse: that I wasn't worth anything. Over time, I was able to mimic her behavior and love myself. Without her, I would not have been able to break down my entrenched belief system and mirror back to myself what I most longed for. But once I did, I was able to hold this for myself as she so caringly showed me. This is when the deepest healing began to happen. Once my heart understood my worth, it was easy to begin to see myself in a loving, healing way. Through experimentation, inner guidance, and commitment, I learned what my body-mind system needed to heal. Reparenting yourself is an opportunity to go back and heal the damage that was done. It is also the act of taking full responsibility for your needs, so that you are not relying on others to do it for you. This allows you to be in relationship with all of the parts of yourself, instead of feeling that you have holes or deficits in you that need to be filled by others.

There are many ways to reparent yourself. As you tune in, you will know what is most nurturing and healing for you and for all the parts of your system. What is most important is that you set time aside for yourself, to heal and nurture your needs. Most of us as children craved more time with our parents. Now, we have the ability to create that time for ourselves. Even if it means waking up twenty minutes early each day to do some self-care, what you are giving yourself and the benefits this will yield are invaluable. Be committed to yourself. Whatever you decide works best, stay with it. It will be the best investment you make, because it will affect you and everyone and everything around you. Learn to communicate love to yourself through words, affirmations, how you structure your environment, and the people you choose to have in your life. Let yourself experience love. As you fully understand the healing power of love, it will be easier to eliminate the negative situations, patterns, and people from your life. Find actions that feel nurturing and loving and that help replenish your life force. Make a list, so that when you are feeling low, you don't have to think up things to do; you can go straight to choosing something from the list. Be in touch with all aspects of yourself. Even if it is just thoughts and feelings that come up, and you can't seem to place or make sense of them, tune into them with compassion anyway. Welcome all parts and aspects of yourself. Embrace all that you feel as you pay attention to what your present experience is.

Kristina
2010

I don't ever remember a time in my life where things went smoothly or of feeling a sense of safety and well-being. It just seems like I've always been struggling to keep my head above water. And most of the time, I am not able to connect my sadness with anything. Every now and then, the thoughts and memories are able to come together in an awkward fashion with the emotion. But usually there is no break in the enormous dam that separates my memories from my feelings. When I really need to cry, and I feel the pain inside, but I can't get it to move past my throat, the tears stay all welled up behind my eyes, and the pain races around my heart with no place to release. Sometimes it gets so bad, I feel I have to hurt my body. I have to create physical pain, so I can feel and touch it. It is the only way I feel human. Otherwise, I'm a robot, just going through the motions, a Tin Man, with no heart.

Today was one of those days. The sadness stuck in my heart. I stayed busy, ate junk food, and emailed everyone I knew, but still no shift. Finally, when I had had enough, I laid down very quietly on my bed, put my hands over my heart and asked, "Who is sad?" And I saw this little me, probably about seven, and I started to remember what it was like when I was seven—always alone, needing someone to help brush my hair, protect me from the abuse, and just give a damn. But no one ever did. And here I am alone again with no therapist, sister, or friend—just me with me. But there's a great power when I go within, and I'm the one making the effort. The exchange multiplies and moves beyond a solo act when I parent my inner child. Divine love always shadows my own, and maybe even guides me as to how it is done. Especially when I give myself the message that says, "Little one, you who felt you were never enough, who didn't get anyone's time or love, who had to wait all these years for someone to come and embrace you, here I am. I have come for you. I love and cherish you, and you have always been enough." In this small quiet act, a profound gift I give to myself, I release my pain and set my young part free. The feelings that have been trapped inside start to come up through my heart, chest, throat, and eyes, and I feel the warm tears roll gently down my cheeks. Not too many, just enough to release a little sorrow. I am safe in my own arms, in the energy of love I have found for myself and all the parts of me. I am lighter. I feel connected to myself in a new way. I feel wholeness and a steady flow between my mind and emotions. And I feel loved—yes, loved. Love that can never leave or be taken away, that is held forever in my heart.

KRISTINA: Although healing is not meant to be done alone and without support, love, and assistance from others, *we* are ultimately the ones that we have been waiting for. By meeting ourselves consistently and unconditionally, we find deep healing and integration. Our parts begin to trust, open, and let go. We form a relationship with all of the parts within our own being and are then able to be in healthy mutual relationships with others, no longer looking to them to take care of us. This is freedom, as we can be in our own power to heal and be whole.

Your young parts need to be reparented so they can develop healthy beliefs and ways of being. This often takes learning what appropriate parenting actually is and creating healthy routines and structure in your life. In this way, you begin to form a foundation to create new rituals and memories, ones without old unhealthy patterns. Sometimes, it might be helpful to go back into a memory with a part that is stuck and rewrite the story. Through reparenting, you unlock from what you learned and experienced in the past and are able to internalize a new way of understanding and being.

Kristina
2010

If I could, I would go back in time, and find myself at the age of four. I would reach right down and pick my little self up and gently carry her to a soft, oversized chair, placing her gently on my lap. Yes, I would wrap a warm soft blanket around my small little body, letting me fall safely into myself. I would sing soothing songs that spoke of far off lands where fairies lived and gnomes walked free, and everyone was nice to each other. And there was no hurt, and I could be very, very safe there. And my little one, on my lap, would fall asleep in my arms, somehow knowing nothing bad could happen to her. I would whisper to my young self how she was loved just for who she was, for the wonder of her being. I would tell her that she has unique gifts and talents and unlimited potential, and that the Universe is blessed with her creation. And me ... I would finally breathe, letting all the fear go, knowing that I had found myself, wrapped in the safety and love of my own arms.

KRISTINA: As a child who grew up in a great deal of neglect and abuse, assumptions about life were imprinted on me through experience rather than through any direct teaching. I learned that intimate relationships were not safe and always included an element of pain. I also felt that I was powerless in the world, and that appropriate boundaries between people didn't exist. I never knew what love felt like and how it was to be nurtured or cherished as a human being. I didn't have a clue as to how to take care of my needs or even how to identify them. I believed that it was bad to have wants or needs. I actually felt that even existing and taking up space was an inconvenience to everyone else on the planet. This was normal for me. I never knew anything else. I had to start from the very beginning, from the infant stage, showing up for myself by learning what my basic needs were and how to meet them. What did safety look like? What did hunger feel like? I had to learn how it was crucial to know my physical needs on the most primal level and begin to heal from the beginning. What did it feel like in the womb? What was lacking? What was needed? How do I go back and heal the growing fetus? What did it feel like to be a child? What was lacking? What was needed? How do I go back and heal the young child? And I continued through the moments, days, months, and years of my life.

In the beginning of my healing process, someone from outside of me had to help me understand what babies and children need. Babies need structure, routine, safety, and to have their needs met by parents and adult caretakers. A new "normal" that I had to learn about was what supported the development of healthy, happy children that was so vastly different from what I experienced in childhood. I had to learn that when I am thirsty, I drink. When I am hungry, I give myself food. When I feel raw, unprotected, and sad, I draw into myself, and offer myself protection and safety as I nurture, comfort, and give solace to the suffering parts of myself. I worked to create safety both from outside harm and from any unkindness I would do to myself. Understanding and creating boundaries to protect myself from anger and violence, I began to learn for the first time, that I am worth these precautions and protective measures.

Learning how to parent myself did not come overnight. It took a lot of time and hard work to feel I was worthy of such attention, and that it was not only okay, but my birthright to have such basic human needs met. I had to not only learn this new behavior in my head logically, I had to learn it in my heart and whole being. I had to learn how to treat myself with unconditional love. When I believed that my therapist cared deeply for me and valued me, then I was able to begin to internalize that I was of value, and that something of value needs to be taken care of and looked after with tenderness and attentiveness. I learned that I am good. I came into this world good. I am worthy to be loved, nurtured, and cared for. Meeting my needs, wants and desires is not an extravagance; it is necessary to become whole, healed, and happy. I am able to be the best parent for myself; I do not have to wait for someone else to give me what I need. I am ultimately responsible for my own life, healing, peace, and joy.

During the early and middle stages of my healing, my therapists became my surrogate parents. Through example, love, and guidance, they taught me and reflected back to me what nurturing and self-love look like. I could not have learned how to take care of myself without them. As I worked on my healing in these relationships, I began to know what love really looked and felt like, and how I could learn to trust others and myself. I learned not only what nurturing looked like, but how the energy felt when I received it. And then the shift began, slowly and inconsistent at first, but over time I was able to step into truly being able to love myself, to be present to my needs and wants. I learned to put them first and not brush myself off, but to value my being and existence. I no longer looked outside myself for what I needed.

Merging parts together as a whole

In ongoing work with your trauma, you will need to intuitively sense how and when your parts are ready to blend and merge with other parts and with the more collective energies of your system. Feel when this is appropriate to address this with your parts and how to pace this with your healing process. Once parts have told their stories, healed, and come to understand that the abuse has ended, they will most likely be ready to let go and release their need for a separate identity. You have options as to how to work with them to blend their energy into a more collective oneness. You may continue to feel that these are aspects of yourself rather than distinct parts, and you may also feel their presence in an ongoing way, but they become more background rather than foreground in your daily experience. They are also now more aware of the other parts, and they feel held and protected by the adult self, so that they can all become part of the whole self. Some parts may be ready to be fully released from your body and psyche or to just become part of the energy of who you are. Tune in to what feels right for you and allow this to unfold in your ongoing inner dialogue and healing process. At times, parts may be ready to be released even if you haven't fully identified their memories or stories. They may be holding feelings or pain from the trauma, and as you work your healing process, they may be ready to release the pain from your body and psyche to free you from being mired in the past.

Kristina
2011

I let my voice go down, down, down to all parts in my system, so that everyone can hear my voice. I speak especially to the part who is feeling raw, heart pain. I feel your pain in my heart. Please find a safe place to be inside, I am coming to help you. I align to inner stillness and feel my true Self more and more present.

A:	Hello everyone, I am here. Please come talk to me if you need help.
C:	I am trapped in this body, and I want to get out.
A:	How did you get here?
C:	I don't know.
A:	Where do you want to go?
C:	I don't know. Outside. Outside of here.
A:	Oh, can't you just leave, and go where you want to go?
C:	No, I'm trapped. I can't get out.
A:	Oh, that must feel terrible. Is your heart raw?
C:	No, that is not me.
A:	I'm not sure how to get you out of the body. Maybe if we create a door of light, you can pass through it. Do you want to try it?
C:	Okay.
A:	Once you pass through the door, let's put you in healing light. Maybe, you will wait for the rest of us in this healing light, and when we pass out of the body, we will all merge together.
C:	Okay.
A:	Do you have any information or memories that you want us to know before you go?
C:	Just sadness. So much sadness. And so much loneliness.
A:	Do you have memories with these feelings?
C:	Yeah.
A:	Hmm.
C:	I don't want to stay in this body anymore.
A:	Okay, I understand. I will guide you through the door and into the light.
C:	I want to say goodbye to everyone and tell them I will be waiting for them on the other side.
A:	Okay, I will wait for you. (As I am holding space for this part to be ready to go, I feel a sadness, as if I am losing a part of myself.) Did you say your goodbyes? Are you ready to go?
C:	Yes.

(As I help this part cross into the light, I physically feel the heaviness in my body and the rawness in my heart begin to lift and go away completely.)

Becoming conscious leads to healing and wholeness

HEATHER: As you work at these different levels and use whatever modalities are most helpful for you to gain more consciousness of these lost memories, feelings and aspects of yourself, you are able to move into deeper levels of healing and integration. To avoid bringing these lost parts of the self into awareness means that you are operating out of only a portion of yourself and often playing out unconscious patterns in a way that is hurtful to you and your relationships. To stay unconscious is to stay out of balance and to live in disharmony rather than integrated and in wholeness. The path of deepening in consciousness also enables you to see your life and your journey in a larger context and to feel held by the consciousness and love of the cosmos.

KRISTINA: We do not need to fully heal to become whole. We become whole when we embrace the present moment and all that is presenting itself within us, both what is conscious and unconscious, denying no experience. We hold the light and dark, the joy and pain, and all of our experience. We allow all feelings, thoughts and memories to come forward, without editing or pushing any away. At first, the process can seem overwhelming, but as the work is paced and better understood, shifts begin to happen naturally and effortlessly. Old imprints and patterns formed from the past, release, and you begin to move deeper into a healing journey. You create a new way of being in relationship with yourself, no longer fragmented or disconnected from aspects of yourself. You are also able to be more in stillness, letting deeper energies and feelings from the past move through you. You have more energy as you are no longer needing to keep parts of yourself buried or kept at bay. You feel more alive, more present, and more able to trust your inner and outer experience.

Kristina
2005

When I was a child, I mastered the art of running away. I would shove as much as I could into a brown paper sack and head straight out the front door. One time, I made it halfway up the street before my father found me and coaxed me back to the house. I was six then. It was the first time I remember physically trying to run away, trying to escape the pain at home. I was born with an instinct to run, and sometimes, despite the odds, I would try. But I was always caught, dragged back, and abused again. I guess it happened so much that, at one point, my legs just quit working that way. The men from the cult would sadistically play with me, by putting me down, watching me run, and then catching me like a wild beast fleeing for its life. I was a frantic field mouse scurrying around in a corner while the fat lap cat waited for the right moment to pounce, knowing all the while that the meal was his.

When I couldn't physically get away from the abuse, I would fold up inside of myself like a dying flower. When the pain was at its greatest point, when it felt insurmountable, like I wouldn't be able to survive one more moment, everything went still and quiet. I became numb to all feeling. It was like someone coming in and turning off the faucet to all emotion. I became a desert, and my land began to crack into pieces, because there was no moisture to keep it together. And these pieces became their own entities, holding onto separate memories. Most of the land lay so dormant, it had become forgotten. And then one day, there was a marvelous rain shower. And I began to once again remember and feel some of the pieces from the desert place. And the rain came down, and the pain ran deep through its cracks. But the rain also brought new life, as it often does. And even though the flowers had died, they left behind their seeds. And it wasn't long before some of the most amazing flowers began to bloom. And I gave the flowers names, because they were noble and good. And even though they had lain under the dry ground for so long, they were still alive. And now, as I look out over my land, it is filled with lush green grass and glowing with colorful, radiant flowers that are full of life-giving energy.

When we claim all of who we are, we stand in our authentic truth and power. Coming into full and right relationship with ourselves prepares us to go deeper into the healing process. This path of healing takes courage and tenacity, but it leads us to empowerment, freedom, and wholeness. No longer victimized by the past and by our external experiences or internal fragmentation, we reclaim all of who we are and take responsibility for our lives.

I am a Warrioress
a Warrioress of the Heart
I am Queen
of the domain of Myself
I am able to respond
in all situations
from the knowledge of who I am
My actions are who I am
My beliefs are who I am
All I do is who I am
That which is outside of me
stays outside of me
That which I choose to let in
I own and acknowledge
How can you be responsible
if you do not own all aspects of yourself?
How can you be accountable
without being Queen over your own domain?
How can you serve your consort, your children, your community
if you are unwilling to acknowledge and answer for yourself?

—words of the Irish goddess Maeve from
The Goddess Oracle: A Way to Wholeness through the Goddess
by Amy Sophia Marashinsky

CHAPTER 6

H - Healing

We now go deeper into the healing process as we move around the ARCH medicine wheel and come to the final quadrant and the direction of east. Again, all aspects of the wheel are interconnected. As we come into alignment, we gain a remembrance of our deeper essence and develop a witness self that is able to guide the vulnerable parts of the self through the healing journey. As we take in the support that is there for us in our lives and experience healing relationships, we feel seen and heard, and we learn to hold ourselves in more compassion and have the courage to move forward on the healing path. As we grow in consciousness, we get to the roots of our pain and trauma and bring what has been hidden in the shadows into the light to heal. Now, as you move into the east on the medicine wheel, allow yourself to give thanks for the healing that you have been experiencing in all of the work that you have done up to this point. Open your heart and honor the healing energy that surrounds you and is within you. Allow yourself to step more deeply into the process of healing the wounds from the past to free you to live more fully in the joy of the present moment.

This Healing section of the ARCH model will offer you guidance for turning into your wounds and healing your trauma more fully. In this chapter, there will be ideas and suggestions with the intent to make your healing toolbox your own. Hopefully, you will begin to create your own methods and share them with others. The healing journey that you will embark on is sacred uncharted territory. As you gather all the lost parts of yourself and bring them home again into your heart, you will enter the deepest and darkest places of your being. To touch the soul of another human being is to walk on holy ground, especially if the ground you walk on is your own. Listen to your deepest truth, follow the pull of your heart, and trust where the process is taking you, because it will lead you back to your true self.

Preparation: Creating a healing environment

De-stress your current life

It becomes critical when working with your trauma to establish and maintain solid levels of safety and balance, externally as well as internally, as you move through the healing process. This sets the stage for the work to be healing and not re-traumatizing. If you have ways to contain the intensity as well as holding the connection to your present life and experiences, you do not become consumed by the trauma or overwhelmed. Instead, you are able to come from a heart-centered space, folding in the wounds of the past into the present moment.

KRISTINA: This is the time to make efforts to de-stress your life and create a more concrete sense of safety for yourself. Stress tends to bring the body and psyche into imbalance and instability, often exacerbating the painful feelings and memories that are emerging. Stress also makes it harder to stay centered and to have the adult part of you in charge and out in the world to make decisions and be present in your relationships. It might be helpful to fully examine what in your life is causing stress that can be modified or eliminated. Also, it may be helpful to have a list of activities that are calming and grounding for a quick resource of ideas to release stress from your body and mind when trauma is up and more active. By reducing the stress in your life and knowing how to bring your body and mind into balance, a level of natural healing can take place.

Examples of things to do in order to de-stress your whole system—body, mind, and spirit:

- Avoid loud, crowded, over-stimulating areas (like shopping malls)
- Have a daily structure or routine
- Avoid unnecessary arguments, confrontations, or stressful situations
- Let go of or create stronger boundaries with any relationship that is causing you stress
- Drop time-consuming activities that exhaust you or aren't supportive of you
- If you are working, make sure that you keep your work hours in balance to have time for what is nurturing for you personally

Ways to engage in self-care that also reduces stress and calms your system:

- Organize your house
- Take a daily nap
- Watch the sun rise or set
- Take a bath with Epsom salt
- Cook and eat warm, nourishing food
- Take long walks in nature
- Spend time with animals
- Enjoy recreational or playful activities
- Meditate
- Weight lifting or doing cardiovascular exercise

Kristina
2005

For the past few days I've been dealing with a lot of sadness, anxiety, and pain in my whole body. I have this racing thought that I'm not safe, and that I need to run and hide to protect myself. But, for the life of me, I can't find a place that feels safe. Maybe, it's because all of the scary things that I'm running from are inside of me. Still, it keeps my heart racing, and I have an overall sense that I am in danger and need to lock myself in a closet with a soft blanket. The pain and anxiety intensify and lessen, back and forth, across the day. When I feel my sadness is at its greatest, my body naturally wants to completely shut down. I feel it happening. It first starts physically, and it becomes hard to move. Next, my emotions start to fade out, and everything becomes very quiet and flat. Yesterday, I probably hit that space about twenty times. And then something from my outside world would pull me back into stress again.

When it was finally time for me to go to bed, I grabbed my favorite blanket and crawled into bed. My husband came in to say goodnight, and I asked him not to leave me. I told him what had been going on, that I didn't feel safe anywhere, that I wanted to run, but didn't know where to go. And at the same time, I wanted him close to me. He asked me if I wanted him to run his fingers through my hair. And I said, "Yes." He tucked me in tight, spoke to me quietly with such kindness and caressed my head. I started to cry. I finally was in a place I felt safe to be able to feel young and let my pain out through my tears. My system didn't have to shut down to keep functioning. That was healing to give my young parts a safe place, with a safe person, and enough time to let them feel their sadness and pain. I fell asleep, and this morning I am doing okay. I'm not depressed or anxious, I still have feelings of sadness and of being young, but I am centered in a more adult space, and able to turn in and take care of my young parts.

(Please refer to meditations in the appendix to help you de-stress and align with stillness.)

Create a support team

It is important to establish clear boundaries for yourself in your relationships, especially with family members if you are dealing with trauma from your childhood. Be discerning about who you share your process with so that you can allow your healing to unfold at your own pace. In these early vulnerable stages of the healing process, it is not helpful to share your process with more than a few trusted others. You don't want or need to be dealing with other people's questions, reactions, or possible skepticism about what you are experiencing. Have your support system in place, consisting of a few people you trust in whom you can confide and who will listen and support you in your process. You need people who will listen without giving opinions or advice, who can keep what you share in confidentiality, and who will provide support and hold you emotionally, and at times physically, when you need it. One of the challenges about opening to your healing process is that you never know where it may lead you. You are embarking on a journey into the unknown, and it can feel vulnerable, frightening, and disorienting.

HEATHER: There is a powerful ancient Sumerian story, the myth of Inanna, about a woman who sets out on her healing journey, a journey to the underworld to reclaim the lost parts of herself. She does not start on her path until she has made sure that she has a trusted companion by her side who will hold a "safety line" for her as she descends into her process, in order to ensure her safe return. The name of this friend and companion was "Ninshubar" (pronounced NIN-shoo-bar). Make sure that you have a Ninshubar as you enter into your healing process, someone who will "watch your back" and be there for you when you may feel overwhelmed or disoriented.

Build safety in your life

KRISTINA: Once you have found your "team" that you can rely on, you can start to build safety that will be instrumental in healing within relationships. As you move through the healing of your trauma, you will come to better understand when it is important to rely on your team, and when it is more beneficial to hold and work the process on your own. Be compassionate with what you are undertaking. Often for those coming out of childhood abuse and neglect, it is a new experience to find and trust people, as we have so often been alone and not had others we could depend on. It can also be a new experience to trust in yourself and in your capacity to heal and to say "no" to further abuse. If your early life was imprinted with trauma, it is hard to imagine that life can be different from that. Allow yourself to open to that trust. Like a seed planted in the fertile soil of the self, as you nurture it, it will grow.

Kristina
2004

Why is it that I'm so depressed? Why is it that I don't care anymore? I know that I'm supposed to, but I don't. People are telling me that I need to care, need to work, that I deserve to heal. But I just don't care. What makes me worth it, worth the fight? What happens when I'm the only one who can fight my own battle, and I have no desire to? I picture myself on a field, just me among the wounded in a fog, and the people on my side are shouting at me to draw my sword and start fighting, but I stand there, looking at my feet, and I can't move. My shoulders are hunched over. I have no energy to even budge, and no one can move for me. So I continue to stand there, listening to the voices, but still, standing still. What's wrong with me? Where did all my fire go? Where's the force, the drive that has left me? How do I create something from nothing, from inside of me?

I see myself as a child, in that field, with the fog, the wounded and the dead. No daisies grow here. No laugher or innocence. My childhood was a battlefield, not a playground. I was all alone then; all alone, fighting on my field. I fought hard to stay alive. No children singing, no carefree play or lazy summer afternoons without the undercurrent of high alert. My field was cold and full of bleeding hearts. I was alone, and sad, and always fighting. Sword drawn. Running fast and swift. There was strength within the instinct to survive. Now, there is less strength, and I feel more weighed down with depression that keeps me looking at my feet. They yell to me from the sidelines, "You are worth fighting for your life, you deserve to heal! It must come from within!" I look at them, as they look at me. "Fools," I think. "You are wasting your time on me. I'm a one-woman team with a losing record. Leave me. Let me be." I look around me, alone in my field, surrounded by sad memories and hopelessness. What is my strategy to get past the endless lines of nightmares, heartache, memories of abuse and despair? No thoughts come. No desire is felt. I stand still, staring at my feet, with the sound of distant cries gently falling onto my heart, "Don't give up, you are worth the fight," and somewhere deep down, the quiet message seems to ring true.

It is an act of courage to finally take that step to value yourself and choose to heal. No matter how many people may be there to support you, you have to decide that you are worth saving and allow yourself to take the first tentative steps towards healing and wholeness and joy.

Returning again and again to Alignment to support your healing process

HEATHER: As you work through the healing process, it is important to remember and return to the ways of coming into alignment to support you and hold you in the healing journey. Sometimes, as Kristina experienced, it is challenging to find the motivation to continue on the healing path, given that it often feels painful and endless. It is hard not to feel at times utterly alone and overwhelmed and to wonder if it is worth the effort. Another way to seek support and to feel held by energies larger than yourself is to open to your connection with the Earth and the sky to remember that you are a part of the expansive web of life and of all that is. This can give you a larger perspective on your experience and give you a sense of being held in energies of love and wisdom that are beyond you and also in you. These energies can help guide you and hold you in those dark times. In doing this, you are not disengaging from yourself and all that you feel; it is rather about opening and expanding and knowing that the intensity of your experience is part of the sea of all that is. It is a reminder that you are not alone in the process and that there is meaning and purpose for your life that is beyond your comprehension. This can support you in living in the mystery and in times of not knowing and can give you some sense of calm in the midst of the inner and outer storm.

When I lived in Los Angeles and had times of feeling overwhelmed by the stress in my life and my own healing process, I would seek refuge in the mountains of the Sierras. I remember the sense of calm that I would feel when on a mountaintop gazing over the expansive vista below. At these times, my feelings of overwhelm and my worries seemed to melt away and become minute compared to the vastness of the mountains and sky. Later in my life, I learned to open to a sense of expansiveness by taking time each day to call in the four directions and open myself to the energies of the Earth and sky and Spirit. This ancient practice, which is also part of walking the healing medicine wheel, reminds us of the boundlessness of the cosmos and the energies of infinity that are beyond our human comprehension. It also dissolves the ego and helps us remember that we are part of the oneness and interconnectedness of all. This practice is centering, grounding, and expansive all at the same time.

Using the medicine wheel to connect to the Earth and sky and four directions
This meditation practice is similar to the medicine wheel meditation discussed in the Alignment chapter, but now you are expanding the meditation to bring healing to your heart. To do this, find a quiet place and stand in the center of your room or outside in an area where you can have privacy. Orient yourself to the four directions. Take a few minutes to turn and face each direction, starting with the east, then moving clockwise to the south, then west and then north. Honor the energies that flow from these directions and call them in to hold you as you center yourself in these four directions.

Then, honor the energy of Mother Earth and the energies of the sky. Visualize yourself as a bridge, a conduit, allowing the energies of the Earth to ground you and keep you rooted in your body and in the nurturing connection with Mother Earth. Then, imagine the energies of the sky filling you, coming down through the top of your head and flowing through your body down into the Earth. Let the energies of the Sun, Moon, and stars fill you with healing light. Then, honor the energy of the center, the center within you, your heart, and the center of all that is. This is the place of stillness, of peace, and of all possibilities. You are safe from any outer stress or inner turmoil. This is the place where you remember and reconnect with your soul self, your consciousness that is beyond time and place. This is your true home. Take a few moments to breathe in and out deeply, allowing yourself to open to this centeredness and stillness. Feel how you are now held in the center of these energies of the Earth and sky and Cosmos. You are not alone. You are one with all that is, and you are held in safety and in unconditional love and in the wisdom of the Earth and of the Cosmos.

Now visualize the energy of the Earth merging with the energy of the sky at your heart. Breathe in and out slowly and deeply, feeling this healing energy of the Earth and sky filling your heart. Feel your deep alignment with the Earth and with the sky. As you are centered in your heart, draw in your emotions and all aspects of yourself into your heart. Honor the full range of all of your experiences as they present in the moment. Hold the wholeness of who you are in your heart. Continue to breathe in and out slowly, honoring all that you have learned and all of the ways that you have evolved through the times of pain and of joy in your life. Breathe in and honor all of those experiences and allow them to feel held in the loving, healing energies of the Earth and the sky that are flowing through and surrounding your heart.

Now, continuing to keep part of your focus on your heart, begin to also feel and sense the energy field around your body. Feel the spaciousness around you and gradually allow yourself to begin to feel your energy field expanding further and further out. Expand more and more until you feel the connection between your heart and the crystal core at the center of the Earth. Then allow yourself to feel your energy expand out to the brilliant healing light of the Sun. Continue to feel your energy expanding further and further out to merge with the heart of the Cosmos.

Feel your heart pulsing with the rhythms of the Earth and Cosmos as you breathe in and out deeply. Allow yourself to simultaneously hold the awareness of your heart and your earthly experiences with the expansiveness of your energy merging with the Cosmos. You are in this body and you are one with all that is. Breathe in and out, holding the sense of mystery and wonder as you honor yourself and your oneness with the Cosmos. Then, gradually, when you are ready, bring your full awareness back to your body. Gently draw in your energy, breathing in and out as you return your focus to your heart and your body and the present moment. Then, gently, giving thanks, open your eyes.

KRISTINA: It is also important to continue to stay connected with the deeper stillness inside as you work the wounds of the body and mind. The more you build the space of peace inside, the more it will grow, and you will have easier access to it. This will allow increased safety for the more intense emotions and memories to emerge. This will also help you stay grounded and able to integrate the wounds of the past into the stillness of the present moment. Your pure inner state is like space. Your thoughts, feelings, memories, and beliefs will come and go out of this pure state of consciousness. You always have access to complete peace, joy, and love, but at times it will seem difficult to hold to this alignment, as your body and mind will come back to express themselves through memories, nightmares, body sensations, and feelings. Your body's experience and what has been hidden in the unconscious part of you wants to be seen and heard. Your body needs validation for what it has been through, and what has been held in your unconscious mind needs to be brought into the light of awareness.

It is easier to align to your true nature and inner stillness when the pain and trauma of your body are not so charged, intense, and heavy and do not keep coming back, demanding to be noticed and healed. It is important for your body to rest and to not be in a constant state of stress or hypervigilance, but your physical system will need help to shift out of this hyperarousal when it is activated as you work through the trauma memories and feelings (this is discussed below in the section on how to heal at the physical level). As your mind and body heal from trauma, you pull in the fragmented parts and become more whole and integrated, more at peace. After the memories are brought into the light of consciousness, your body and psyche are more ready to let go of the pain, and they begin to lighten and feel more freedom from what has been held so tightly inside.

In this way, you do not bypass what is rising up and calling out. And at the same time, you do not simply indulge in the wounds either. It is important to not become overly focused on the memories and feelings of the past in a way that you become mired in them as your only sense of identity. That will keep you locked in the trauma of the past and controlled by the thoughts, feelings, and beliefs associated with it. This process of opening to the wounds and allowing the healing to occur and to set you free is a dance, a movement of grace, back and forth, in and out, again and again. It is about allowing healing into your body and your psyche, and then finding rest back in your center, your soul self, and the inner place of peace. If you are able to align to stillness during the trauma work, you allow the difficult emotions to come up and move through you as a way of cleansing the body/mind/spirit. Sometimes, all that is needed for deep healing of certain layers is to allow the wounds to come up and out of the body instead of keeping the trauma trapped inside, circulating, and causing disease in your mind and physical body by creating blocks of dense energy.

Holding onto the trauma keeps you trapped in the past and not able to be in the present moment. If instead you stay in the present moment and let the experience of emotions, pain, and wounds come up and move through you, you are able to allow this flow and then fold the wounds into your heart with compassion. When you are in the witness self, you remain aware that the trauma happened in the past and is no longer happening in the present. The feelings are only reminders of the past. They comprise information that is trying to purge, so that your body and mind can rebalance their energy. In this way, by staying in the witness self, the trauma is seen and felt but not re-lived and re-enacted internally as if it is happening in the present moment. Staying aligned with stillness also helps keep a clear understanding that this is a phase, and that these feelings and body sensations are fluid, and that the pain is not permanent. It will eventually pass. We are then able to hold more of the wholeness of life with a sense of gratitude and to focus more on what is good and positive in our current experience. Holding this gratitude keeps us from spiraling into a negative pit of hopelessness and depression.

Working with challenges to healing

Dealing with triggers, dissociation, depression, anger, dreams, nightmares, and flashbacks

As you begin to open to the memories and feelings from the past that are emerging, honor your process and allow yourself to pace this in a way that feels safe for you. Often, as you begin to work the process, you may experience flashbacks, nightmares, or feel more reactive to triggers that bring up the trauma memories. It is important to seek support as needed and pace the process so that your life stays in balance as much as possible. Allow yourself to take time to focus on daily activities and nurturing "distractions" to give yourself a needed break from the turmoil of the trauma.

Triggers
Our wounds usually occur in relationships, so it makes sense that we also need loving, supportive relationships to heal. To do this, we must be in relationships in a way that we are relating consciously and with awareness of our feelings, projections and how any unhealthy patterns are playing out. Otherwise, we tend to place the blame for our hurt and confusion onto our significant others. If the feelings tied to past wounds are not worked with consciously, they will continue to be activated in our current relationships, and we will constantly be in reactivity mode, unconsciously replaying and reliving the past in our present. But if we are willing to look deeper into our intense reactions in our relationships, these can be messengers or indicators that can potentially guide us towards becoming conscious of past wounds in order to heal them. Then, we can start to take responsibility for our own behavior and use our feelings and reactions as signposts helping us as we trace back to the underlying wounds that are calling out to be healed.

If in your childhood it wasn't safe for you to express your feelings, you most likely stored them away inside or disconnected from them. And you may have tried to shut yourself off from the people that hurt you, so that you could move on and function in the world without feeling too vulnerable. These ways of coping were a way to protect yourself and survive in a traumatizing environment. If you do not consciously step into the healing process, as an adult, you will tend to carry on this pattern of suppressing your feelings, especially in close relationships. If you lack the ability to be vulnerable and authentic, it can make it extremely difficult to be in a rich, deep, and fulfilling relationship. It will also be difficult to let yourself feel negative emotions (such as sadness, disappointment, or anger) in your present relationships without having this activate fear or wounds of the past.

Once you feel triggered and become reactive within a current relationship, then core beliefs from the past tend to come up with the feelings of hurt or woundedness. If you were abused as a child, you most likely internalized the abuse and believed that there was something wrong with you at a core level. It would have been too threatening at the time to believe that your parent or other significant adult on whom you depended could be the one at fault. So this then activates a tendency in your current relationships to form beliefs about yourself that are false and destructive as you try to understand and make sense of your intense and often out of balance reactions to those that you love and are in relationship with in the present. When you trace these reactive feelings in your current relationships and connect the dots further and further back, you are able to find the root cause of the wound and the incorrect beliefs that you formed during and after the abuse.

The triggering of old stored emotions and memories often happens in the present in your closest relationships. You may feel as if your emotions come out of nowhere or feel far more intense than the interaction in the present moment would seem to call for. This tells you that the feelings you are dealing with are most likely from your old wounds. At these times, it becomes important to turn towards the feelings and begin to trace them back to their source, so that you can bring these feelings and memories into awareness and open to the potential of healing them. You can be triggered, not only in your relationships, but by almost anything from your external experience that is a reminder of the past trauma. It could be a certain scent, a sound, a color, a tone in someone's voice, or a way you are touched by another. If you know that certain situations or stimuli tend to trigger you, it is important to have a way to respond, so that you are not living in a state of constant reactivity and fear.

When you first feel the reactivity rising up, it is best to find distance and space from others, so that you can breathe, get centered, and gain more clarity about what is happening. This can be the most challenging step to take. It is helpful to learn your personal "red flags," feelings or reactions that indicate to you that the trauma from the past has been activated. You might also need a reminder for yourself or have something that you do so that you can pull yourself out of the situation. For example, you might wear a rubber band around your wrist, and as you feel the familiar surge of emotion coming, you might snap the band as a signal to remove yourself before you react. Or you might want to carry a special stone or wear a certain object to help remind you of healthy steps to take to find distance and space to breathe back from reactivity. Next, it is important to calm your system down. Find what works best for you in the moment. It might be to take a brisk walk or to take a shower or to meditate. Preparing in advance a list of options for helpful grounding and calming practices might be useful, so that you are not trying to think of something in the moment.

Once calm, try to ground yourself by becoming very clear about your present reality. Try using any or all of your senses to do this. Look around you. Feel the ground beneath your feet. Remind yourself that this is your current reality, and that you are not back in the past. Begin to question what your mind is telling you about your situation. Try to distinguish what you are feeling from what is actually occurring in your current reality. Then, tune into where the impulse came from. Does it have a place of origin in your body? Can you count down and open up into your inner experience? If you are able to get closer to the wound, you can start to bring it into consciousness and begin to work to heal it.

Kristina
2004

While traveling with my husband, he told me that he felt like I kept getting on him about one thing or another. He finally said that he had had enough and told me to stop. Actually, his words were, "Stop, please, just stop." I immediately defended myself and then felt intense anger and an abrupt desire to shut myself off from him as if to protect myself. At the time, I didn't realize that my feelings did not match the situation, I just felt justified anger and a desire to shut down. The next day, I started to feel pain in my heart. So when I had a little time and space, I let myself go through the process of turning into the pain in an effort to heal. This is how the practice looked:

While placing my hands on my heart, I talked to the pain, "I am letting my voice go down, down, down to the pain in my heart, and sending a message that I am here. I am here for you. I love you. I am here to hold you and give you what you need. Do you know what you need?" I received the answer, "Healing light."

So I responded, "I am going to send down healing light to you. I am holding you in healing light and love. I am here. You are safe. I see you. I hear you. You are loved. You are wanted. I am pulling in all the pieces of your suffering and pain, pulling them into wholeness to be held in my hands. I am stroking your head and loving you. That's right. I see you. I am here. And you are being held against my chest, against my heart. That is healing you. Light is surrounding you and absorbing your pain. I am going to hold you safe. You are loved. You are safe."

After doing this inner dialoguing to let my young parts feel held in love and safety, I let the feelings of pain in my heart come up to the surface to heal. I held the feelings of a young part, of not being loved, and the feeling of rejection. I held and healed the feeling of not being good enough and the feeling of not being lovable. I healed the shame of doing something wrong and the feeling of shame for who I am and what I did. I helped to heal the feelings of being bad. I then said to the young part, "I'm just going to hold you, surround you in light, and hold the shame. I will hold the feelings of being bad and unlovable. I love you. I see you. I feel you. Come to me. Let me love you and hold you and surround you in light and love. You are not bad. You are good, and you are lovable. Just because someone got mad at you in the past, doesn't make you bad. Just because someone is very angry with you, doesn't make you wrong. It's okay for you to have feelings. It's also okay for other people to have feelings. It doesn't make anyone bad. It's just different energies inside of us. You are still the same inside—lovable, kind, whole, and connected."

Whatever words came to my mind, I said back to myself, uncensored. I trusted that the loving words that came forward were the exact words that I needed to hear to be healed. And I kept saying what came up, until I felt that something inside took hold and started to trust and believe what was being said. At first, the pain rising up just needed to feel safe and loved. And then, it opened up deeper, and I felt the energy begin to change from pain to shame, and the words helped me understand that the wound was deeper than my experience with my husband, that this was pain that was experienced as a child with my mother.

As I continued to dialogue with the feelings arising, I became aware of how the emotions that had been activated in my experience with my husband were *really from this young child part's experience of my mother and the wounds of not feeling seen or loved by her. I kept holding the pain with love and light, using the safety created as a space to counter old beliefs and introduce new ways of thinking about emotions and how they relate to me as a person. As I worked with the emotions and beliefs at the place where they were formed and shaped, I could feel they were truly being healed at an organic level. As I stayed present and connected with myself in the feelings of the pain and shame in a safe way, I experienced being able to hold negative emotions and not shut myself off from them.*

I stayed with the exercise until I felt a significant shift in the emotions. I felt the pain lift from my heart, and my body began to feel lighter and more integrated. I naturally started to feel more present in my environment and in my relationship with my husband. I felt a healing take place with the past and with the present. Only in the present can I drop the illusions of the past and begin to heal. The past brought pain, and thinking about the future may evoke anxiety. But in the present moment, I am able to look deeper into the emotions, find the wounds, and surround them with love and understanding. I give them a voice, take care of their needs, and show these parts of myself that they are safe, valued, and worthy of love.

Dissociation

HEATHER: Dissociation is a coping mechanism that protects us when we are in a situation that feels too overwhelming or painful to handle. It involves a way in which our minds and emotions disconnect from the trauma in order to allow us to endure the experience. It is similar to the way in which one would physically go unconscious if injured or in overwhelming physical pain. While dissociation is a protective way of coping in the moment, it often leads to ongoing disconnection from the feelings and pain of the traumatic event. This can complicate the healing process, since we tend to split off feelings, thoughts, body sensations, and beliefs from the experience. To heal, it is important to reweave these fragmented aspects of ourselves to become more integrated and whole.

Kristina
2000
Body and Soul

Here I lie,
Body and soul
Separated.
Here I lie,
Wondering why …
Watching my body take the abuse
As the question echoes through my mind …
My soul soars higher.
Here I lie, then and now,
Feeling I must be worthless,
Like dirt, not fit to be spit upon.
My soul soars higher and higher,
My body lies motionless.
Time passes …
My soul returns to be one with my body for a moment …
She touches my body with past pain,
And my lifeless body begins to feel,
If only briefly,
The body feels,
And the soul again returns to the sky.
Here I lie …
Body and soul separated.

Kristina
2007

I'm feeling so sad. After my session with my therapist today, I felt better, because I knew she heard me and cared about me. My heart stopped hurting so badly, but I still feel young, and now my heart is starting to feel raw again. I'm starting to cry. My cell phone keeps ringing, but I can't answer it. I don't think I can talk to anyone.

Thoughts and images arise from within me. Why would my mom pin me down and keep telling me, "Shhh ... shhh ... shhh"? Why does she want me to quiet down when they are trying to hurt me? I'm kicking and kicking until I can't move my legs anymore. It happens too quick, and I can't get out of my body fast enough. And I'm looking right at her face, and she is just inches away from me. I am screaming and screaming, and she keeps saying, "Shhh ... shhh ... shhh." And then all of the features on her face start to blend together, and I can't make out her face anymore. And my heart is breaking, because she doesn't grab me and pull me close to her, and because she doesn't make them stop. Maybe it's because she doesn't see me anymore. Maybe I've become invisible to her. Because I know if she could see me, she would grab me and hold me tight. I'm going numb. No more crying. I'm invisible.

Here are some common signs of dissociation:

- Experiencing feeling detached from yourself (from your emotions, body, thoughts)
- Unable to recall information from the past
- Having few memories of early childhood
- Often feeling spacey or having problems with concentration

At the extreme end of dissociation, you may have symptoms of dissociative identity disorder which include such symptoms as:

- Absence of memory from past events or periods of time (could be days, weeks, or months)
- Changes in the tone of your voice, feelings, or behaviors, in different situations as you switch into different personalities or distinct parts

Dissociation is activated by intense stress or any situation that reminds you of the past trauma. So to heal, it is critical to first establish a sense of safety, so that the inner parts of you can trust that it is safe to stop disconnecting or splitting off. The more that you experience dissociation, the less you are capable of feeling a range of emotions and the less you are able to feel fully in yourself and able to engage in life. When you have a trauma history, you will tend to split off from intense feelings and experiences under stress in an effort to protect yourself as well as for survival when you do not feel safe and when you do not have a secure or safe relationship to rely on. The fragmented parts of yourself need to experience something in the present that is different from what they went through in the past. When your parts feel heard and their needs are met through empathic attunement and accurate mirroring, then it gives them the ability to pull together their energies, to feel what needs to be felt, and to remember what needs to be remembered.

If you did not have a secure attachment with a parent growing up, then it was hard to feel safe in childhood. There was no nurturing context in which to work through the experiences of trauma or emotional injury in order to heal. Without this secure attachment, it is also difficult to have formed a solid or secure sense of self. This means that you also have to learn to care for and love yourself and learn how you can be a healthy parent for the internal young parts of yourself. You may not have had healthy parenting in childhood because your parents had their own trauma histories. Patterns of abuse and neglect are often passed down from one generation to the next until someone in the lineage stops the pattern by choosing to heal. Unhealthy parenting may include abuse, neglect, or a lack of being able to clearly see and care for the child in their own unique way of being. Also, dysfunctional parenting is more reactive in nature (often associated with the parent's childhood wounds) and lacks empathic attunement to the needs and feelings of the child.

Some of the characteristics of unhealthy parenting include:

- Enmeshment or difficulties with appropriate emotional boundaries
- Overprotective behavior
- Abusive behavior
- Abandonment or neglect
- Unpredictable ways of relating
- Inconsistent behavior

- Chronic depression and an inability to attune to the feelings and needs of the child
- Avoidant behavior
- Passive behavior or withdrawal
- Lack of empathic understanding or mirroring
- Need for the child to be an extension of the parent rather than a separate self

KRISTINA: Dysfunctional parenting patterns such as these tend to create difficulties for the child in developing a healthy sense of self or being able to connect with her or his own feelings and needs. The child learns that it is safer not to share feelings, talk, or be seen. But the child has critical emotional needs that must be met. This creates inner conflict. The child may try to disconnect from needs, feelings, and painful experiences as a way to resolve the conflict. But the conflict can never truly be resolved this way. If you are able to identify and connect to the hurt child parts inside and understand the needs, and then have the parts re-experience the conflict in a different way by experiencing being in a consistent, safe, and loving relationship, this allows the parts of the self to feel loved and to know they are now safe to be seen and heard and to have their needs met. Then, they are able to reintegrate their memories and feelings from past painful experiences. This then also allows them to fully grieve, heal, and let go of the trauma.

HEATHER: If you have not had an experience of secure attachment with a parent or a loving adult in your childhood, it is important to experience a model or template of this in a healing relationship, most likely with a therapist who has training in attachment difficulties. This can help you to internalize an image of a loving parent that you can hold within to be there for the young parts of yourself. It is possible to meditate and form an image of a loving parent that you can begin to internalize.

Some basic needs that young parts should experience and receive (either from a therapist or adult part of self) in order to stop the inner conflict and dissociation are:

- Safety
- Unconditional love

- Ability for healthy dependency on another
- Sense of autonomy and feeling respected
- To be seen and heard
- Stability
- To feel empowered

When you begin to resolve the inner conflicts and start to heal the parts of yourself, you no longer need to dissociate or maintain a disconnection from the feelings and memories of the past. You then are able to begin to integrate these emotions and memories and to have more of a stable and coherent sense of self.

These are some signs of being more connected to yourself in an integrated way:

- Calm, deep states of peace and rest
- Behavior that is not reactive
- Positive thinking
- Ability to concentrate
- Capacity to trust others
- Good judgment
- Sense of confidence
- Patience
- Involvement in daily activities
- Ability to ask for what you need
- Self-care
- Enjoyment of life
- Expressing your creativity and gifts
- Solid sense of self

In working with your trauma, it is important to know the difference between when you are dissociating and when you are fully grounded in yourself. It will be much safer, easier, and more effective to work with your parts and integrate the memories of the past trauma if you are in your body, grounded, and centered, so that the work is healing and does not become re-traumatizing.

Kristina
2005

I had a session today with my therapist. I can't believe how much easier the work is when I'm not floating. I think it is so natural for me to dissociate, that I don't even notice when I'm doing it. But there was a big change when I got back into my body. The work was a lot easier to do. Working with my young parts, I tried to get them to own some of the anger. And today, I think we did, even if it was just partially. My Little One felt it and actually voiced it! That's a first. That's movement! And it's huge. I told my abusers, "NO!" My young parts actually stood up to them, when they usually experience just being terrified. It was a breakthrough to be able to say, "NO, go burn in hell." My therapist helped support me in getting there and expressing it. I felt more empowered and felt a greater sense of being able to take care of me! It was a fantastic feeling. It was so healing. My depression has lifted, and I'm feeling better than I have in a long time.

KRISTINA: If you have a history of dissociation and have become used to being out of your body, it may take time and work to establish a new baseline for being more present in yourself. The feelings of "floating" can actually become addictive, as some parts might like the spaced-out feeling more than the experience of being fully present when it also includes integrating painful or sharper feelings.

Here are a few techniques to use if you feel you need to be more proactive with grounding yourself throughout the day:

- Stretching
- Going outside for a walk or to breathe fresh air
- Being with people
- Splashing cold water on your face
- Spending time with nature or pets
- Fixing something
- Cleaning or organizing a room

- Listening to music, dancing
- Lying on the ground outside
- Doing push-ups or movements to strengthen and feel your muscles

HEATHER: It is important to become aware of when you feel you are dissociating or when you feel a pull into the "underworld" of the emotions related to the trauma. At times, it can feel as if this is how life will always be, and that your daily life will always consist of being in survival mode, trying to endure the waves of dissociation, depression, disconnection, or overwhelm that are often the aftermath of early severe trauma. Remember that you now have the tools to support you in your healing process, and as you take those first courageous steps to face these feelings, it opens the door to healing and to being in a new reality with different and more positive experiences and possibilities.

Kristina
Gathering me

Nowhere left to turn, I go inward. Last night, when the sadness and feelings of wanting to withdraw started to set in, I was praying for the day to end, so that I could find refuge in sleep. I curled my body into a cocoon of blankets, hoping that tomorrow would open to relief. It didn't. Stumbling my way through the morning routine, I am wanting a natural switch to come over me to stop the depression from spiraling down and the dissociation from becoming ever more present. I don't succeed. Driving is difficult. Conversations keep ending in a drawn-out lag. I am unmotivated to even move.

It is time. I gather my notebook and pen and fight against the downward pull. I am the hero of my story. No one else is here to save my day. I open up to myself and start the process of gathering myself in. Thirty minutes later, I close my notebook, gently laying my pen on top of its cover. It is done for now. The depression has almost lifted completely. The dissociation is nearly gone. I am quietly respectful of the sacredness of such a seemingly easy task, taking a little time and attention to spend on myself—how simple, at times, and yet very profound. I am able to heal myself.

Depression

Trying to understand why your system is feeling overloaded can be very helpful in lifting depression. Remember that when you are doing this deep healing work it is important to reduce the external stress in your life. Otherwise, your adult self can quickly feel overwhelmed in the present while your young parts are overwhelmed with the pain from the past. This can lead to feelings of hopelessness and depression. Reducing external stress and gaining access to information about what is going on deeper inside can allow you to work the process in a healing way.

HEATHER: Clinical depression is different from grief or sadness. When you are experiencing clinical depression, you are more likely to feel mired in feelings of depression as well as experiencing reduced energy and a lack of motivation or interest in activities that you normally would enjoy. Clinical depression is also usually accompanied by changes in sleep and eating patterns. This can include insomnia or sleeping much more than is usual for you. It may also include weight loss or weight gain due to difficulties eating or overeating. You may also have feelings of worthlessness, hopelessness, fatigue, and a lack of pleasure in life. Especially if you experience this type of depression for two weeks or more with your sleeping and eating patterns seriously affected, you may need medication to help your body come back into balance.

It is important, however, to also work this at the emotional level to get to the root of your depression. Depression can be a way of attempting to numb or keep at bay deeper levels of trauma or painful emotions. It may also be related to feelings held by younger parts who are stuck in pain from the past and in feelings of helplessness and hopelessness. It can also be the aftermath of gaining more insight into aspects of your trauma. The efforts to integrate your feelings of loss, sadness, and betrayal might become too much for your system to handle if it comes all at once or too close together. Honor your depression as part of the healing process but seek support so that you don't stay stuck in this darkness or "underworld" experience for too long. It is important to reach out and be in connection with a therapist or someone you trust to help you know how to explore the deeper meaning of what you are experiencing and then know how to return to the light of day and the "upper world," deeper, wiser, lighter, and more integrated.

Kristina
2001
The Darkness within

I sink into the gray of winter.
The still darkness deafens my soul.

Slipping further with nothing to grab hold of,
I am free-falling through space.
Hopeless of being able to stop myself
From aimlessly, eternally free-falling.

The thick black darkness encircles me ...
There is no escaping it.
It victoriously laughs as my breathing begins to crawl and my limbs fail to move.

The battle is over.
No more strength to fight.

The darkness closes in on its prey ...
Becoming a part of who I am,
Convincing me that we are one.
Never again to be free from the darkness that has seeped through my being and consumed me.

KRISTINA: I had not experienced depression until I was about two years into my trauma work. At that time, I made a major move, which left me separated from my therapist, friends, culture, and all outside safety and support that I had known. We moved from the South to Washington, DC, which was like moving to another planet. I began working nights to make ends meet. I also started working with a therapist who said that she was well trained in trauma; however, she quickly diagnosed me as a borderline personality and wrote off what I was experiencing as attention seeking and not due to trauma. I felt utterly alone in my ever-present nightmare. Everything inside me seemed to shut down in an effort to survive, and I went into a full-blown major depression. I was then referred to a psychiatrist, which led to years of trying to manipulate multiple medication cocktails, from Adderall to get me going in the morning to Ambien to help me fall asleep at night, and everything in between (including various antidepressants, mood stabilizers, and antipsychotics) to get me through the day. Not surprisingly, the depression didn't lift until I found a different therapist and started working with what was really going on—the underlying trauma. As I worked my way out of major depression, I began to realize that there seemed to be five core reasons why I would tend to experience a depressed state:

1. A distorted or false thought or belief that I held
2. A deep need that was not being met
3. A feeling or emotion that was trapped inside my body that needed to be released
4. Too much stress that led to feeling overloaded, which resulted in my system shutting down
5. A young part inside that was stuck in a freeze state of trauma

These experiences tended to occur deeper in my psyche, so to gain access to help and offer relief to these younger parts, I had to meet them where they were.

In this section, we will look at specific ways to shift out of depression and facilitate deeper healing. It might be helpful to start with directly communicating with the depression through dialogue, the same as you would if it were an aspect of yourself. Also try to assess if there is anything in your current life that is creating thoughts and beliefs that need to be addressed and dealt with. Maybe the depression will tell you there is too much stress; maybe there is a concern, or something needs to change, such as a relationship or job. Once these issues are addressed, see if you can go deeper, by sensing into what might be underneath the surface layers of sadness or depression.

As you come to better understand the depression you are experiencing, you will have greater access to what is needing to be addressed underneath it.

This will lead you to the root causes which, once met, seen, felt, and healed, will be ready to let go. It is important as you do this work that you hold the awareness that the depression is just part of you, not all of you. This way, you are able to have enough space to reparent and meet the needs of your wounded parts. As you allow yourself to connect with your witness self, you can address the depression without fearing that it will overwhelm you or consume you. However, if you have difficulty maintaining this co-consciousness and allowing the witness self to facilitate a dialogue, seek help from a therapist or a trusted healing other.

Keep working with the depression until you find something that will help meet your deeper needs. This might become a back and forth dialogue, as the pain seeks to find love and safety. If you cannot find a way to help the sadness release, then offer ways to just be together in the suffering. This allows the depressed part to feel seen, heard, and held. Sometimes, the depression is so deep that you may feel helpless, overwhelmed, paralyzed, and cut off from your emotions and from any sense of motivation. At these times, it may be challenging to do the inner dialoguing.

Here is an example of how Kristina dealt with this type of depression:

Kristina
2012

"Don't stop!" my high school cross-country coach would yell at us. "Whatever you do ... just don't stop. Jog, walk, crawl ... but don't stop moving." The depression sometimes would be so difficult I felt I couldn't physically move. I would lie in bed and hope that some big rock would come and cover me up. At times, I would even be despondent. It was as if the trapped emotions inside my body made my system shut down and cut off from feeling them and also from everything and anything else living and breathing in my life. I felt physically and emotionally deadened. But there was one thing that I could still move—my mind guided by my heart. Even if all hope of getting better and moving past the numbness of depression was gone, I still could find a spark of some desire to heal, to be free. And with that particle of desire, I envisioned white healing love move into my being, coming in through the crown of my head, down through my body

to my toes to fill me with divine love, to move into the dark heavy places where the pain and trauma were stored. Slowly, softly the light surrounds and moves into the wounds, filling them with healing energy. I let my body fill up with light that begins to restore it to its natural state of being, whole and alive again.

Gaining strength, I then ask for a loving other to walk with me for a while. And even if I only gain enough energy to get a bite to eat or take a warm bath, it is a powerful message to myself that says it is okay to be sad, to feel and even be depressed. These acts are me showing up for myself and demonstrating that I am worthy to be taken care of. And these small steps lead to bigger steps, and the healing process grows. I move more into my wholeness each time I turn inward. My body and all the splintered-off pieces of my soul begin to heal. And I learn that it is safe to integrate my sadness and anger when they come up. I don't have to split off from my feelings. I don't have to be numb. I can relax into a feeling, into my authenticity. This must be what it felt like to Pinocchio, when he changed from being made of wood into a real boy.

HEATHER: At times, the depression can be related to being in a freeze state, which may have been a way of coping with the trauma in the past. As Kristina expressed, you may feel empty, unmotivated, heavy, numb, and unable to move. At these times, it is very helpful to do something that allows you to move and take action and begin to break out of the freeze state. Even if it is just to go for a walk or stand up and move around the room. Your witness self is reminding you that you are not locked in the trauma of the past and are safe now. Look around you and actively take in the surroundings of your present reality. As Kristina did, it is also helpful to meditate and visualize taking in warm, healing light. This can also help to thaw the frozen parts of yourself and allow you to feel held in safety and love in the present moment and remind your young parts that you are not mired in the trauma of the past.

KRISTINA: As you begin to work with your depression you will often find layers of emotions underneath the depression. As you work through one layer, another might come up ready to process, heal, and release. Emotions hold a lot of energy that we do not have access to as long as the emotions stay stuck.

Once found and released, we are able to integrate this energy back into the wholeness of our being. Our energy as a whole shifts from being in survival mode to that of creativity and thriving. At times, it might be too hard to separate from the depression or intense energies that come up from deeper down inside. If you feel you cannot find distance enough to work with the underlying wounds, just try working to release some of the energy. Turn inward and hold yourself in a safe space or in healing light. You might find it helpful to take a break from working on your emotions to ground yourself, and then come back to the process from a more centered and aligned space. You might also need to reach out to your therapist or a trusted healing other to hold space for you as you do this deeper work. It is important to feel that you are not alone in the healing journey.

Kristina
2010

I've spent the last week in depression. Even though I have fought hard, it has slowly taken over my body. What makes it so unmanageable is that I feel it debilitates me, leaving me feeling I don't have much ability at all to help myself. I tried meditating, praying, exercising, doing anything that could counter the sadness and offer me a scrap of joy, but nothing has worked. My efforts turn to distraction, and I start eating, sleeping, and trying to zone out. I feel numb in a body full of emotion. I just can't get to it. It's stuck inside, somewhere down deep. My life on the outside feels close to perfect for me and does not match my internal reality. What is wrong with me? I reach for my contact list. Somewhere on it is the name of a psychiatrist who will give me meds. I did this routine for years, it never really helped. I feel desperate.

I decide to make one last effort to free myself from this prison. I sit down on my bed, and then gently lay myself back and become very quiet. It is time to go inside and find what is lost. What is stuck and screaming for help? It is time to do for myself what was never done for me. Time to care enough about myself. I try to speak to the depression.

The depression takes form, and a young me climbs up onto the lap of the adult self. And I hand her a blanket and wrap my arms around her. I begin to dialogue and allow her to drop into her feelings. I place my hand on my own heart as I also visualize myself placing it on my little one's heart. I breathe deeply. I let the breath touch the sadness around my heart and begin to melt the walls, and I see them slowly go away, and a flood of tears begins to flow out of my heart up through my chest. The tears are finally able to break free from my heart and move up through my throat and eyes. The sadness flows freely from my body. As my little one who has held this sadness for so long cries, she begins to dissipate into the healing light above her. I have helped to release her, and she is healing me. I feel connected to myself in a new way. The depression doesn't hold me prisoner to my feelings anymore. I let the sadness wash through me, cleaning out the wounds a little deeper.

KRISTINA: Sometimes fear is what keeps us from connecting to deeper emotions. Fear can shut us off from feeling and keep us disconnected through depression. Depression has often stopped me from making any movement in life and from progressing with my healing process, but often I find what lies just under the depression is fear. Fear may also be trying to buffer or distance you from feeling the pain or more intense emotions of anger and sadness. It sometimes feels safer to feel depressed than to risk getting hurt, feeling vulnerable, or facing the feelings that you fear are going to be too much to handle. These were some of my fears: What if I open up and look at my past, will it consume me? What if I become vulnerable with someone and share my deeper feelings, will I be abandoned?

Kristina
2010
Tick Tock

I listen to the ticking of the clock as the hands go 'round and 'round its stalwart face.
    Tick tock. Tick tock.
    No thought or feeling can it have, as it methodically keeps time.
    Tick tock. Tick tock.

No sorrow or longing. Joy or peace.
Tick tock. Tick tock.
It breaks through the silence of the sterile, immaculate room.
Everything is in its proper place.
The wood is polished, and the sheets tucked in military style as the clock keeps perfect time, holding it all together.
Tick tock. Tick tock. Tick tock.
And if by chance the clock should stop, what would happen to this room?
Paintings drop and crash onto the floor.
Feathers burst from their casing.
An outright revolt as clothes march right out of closet doors.
Tick tock. Tick tock. Tick tock.
And maybe ... only tears will flow, no revolts or falling objects. Just small, simple tears that soften the heart, and release the pain ... allowing the clock to give way, if only for a moment in time.

KRISTINA: When depression presents itself strongly enough, it is hard to get to the feelings and wounds underneath that are actually desperate to heal. It is important to work with the fear if you want to get past the depression. If you wait until there is no fear in order to work on healing, it might never happen, or the process will be very inconsistent, as the fear comes and goes. You can work with depression and fear at the same time. Gently and gradually opening up the feelings of fear, you can come to better understand the thoughts that are creating the feelings. As you work with the fear, the depression will lift. Usually, this is an effort that moves back and forth between depression and fear. But it is important to continue to try and tolerate both feelings, while continuing to move forward with the right actions to heal the underlying wound. Being able to tolerate both feelings at the same time might be difficult, but you can work with the fear and create enough safety to allow space for healing work to be done.

As you face the feelings rather than avoiding them, their power over you begins to dissipate, and even the fear can flow and become a current within you, rather than overtaking you or being an impenetrable wall blocking you from the deeper feelings within. Taking time to respect the fear by being present with it, feeling it, giving it space, and making efforts to better understand it will be greatly beneficial in the long run. Fear can offer profound wisdom relevant to what will create a more effective healing environment. For example, the wounded parts of yourself may need you to give them more reassurance, support, or containment. Sometimes, the fear may seem irrational based on your present reality. If this is the case, then the fear is showing you what needs to be worked out first from the past, before your system will feel safe to do the deeper healing.

If you have tried to work with fear as you would another part of your system, and it keeps presenting itself, then it might be more appropriate to just experience the fear, welcome it to come up, and hold loving space for its healing. It might be energy that needs only to emerge, through holding loving space, and then releasing it from the body. Working with the fear, depression, and deep wounds becomes a loving dance if given the proper setting. And when given adequate attention and care, this will allow closed gates to open wide into the depths of your heart.

HEATHER: A phrase I learned long ago from Starhawk, a powerful healer, activist, and teacher was, "Where there is fear, there is power." It took me years to finally understand that fear blocks us from these deeper aspects of ourselves, and when we finally face the fear, we open the doors to our deeper feelings and, in doing so, recover more of who we are and reclaim the gifts, wisdom, and power that have also been trapped behind the wall of fear. We then are empowered to be more fully in the truth and freedom of our authentic selves.

Here are some other ways to work with stuck energy in the body or psyche that often contributes to depression:

- Free association writing for twenty minutes or more
- Expression through art
- Acupuncture or other forms of energy work
- Yoga
- Dancing or doing qi gong or any form of meditation in motion

Through these practices, you can open up space for the energy to move and be released from the body. When the feelings finally come into awareness, you can meet them with your adult witness self or in the space of inner stillness with healing love.

Working with anger

KRISTINA: Anger is an emotion that can be particularly hard to access and express, especially for women, who have been taught that being angry isn't "nice" or spiritual and that anger should be suppressed or bypassed. Often girls and women are punished or silenced through fear or shame when anger is voiced, and we respond by going into sadness instead. But it is important to stay with the anger, to feel it and claim it. In this way, we direct our anger appropriately—not inwardly, but rather to those who violated us. Anger holds our sense of power and full capacity and can move us into right action.

HEATHER: Anger is also a healthy and normal response to experiences of being violated, neglected, or traumatized. Reclaiming the anger is key to reclaiming the full spectrum of your emotions and sense of self. It is also a reminder to your young parts or the aspect of you that experienced the trauma that the abuse was wrong and was unjust and undeserved. Healing is about coming back into balance, harmony, and right relationship. It is only when we honor our anger that we claim the truth of the violation that we experienced and take a stand for self-care, for justice, and for coming back into right relationship with ourselves. Anger is also a way of being in right relationship with the abuser by holding fast to the importance of justice and of the rightful consequences for the wrongdoing and violation. Also, if you don't directly acknowledge the anger, it is likely to manifest in unhealthy ways and come out covertly, indirectly, or even worse, be directed at yourself. Repressed or suppressed feelings do not go away. They get expressed in disguised or indirect ways or manifest in physical symptoms or illness. They also lead to depression or fatigue in that it takes a great deal of emotional energy to keep these feelings at bay.

Kristina
2001

Under the Surface of the Cool Calm Earth

Simmering ...
For years, the anger has been simmering.
Hot ... steaming hot ... fiercely hot ...
Boiling under the surface of the cool calm earth,
It is boiling strong.

Eruption!
The anger unleashes itself from the Earth's bondage.
Spitting.
Screaming.
Raging.

Flying wildly into the clouds.
Raging red fire ... lashing around in the air.
No reason. No logic.

Too long, it has been trapped.
Stuck.
Imprisoned.
Given no voice. No existence.

Anger—roaming like a ravenous wolf looking for its prey.
Prey that can never be found under the cool calm Earth.

KRISTINA: It is important to find the parts of you that may have a hard time expressing anger or experiencing conflict or confrontation. We need to reparent our young parts around any false beliefs they might have developed and teach them that anger is healthy and is a way of protecting of ourselves.

You can also instill the sense of being valuable, so you understand that you have the right to push away what feels harmful or hurtful. As you feel your value and worth, you are able to claim the anger about what was done to you, that you did not deserve it, and it was not right. Often, there is one part that holds most of the anger, and other parts that are terrified of it. It is important to bring all of your parts into an understanding of the process, so that you can continue to work together to bring them into safety and love and help them to not be in inner conflict with each other. As you allow all of these parts to open to their feelings and experiences, the inner blocks begin to melt away, and your true self begins to emerge.

As children coming out of trauma or abuse, we probably have little experience of seeing anger or conflict expressed appropriately. We have a limited idea of what conflict looks like, other than that it usually involved hurt, destruction, and some form of turbulence or chaos. Because of this, you may tend to shy away from situations that might involve conflict, even to your own detriment. This is true especially if your coping style was flight or freeze. It is important to explore different ways of expressing anger and discord that can feel safe, productive, and protective of oneself.

HEATHER: At the other end of the spectrum are those who used the fight response for self-protection, and then your problem with anger is a tendency to be reactive and to respond with aggression to any emotional slight or experience of feeling unsafe or hurt. While these angry outbursts are an effort to avoid pain, they actually now in adulthood lead to unnecessary conflicts and even to ruptures in significant relationships. The challenge then is to learn to honor the feelings of anger but to discern when the intense aggressive feelings are related to the past and not in balance with what is occurring in the present moment. Gradually, you separate the pain from the past from the experiences in the present and are able to bring your anger into balance and learn to deal with conflicts in your current life in a healthier way. Then, your expressions of anger are able to come from a clear place in the present rather than from an unconscious reaction out of the fear and pain from the trauma of your past.

Kristina
2005

Today in session, I worked on the memories of the man that used to come into my room at night. My therapist helped connect me to my four-year-old self. After I had cried about my sadness, my therapist gently pushed me to get to my anger about it. I was pretty sure that that wasn't going to happen, because I didn't have any feeling of being angry. But I was still doing self-destructive things, so it had to be in there somewhere. She strongly urged me to throw her footstool at the door. I didn't want to, because I thought it was an inappropriate way to show anger. I thought hitting the couch would be a nicer way to approach it. But she kept encouraging me, and finally I connected to it and really felt like I was angry at my abuser, and that it wasn't my fault, and so he (the footstool) deserved to be put through the door. It empowered me. For some reason, having something tangible in my hands and taking action felt good. My therapist said that it was time for me to take my power back, that he had had it for too long. And she was right. After throwing that object as hard as I could against the door, I felt all this anger inside. My therapist said it was probably just the tip of the iceberg, and I think she was right. When I got home, I felt that more anger needed to be released. I found a shovel and went into the back yard, and with all my strength and might, I dug a hole, again and again, plunging the shovel into the earth. He became the dirt, which I shoveled, crushed, threw, plowed, and chopped. The dirt is outside of me. Not in me. Not anymore. And when all the anger was released, I dropped down on my knees and felt the earth, fists full, holding it to my chest, feeling its coolness against my skin, bringing me home again to myself.

It is important to give anger a safe and contained physical outlet as a way of release. You can do this in a variety of ways, such as:

- Taking a quick run
- Dancing

- Drumming
- Ripping up paper
- Smashing old dishes
- Chopping wood
- Doing aerobic physical exercise
- Punching or kicking a pillow

KRISTINA: After releasing the anger, it might be helpful to continue to connect with any deeper feelings that might be tied to the anger. This would be a good time to dialogue with your younger parts. Allow yourself to explore whether there are other layers or feelings beneath the anger as it is released.

HEATHER: Another way to work with your anger is to say out loud or in writing what you wish you could say to your abuser. Allow all of the anger and feelings of injustice to rise up, and let yourself say it, yell it, or write it out. Keep going with this process until you feel some sense of release and relief. You may want or need to do this more than once. If you write out what you wish you could say to that person, you may then want to burn the paper, and let the anger be released to the fire. At times, it is possible to have a direct conversation with the one who has hurt or abused you. This can be part of the healing process. However, I strongly recommend that you let yourself have the uncensored conversation first in which you let your anger have full expression. Then, after honoring all of your feelings, you can work through how you want to approach the conversation with the person if this feels right to you as part of your healing process or in an effort to get resolution or closure with the person. If you do not feel that the person would in any way be open to this conversation, take time to assess whether having direct conversation would be healing to you or further traumatizing. If it is not going to be helpful or possible to have that direct communication with the person that hurt you, it can be important to let yourself express this anger in the context of a therapy relationship or with a supportive person in your life. This allows the adult part of you and all of your young parts to feel truly heard, seen, and supported.

Kristina
2005

It was difficult to connect to my anger at first, but the more times that I said out loud what I was angry about, and the more I hit the couch and let it out of my body, the more I began to feel it and connect with it. And when I was done, I was tired, especially the young parts inside of me. And then, I began to feel sad. The words fell from my ears to my heart, and I started to hear myself, what I was saying about me, not someone else, but this was about me. And my little one began to curl up, she wanted to hide and be protected from everyone and everything. But my therapist just let her love flow out towards me, and I felt seen, safe, and cared for. And I learned that it's okay to let someone in when you are angry and hurting so badly inside, because not everybody is going to come in and take advantage of that. This time, I felt it was going to be different. This time, I was going to be loved.

Dreams, nightmares, and flashbacks

Dreams, nightmares, and flashbacks are also some of the ways that your wounds may try to get your attention. These wounds remain hidden in the subconscious until your system feels that it is time to start letting bits of the trauma come up in order for the body and psyche to release, heal, and come back into balance. Having these experiences can sometimes feel terrifying and out of control, but how you work them can make the difference between being re-traumatized or having this be part of a healing process. If you can reframe these experiences, as horrible as they may feel, as messages of what needs to be seen and brought into consciousness, then you can remain open to what is coming up. Rather than getting caught in fear or trying to block or distance yourself from these experiences, you are again able to open to what they are trying to show or tell you, and you are then able to heal and hold the wholeness of who you are.

Dreams

KRISTINA: I have always been an active dreamer. Some dreams are so clear, it feels as if I am literally living in a parallel universe. At other times, the dreams are confusing and full of emotion. I wonder if my subconscious is trying to pull hidden pieces of thoughts, experiences, and feelings together in a desperate attempt to make sense out of the endless disorder of the past. If trauma is added to the mix, it feels as if the crevices of my mind and psyche are at a breaking point having contained things for too long, and all of the information is being spilled out into some twisted Cirque du Soleil dream world.

Even though dreams can be hard to decipher and understand, I have found over the years that they can be invaluable clues about myself that I have had little prior access to in a conscious way. Dreams can have multiple meanings and purposes, but often for me, they seem to be messages from parts that are trying to release pain or sort out inner confusion in order to heal. And if I take the time and make the effort to listen and try to understand the messages, I can learn more about myself and what is still in need of healing. It then becomes more of a process of turning my attention inward and seeing, on a multi-faceted and deep level, that all parts and all stories, even pieces, are important and valued. It is like gathering little gems of information, whether the dream is about a specific memory, a core belief, or a feeling. This precious information is vital for my system as a whole to heal. Dreams should be seen as useful insights into our inner world. When paid attention to, they can offer great amounts of support in overcoming depression and lessening reactive behavior, moods, and thoughts.

HEATHER: It is also important to realize that there are many types of dreams. Dreams are one way that the unconscious mind can begin to communicate and give you messages about the feelings and memories from the past that have been buried and that are now ready to come into awareness. Other dreams may reflect your more current processing of the events of the day or efforts to work through problems in your life. And some dreams may be guidance or messages from your soul self or from your spirit guides in other realms. These dreams often feel very vivid and may not be imbued with a lot of emotion but are often giving you powerful messages that support you in knowing that you are not alone, that you are loved and are being supported in your healing journey.

As you pay attention to your dreams and work with them, you will begin to more easily differentiate the different types of dreams and how to best use them to support you in your process. Research has shown that if you make it a regular practice to record your dreams on a daily basis, you will have an easier time remembering them more frequently and consistently. So even if you do not believe that you dream very often, try to begin to journal each morning and record what you do remember, and you are likely to find that your ability to remember your dreams will increase. Developing a relationship with your dreams allows you more entry to what is held in your unconscious as well as stronger access to your intuition and the wisdom of your soul self.

Flashbacks

Flashbacks are intense, vivid moments of remembering, seeing, or re-experiencing traumatic events that have happened in the past. They are often precipitated by some experience in the present that evokes the memory of the trauma. At times, it can feel as if they are coming out of nowhere. When a flashback occurs, it may be an indication that the trauma held in your psyche is ready to come into consciousness. Because having a flashback literally feels as if you are back reliving the traumatic event, it can be overwhelming and hard to disengage from.

When you begin to recognize that you are in a flashback, try to start aligning with your witness self, so that you can begin to help calm your system and bring yourself back into the present moment. One way you can do this is by breathing in and out slowly (using the count of five for each in breath and out breath). Take a moment and look at your surroundings and help ground your body and psyche in the present moment. As you breathe in and out deeply and slowly, calming your system, gaze at the objects that are around you. Name them silently or even out loud, noting their colors, shapes, and textures. This helps your psyche to remember it is in this current place and time and not still in the trauma from the past. Take time to allow your body to fully shift out of the stress response, and then, once you are calm, you can begin to explore what the trigger was for the flashback and what feelings and memories were rising up from your buried trauma. The more that you can work consciously with what is coming up from the deeper layers of your unconscious, the more you are able to release, heal, and integrate. This then leads to having fewer flashbacks and disturbing dreams or nightmares.

KRISTINA: When working your way through a flashback, nightmare, or disturbing dream, and back into the present moment, try to notice what is going on internally in the present moment. What is your body telling you through thoughts, feelings, and sensations? Try to gather and understand all of the information that you are being given about what happened to you in the past. If you write it down, this helps to give you a safe container for the experience and a way to return to it later and work with it more consciously at another time. Remind yourself that your body and psyche are trying to heal, and that this is part of the process. Try to bring yourself, as fully as you can, back into the present moment. You might need a cup of warm tea, a soothing bath, a soft blanket, or some movement to get you back to the present and into feeling safe. It is also important to send a message down inside to all parts of yourself that you received the information, that all parts are now safe, and also to inquire as to what may be needed to bring every part into peace and healing and out of the trauma state.

For years, I had dreams, nightmares, and flashbacks. Often these would occur along with having night sweats, which had me doing multiple rounds of changing bedclothes and sheets that had been soaked through in the night. In the beginning stages, I was terrified and exhausted and wanted it all to go away. Taking a double dose of a prescription sleep aid each night helped quiet the night experiences, but that had other side effects, so there came a time when I had to choose to face what was coming up at night. At that point, I began, during the day, to work out the images and experiences that were happening at night. The more I worked these in the daylight, the less often I had flashbacks or nightmares at night, and the more healing and integrating the process became.

Kristina
2013

Dream: I was probably around the age of eight, and I was lying in bed with my mother. It was night time. It was just my mother and me, and I was sleeping next to her. Then, I was startled out of sleep by my mother being on top of me. She had her hands around my neck, and she was strangling me. I was flooded with powerful emotions that were running violently through my body. I was fighting to get her off of me, which I finally did.

Breathing heavily and still in a panic, I asked her why she was trying to kill me. She responded that she was sorry, but that she was so full of rage, that sometimes she couldn't control where it went or who she took it out on. I got up and went to my bedroom, which wasn't far from hers as it was a small house. I shut the door behind me and quickly dropped to the floor, looking for the shadow of her feet behind the door. She was there. She had come back to kill me. I started breathing hard, planning my escape. I looked again under the door, and she was gone. I quietly opened the door and ran towards the back of the house. She heard me, as I ran for freedom. And then I woke up.

Now, in the present time as an adult, I am thousands of miles away from my childhood home, and many years have passed since being eight. I lie in bed on my back with my heart racing, full of fear, deep sadness, and disbelief. I have always known and understood that my mother's moods would quickly change on me. I knew she kept a rage in her that was very scary. But I had no idea that I had parts inside that held beliefs and emotions from so long ago, forgotten by the adult me. These emotions have been tucked away for years, so I wouldn't have to keep feeling the devastation of being raised by an unstable and abusive mother. Breaking myself into countless pieces, I gave myself a chance to live. Now, reclaiming the lost and broken parts of myself, I begin to pull in my whole being. The lost, destitute, and forgotten, it is all part of me.

I then send love and healing and do an inner dialogue with this eight-year-old part.

Here are excerpts from the inner dialogue:

A: *Can you tell me why you sent this message in a dream?*
C: *It's safe that way, because then no one knows I sent it.*
A: *Well, then, you are brave for coming forward. Why do you send the message?*
C: *Because I am trying to get it out of my body.*
A: *Can we talk about it?*

C: *Okay.*
A: *Did this happen to you? Did the mother get on top of you and try to strangle you?*
C: *No.*
A: *Why do you send a message like that then?*
C: *Because that is how it felt.*
A: *What do you mean? Did it feel like she wanted to kill you?*
C: *Yes.*
A: *So the feelings, those were yours? I mean something that you have felt with your mother was extreme fear, and a feeling that she was going to hurt you, and that she wanted to kill you.*
C: *Yes.*

I took time to hold this part and comfort her until she felt safe and at peace. I was then able to go back to sleep.

HEATHER: This dream is an excellent example of the ways that your dreams may give you messages through images or metaphors. Allow yourself to sit with the dream, to meditate on it or to dialogue with a character or young part in the dream in order to discern what its message is for you. I would encourage you to avoid dream interpretation books. While some dreams hold archetypal images or symbols, most dreams are profoundly unique and emerge from the unconscious, giving you very personal information and messages to help you to heal and become more conscious.

Kristina
2013

Throughout the fifteen years of working to heal my trauma, I would have a recurring dream about a staircase. In the dream, this staircase was in my grandfather's house, and I was repeatedly trying to get to the top, so that I could open the door and gain access to all the family secrets that I believed were hidden there. What these secrets were, I had no idea. But in the dreams, I felt that the room behind the door at the top of the stairs held them all. Often in the dreams, I would be at the bottom of the stairs, going through clutter and boxes of papers, photographs, and all sorts of junk, trying to find pieces of information. But I knew that what I really needed was at the top of the stairs behind the door. Throughout the years of working the healing process, in my dreams I would also be making my way further and further up the staircase, each time getting a little closer to the door before I would wake up. The furthest I got was being able to place my hand on the doorknob and begin to turn it. When I had healed most of my past trauma, I stopped having the dream.

What was always curious to me was that, through all the times and many years that I had this dream, to my current knowledge, my grandfather did not have stairs in his house. I was never aware that there was ever a second floor. My grandfather, my father's father, had a very large and spacious home right off the main square in a small town in the South. Across the street were a few townhomes and a gas station that my grandfather owned as well. Further outside of town, the family also owned many acres of land where they raised cattle. I remember as a teenager, being shown a good-sized cemetery, where many of my ancestors were buried. I was curious when I noticed that many had the Masonic symbol on the gravestones. Other than these properties, and a few others further out of town, I had never been told about any more in town. Sixteen years after my first flashback came of a satanic ritual being performed, I was back in this small southern town of my father's lineage in an effort to finally put more closure on my past. My father had died a year previously, and I had not gone back for the funeral.

When I did return, I sat by my father's grave. I was alone in the small cemetery, and I called out to his spirit to come sit with me for a while. Out of nowhere a strong wind blew through the stagnant, hot, humid air, starting at my feet, and moving all the way up through my hair. I spoke from my heart, with a complete sense of letting go, of all that was done and had happened between us. I thanked him for giving me life and for the times of kindness that he showed me. I was able to hold the complexities of his being human. I had also brought one request that I wanted of him. I asked him to show me a sign. I explained to my dad that one of the most challenging things about healing from my trauma was not being able to have any direct process with the others *involved, and this made it hard to feel I had complete closure. I told him that I had gained an understanding about my past and felt that my experiences were confirmed over and over again in different ways. But nothing felt like solid enough validation to me, because it never came from the source of the abuse. "Oh, well," I said to him. "You are now gone, and it's too late for that." Still, I held on to the wish. As I walked through the cemetery to my rental car, I had the thought to go by my grandfather's house. It was in town, not far from the cemetery. "Why not?" I said to myself. "I can say goodbye to more of the past, it can't hurt."*

It had been twenty years since I had last been to the house, and as I pulled up I noticed the windows were boarded, and it looked as if it were vacant. As I walked around the grounds, there was a familiar feeling, as not much seemed to have changed from so many years ago. The pomegranate tree, with its fruit that I ate as a child, was still able to produce its magical seeds, as the branches had grown much taller than when I was a child. The large veranda wrapped around the right side of the house, still offering its cool shade. Even though the house seemed to be locked and boarded up, I decided to try the front door. With just a gentle push, the door opened up to a wide entryway that led into the vast living room with high ceilings. It was all exactly how I remembered, except one important addition that felt like it had been extricated from the countless dreams of my past and placed in solid form right in front of me. It was a large staircase, leading to a second level. I was shocked, frozen in the implications of what this could mean.

A woman's voice startled me from behind, "They put the staircase back in just a few years ago." Her voice broke my freeze. "Oh," was all that I could say. "They have to move this house by tomorrow, as it doesn't have a foundation, and it is not up to proper regulations for the town anymore. You shouldn't be here," she said. Over my shoulder, I called back to the woman as her head was still peering in through the front door, "This was my grandfather's house and had been passed down through multiple generations until a few years ago, when it was sold outside the family. I guess that's when the stairway was put in." "Well, yes," she replied. "The new owner remodeled the upstairs by creating four bedrooms and a bathroom. It really increased the value until it had to be moved, what a pity." Her words seemed to trail off as something deep from within me took over. I took a quick breath and without much thought, I began to walk up the stairs. I vaguely could hear the voice from below calling me to come back down and leave the house, but something much larger than myself was now helping me move up the staircase, one step at a time. Reaching the top, I was able to turn the door handle, and for the first time, finally, I pushed the door wide open.

The space that I entered was massive. It must have been the full length and width of the house, and she was right, there were four bedrooms and a bathroom. Walking through the empty rooms, I noticed the large windows. They looked exactly the same as the trauma memories that came up as an adult, small-paned glass windows from decades ago, creating the long rectangle-shaped windows that went from floor to ceiling. I felt a sudden dropping sensation as I began to take it in. This was the room of secrets, the place where the abuse happened. I touched a window pane, somehow reaching for something that felt real. A memory comes back to me, and I realize that I am looking out the same window I had forty years earlier. I was in this room. It was night, and I was by this window, waiting to be taken for a satanic ceremony. I was cold and terrified and as I waited in anticipation for my mother and grandfather to come in, I watched a gentle rain begin to fall on the window panes. This partial memory of watching raindrops fall against glass is one that I have always had but could never understand the significance of why it kept recurring. As I touch the window pane, I feel myself as if I am back touching it again as a child. Somehow, back then, in my tiny, young body, I felt myself become the glass. I knew terrible things were going to be done to me, but somehow, they wouldn't be able to touch me. At some point, I wouldn't feel it, and it would be as though it was running off me, like raindrops do when they hit the smooth surface of a window pane.

As my past and present were meeting in a space that felt dreamlike and very real at the same time, I was startled back into the moment, as I heard the woman from downstairs yelling out. It was time to leave. She was waiting for me at the bottom of the stairs. She showed me out, and I thanked her for giving me some time. I told her that I was the great-granddaughter of the people who once owned this house. I asked her about the other properties behind the house and across the street. Some I had even lived in for short periods of time during my childhood. She said to me, "That house over there, kitty corner to your grandfather's house, was your grandmother's house that she grew up in." "Oh," I responded, "I actually didn't know that." After all of the years of spending time in this small town, I had never been told that the house just diagonal and across the street from my grandfather's house was my grandmother's (my father's mother) childhood home. "Yes," she went on, "right next to your grandmother's house is the Masonic lodge. It's the first building on the square that is in the center of town."

My knees weakened and almost gave way. I crossed the street diagonally and walked over to my grandmother's house. Now, it was also all boarded up. I then turned, took a deep breath and faced the Masonic lodge. Here I was, literally facing my past trauma, and the source of the terror that had controlled my life for so long. I approached the building and peered through the window on the door. There was a sign that stated the days and times of the weekly meetings and ceremonies. It was still an active chapter. A date on a plaque was on the outside, indicating it was founded in 1907. The Masonic symbol, just above the date, was the same symbol that kept appearing through all my nightmares and memories.

Once inside the rental car, I sank back into the seat, and tried to take it all in and shake it all off at the same time. Just a few hours earlier, I asked my father for the validation I had so longed for, just an ounce, to give some accuracy to what I had experienced from my past and all my suffering. Was this it? Would it be enough? For years, I had so badly wanted to have something confirmed, but in this moment, I came to a subtle but powerful realization, that maybe, just maybe it never actually mattered. The validation that I so wanted from another was most powerful when it came from myself.

HEATHER: This recurring dream that Kristina had of the staircase (leading to long held secrets of her abuse) is a profound example of how dreams can help us to piece together or confirm aspects of our memories to create a more coherent whole. And some dreams are messages from higher states of consciousness, either your own or from other beings or spirit guides from outside of you. These types of dreams and messages can come as divine gifts and guidance in times that we feel lost, alone, and overwhelmed in the process of healing our deepest wounds. And Kristina's experience at her grandfather's house is an example of the synchronistic events that come when we need guidance, validation or support in the healing journey. It is a reminder that we are not alone but are held by energies larger than ourselves.

Kristina
2004

Dream: I was driving with a friend to see a particular movie. On our way to the theatre nothing seemed to come easily. It was hard finding a parking space, and danger seemed to be around every corner. It felt as if we were constantly trying to avoid becoming victims of some act of violence. We finally found the movie theater, which was inside a mall. My friend had never seen the movie before, but I had. I was telling her how good it was, and how I was glad she had come to see it. There were quite a number of people gathered outside to also see the movie. Once the doors opened, we entered into the huge movie theatre. It must have been twenty stories high. It was almost completely dark inside with just enough light to see where we were going just in front of us.

I told my friend to hurry and find a place to hide; even though there were hundreds of different places, we were on a time limit. The rules of the game were being spoken over a loudspeaker, as we were trying to find a place to hide. I found a hiding space way up high and settled in. It was the farthest away that I could get from a woman that was standing in the front on a platform, holding a microphone. She seemed to be in charge. Then, when she felt the time was right, she released a large bird. The bird would search through the theatre and pick someone out of their hiding place, and they would be taken by the bird to the woman at the front. I wanted to be the last one found, as I had a feeling that being picked also involved some element of pain. I felt hopeful, because I had found the best hiding place. All of a sudden, I could hear the bird screeching beside me. I stayed very still hoping it would pass me and get someone else. But it didn't. He reached out, and his claws sank deep into my arm. Despite the fact that there was no blood, it still felt very painful. I knew that my time was up, and I was going to be taken back to the lady who was front and center on the stage. I couldn't believe that I was the first one picked up.

I began to feel everything around me go dark. I had a sense that I was rising up in the air, beginning to float effortlessly, and then being guided down to be by the woman. As I was descending, I looked at my arm where the bird had put his claws into me. There were sparkles of light flickering around the wound, and I could see the light was healing me. When I reached the woman, she asked me, "What is weakness?" I didn't know what she was talking about. She said, "Everyone who comes to the theatre to see the movie is damaged or broken in some way. Those that have the greatest damage are the ones found first by the bird." I began to dig around in my purse, until I found the object I had been looking for. I pulled out a compass and held it up. She looked at it and, in a sad way, said, "Oh my, your compass is broken, it could never tell you which way to go. Come with me, and we will get you a new one." I followed her into a room that was full of bright white light. There were all sorts of gadgets. She looked around and found a beautiful new compass, and she placed it in my hand. She threw my broken compass in a box with a lot of old broken compasses. Love and gratitude poured out of me towards this woman as I felt she had healed a fundamental element that was so vital to me. For how could I follow my own path, aligned to my inner truth, while using a broken compass?

HEATHER: This dream is a beautiful example of the ways in which, at times, we are given healing experiences in the dream state. When this happens, take time to write down the dream and the messages and guidance that have come to you to allow them to more fully and consciously integrate.

For others, it may be hard to go into a deeper state of sleep or access dreams. Often, young parts that were abused at night are hypervigilant and stay awake during the hours the rest of the body might be asleep. For someone with trauma, it can feel as if part of them is awake all night while other parts sleep. This can lead to waking up exhausted in the morning or difficulty falling asleep or staying asleep at night. It helps to have a structured and consistent bedtime routine that fits your lifestyle. Some general rules are important in helping to calm your body and nervous system before bed. Here are a few suggestions to help with sleep issues:

- Take a warm bath at bedtime
- Use lavender essential oil to relax your body
- Use a heating pad on your shoulders or back when you first get into bed
- Listen to a guided sleep meditation
- Listen to binaural beats in relaxing music with delta waves
- Do not watch TV or use a computer within 30-60 minutes before bedtime
- Take melatonin or a GABA supplement
- Use CBD oil
- Make a mental list of the things you are grateful for and be in the energy of everything that is going well in your life as you fall asleep
- If you are in a healthy, supportive relationship with a spouse or partner, ask that person to hold you in the night and remind you that you are safe now

It is helpful to have your young parts participate in the bedtime routine. You might want to show them through your eyes how you are locking the doors and windows, and then you can tell them that the bedroom and house are safe. Show them, as they look through your eyes in the mirror, the adult body that they are in, and let them know that you will keep them all safe through the night. Once you are in bed and ready to sleep, send a message down to all of the parts inside, counting them down into their safe places where they have everything they need. Let them know that night-time is a time for sleep, and no one is to be awake or active at night. Help those parts that feel lost and alone by mentally creating a safe place inside where they can be at night. This work can be done during the day, so all parts have a place to go at night, prior to sleep. It might also be helpful to have a safe object to hold at night that supports younger aspects to feel safe and protected, such as a stuffed animal or soft blanket.

If you have put everything in place with your parts, done a bedtime routine, sent a message down to all parts that it is now time to sleep, and you still feel an undercurrent of anxiety or hypervigilance, then you might want to work specifically with the part that is up. This could involve a dialogue to address the concerns of that part. You might also need to bring your young part into your heart space and hold this little one to bring calming energy and safety directly to the part. Sometimes, holding a stuffed animal up to your chest, rocking back and forth, humming, or holding it to your heart while saying, "Everything is going to be okay," can bring comfort to that part and soothe the anxiety.

HEATHER: It may also be important to allow yourself to use natural supplements or medications as necessary to balance your sleep cycle during stressful periods of your healing process. If you are consistently not sleeping well, this will reduce your capacity to cope and deal with the stress of opening up more fully to your emotions and the wounds and memories of the past. Allow yourself to honor what you need (physically and emotionally) to feel that you have the support and ongoing safe container necessary to work through this more intense aspect of the healing process.

It can also be helpful to call in your spirit guides or helpers to protect you and guard you through the night. Call in the energies of the four directions and ask your spirit guides to surround you with healing, protective white light and to hold you in safety and love. This can help your young parts as well as your adult self to feel that they are protected and watched over through the night, so that you can rest and sleep more easily and deeply.

Some common blocks or obstacles to the healing process

HEATHER: It is important to remember that healing is not a linear path. It has ups and downs and detours and plateaus. It also helps to remember that, at times, just before or after a critical breakthrough in your process, you may experience an internal backlash. This is because, while your deepest self may be committed to the healing process, parts of you may feel threatened by the changes that you are making. We each have developed different patterns and coping mechanisms to protect ourselves from the wounds of past trauma and our painful emotions. As we dismantle these protective mechanisms, some of our parts are apt to feel endangered and try to block the healing process or act out in an effort to stay in familiar ways of being. It can help to know that this is a natural part of the healing journey. When you feel inner resistance or blocks arise, try to tune in and dialogue with the part that may feel unsafe. In this way, you can help that part to understand that you are working to create more safety and joy for all of the parts of you, and that no part will be disregarded or left out. Honoring that these blocks and experiences of resistance are part of the healing process will allow you to then hold the wholeness of who you are with compassion.

Denial

KRISTINA: When it was finally safe for my trauma to start coming out, there were times when my system seemed to go into automatic resistance. It was almost as if I had some internal detector that set off an alarm that my system was in danger. I had spent years being in relationships in which it was not safe for me to let out my secrets, and I had developed a way to systematically shut myself down. Even if the present experience was now different, it was hard to open up the past. This process seemed painfully slow at times, and I had to be patient with myself and realize I was unwinding a lifetime of hurt and abuse. Denial also became a way of gaining space from information that was coming up, that was too painful to immediately accept. I would, in one moment, have an undeniable sense that I had been abused and, in the next moment, I would feel as if nothing had happened. It seemed I could never have strong enough proof to completely believe that what I was presently experiencing was because of something that had happened to me as a child.

    I came to a point where I had to want to heal and become whole more than needing to have the memories that were coming up be verifiably 100 percent accurate, because I was never going to get that. I had to choose to step out of denial when it would arise and derail me. I learned how to just hold space without judgment. I wasn't collecting evidence for a court trial, so

I began to let what was coming up just be. Over time, as I stopped denying that my experiences were authentic and accurate, I also stopped denying parts of myself. When I was angry, I let myself feel the emotion without stuffing it. When information came in through dialogue, dreams, and memories, I allowed it space, instead of rejecting it. I brought everything into my heart. And, in response, my heart started to open up and heal.

Kristina
Dream 2009

I had a dream last night that I was back in the small southern town where I lived until I was four years old. In the dream, my father still owned the family land and property there. He was renting out homes and other types of buildings like his father and past generations had done in reality. In the dream, my father had continued owning and renting out property, and I had driven back to the land to see a Mexican family that lived in one of the small rental homes. (This family had actually lived in this home for part of my childhood. They tended to the small farm and cattle that were being raised on the land.) In the dream, my father was going to do something terrible to them, so I had gone back to warn them to move and escape danger. They were a young family with small children. After I had gotten to them and warned them to move, I had gone out further into the ranch land to see my father. Once I found him, he began to show me the buildings and grounds. My father then became distracted with something and walked off.

Out of curiosity, I decided to go inside one of the small buildings that was nearby. When I went inside, I almost immediately saw the doorway to the secret room that has routinely been in many of my dreams throughout the years. In my past dreams, whenever I got close to the door, something happened, and I was not able to get in. Something blocked or distracted me, or the door was locked, or I woke up. But this time, when I approached this entrance way, knowing it was the secret room, I was able to go inside. I was surprised but also had much anticipation because I had been waiting for so long. I was also scared, because I was afraid my father would come back and catch me. So I quickly moved through the room. It was filled with filing cabinets, books on shelves, and boxes full of paper and other items I couldn't see clearly. I knew it was all the secrets from the cult. As I was looking around the room, I turned to see two flip boards. I gasped. They were the flip boards that I had always remembered from my childhood, but they would flash into my memory as just an image, I could never place where they came from or why I was remembering them. In the dream, there were two flip boards on two easels. I walked up to them with a strange awe. This is what the group leaders used when they were teaching me certain things when I was a child. I reached out to touch the boards. I couldn't believe they still existed after all these years. I had forgotten almost everything about them. But here they were, right out of the past. Contained within these boards was everything I was taught to believe: how to dim my light, lose my identity, and become one with the dark. I finally had proof that all this stuff existed. As I went to flip open the first paper, to see what was written inside, I woke up.

HEATHER: It is important to honor the insights that come in the dreamtime. This is a powerful way in which your unconscious as well as your intuition, inner knowing and soul self are guiding you in your healing process.

Confusion

Our minds will lead us into states of confusion just to keep us spinning at the surface level and to keep our underlying feelings and memories at bay. This is another way that parts of us may be trying to fend off the inner pain or deeper knowing. But if we can drop out of the level of the mind and into the heart, we will be led again and again to what is our truth. Sometimes confusion can come through cognitive dissonance, when it is difficult to hold conflicting ideas and beliefs at the same time. For example, this may happen when memories start to unfold that have elements of abuse about someone we love, and we have only held one way of viewing or remembering this person. The experience creates cognitive dissonance; how can someone that shows love and care for you also hurt you?

HEATHER: Confusion can be an emotional defense, but it is also a common facet of the healing process. As you begin to allow the memories and feelings of the past trauma that were buried in the unconscious to emerge, it can feel disorienting, unsettling, and confusing. Honor that this is part of the healing process. You are releasing the old, familiar coping patterns and sense of identity and stepping into the unknown. As you hold this period of confusion and uncertainty with compassion, you will begin to heal and will slowly gain more understanding of your past and a clearer sense of your true self.

Fear

KRISTINA: There is so much fear around what is hidden in the shadows of our being, the things that have been tucked away for years, because they have been too painful to bring into the light. Depression and suffering come in the present, not from the traumatic events themselves, but from our inability to face them. We fear that if we open up to the wounds, we will be consumed with the pain and darkness or that the process will never end, and our lives will be taken over. But this is not so. If we find the proper support, grounding, helpful tools, and the courage to open to our wounds, we can have a loving and healing experience.

HEATHER: Remember Starhawk's words: "Where there is fear, there is power." Fear can block the healing process, but fear is also a response to the dismantling of the walls that have kept your feelings and memories at bay. Honor the fear and remember that it is also the doorway to regaining your power and true self.

It is not that you must be free from fear. The moment you try to free yourself from fear, you create a resistance against fear. Resistance, in any form, does not end fear. What is needed, rather than running away or controlling or suppressing or any other resistance, is understanding fear; that means, watch it, learn about it, come directly into contact with it. We are to learn about fear, not how to escape from it, not how to resist it through courage and so on. —J. Krishnamurti

Blame

KRISTINA: For years, I stayed stuck in a cycle of anger and in the feelings of being a victim of abuse as a child that was beyond my choice and control.

There were times I believed that this should not have happened to me, which was healthy initially as I reclaimed my anger, but eventually, I blamed God and spread anger onto everything around me. I so badly wanted to change the reality of what had happened to me and the effects that it was currently having on me and the ones that I loved. I compared my life to the lives of others and grew increasingly resentful and depressed that I had been dealt such terrible cards, while others seemed to skim by in life. It just wasn't fair.

As an attempt to try to make sense out of the abuse, I came up with some possible reasons as to why I was given these life experiences. One reason was that perhaps my soul desired to have these experiences, so that it would open possibilities for soul expansion and to gain greater wisdom. Another reason was that, through learning from my experiences, I would have the opportunity to better help others. In the end, though, I really don't know why I had to endure the abuse and neglect that I did. But the point is, I did.

I had to learn to not give in to these thoughts of blame and the questions as to "Why did this happen?" that ultimately led to suffering. I was never going to find an answer that was good enough to satisfy my mind, and more importantly, take the pain away. What I came to realize was that this was the reality of my life, and how I chose to live with it was now up to me. This allowed me to drop into the anger about the abuse, without adding the suffering of needing someone to blame for it. This is different than holding someone accountable. When you are in a space of blame, you tend to expect someone else to show up and make it better. You hold this sense that you have been wronged, and now someone must fix it to make it right. When you are caught in this way of thinking and feeling, you give your power away and stay dependent on others, instead of showing up for yourself and fully claiming your own healing process and life.

Many of us who were abused in isolation, being helpless and alone, have an aversion to the idea of being back in pain, having to deal with it all by ourselves. At times, even the word "alone" would make my heart go numb, empty out, and lock up. Somewhere inside, deep down in a young part, I had the haunting feelings that bad things happen when I'm all alone, and I become powerless and unable to help protect myself from the hurt. And that was true when I was a child. So being alone became synonymous with feelings of hurt and being without power to do anything about it. It is no wonder that, when I felt pain as an adult, I sometimes turned, out of instinct, to find anyone or anything to cling to.

It is important to understand the difference between being the primary one responsible for our own care and doing it all alone. When we turn inward, we are able to be with our thoughts and feelings, so that we can tune into what our body and soul are trying to communicate directly to us. We find our own answers and guidance as to what is needed most for our healing and growth. We can then experience the sense of aloneness differently, as we are now with ourselves in a way that is nurturing, loving, attentive, and real. Healing becomes true to who we are, and we are able to experience lasting, long-term changes and results.

Shame

KRISTINA: You may also feel blocked by feelings of shame and a sense of being defective or "broken" because of your trauma. The feelings of shame may also be reinforced by false beliefs that the trauma was somehow your fault. If not addressed, the shame becomes a wall that conceals the wounds and keeps the young parts of the self imprisoned in feelings of inadequacy or worthlessness. Allow yourself to name and address the feelings of shame and to see these feelings as a reaction to or a way of internalizing the trauma without getting mired in the beliefs that arise from these feelings.

Shame is different from guilt. As I worked through my trauma, I had guilt about things that I had done, but the shame was about who I was. I felt that I was bad because I was involved in something that felt wrong. Somehow, with shame, the negative feelings about what happened to me became transformed into negative feelings about myself. Being the victim of wrong actions and feeling traumatized morphed into negative feelings about who I was. I had to come to understand the shame and where it came from, so that I could separate out what was done to me from me as a person. Until we are able to let go of shame, we may feel unworthy to receive love—from ourselves or others—or to fully enter into a healing process and develop a solid sense of self.

It is important to gain the ability to hold the awareness that you have experienced bad things and that wrong has been done to you, and at the same time that you are still good, whole, pure, and lovable. You can feel shame *and* still know you are good and pure. Allow yourself to feel the shame, and at the same time honor the purity and goodness of your true nature. As you are able to hold both the feelings of shame and the awareness of also being good and pure, you can heal and release the shame and come into wholeness.

Taking on a false sense of responsibility for the abuse or trauma can reduce the feelings of helplessness and give you some sense of control, even if this illusion increases your sense of shame. It may also feel safer to feel shame rather than the intense feelings of rage, sadness, and fear that might otherwise overwhelm you. If my abusers were the ones that did wrong to me, and I was innocent, pure, and good, then what? If it wasn't my fault, what is the meaning of all of this? And if it involved abuse by family members, and I wasn't responsible for what happened, then it means the abuse happened at the hands of the people who were supposed to love me, take care of me, and keep me safe. Once brought into conscious awareness, this can often lead to feelings of distrust and of not being worthy of basic love. Feelings of betrayal or having not been protected by a parent or caregiver are sometimes the deepest and most painful wounds to heal.

As you face and come to understand that the childhood abuse, usually done by a trusted adult, had nothing to do with your own value, you are able to give the shame and guilt back to the abuser. You can literally, with your intent and imagination, gather the shame from your whole being and give it back to the person it belongs to. As you are able to give back the shame and be in your own energy, you can drop deeper into your own feelings and beliefs. You are then able to more fully work the wounds underneath the shame, layer by layer, and allow yourself to go to the depths of uncovering core beliefs and deep-seated emotions for ultimate healing. As you heal shame, you are able to shine in your inner light and be in alignment with your true gifts and wholeness. As you work with the parts that hold shame, they heal, and you are able to reach your greatest potential and follow your unique path.

Kristina
2009

I work so hard to heal the wounds inside, so the nightmares will go away. I get glimpses of the impact that healing could have on me, moving from who I was to who I could become, free from the heavy depression and pain I've been holding all these years. Light. Free. Capable. All that negative energy transmuted. Opening to my divinity and inner genius, to what I could be. And something sharp from my heart slips up my throat, up, up to my head, and taunts me with the thoughts, "Who are you? Something great? Someone special?" And I think to myself, if only for a moment, "Yes."

Acting out

HEATHER: Another potential block to healing is acting out. This frequently occurs if a young part is not identified consciously and has no other way to communicate the unresolved trauma. Those who have experienced early childhood physical or sexual abuse tend to unconsciously seek out abusive adult relationships. The young traumatized part is replaying what happened in an effort to bring the wounds into awareness and to heal and resolve what happened in the past. Unfortunately, the adult and young parts are then re-traumatized in a way that parallels what happened in childhood. This is why it is so important to be aware of the parts of yourself and to make sure that the witness self or adult self is making choices that are protective and healing for all aspects of the self.

At other times, certain parts may act out when there is a significant breakthrough in your healing process. This may be because they feel threatened by the changes and are trying to sabotage the process. Also, at times, certain parts may fear that they will no longer exist if you heal and work through the trauma. By engaging in inner dialogue, you can reassure those parts that their feelings and needs are being taken seriously and that the healing is for all of you (not just certain parts of you) to feel seen, heard, and held.

Another form of acting out occurs when the adult self does not take responsibility for the healing process and allows the young parts to take charge of the self. This can lead to impulsive, rebellious, or self-destructive behavior. It can also manifest in relationships in dependent behavior or in destructive acting out in a conscious or unconscious effort to be rescued by another person. This can take place in love relationships, in a therapy relationship, or in a relationship with a healing practitioner or spiritual teacher. If not worked consciously within yourself and in the relationship, this can result in emotional regression and acting out in the relationship in a way that both derails a healthy adult relationship with the other person and blocks an internal sense of adult responsibility and empowerment for healing the young parts of the self. The young parts may also then feel neglected, angry, resentful, and abandoned, while the other person in the relationship (unless an experienced therapist) may feel confused, unsettled, or threatened by the volatility of the relationship. It is important to take full responsibility for your own healing journey. This does not mean that you have to heal alone, but it is important to let go of the belief or longing that you can be healed by or through another without your own intentional and full participation. It is profoundly empowering to realize that right now, in the present moment as an adult, you can be the healing other that you have been seeking. The young wounded parts of yourself are then never alone or uncared for. The loving conscious parent is always there for them.

Other challenges in the healing process

Hitting times of crisis

KRISTINA: There were many times in the beginning phases of my healing journey when I encountered times of crisis. Even to this day, as I reflect back, it is still painful and hard to remember those times of intense difficulty. Some days had to be taken in each moment, step by step, until I made it through to the other side. There were times when I felt my psyche was literally splitting apart. It felt like so much was deconstructing internally, that there was little energy or mental organization left to manage my external life in the world. Those were horrific times, when I felt like I would never get through the darkness of the journey.

It was when I felt most hopeless that I resorted to all sorts of destructive coping in efforts to contain and control the inner turmoil. Trying to numb out the horror that was invading every facet of my life, I was desperate to shut it down, so that I could find even a sliver of space to be free from the pain. I resorted to drinking too much alcohol, cutting my body, not eating, and misusing my prescription medication. But this only slowed the healing process down and created more distraction and chaos in my life. It was helpful for a time to have an agreement in place with my therapist that I would work with my trauma in constructive ways and not give into my impulses by acting out. As I better understood what my system needed to feel safe, I was able to create a structure that could support me. This allowed me to work the deeper trauma in a way that was more contained, while allowing my parts to feel held, met, and understood. I learned when to open to the wounds and how to safely put things on hold. I became better at asking others for what I needed as well as showing up more for myself.

When you understand where the destructive impulses are coming from and what those parts of you need, you can more adequately hear their call for help. The parts of you that developed out of your trauma have different perspectives and ways of holding and working the experience of the abuse. It is necessary to get all of your parts "on the same page" regarding what coping behaviors are healthy and which ones no longer serve your whole system. When all of your parts are collaborative in the work, this creates balance and unity and provides space from the need to act out. This makes it possible for your adult self to step in and reparent the more traumatized young parts by taking care of their needs without being overtaken by their impulses.

Sometimes, you may need external structure to help create space between the impulse and the acting out. It can be helpful to have an agreement about what steps to take in times of crisis as well as what behaviors are not acceptable ways of coping. Having a contract on hand or as part of a "crisis" folder, so that agreements and next steps can be easily found and followed during times of inner turmoil, allows the process of dealing with a crisis to be clear, structured, and easier to manage. This can also feel healing for your parts who felt unsupported and left alone during times of chaos and abuse in the past. As the wounds come back to the surface, and you meet them in a loving way, with support, you are giving your young parts a powerful message that this time, it is different. As the pain surfaces, it is met with love, concern, and attention, so that it can be brought into healing.

For many of us, during the abuse, we learned to cope in any way that we could, because we were alone and didn't have other resources. Each time my therapist held me to a contract, the message was sent throughout my whole system that it was important and that it was safe to do this healing work. It also reinforced the message that I mattered, and that I was worth protecting, even if it was from myself. Also, through the safety, trust, and alliance formed in the therapeutic relationship, I was finally able to turn my anger away from being directed inward at myself and instead turn it towards the appropriate people (the abusers) outside myself. It is important that a contract for safety be seen as a support for healthy behavior and self-care and not as demeaning, because extra structure is needed during times of crisis. Maybe it is helpful to frame it for yourself that the crisis is simply a time when your system is dissolving or in chaos as it is breaking down and transforming from one state of being into a new state of being or existing. It is generally a good idea for the safety contract to be in writing and agreed upon by all of those involved in the healing process (such as you, your partner or a family member, and your therapist) as well as including all of your inner parts. You can briefly explain to your parts what behaviors are not okay and what steps to take for healthy alternatives.

Warning signs and triggers of a crisis could also be addressed, so that the contract becomes more proactive and supports decisions that feel empowering and is less about managing self-destructive impulses and behaviors. When you are in a reactive mode to your inner feelings and experience, you tend to replay the painful patterns of the past. When you are able to be proactive, you can create a new way of engaging with your trauma. You then have the safety contract in place so that you can make healthy choices when possible and know what steps to take when you feel overwhelmed and experience the impulse to cope in an unhealthy way. A safety contract can also be a place to have a list of "red flags" or behaviors that can alert you that you are starting to enter into crisis. Once aware of these precursors, you can take the steps needed to avoid going into a downward spiral.

Contracts can be signed and dated, so that behaviors can be monitored as an indicator of progress. Using a safety contract allowed me to do the deeper healing work, which then continued to decrease the intensity and complexity of the trauma coming up. As I continued to heal, I naturally grew out of needing the external structure of a contract and was more able to internalize and integrate healthy ways of being.

Suicidal thoughts or feelings

HEATHER: In the intensity of the deeper healing process or in times of crisis, feelings of wanting to die or to commit suicide may arise. As the pain from the past surfaces, you may forget that this pain comes and goes. The suffering can feel overwhelming, as if this has been and will always be your reality. At these times, suicide may feel like the only way out of the pain. It is important to be able to talk about these feelings with your therapist and to have that external support to help you remember that this intensity will come and go. The safety contract can be an important tool in these times in helping you to hold steady, to resist the impulse to harm yourself, and to trust that this dark night of the soul will eventually open you to the light of a new day of healing and hope.

KRISTINA: At times, when my trauma was up and activated most intensely, all I could do was curl up in a fetal position and wait for it to pass. With every inch of me physically and emotionally in pain, I felt myself as if I were in a hurricane of energy, and I sought refuge in the eye of the storm. When I tuned into myself and dropped into the sense of deeper presence—my soul self—I found complete stillness. From here, I would rest in the calm that was not transient and allow everything else to move around and through me. Sometimes, in the midst of a crisis, this might be all that you can do—to tune in, find the eye of the storm, and let the intensity pass.

HEATHER: The adult self may not be strong enough to manage these suicidal feelings or impulses, and you may have a part that takes over that is convinced that this is the only way out. At such times, you may need to have increased external support to hold you through the crisis. This may involve more intensive family support or care by friends or even hospitalization. While being in a psychiatric hospital can often be as stressful as it is therapeutic, it does give you external protection and a safe holding container for your parts until your adult self is more centered, stable, and able to be protective for your whole system.

KRISTINA: As you work through your healing process, you begin to absorb the fact that the bouts of pain come and go and eventually begin to release more and more. You comprehend that life is a journey and that change and movement are the truth of our existence. Nothing stays the same except the pure state of consciousness that runs through us and is always present within us. As you experience the truth of this more in your healing process, your witness self can remind the other parts of you that the feelings of pain and of being in crisis will pass, and that they are like the storminess on the surface of the sea. Deep beneath the winds and turbulent waves lies the calm and peacefulness of the ocean depths.

While there is much that you can do in your own process to heal, it is also important to set up a support system for yourself in this process. As you work through deeper issues, it is helpful to work with a therapist or healing other and to have increasing support through more contact with trusted family members, loving friends, or others who understand the healing journey. Many of us who have experienced trauma or abuse have difficulty with trust, and often there is a tendency to withdraw or avoid seeking help. In times of stress and vulnerability, isolation can sometimes feel safer than reaching out for assistance. But if you have the needed support in place for times of crisis or emotional overload, then accepting assistance and learning to trust can become an important part of the healing process.

Taking medication to support your body and mind and to calm extreme emotional states can be helpful in maintaining balance and overall functioning while healing deeper layers of trauma. It is important to keep in mind, however, that medication can help support, but cannot alone solve, fix, or heal the trauma. It is tempting to want a magic pill to "make it all better" and take the pain and angst away, but healing is a process. Fortunately, this process has the potential, if worked through, to significantly transform us on all levels.

Medication is helpful to use if you are not able to keep yourself balanced enough to work through the trauma. Medication can help stabilize your body if stress or heightened emotional states have triggered significant sleep disruptions or eating difficulties. These can be signs of biochemical imbalances in the body, and medication is helpful in stabilizing your system. However, for long term and permanent healing, it is necessary to work with the trauma and the emotional roots of the imbalance.

Working with addictions

HEATHER: If you have a trauma history, it is common to have issues with addiction. Using drugs or alcohol in excess may be a way to numb out the pain from the past or to keep intrusive memories at bay. Addictions can also be related to low self-esteem and distorted beliefs about yourself as a result of the trauma, which can then be used directly or indirectly as a form of self-destructive behavior. Using alcohol or drugs in an addictive way can block or derail your healing process. Addictions often begin as an attempt to cope with underlying intense emotions that don't feel safe to experience but end up exacerbating and intensifying these feelings and increasing your sense of being overwhelmed and out of control. They also take the adult self offline and allow younger parts to take charge of your system. When under the influence of drugs or alcohol, you are more vulnerable to being flooded by feelings from the past as well as more susceptible to re-engaging in unhealthy patterns that repeat past trauma.

Addictions and other unhealthy ways of coping need to be addressed in order to help you feel safe and to support the adult self in being in charge of your system. The addictive behavior must be dealt with before deeper emotional work can be done in a safe manner. This might be an ongoing process throughout the healing journey because crises tend to trigger setbacks, and it takes time to learn new healthy ways of coping and dealing with intense, underlying emotions and issues. It is an important part of the healing journey to be patient with yourself when you feel you have had a setback.

KRISTINA: It is helpful to take time to understand what role addiction plays for you. You may have developed protective parts that had good intentions to keep you from further hurt or pain, and that were using the only tools that they knew to keep the pain at bay. As you gain an understanding and control over your addictive behavior, you can then explain to all your parts what behaviors are harmful and what ones are healthy, which will support your healing process and overall sense of well-being. Addictions can also be used as distractions, to keep you occupied at a more surface level. But as you move away from temporary fixes or ways of numbing, you are able to go deeper into true healing and authentic living. When you tune into the pain instead of into avoidance, you are able to heal the deeper layers and be set free from the wounds of the past.

Sexual intimacy

KRISTINA: For years, I was in a marriage where there was little physical affection, and touch was mostly experienced through intercourse. Coming from sexual abuse which at times was experienced with emotional intimacy with the abuser, meant that sex in my marriage often felt like a re-enactment of my abuse. It literally seemed to unfold as my abuse did in childhood. I don't remember being physically nurtured outside of these abusive experiences. The same pattern played out for most of my marriage, until it was directly addressed and worked differently. The adult part of me knew that my husband needed sex, and as an adult willing partner, I wanted to give that to him, which I did. But for many years, it was at my own expense. Because we were not able to consciously work through what was needed in the marriage and how to navigate intimacy in a balanced and safe way, sexual intimacy became a distancing act instead of a way to bond more as a couple. I would often handle sex by dissociating during the act and by getting it over with as fast as possible. And then once it was over, I would often jump up and engage in self-destructive behavior, as an effort to shut down the emotional pain and turmoil as quickly as possible.

HEATHER: If you have a history of sexual abuse, this can become easily activated in your sexual relationship with a partner or lover. It can be very hard to separate out the feelings and beliefs that resulted from the wounds of the past with current adult experiences of sexual intimacy. It is important to hold yourself with compassion and be open with your partner about your feelings and needs so that you can experience sexual intimacy in a way that feels safe, loving, and connected. Otherwise the relationship will feel re-traumatizing to you.

Kristina
1999

It feels like my husband and I have been growing further and further apart. I don't know why, and it is all so confusing, because he matters so much to me. Last night, we were lying in bed, and just the way he kissed me, I felt his love, and it made me want to feel closer to him. I think we were both surprised, since most other times it feels so fraught to be sexually intimate with him. So we had sex, and it was wonderful. We were both passionate and present, and the act brought us together again. Afterwards, he was tenderly holding me, and I thought about the people from my past who had abused me and who had stolen from me what was meant to be so intimate for me and my husband to share. I thought about how I was robbed of my innocence and purity. And I cried.

My mind then opened up to a memory of me being in a dark closet where a man was grabbing my shirt, threatening me not to tell anyone. This is all I remember, so I don't even know what it was I was being silenced about. In the memory, I was terrified, but in that present moment, I was all mixed up in anger, sadness, and fear. I so wanted to get away from these feelings and the experience I was having. I turned to writing, giving my emotions a place to go, and it helped. Afterwards, exhausted, I just wanted to go to sleep. My husband was confused and sad as to why I shifted and wanted to withdraw from him. I got up to leave the room, and I told him that I was sorry that I couldn't be with him, but I was trying to work through what was coming up for me. I told him that I just felt so empty, I had nothing more to give tonight. Before we went to sleep, he told me how much he loved me, and I just laid there in silence, thinking to myself, "I wish I could believe that." I wondered how anyone could love me. I wondered if I could ever be loved.

Kristina: In my adult life, intimacy in relationships was by far the aspect that was most impacted by my abuse history. Physical and sexual intimacy with my husband was a big challenge for us to face. In its highest form, sexual intimacy between two people is a reflection and extension of their love for each other. Love is not about meeting one's own needs; it is rather about being able to tune in and love someone else in a way that meets their needs. In our current society, sexuality tends to be about using a physical act as a means of self-pleasure, which has nothing to do with loving another. When you add sexual abuse to an already skewed cultural context, for the one being objectified and used for someone else's pleasure, sexual intimacy feels like being abused again rather than an act that is about love or bringing two people closer together. If intimacy is not held and worked consciously, sexual difficulties will grow in a relationship and further divide a couple.

Sexual abuse memories are often held in the cells and body tissues. The body remembers the abuse. Certain kinds of physical stimulation and touch can bring back the abuse as if it were happening in the present moment. This type of encounter can also be charged with emotions and beliefs about oneself that can be confusing if the feelings and sensations are rising up from the past but feel as if they are the current reality. If not handled consciously, sexual intimacy can feel like a re-enactment or continuation of the pattern of abuse from the past. You then end up with feelings from the past that become projected onto your partner as if he or she were the abuser.

(Dealing in depth with the subject of sexual abuse and intimacy is beyond the scope of this book. You might find you need to refer to other books and materials that are written specifically for issues around sexual intimacy. Another consideration would be to work with a couples therapist who specializes in abuse and sexuality.)

Here are some things to consider when one is in a relationship and is dealing with sexual trauma from the past:

1. First and foremost, we must learn to connect with our own bodies and sexuality in a healthy way. How can we expect to connect in an appropriate, loving and intimate way with someone else, if we have

not learned and experienced how to do this with ourselves? If we are lost in our own sexual wounds, how is it possible for our partners to be clear about what we want or need? We must understand our bodies, how they work, and what feels good to us, not just physically but also emotionally, spiritually, and relationally. As you come into deep relationship with yourself first, you come to know your needs and wants, so that you can then communicate these to your partner.

2. If you have been sexually abused, the abuse was likely carried out in secrecy, and there are often deep feelings of shame, anger, terror, and sadness attached to it. These feelings are held in the body along with other fragmented memories. This means that, with any sexual interaction, there will be a reaction from the parts deep inside your system that are still frozen or stuck in the past trauma.

3. It is also important to know that if you experienced early sexual abuse in childhood, this may have been repressed or split off. Often in adolescence when going through puberty and feeling an increase in sexual feelings, these memories get reactivated and may come to the surface or get expressed through sexually acting out. If this was your experience in adolescence, hold that part of yourself with compassion. These trauma memories can also get retriggered later in adulthood through sexual experiences.

KRISTINA: My abuse memories were in large part unconscious until I became sexually active as an adult. It was then that not only images and scenes of the past began to arise, but intense emotions and body sensations became present as well. I was able to work through trauma as I came to better know my sexual needs and how to meet them in a healing way. I did this primarily through dialoguing with aspects of myself as well as with the body parts that held the trauma. It is important to work through any confusion or merging of past and present to help your parts and your adult self differentiate what happened in the past from the reality in the present moment. You can work through the wounds of sexual intimacy with your parts in the same way that you do with other stored feelings, emotions, and memories.

4. How open you are in your primary relationship will directly affect the quality and experience of your sex life. Open and honest communication between partners must be solid and in place. Make this your priority before entering into sexual intimacy with your partner. If there are communication issues inside the bedroom, it likely indicates that there are deeper issues that need to be addressed and dealt with, and there will certainly be problems around how to engage with each other sexually. If there is a lack of clear communication in the relationship around needs, wants, and desires, this must be remedied so that you are able to work with your partner to gain more intimacy in the relationship.
5. If you come from a history of neglect and sexual abuse, you might be in internal conflict around sexual intimacy. Part of you may want to be sexual as a way to be touched, noticed, and seen, while other aspects of you are experiencing the physical intimacy as a violation. It is important to bring all of these parts of yourself into communication and understanding so that all of your needs are met in a safe and conscious way.

KRISTINA: Healing happens when you take charge of your experience and bring what is needed to the situation instead of accommodating another person at your own expense. This often happens while in the "fawning" state of PTSD. Your relationship to sexual intimacy will evolve from woundedness and re-traumatization into healing and connection as your needs are heard, met, and understood. An internal message is sent throughout your system that you are of value and that how you experience sexual intimacy matters.

Here are some practical suggestions:
When you begin working on issues of sexual intimacy with your partner, take it slow. Begin with ways of touch that feel safe and are not re-triggering to any part of yourself. These might be activities such as hand-holding, back rubs while clothed, gentle hugging, or a kiss on the forehead. Stop and pull back if the activity feels in any way abusive, or you feel yourself becoming dissociative or submissive. It is important that you stay centered and in your power, so that

you can communicate about your experience and work it through as a couple. Make sure you have had clear communication with your partner about the process, and that there is an agreement that at any point things can be altered or stopped. It is crucial that both individuals have their own support plan ahead of time about ways to be clear and to honor their feelings and needs in order to stay connected with their process around whatever is coming up for them in the moment. The partner that hasn't experienced past abuse will still need a way to work with their own parts and possible reactions to the process that both partners are in together.

After being sexually intimate, take time for yourself to work through any wounds that were activated in the process, and do self-care around this. Then, it is important to come back as a couple and take time for both of you to talk through your feelings about how it went and what needs to be changed or altered going forward. It is important to keep in mind that, for a certain period of time when you are deep in your own healing process, there might need to be an agreement about other ways of being intimate (besides directly sexual) that can be used until the deeper wounds around the sexual abuse are healed and sexual engagement feels safe.

An example in how to heal past wounds around sexuality:

- Start by grounding yourself in stillness or in the center of your being. Make sure that you are fully in your body, and that you feel safe internally and externally to be in this process. (Please see the meditations in the appendix if you need ideas to help you be in a calm and peaceful state.)
- Guide all of your parts into safety, letting them know in a firm but gentle way that this is not a time for young parts to be out, that this time of sexual experiencing is for parts of appropriate age who want to be involved. You can tell parts that when it is time for younger aspects to come out, you will let them know. (Note: When being sexual with another person, this step is especially important.)
- As you start to explore being with yourself and your sexuality, go slowly, and stay aware of whether you are able to be fully in your body. If you are not, then step back and find your way to a safe place again.

- If at any point you feel you are being triggered with a body sensation, memory, or feeling, stop the exploration and bring yourself and any part that was activated back into safety.
- If it feels appropriate to end any sexual exploration, give yourself permission to do so, and tune more into the healing process. Allow time and privacy to make sure that you are centered before beginning the process of healing and self-care. (Note: When being sexual with another person, it is important to address how this will be handled ahead of time, so that both are clear about boundaries and are in agreement that there will be open communication throughout the process.)
- Take time for the healing process: If you felt triggered, allow that feeling or memory to come to meet you. Welcome it into your heart or to a place that feels safe inside and hold it gently, while surrounding it with healing light. Give that part or feeling the message that the abuse is over, and that everything is now okay. Ask what is needed, and take care of that part. End the process by doing some form of self-care that feels nurturing, loving, and grounding.

Some areas that you might want to address and explore more with your partner while you are working through your trauma:

- How to make love with each other without sexual activity
- How to initiate physical touch
- How to cultivate love, trust, and intimacy outside of direct sexual activity
- How to understand and become clear about the differences between physical intimacy that is about affection, and what types of physical intimacy are precursors to having sex
- What the specific triggers are that are connected with the past abuse

Sex opens us to all levels of vulnerability. It might trigger wounds around past trauma, early neglect, body image, displaced sexual energy from the family of origin, suppressed aggression, cultural influences around gender dominance, feelings of powerlessness, or other emotional and physical vulnerabilities. If you have not worked through enough of your healing to make conscious choices as to how to engage in sexuality in a healthy and truly loving way, then you are apt to continue to be in an unhealthy pattern that re-triggers, wounds, abuses, and fragments yourself. It is important to move beyond sex as a form of demand or obligation used for yourself or someone else's agenda, and step more into an authentic relationship by being honest and open about how you engage in sexual intimacy. In this way, you can mature past "you owe me" attitudes and "I'll do this out of obligation" ways of thinking.

KRISTINA: For the length of my twenty-four-year marriage, there was always some level of difficulty with the act of sex and connecting on a deeper level with my husband. Even long after I had done enough healing to feel I should be free of having any complications during sex, it was always assumed by both of us that our issues stemmed from my having come out of an extreme sexual abuse history. It never occurred to us that I might not be the sole cause of our continual problems with intimacy. It was not until after our divorce, and my being in a sexual context again with someone different, that I realized the error in taking on the entire responsibility for my past complexity with sex. When I was finally with someone who understood the sacredness of sexuality, and how to connect at a heart level first and then come from this place into love making, then I was able to comprehend that a sexual act between two people—being ultimately about love—goes both ways, no matter the extent of sexual abuse from the past.

It can be profoundly healing to be in new patterns of emotional closeness and sexual intimacy that feel safe and loving rather than intrusive and abusive. Sexuality can then become a means to deepen your intimacy with another, align with your true self and sense of empowerment, and expand your consciousness. Deepening into this profound intimacy with yourself and another mirrors our experience of cosmic consciousness or divine love. Sexuality can be a path to spiritual awakening. When used as one of the highest forms of love, it is a profound and sacred gift.

(See the ceremony section for a way to do a sacred cleansing, healing water ceremony to support you in healing and reclaiming your body and sexuality.)

Honoring the process

HEATHER: As blocks or obstacles come up in your healing process, hold them all with compassion. Allow yourself to stay centered in your witness self who can hold space for all of the parts of yourself. This is a journey that takes time. Remember that you may not be able to see the destination while you are in the process. Allow yourself to keep moving forward, trusting that the journey will unfold as it needs to and that it will lead you to where you ultimately need to be going. Learning to live in the present moment, without anticipating what the future will be, allows you to be flexible and open, so that you can bend with the wind in the storms of life. Again, honor the ebb and flow of the healing process. Remember that healing occurs in the liminal space and the vulnerable "in between" experiences of letting go of the past sense of self and old ways of coping and being in the uncertainty, fragility, and turbulence of transition and transformation. Trust that as you stay with the process, you will be guided and carried by the currents of change to the shores of a new way of being and a stronger and more whole sense of self.

Opening more fully to heal

Healing is an act of courage

> *Courage is the willingness*
> *to be afraid and to act anyway.*
> —Stewart Emery

There comes a time, maybe multiple times, when you have to choose to face your fears, and turn inward to finally meet the pain within. It takes courage to face your wounds from the past. Many people stay trapped in patterns of the past and held within programmed thoughts, feelings, and beliefs from early wounds rather than face the uncertainty of stepping into the healing process. To heal involves letting go of a sense of safety that has been created in the known and be willing to jump into the void of uncharted territory. Many people choose to stay with familiar patterns even if it means staying mired in suffering, rather than facing their fear and taking the steps needed to open to change. Healing occurs when you decide to turn inward and open up what has been locked inside the recesses of your body and psyche. It can be frightening and painful at times, to open old wounds, but it is the path to healing and finally reclaiming the treasure of your true self.

Healing means being vulnerable and deciding that you are worth taking the risk to heal and to find your true self. It is an act of stepping out in trust and hope, even when you are experiencing the deepest feelings of fear and despair. And it means being willing to let go of suffering and open to love, even when you feel most broken and unlovable. As you honor that path of healing, you are then able to regain a sense of self-love and learn the meaning of healthy relationships. You let go of false notions of love that are about abuse, dependency, self-sacrifice, or loss of self, and you recover the ability to love in truth, honoring who you are as you also see others for the uniqueness of who they are.

KRISTINA: For the most part, I have been able to live with an open heart, as I believe that this is the natural and pure state of all beings. If we rest in our authentic state and flow with our natural energy current, we live from an effortless place of love and compassion. At some point, I realized there was another side to love, and that was courage. I began to see that I often acted out of what I thought was love, but in reality, it lacked courage. So instead of coming from a true heart space, it was really coming from a type of fear, which was avoidance. I needed to gain clarity on what love really meant to me, and what it did not. I thought love meant no conflict or contention. I thought love was when I put other people's needs and wants before my own. I started to learn that I had to develop more courage within myself so that I could more fully love. First, I had to start breaking down the illusions that kept me safe. I then had to really find my own truth, coming from my heart space, not what my mind was telling me. I had to learn where my motivation was coming from—was it really love, or was it obligation or fear? I began to see that I couldn't unconditionally love others until I had learned to do that for myself. I learned that, sometimes, conflict and confrontation were truly acts of love. I found that if I followed the voice that came from the deep stillness inside, it was always guiding me to what the most loving act would be, for me and others. By developing the courage to then act from this loving guidance, I was able to hold the wholeness of my heart.

> *Owning our story can be hard but not nearly as difficult as spending our lives running from it. Embracing our vulnerabilities is risky but not nearly as dangerous as giving up on love and belonging and joy—the experiences that make us the most vulnerable. Only when we are brave enough to explore the darkness will we discover the infinite power of our light.* —Brene Brown

HEATHER: As we step into the unknown, it is helpful to have a map or model for this process. This ancient archetypal myth of Inanna, Queen of Heaven and Earth, gives us a guide for how we can have the courage to step into this healing journey:

From the Great Above, she opened her ear to the Great Below.
From the Great Above, the goddess opened her ear to the Great Below.
From the Great Above, Inanna opened her ear to the Great Below.[5]

In this hypnotic way, the story of Inanna's descent into her journey begins. She steps away from her familiar world of power and privilege and decides to go inward into the underworld (the subconscious realm) to reclaim the aspects of herself that are buried there. Inanna senses that something is missing in her life, and she feels that deep call to go inward, to find what has been lost. This is the story of the journey to reclaim what has been suppressed or repressed.

Inanna was the primary deity in ancient Sumer (now modern Iraq) as far back as 3000 B.C.E. Her story was written on clay tablets around 2000 B.C.E. and is one of our most ancient recorded myths. Inanna was the daughter of the Moon God and sister of the Sun God. She was "Queen of Heaven and Earth." In this story, Inanna hears the "call of the Great Below" and sets out on a journey to meet with her dark sister, Ereshkigal, queen of the underworld. Inanna's sister Ereshkigal represents the part of Inanna that had been split off

---

5 Wolkstein and Kramer, *Queen of Heaven and Earth*, 1983, p. 52

and buried beneath the surface of the conscious realm. In earlier stories, we learn that Ereshkigal was raped, abused, and banished into the underworld. Inanna sets out to be reunited with her sister (and this lost part of herself). Before she sets out for the journey to the Great Below, she asks her close friend, Ninshubur, to go with her and to stay and watch for her return from the underworld and to seek help for her if she does not come back.

Inanna follows this inner call to go "below," and steps into the unknown. She knows the risks of journeying into the underworld, but she also knows that she needs to do this. As she arrives at the gate to this world of buried emotions and memories, she has her companion, Ninshubur, hold the thread of connection with her as she descends. As Inanna journeys down, deeper and deeper into this unconscious realm, her defenses and coping mechanisms, the ways in which she felt in control in the world, are one by one stripped away from her. She finally arrives in front of her sister, Ereshkigal, naked and unadorned. Ereshkigal, having held the pain of the trauma from the past and being jealous of Inanna (Inanna being the part of the self that has been successful in the world), strikes out at Inanna with rage and envy and kills her.

> *Ereshkigal fastened on Inanna the eye of death.*
> *She spoke against her the word of wrath.*
> *She uttered against her the cry of guilt.*
> *She struck her...*[6]

Having hoped to heal the rift with this lost part of herself, instead Inanna is overcome and undone. She lies dead for three days in the underworld.

> *Inanna was turned into a corpse,*
> *A piece of rotting meat,*
> *And was hung from a hook on the wall.*[7]

---

[6] Wolkstein and Kramer, *Queen of Heaven and Earth*, 1983, p. 60
[7] Wolkstein and Kramer, *Queen of Heaven and Earth*, 1983, p. 60

What a vivid image this is for how it can feel to go into the depths of our pain and wounds from the past.

When Inanna does not return from the underworld, Ninshubur seeks help for her. She finally finds aid from Enki, the god of wisdom. He sends two healing earth creatures who are able to slip unnoticed into the underworld and go to find Inanna and Ereshkigal. They discover the body of Inanna and find Ereshkigal writhing in pain. They are able to see the agony that this repressed part is in, and they hold Ereshkigal in her trauma and allow her to cry and wail and release her pain. With empathy and compassion, they let her know that she is seen and heard. Over and over again, they reflect back her distress and are present with her in her suffering.

Ereshkigal was moaning: "Oh! Oh! My inside."
They moaned: "Oh! Oh! Your inside."
She moaned: "Ohhh! Oh! My outside!"
They moaned: "Ohhh! Oh! Your outside!"
She groaned: "Oh! Oh! My belly!"
They groaned: "Oh! Oh! Your belly!" [8]

On and on these healing beings continue, until finally Ereshkigal begins to calm down. Having felt seen and heard and healed by their empathic mirroring, Ereshkigal, in gratitude, wants to gift them with some reward. The earth creatures refuse her offers of bountiful gifts and ask only for the corpse of Inanna. Given the corpse, the earth creatures revive Inanna with the bread and water of life and help her to ascend back to the upper world. Inanna returns to her home, but she is now transformed and disoriented by this experience and has to take time to integrate her new sense of self.

This is a profound story about transformation and the cycle of life, death, and rebirth that occurs when you choose the path of descent and return that are part of the healing process. Inanna teaches us how to hear the call of the "Great Below" and how to embark on this journey that leads us deep into what is buried within us and through times of darkness in order to heal and reclaim

---

[8] Wolkstein and Kramer, *Queen of Heaven and Earth*, 1983, p. 63

our wholeness and then bring us back again into the light, transformed and renewed. She reminds us that we are not alone in the journey, that we need the support of our friends and those who care for us and who will hold the thread as we descend and return. Inanna teaches us that our initiation experiences often take us to unexpected places and transform us in ways that we could not have anticipated. She also shows us that the cycles of dark and light, sadness and joy, death and rebirth are all intrinsic aspects of who we are and of the mystery of life.

Kristina
2003

> *I want to stop reacting to impulses that arise in me from my external environment. I want to take control of myself and my behavior. I want to heal and stop re-injuring myself. I'm at a turning point, and I'm ready to take care of my unfinished past. I want to stop running away from what haunts me and create something different. I want to decide how I want my story to be written. I choose to be the author of my own fate. I know what I am facing will be hard, and there might be times when I want to run and block the pain. But it is time to face it, time to walk through it. It is time to heal. It's time to change the dance that I've been doing and create a new one. This time, I will lead. If I keep running, it will keep chasing me. If I choose to face it, it will face me, and we will find a way to be together, to heal and grow. And I will give my story a new beginning, and it will end with the most wonderful dance, because it will be my own. And I will move with grace until all the chains fall off of me. My dance will set me free—free to feel, free to love, free to be me.*

The importance of being seen, heard, and having a voice

KRISTINA: Sharing what happened to me, breaking the silence, was a crucial part of my healing process. My suffering, and my being silent about it, was a wound that needed a voice to be heard, so that it could heal. I took back my power the day that I gave voice to my pain. Prior to this, I had lived my whole life in silence about what I had been through, as the abuse and pain I endured were ignored. To the outside world, it didn't happen. The external reality that I was living in was a stark contrast to the experience that I held inside, and so I had to find creative ways to cope and stay sane. One way that I survived was to believe and go along with my abusers' denial and commands for silence and to pretend that the abuse never happened. If no one ever talked about it, it wasn't real. But this created a split between my inner and outer experience.

When I was finally able to give expression to my inner truth, it corrected this incongruence in myself which bridged the gap between the differing realities. This happened, not because my abusers came forward, confessed, and said that my experiences were true, but because, when I gave voice to what had been unspoken and unacknowledged, it created an authentic opening for others to be there for me, to hold loving space, and to hear me and believe me. And this mirroring back allowed me the security to fully break free from the illusions and distorted reality of my abusers and to be able to stand firmly in the power of my truth. It started to disintegrate the deceptive lies that had been created and enforced as the fundamental core of who I believed myself to be.

Giving my abuse expression through words and art was a way to send a strong message to my wounded parts that what happened to me was not okay, and that I was entitled to much more than a life of silence. I was worth being able to speak my truth about what happened to me, and that it was not right. And even though I found and expressed my true voice many years after the abuse had happened, speaking was nonetheless an important part of my recovery. When the abuse happened to me in my childhood, I was alone and made to keep the horrors secret and inside myself. Those secrets became deep seated and then sealed and shut tight. So part of my healing took place when I took back the power that was ripped from me and decided for myself what I wanted to keep quiet about and what I wanted to tell. I was no longer controlled by the threats that had been used to keep me silent in order to protect my abusers at my expense.

The abuse occurred in secret, when I was isolated and alone, and so for my healing, it was critical for me to not be alone when I shared what happened to me. It was terrifying for me to be so vulnerable with another human being, and it took a long time for me to feel safe enough with someone to start opening up the nightmare. But, as I began to share my story with people who I felt I was able to trust, I could feel the trauma that I had endured and carried alone for so long begin to melt away. It was the beginning of the process of being able to heal, purge, and finally let go.

HEATHER: Telling your story gives you a chance to go back into the past, and in a way, do it differently. Part of what causes the trauma to be mired in your body and psyche is the experience of helplessness in the face of the abuse, the lack of any external support, and not being able to take any action to protect yourself or to tell your truth. Going back into the wounding experience, sharing what happened, and feeling held, heard, and validated helps to empower you and finally give you a sense of support and the ability to take action on your own behalf. In the past, the abuse left you feeling silenced, alone, and cut off from the support of others; now you can feel held in a caring relationship, heard and supported as you begin to heal. You learn, through being vulnerable and heard in a safe relationship, that the shame you have been holding was never yours to begin with, and this gives you the option to give it back (emotionally and energetically) to the rightful owner. Breaking the silence and having loving support releases you from the bonds of shame and lifts the heavy burden of keeping secrets. When you find your voice to speak what had been silenced, you reclaim the power that was lost—often lost multiple times with recurring trauma. You demand to be authentically seen in your truth. You step out from the dark shadows into the light, and claim your birthright by honoring your deepest feelings and needs.

Kristina
2005

The sadness that has been pounding away at my heart for the past two days melted away through my tears today. In my session with my therapist, I got to this pain that seemed like it was buried so deep, it was as if I was scraping it out of my soul. And then I was able to send it out of my body through my voice and tears. When I found my voice, it felt so powerful, because for a very long time, I have been without one. I talked the pain right out of me, one experience at a time. And I felt it freely flow and release, one tear at a time. There is so much pain in the memories of my abuse. It feels as if every cell in my body holds part of the story. And today, I physically felt my story being told and heard. My words landed on ears that could hear and eyes that could actually see my pain. I wasn't left alone with my wounds, and I felt this weight lift off of me, right off my chest, a weight that was full of confusion, frustration, guilt, and shame. This time, someone came directly to me and into my heart to help me.

It might be the case that, at times, you do not have someone outside of you to hear and see you. It is important during these phases that you know how to show up for yourself, and how to tune into the wound and pay attention. This inner listening and mirroring of your true self back to your wounds is also very important and can be profoundly healing, even if you have found someone with whom you can safely share your story.

Kristina
2013

I can't escape the sadness. Sometimes I catch a breath, which gives me a sense that maybe the pain is gone, but then, in an instant, it returns, feeling stronger than the last go around. My husband brushes by, in from work and off to pick up the kids. He is good and kind and also vacant to me. The pain increases. I turn to God but feel nothing. I know God could take this from me. Still nothing. I turn inward and feel despair rising, starting to engulf me. I cannot form words to articulate the suffering. I sit in silence as it races inside of me. I keep my body motionless; it is painful to move, to feel alive. I go to take a bath in the hopes that it will bring some comfort, a bit of relief.

I feel such a need to be heard, for the pain to be acknowledged. I want to scream. I want to be seen. Still, I am alone, the bath water growing cold around me. I turn inward and surrender to the pain. Arms wide open, I embrace it. "I am here. I have not left you. I see you. I feel you." I let the pain come and go, release and wash over me. Again and again comes the tide of pain, and with each recession, I feel the unmoving peace that remains. It is all here, the pain ... the peace. It is all the gift. It is all of me, the cleansing, purging, and healing. I am always here, the deepest part of me. I never left. I just lost my way and forgot. But now, I remember. I am enough for me.

Managing the stormy times in the healing journey

HEATHER: It is important to know that there are times in the healing process when it all feels too dark, too overwhelming or too endless. Know that this is part of the process and that the inner storms are helping your psyche and body to release the pain and trauma of the past. In these times, it is critical to have a therapist or trusted other who can remind you that these storms will pass and that you are moving towards healing and wholeness. The healing journey is like crossing an ocean in a sailboat. At times, you see into the distance and are filled with wonder at the ways in which your senses, memories and emotions are opening up in more expansive ways. Then, there are times when a storm sets in at night and you feel lost in the wind and waves of tumult, confusion and emotion. Remember, the storm will pass and the sunrise will return even after the darkest and longest of nights. Remember also, that at times, you will feel confident in your direction, knowing that the shore of your healing and empowerment lies ahead of you and are your destination. At other times, you will feel as if you are a tiny boat, lost at sea, with no bearings or sense of direction or assurance of your safe arrival on the other shore. Your personality self may feel overwhelmed with emotion and despair. But remember that your soul self knows the way and that there are currents and energies larger than yourself holding your boat and guiding you to the other shore. The healing process is a journey of discovery, of releasing, remembering, expanding and returning to wholeness. It is arduous and messy but also beautiful, profound and transformational. Honor all that you feel and honor the sacredness of your journey and hold yourself in compassion during the stormy times.

KRISTINA: When the trauma started coming back to me through nightmares, flashbacks, depression, triggers, and body sensations, I struggled to hang onto any thread of normalcy in my life. It felt as though reality, as I had known it, had been suddenly pulled out from under me, or as if an inner force had erupted, wrapped itself tightly around my body, and then pulled away rapidly, leaving me spinning like a destructive tornado. I tried to make sense of the involuntary information that was coming up and flooding me in efforts to feel some type of control over what was happening. I was desperate for a way to understand the images, sensations, and feelings that came rushing through me, especially when I felt I had no control as to when and how they so intensely rose up within me.

Kristina
2000

Feelings that breed in thick flowing blood

I stare at the clean white paper.
Trying to force my thoughts to connect,
But the stupor buckles in, letting my feelings overpower them.
I am filled with the deep feelings of my soul,
The soul that knows and remembers …

The feelings are racing,
Racing inside …
Running faster to escape being found.
Emotions running frantic
Colliding under my skin …
Faster,
Faster.

Nowhere to hide,
Nowhere to go.
Only to bind to thick flowing blood.
My blood …
Flowing heavy and hot,
Giving my feelings life and energy.

My mind tries to catch a thought,
To make sense of the madness inside.
But my feelings run strong
Like a forceful wind against an old oak tree ...
Whipping around out of control.

So my mind tries to catch a feeling
To make sense of the madness inside.
But the feelings run faster and faster,
Too slippery to be caught,
Too afraid to be found.

And the powerful array of feelings
Continues to explode
Inside my body.
Feelings contained within, only by a thin layer of skin.

My mind is numb with exhaustion
Allowing the feelings to run their course.
I sit in silence, watching the clean, white snow outside my window,
Drifting,
  Falling,
    Submitting to the will of the gentle wind.
The same wind that blows against the old oak tree.

KRISTINA: It became helpful to give a voice to the wordless phenomena and turbulence within me and to provide a structure wherein emotions, images, and body sensations could come up to be heard, seen, and healed. This helped to create a bridge between the gaps of time and forgotten information about the trauma that had happened to me at an early age (including how those memories and wounds were encoded) and how the memories and feelings were coming up in the present, so that my system as a whole could heal. I found that giving a voice, whenever possible, to the silenced feelings and sensations tended to give life to what had stayed quietly buried for years deep inside my unconscious and in my cellular memory. It was amazing to find that the knowledge held within this framework led to more associations with fragments of other dreams, memories, triggers, and flashbacks. And by connecting the dots, a more whole and complete story would begin to form. As the memories were finally able to be gathered together with all of the parts, thoughts, feelings, images, sensations, and beliefs, I began to feel a stronger integration of the self. The flashbacks and nightmares became less frequent, the depression lifted, and I could then experience life more fully in my present reality. Most of all, I began to feel integrated and whole as the pieces of myself were being woven back together again.

Kristina
2000

Memories are coming back in pieces; nothing is making sense. I watch the memories unfold like I am watching a black and white movie about a little girl that isn't me, and yet I am left with feelings of disgust, filth, and fear. For two weeks, after having experienced fragmented memories, I'm having nightmares and night sweats almost every night, often multiple times a night.

Kristina
2000

I was taking a bath as I typically like to do to calm my nerves. This time, I had a candle nearby as the electricity kept shutting off and coming back on again. As I looked at the candle, I had a flashback. I am no longer looking at a single candle with a single flame. I see an iron candle stand, holding five lit candles. After my bath, while in bed, my husband comes in holding a candle as the electricity is still out. He crawls into bed and gently blows the candle out. I am filled with terror. Frozen, I lie silent.

Kristina
2000

I have spent a good deal of time trying to accept that there are young places inside myself that exist as if they were real and alive, with their own thoughts, feelings, and memories. And maybe there are not just young people, but teenagers and even adults as well. I'm trying hard to understand what happens to the brain and my whole body when it experiences trauma, and how my cells can hold my stories too. How can this be? Is this why my skin crawls, and I feel I am being violated when my husband touches me in a certain way, even though he has never done anything to hurt me? Is my body talking to me, trying to tell me something, warn me? My therapist encourages me to be open and honor what is, and what is happening on the inside. And that maybe I am more than what I outwardly present. It sounds strange and a bit frightening to me; however, there is something inviting, almost liberating about this idea.

KRISTINA: It took me a while to realize that the experiences I was having weren't going to just go away. There was no way around it, I had to go straight through it. I began to tune in, to pay attention, to gather the pieces and respect the process. Then, true healing began to happen. I started to work with my body and the sensations I was having as if I was dealing with an aspect of myself. With the idea that woundedness was trapped at the physical level, I began to work with it directly to heal and release it from my body. Sometimes, my body would communicate back to me through feelings and other sensations. If there were no words or parts that came up while communicating with my body, I would offer another way for the emotion or sensation to heal and then release. However, if it felt like I was working with an aspect of myself, I would find a way to communicate with the part.

Remember as you embark on this process you might go through times when you doubt the feelings and memories that are emerging are accurate. You may wish that you could return to the denial or repression that you experienced before. You may often feel as if you are going crazy or "making it all up." This is part of the process and is a natural resistance to diving into the pain and memories from the past. The memories were too overwhelming to experience earlier in your life, and you will need to remind parts of yourself that it is safe now to open up to these thoughts and feelings.

HEATHER: As these trauma memories emerge, it is important not only to name them and allow them to come fully into your consciousness, but it is also healing to allow yourself to feel empowered to take actions that feel nurturing and supportive of yourself. Trauma becomes encoded in the body and buried in the psyche when there was no possibility for action at the time or adequate healing afterwards. Honor the profound courage that it takes to allow these memories to surface, then do a healing ceremony or take some action to nurture yourself, to help young parts feel supported and to enable further integration of the healing process. It can also be profoundly healing to share your story and memories with someone that you trust, who can hold space for you and hear you and support you in this process.

As much as it can feel unsettling and even frightening when these memories, feelings, and sensations begin to rise up from the past, it is also an indication from your deepest self that it is now safe for you to regain connection with what happened to you. It is time to heal. Regaining the understanding of the trauma and what you experienced in the past is likely to be a piecemeal process with fragments of memories, nightmares, body sensations, and feelings all giving clues to what happened, instead of a direct full memory. Hold this process with compassion and realize that you are gradually weaving together a tapestry that will take time before you have a sense of the larger picture or story of what occurred.

When you endure intense trauma, your system learns to go numb and to split off the feelings so that you are not paralyzed and incapacitated by the pain. You may begin to live in survival mode with a reduced range of emotions and may even have more restricted bodily sensations of pleasure or pain. Both an absence or restricted range of feelings as well as times of being flooded by feelings that seem to arise out of nowhere are indications of past trauma that has been repressed or fragmented. As you engage in your healing process, the numbing begins to thaw, and feelings that seem disconnected from what is going on in the present and even from any memory of the past may rise up more frequently. It can feel frightening to suddenly feel overwhelmed by intense anger, sadness, or terror for seemingly no reason. Trust that your psyche is trying to help you to reconnect with these feelings from the past in order to allow you to heal and release them. Give yourself permission to honor these feelings and to engage them in a dialogue to see if you can trace them back to their roots. At times, you may not be able to gain any insight about their source or what experiences in the past they are connected to. It is still important to allow the feelings to flow through you. When you feel flooded with an intense emotion, it is usually an indication of a trauma trigger. Do not act on the emotion or attach it to your current reality. Let the feelings, like a tidal wave, come and then move on. Focus on self-care and stay afloat in the moment, knowing that the intensity will pass. At a later time, from a calm and centered place, you can explore more of what the messages and meanings of these feelings may be for you.

Kristina
2007

At times, the men from the group would come for my sister and me. It was usually at night. My parents never stopped them. They lay still in their beds as we were lifted out of our own and taken swiftly down the corridor through the house. When we passed by my parents' door, I would let out an inner scream for help, but no noise would rise past my throat. They took us through the kitchen, out the back door, silently slipping us into the back seat of the waiting car. There was no fight. No screaming or crying. Everyone knew their role to play, even me, at the tender age of four. I don't know why I never yelled out for my mom or dad to save me. Maybe I was too frightened. Maybe I was too well trained. Maybe I knew they wouldn't come to help us.

Terrified and unprotected, we were abused in the darkness of the night by the darkness of men's souls. We experienced abuse that was unspeakable, unbelievable, and almost unendurable. We were stripped of virtue, purity, and innocence, and of everything we knew to be good and whole. Then, we were brought back to a shell of a home inside the shell of our beings. We were dropped off in the kitchen where we had passed through just hours before, only now returning in the light of the morning sun.

In those moments after we were returned, with my sister by my side and my mother in front of me, I felt as if I was completely alone. As my mother spoke to us, her eyes gazed past me. I was invisible to her. The secrets inside of me took on their own life forms; having nowhere to go, they were racing through my body, enclosed within the walls of my skin. Inside I was yelling at her, crying, shaking for her to notice me ... hold me ... want me. Yet I only received her blank stare and felt her absent heart. And the lesson over and over again to me was that I was nonexistent in my mother's world. I was worthless to her. There was no belonging. No maternal bond. No yearning. No love. I was watching and learning how to stop myself from feeling, wanting, and needing anything from her. Each time, I suffered an emotional death, within arm's reach of the vessel that carried me and brought me into this world, only to be deserted and left alone in her presence, knowing that she would not fight for me and feeling that she didn't care or want me. As I stood before her, I was immovable. The pain drained out of my heart into every limb and cell. Only my eyes stayed fixated on the woman who was silently teaching me how to merely survive.

KRISTINA: For years, I had access to only a limited range of emotions, and within that range, I had only a small degree of variation. As I became sexually active, the range became even more narrow. When I gave birth to my first child, I felt myself growing numb and even more cut off from all emotion and feeling. I began to feel as though I were hollow inside, as if I were a "Tin Man" with no heart at all.

Kristina
2001
Safe and Raw Inside

Numbness is a place I go deep within my soul.
I retreat from all feeling,
To a hollow place inside.

Too much, too heavy,
I must run,
I must hide.

Safe.
I am safe.
Numb.
I am numb from all feeling.

I stay protected inside the walls of my heart,
from the feelings I hold inside.
Safe from the pain whose roots grow strong and deep within me.

KRISTINA: Through healing the wounds, I had to claim, bring back, and integrate aspects of the trauma that had been splintered off. This included the intense emotions that were stored and trapped deep in my body and psyche. The doorway out of the trauma states of fight, flight, freeze, or fawning is through feeling. When we connect again to trapped emotions, we emerge from numbness and begin to connect the pieces together again. This allows the feelings to have movement and flow, giving us the ability to release from the trauma loop and let go. If we are able to put words, sensations, beliefs, and thoughts with the emotions, we integrate deep-seated pain and bring it all into healing.

HEATHER: As you work through the memories and feelings of the past trauma, you no longer unconsciously and instinctively respond to stress with the old coping mechanisms. This frees you up to develop new and more healthy patterns in your life and develop a more extensive and nuanced range of coping skills and ways of managing stress. As you no longer need the protective methods such as fight, flight, freeze, and fawning that were crucial to your survival at the time of the trauma, you are able to feel more safe in your body and in your life.

The ebb and flow of the healing journey

As you let go of the old ways of coping, you begin to allow the fear and feelings related to the trauma to emerge. In the beginning, when you are connecting back to the trauma and no longer shielding it with these protective barriers, you can feel overwhelmed with the emotions that rise up that you have kept at bay for years. It might feel as if someone has opened a floodgate, and the waters of emotion are overtaking you and threatening to drown you. It is important to honor that letting go of the old ways of coping will activate inner fear and intense feelings of vulnerability. However, if you are proactive, and take the time to work with the feelings and wounds that are coming up to heal, you can better hold a steady balance as the body and psyche heal, release the pain, and begin to let go of the past. Then, you also begin to feel these tender moments of transformation and the glimpses of the true self that is emerging.

Again, honor the ebb and flow of the healing process. These moments of healing and transformation are also interspersed with times of feeling overwhelmed and alone. You have left behind the familiar ways of coping and are traveling through uncharted territory. And at times, you may feel that the process is too long and hard. Hold all of this with compassion and know that other travelers have been in the mystery and uncertainty of this journey before you.

Kristina
2010

Writing about the feelings, ideas, and thoughts that lie so heavily in my heart: When will the sadness end? What if there is too much inside? I feel so far from any light. It hurts to breathe and to just be alive. My bones hurt. My skin hurts. How do I move this hurt, this sadness? I've tried everything I know how to do, every act to self-soothe, and to be kind to my inner self. But the pain doesn't budge. Other people cannot lift it, and it's too difficult to connect or to move outside of myself. And God is too slow and has chosen not to help ease the pain of my heart. I'm tired, so tired. I am sad, so full of sadness. I beg the tears to come, wash over me, to cleanse me. If this sadness could talk, if my heart could speak, what would it say? If I allowed it to speak and did not hush it up, what would it whisper to me? "Alone. I am suffering alone. The sadness is too big for one little person. Why does no one come? My mother and father see me in pain and do not help me. My pain, it has no words. Sometimes, it can't explain itself. It is just sadness. There is no love, no sense of being wanted. I don't remember being held or helped or cared about." I want to put it all in a black box. Bury it deep in the earth, so I can't see it or feel it anymore. And if I can't separate it from me, then bury me down with it. Bury me down deep, deep, deep, where no one will find us, where it stays dark forever. There, where I can finally close my eyes, and they don't open anymore.

HEATHER: It is also important in these times to have an ally, either a therapist, healer, or friend that you can turn to for support and for the reminder that this time of intensity will not last forever. In the moment, it can feel as if the trauma, fear, sadness, and sense of being overwhelmed are all that has ever been, and all that will ever be. It is important to have a "Ninshubar," one who can hold the thread for you as you journey through this underworld, to remind you that this is a process of healing and that you will return to the light again, stronger, transformed, and more whole. It is also important to strengthen the adult witness self in you who can be the guide and support to the young parts who will often feel overwhelmed and who might not have the strength or capacity to understand the full meaning or purpose of this journey.

Kristina
2010

Sitting cross legged on my bathroom floor, I look squarely into the wall mirror. Me. I look directly into my own eyes, searching for something that lives and breathes deeper inside. I look past the blue irises, falling into the blackness of the pupils. Grief, shame, sadness, I feel them moving inside. I'm trying to find the pieces and put them together and make sense of why these feelings have come up again inside of me. I am trying to remember something that happened so long ago, years and years ago. Why does this come up again for me now? Why do I feel it as though it was yesterday?

Touching the raw sadness, time stands still, and I fall into the hurt and betrayal, into the depths of my soul. There she is, the hurting child, the same as she was years ago, in this present moment. She's been waiting to be found, to be lifted up, held, and loved through the pain, loneliness, and shame. I cave into myself, arms curled up to my chest, as I fall over onto the hard, cold floor, letting the burning emotions move up and through me ... raw burning flesh singed with the blistering pain of anger, shame, and a need to be loved and wanted. Holding onto the child inside, I hold space for the existence of her, all of her. And so she is heard, validated, appreciated, honored, and loved. She so needs to feel loved.

KRISTINA: As you heal the layers of trauma and wounds, you might feel as though you need to "cocoon up," turn inward to find safety and rest, while your system heals and rebalances. Find the space to honor the process, as your body and psyche reconfigures and transforms. Once the healing is complete, your system will "level up," and you will begin again with the next layer. It is a process as the wounds heal, and the layers release, as you continue to come back again to the ever-present energy of peace and love that is within you.

Healing on all levels: emotional, physical, mental, and spiritual

Healing at the emotional level

Throughout the book, we address healing at the emotional level and the importance of honoring and reclaiming all of your feelings, those that are conscious and unconscious. In this section, we will address more in depth how to also heal at the physical, mental, and spiritual levels.

Healing at the physical level

HEATHER: After years of doing therapy with people with complex PTSD, I realized that traditional therapy was not healing the symptoms of trauma at a deeper level. While it is healing to be able to talk through what was experienced and to feel seen and heard and held in that process, it does not fully release the effects of trauma on a physical level. It is important for the body to heal as well as the mind and heart. For so many, trauma occurred in the context of feeling trapped, held down, immobilized, or not being able to take any action to escape or to defend the self. This can contribute to an ongoing experience in the body of being in some way frozen in the traumatized state. The body continues to hold the memories of what happened even if the conscious mind has no recollection of what occurred.

Also, another frequent aspect of complex PTSD is dissociation and not feeling present in or fully connected with your body. If you dissociated to cope with the trauma, you may feel as if you are still disconnected from your body. Many of the clients that I worked with have spoken about feeling outside or "beside" their bodies rather than in their physical bodies. And others have talked about feelings of depersonalization or experiencing a chronic sense of detachment as if nothing is real.

It is important to support your body in releasing the experience of the trauma and in healing. This then allows you to begin to feel more safe in your body and more in connection with your physical self. To support the body in healing, there are a number of approaches that can be helpful. Myofascial release and massage can be helpful in releasing body memories and calming the body. Other forms of body or energy work such as reiki, tapping (EFT), or shamanic work can also be profoundly healing.

Here are some ways that you can actively support calming your body and being more in tune and connected with your physical self:

Listen to your body: Pay attention to your body's symptoms or to areas of stress, tension, or pain. Take time to dialogue with your body and to tune into the messages that your body is giving you.

Allow yourself to be in your body again: Take time to reconnect with your body. Yoga, massage, or doing walking meditations are all helpful ways of beginning to come back into your body and feel more present in a physical way.

Movement: Engage in physical postures and movements that are empowering for you and that help to heal the trauma experience of feeling helpless or immobilized. You can use different yoga poses in a healing manner. If you are feeling ungrounded, try doing the mountain pose. If you are feeling anxious or vulnerable, try doing the child pose. Also, martial arts, weight lifting, dancing, shaking or active movements can be effective in shifting you out of a freeze state to release the trauma held in the body.

Calming your body and nervous system: As discussed earlier in the book, PTSD can lead to an ongoing heightened state of arousal in the autonomic nervous system (including increased heart rate, blood pressure, and shortness of breath), increased cortisol levels in the body, and a hyper-reactivity of the amygdala (the part of the brain that monitors threats). This means that with more severe PTSD or complex PTSD, the body never returns to a true calm, baseline level.

In 1994, Stephen Porges, MD introduced the polyvagal theory and showed how the (with its two branches, the dorsal vagus and the ventral vagus nerves) play a crucial role in managing the autonomic nervous system. The dorsal vagus, when functioning normally, helps the body shift between arousal and relaxation. But if the sympathetic nervous system is overactive due to trauma or high levels of stress, the dorsal vagus nerve triggers the freeze response. The ventral vagus branch affects the body above the diaphragm and helps to give more nuance to our body's responses to stress and also is attuned to social engagement. Learning to tone and balance your vagus nerve can help to calm your body and your nervous system.

There are four primary, simple ways to do this on your own:

1. Slow breathing: Breathe in and out slowly to a count of five.
2. Valsalva technique: Try to exhale while keeping your mouth closed and holding your nose. This builds up pressure in the chest that increases vagus nerve tone.
3. Humming or chanting: This balances and supports normal vagus nerve functioning.
4. Diver's reflex: Splashing water on your face or holding ice cubes to your face also calms your body, slows down your heart rate, and increases vagus nerve functioning.

Opening to birth trauma and preverbal wounds

HEATHER: Since we do not begin to encode memories in the hippocampus in the brain (allowing the conscious access to the memories) until about age three, working with preverbal trauma experiences presents a challenge. Preverbal trauma is stored in the emotional part of the brain and in the body in the form of body memories. When this early trauma is triggered, you may feel flooded by anxiety, sadness, pain, body sensations, or terror without understanding why. This can be frightening to the adult self who may suddenly and unexpectedly feel co-opted or overwhelmed by the feelings of this young part. To heal, it is important to honor and work with the trauma of these preverbal aspects of yourself even if you are not able to access the information about the trauma or gain a clear understanding of the events that occurred. By honoring the truth of what your body and emotions are telling you, you can hold, calm, and heal these young parts without having the full content or context of more conscious memories. In addition, as described in the example below, you can also work through meditation, dreams, hypnosis or shamanic journeying to access and help heal this preverbal trauma.

Kristina
2001
Maternal Irony

The day has arrived,
And the angels have come.

The air is clear, calm, quiet.

The mother's womb is sliced open, all according to plan.
And the babe is taken,
Blue, gasping, early … too early … eight weeks too early.
The evening air is broken, as a team of doctors in a flurry of color,
Try desperately to save this little one.
Men and women breathing quick and heavy,
Running, pacing, playing god.

The angels are hovering,
Standing still,
Watching with wisdom.

The mother, full of drugs, lies still as death,
Too lifeless to move or to feel.
The baby is whisked away.
Gone
Gone
Numb

The great machine, that men have created, plays God.
Separated for weeks in a clear, sterile box,
It strokes the breath, keeping her alive.

The lungs take hold,
The weight stays on,
The empty baby is placed in the arms of the empty mother.

The angels are hovering,
Standing still,
Watching with wisdom.
They keep returning as this little one grows,
Whispering in her ear, "You are not alone, we have never left you."

KRISTINA: When I was an adult, I was told my birth story by my mother. As startling as it was to hear, I was not shocked. It helped me put the pieces together as to why I had so many primal needs and feelings, such as a deep sense of yearning to connect, to be held, and nurtured. I was taken two months early by a planned cesarean section. There were no medical reasons for this. At the time of my birth, my lungs were not fully developed, and I was less than four pounds in weight. I was taken to another hospital about thirty miles away where I was intubated and held in an incubator. I was kept there until I could breathe on my own and no longer needed a feeding tube. Shortly before my conception, my mother's mother, to whom she was very close, committed suicide by drowning herself in a nearby lake. This left my mother completely devastated. She would often have full-blown anxiety attacks, so the doctors put her on valium to better cope with the episodes. So while I was in utero, I was bathed in the waters of my mother's depression, anxiety, and medication. It only makes sense that I absorbed her physical and emotional states and, on some level, felt them as my own. When I was brought home from the hospital, I joined two other siblings, a three-year-old brother and a fifteen-month-old sister. Needless to say, my mother was overwhelmed raising three children under the age of three. Lacking emotional and financial support, and being unstable herself, she was relieved when I was a "good" baby and didn't demand much, even to the extent of not crying out when hungry, such that I had to be awakened to be fed.

So how do we go back and work with preverbal wounds? It is critical to get to the root cause of trauma, where core beliefs have been formed, to help release unhealthy patterns that continue into adulthood. If we have an understanding that time isn't linear (as we are coming to realize now through quantum physics), and that all information and experiences can be accessed in the present moment, then we just need a way to open to what is already there. One way to do this is through entering a meditative state or going into a still place inside, where we are able to quiet the external and internal noise, and, through intention, bring ourselves back to where the wound is still active and alive.

Below, I describe experiencing going back into being in utero, as I imagine myself back in the womb of my mother. As I sense into my body and any physical sensations and feelings that are coming up, I pull them into my heart, and listen closely. What is my infant self-experiencing? What is she needing? How can I help her heal?

Kristina
Journal: Working the baby in utero

Connecting to the stillness inside, I let my intention take me back to being in the womb of my mother. With my eyes closed, I am in darkness and surrounded by my mother's waters and energy. Writing with my non-dominant hand, I let the baby express what she is feeling: "Rejected. Unwanted. Alone. Needing. Desperate to connect and feel wanted. Sadness upon being in the womb."

Adult self: "How can I help you? Can you connect to your spirit guides, angels, or Divine energy? Try to connect now. Through the darkness, reach out. Feel for the light, it is there. Let it come to you. Let the light surround you and protect you. Let it fill you with love and peace. Feel the connection to Divine love. You are wanting it from the mother, but she can't give it to you, but the energy of the Divine can. Let yourself be surrounded and infused with the love of the Divine. Connect and play in this healing energy, as it brings you into peace, so that you feel safe and whole. When you want to or need to, keep turning into this unconditional love, and let the light fill you." *And now, I sense into the baby me. I let her express herself through written words with my non-dominant hand.*

Baby self: "Pick me up. Hold me. Want me. Love me. Love me. Love me. See me. See me. Hear me. Hear me."

Adult: "Hi, baby Kristina. Look to the Divine. Your mother cannot help you. She has nothing inside. She is hollow. Look to the light. Try to feel Divine light coming down, down, down into your heart to fill you with love and to heal your hurt and wanting. Feel the light enter your heart. See it surrounding you. Feel the love fill you up. No more wanting and needing. You are filled with Divine love. Look and connect to this love. Oh, sweet little baby, breathe in pure love. If you need to nurse, the Divine will feed you. If you need to be seen, the Divine will see you. Feel the Divine mother take you into her arms and connect with you. You are perfect. You were created perfectly. You are cherished, loved, and wanted. Let this knowing move through every part of your little being."

Sometimes, it is helpful to use a doll or stuffed animal to represent your baby self. In this way, you project your infant part onto something tangible, outside of yourself, that you can hold, love, and care for. This can be a powerful exercise. Healing happens as you take the time to be with this little one and to nurture and re-parent the infant self. As you hold, feed, connect with, and love this part of yourself in a tangible form, you can hold the doll close to your heart and send it love until you feel the layers of neglect and abuse begin to melt away and heal.

HEATHER: If you are in therapy, it can be challenging to actively work these preverbal wounds because they are not easily expressed in words. When these wounds are activated, it is important for you to feel held and seen in this level of primal vulnerability. For me, these moments in therapy often involved sitting in silence with my client and letting them gaze into my eyes, much like an infant would with her or his mother. The young parts of the client are needing to feel seen with love. I often have felt the fear and yearning in my client's eyes as they stared into mine. I would allow myself to feel my heartfelt love for them and let this come through my eyes to hold them in a loving gaze. It is also important in therapy to know the value of expressing this care in physical touch —through a hug or touching the client's arm or holding their hand. It is critical as a therapist to know the healing power of touch as well as the abusive ways that touch can feel for many clients who may experience it as intrusive and unsafe. This is where it is important to be discerning and clear about what you are working developmentally with the client and how to also honor the boundaries of therapy by staying aware that you are working with these early parts in the context of being with an adult client. As a therapist, stay in professional consultation about this to ensure that you are working with the use of touch in a clear and healing way and stay in conversation about all of this with the witness self and adult part of your client so that the touch feels safe and therapeutic and not confusing or re-traumatizing.

Other forms of healing that can help preverbal wounds include bodywork or energy therapy, such as:

- Reiki
- Doing healing work in the energy field
- Emotional freedom technique (EFT)

- Eye movement desensitization and reprocessing (EMDR)
- Zero balancing
- Sound and light therapy
- Therapeutic massage
- Myofascial release
- Shamanic healing
- Acupuncture

Working the wound of neglect

HEATHER: If you have experienced early neglect, you may have difficulty with self-care and with a sense of self-worth in your adult life. Childhood neglect often results in longstanding difficulties with food (such as avoidance of eating or a tendency to binge or over-eat) and with having an unhealthy or lack of connection with body sensations. You may have a distorted sense of your body. You may also have internalized feelings of worthlessness or shame in an effort to make sense of the lack of parental love. It is important to allow yourself to open to these feelings and to trace them back to their roots, so that they can be healed. It is also important to experience being loved and cared for in a healing relationship to help you to internalize a more positive, nurturing parental image to allow you to begin to care for the young parts of yourself rather than repeating the pattern of neglect that you experienced in your childhood.

Kristina
2003
A memory from early childhood

Out of boredom, my eyes shifted from the ceiling and settled on the far corner of the hallway. Although I was a few feet away, I could see the small, beaded up doodlebugs, enough of them lying together to make a small pile. Intrigued by the random assortment, I scooted closer, my nose within inches of their countless legs, protruding out from their dead, crisp shells. I began to count them, one ... four ... ten. And then, all at once, the light I had been so patiently waiting for silently appeared from underneath my mother's bedroom door. She was awake, and it was well before mid-day. I wondered what the special occasion was. I waited as long as I could bear it, not wanting to rush in too quickly and send her into an irritated frenzy, one that would send me flying right back into the dim hallway. I had learned through painful experience that I must handle these situations as delicately as playing the game Operation. As in the game, if you get too close to the metal edge, you will get a good zap. I must remain invisible and blend into the outer darkness of the room, which was now slightly illuminated by the light emanating from the TV screen. I quietly, and ever so slowly, opened the bedroom door a few inches. I began to scan the scene and take in the familiar images that filled my childhood. The muted TV was tuned to QVC, a home shopping network. I watched the women wave their arms around and move their lips, trying to sell the most current styles of jeans and purses. The models looked just like my mama. Big hair. Big makeup. The only noise in the room was emanating from a small black radio with a foil antenna, set on top of an old brown bureau in the corner of the room. Rush Limbaugh blared from the speakers, ranting about abortion, something I didn't care to understand.

And there was my mother on her bed, propped up by large feather pillows. She looked like a queen of sorts. Not like one from a fairytale, where one is born into royalty. It was more like a role she had stolen, tried to wear, and demanded that everyone else treat her as if that were the reality. In front of her lay her treasure chest, her gold and silver that transformed her from a lowly peasant into something grand, bigger than life itself. It was her portable vanity that held a large percentage of Daddy's income including her Neiman Marcus facial creams and top-of-the-line mineral makeup. The display seemed limitless, tubes of all shapes and sizes, some promising youth and radiance, all in a single application. These were all to be applied with a certain pressure to specific places of the face and neck. It was a science, really. One that I learned as a silent apprentice watching intently as my mother meticulously applied each layer. As Mama worked, her movements were smooth, effortless, like a creature thriving in its natural habitat. I was an intruder on Mama's sacred ground, one I yearned to be a part of. I found myself coveting each item in Mama's vanity. Not because I wanted to own the exotic creams and makeup, but because I wanted to be them. I would imagine being touched by Mama, like she touched her powder brushes. Then she would have to look at me, notice that I existed. She would need to hold me, and I would be able to feel the warmth of her skin.

Once the creams were applied, the makeup came next. This was truly an art unto itself. My own mama was an artist. Every day starting with a blank canvas of skin, then creating a personal mirage out of mascara, blue eyeshadows, and blushes of various shades. It was a stage act of sorts, trying to cover up the truth and create something that wasn't real. This was a thought that I would never divulge to Mama, knowing she would consider the idea to be sacrilegious and probably enough for her to disown me. First came the foundation, applied generously all over the face to conceal all traces of imperfection, blemishes, wrinkles, and last night's love affair. This was followed by loose powder. Next, she would move on to the cheek area, then the eyes, forehead, until eventually the whole face was altered, and a queen was created. I would fantasize that once she had finished her daily ritual, she would be able to focus on something else. Maybe on me. But that would never happen. She would carefully begin to close each tube, container, and makeup item and vigilantly put them back into their places. I envied her holy objects, and the time and attention each one received. I looked down at my own small frame, not small enough to fit into her shrine. In my dirty clothes and uncombed hair, I had no place among these things of beauty. Mama was done, and my hope of being noticed and loved by her slowly began to vanish away, just as Mama would behind her closet door.

KRISTINA: For me, neglect was one of the deepest and most entrenched wounds to heal. Maybe it is because it started so early and was prevalent throughout my childhood. I worked for years to unhook from the heavy yearning and aching sadness of not being wanted, good enough, or valued by those from whom I most needed it. This was a wound that, when it emerged, would often overtake me. I sought for years for any place I could find to have this wound of neglect filled, because the open pit in my heart felt bottomless. Of course, no one could heal this for me. No one could go back in time and be my parent, although this was what I ultimately yearned for—a mom and dad who wanted me and loved me.

At first, I didn't even know where to start in learning how to love myself. I had very little positive mirroring and no experiences of being cherished. And I needed someone to show me how to take care of myself, and that I was worthy of being noticed and loved. The first time I experienced someone looking at me like I was truly cherished was with a therapist. Somehow, she was able to look past all my acting out and see beneath the protective defenses and into who I truly was. And I felt it. A message was transmitted through every cell of my being that, if this woman could cherish me, then I must be worthy. In time, I was able to take this knowing and reflect it back to myself. It was slow going at first, but with each intention and act of self-love and compassion, I began to heal the devastating wounds of neglect and learn to honor and love myself, just for being me.

I found photographs of myself at certain ages when the neglect was most intense, and I made an altar, a special place where I could put a picture of myself, light a candle, and set an affirmation about being enough and being worthy, valuable, and lovable. I would add objects to the altar that honored me and reminded me that I was worthy to be noticed. I would sit in front of these sacred objects and light the candle, as if bringing in divine energy to all the neglect that was in my heart and to feel seen, honored, and loved. As I took in the energy of the flame as divine unconditional love, I would release and give back to it all the pain of the past. Layer by layer, I aligned with the belief that I was enough and worthy of being cherished.

Healing at the mental level

KRISTINA: The ego or mind's main job is to protect and express our individual sense of identity, but if it is not led by and in balance with the heart and true self, then it creates a sense of separation from ourselves, each other, and the planet. But the truth is, divine consciousness runs through every sentient being, and nothing is separate from this pure consciousness. However, when we believe our thoughts and perceptions to be true, we believe ourselves to be separate, until we align back to the interconnectedness of all that is.

We can absorb thoughts and perceptions from others, the media, and even from the collective unconscious. These thoughts can often be negative and harmful to ourselves and to others. This is why it is important to challenge the thoughts that pop into your mind and not simply believe them to be true. If you don't automatically believe them or buy into them, their influence will not have sufficient energy to live within you or to control you. When your thoughts lead you to feel fear, anxiety, shame, guilt, despair, or other heavy, dense feelings, you must first challenge them and ask, "Is this thought coming from an outside source?" If the answer is yes, you can name them as intrusive, distorted, or predatory thoughts and withdraw your power from them. You can turn your attention away from them and not give the thoughts any further energy, and over time, the thoughts will decrease and dissipate. If you stay vigilant about challenging your thoughts and aligning to deeper stillness, you will remain more in peace, joy, and freedom.

If your thoughts are coming from within you, trace them back to their roots. Your thoughts are often related to your experiences from the past and are filtered through your perceptions, beliefs, feelings, and fears. When your thoughts have an emotional charge, they tend to be connected to your wounds, meaning that your personal wounds will energize the thoughts you choose to believe in, in ways that others without the same wound would not. For example, the thought, "I am not worthy to receive love," will feel more real if you come from a childhood in which you felt you were not loved by those who raised you. You might have a painful wound in childhood of feeling that you could not do enough to be noticed, appreciated, or loved. When this happens, it is very hard not to believe the thoughts that come up in your mind about not being worthy of love, because it has the added sting of an unhealed wound attached to it. Also, it is important to discern whether the negative thoughts are related to your efforts to explain or understand your past painful experiences or are based on your projections or on a distorted sense of self. It is important to analyze your thoughts and follow them back to their roots to assess whether they are connected to a wound that needs healing.

Sometimes, our thoughts are shaped by the messages that we received growing up. For example, if you grew up with a parent who constantly criticized you, then you might internalize these criticisms and believe that you are never good enough. As you examine your thoughts, try to trace them back to their origins, to see if they are coming from emotional abuse. This will then allow you to release the thoughts that are not valuing of you or true to who you are. If the thought is your own, it is important to then discern whether it is coming from your woundedness or from your true authentic self. Thoughts coming from your heart or from your deeper awareness feel alive, empowering, organic, and creative. These thoughts are full of life, love, and connectedness. When you are in the flow with pure consciousness, you have the ability to come from the heart with thoughts and actions that are in balance and serve a higher good. This brings you a source of loving healing energy, as you are centered in the truth of yourself and in balance with all that is.

If the denser thought forms are coming from deeper within you and from the pain of the past, you must meet them, so that you can heal the wound that is connected to creating these thoughts. As you heal the thoughts connected to your wounds, the perseverating thoughts—the ones that get caught in loops—can finally unhook and let go. As children, we take in our experiences and fill in the gaps with our own perceptions as a way to make sense of things. Children tend to internalize trauma, feeling that they are responsible for it.

Kristina
2005

I was frozen in fear when the men from the group would take me. Something inside me would plead for my parents to stop them and protect me, but they didn't. I was left in silence, observing the movement around me. It made me feel like maybe I wasn't worth being protected at all, and that my parents must not love me enough to feel I was worth protecting. I felt violated, used, lifeless, but often could show little of my woundedness in a visible way. It was the deeper wounds inside that couldn't be seen that always stayed with me. My thoughts that formed around these wounds are still alive and still whisper within me in the present, "I'm not worth it. I'm not lovable. I was never good enough to be loved."

As you uncover the wounds from the past and allow the feelings associated with them to emerge, you can also dismantle the thoughts and beliefs that were formed as a way of trying to make sense of the trauma. To change the belief system that is not true to who you authentically are, you must go back to the origin of where the thoughts, feelings, and beliefs started. You need to feel the feelings and separate them from the beliefs. Here, at the site of the wound, it is important to find the part that internalized the abuse, so that old distortions can be healed and released, and new beliefs and thoughts about yourself can be formed.

You need to also consider that you might have parts within you that are not in connection with each other. For example, if a young part holds the belief that it is bad, but the adult self does not, then there will be internal cognitive dissonance. As you meet and work through your feelings related to the trauma, you will be able to resolve the inner conflicts and move more into integration and wholeness. As you are able to heal and reparent the wounded part, you can let go of the thoughts and beliefs that formed out of the abuse. Then, you can open to new thoughts that are based in truth and self-love.

Delusional thoughts and beliefs

HEATHER: A delusion is a thought or belief that is not based in reality. However, from years of clinical experience and my past research into delusional thoughts, I have come to realize that they are profound metaphors and expressions of the past abuse and the young parts' efforts to make sense of what was inexplicable and unbearable for the child self. For example, I had a young psychotic woman in therapy who was sure that she was being monitored with cameras and hidden microphones everywhere she went. She was terrified that the mirror in my office was a two-way mirror allowing someone else to watch her and record our conversations. These thoughts and beliefs were a symbolic expression of the level of intrusiveness that she experienced with her mother and the lack of physical and emotional boundaries in her home. She also had been sexually abused by her step-father and felt vulnerable to further emotional and/or physical violation at any moment. This left her feeling hypervigilant and paranoid that every situation that she was in was likely to lead to further abuse and violation of herself and her boundaries in some way. It is only through healing and beginning to experience a different reality in which there can be a sense of safety and trust that such delusional or seemingly distorted thoughts or beliefs can be released.

Inner critic

HEATHER: We all have some degree of negative or self-critical thoughts; however, in my experience as a therapist, those who have experienced childhood abuse are particularly prone to having a fierce inner critic. This critic tends to be judgmental, critical, and frequently fuels and reinforces low self-esteem. What I have discovered through listening to my clients is that the inner critic often initially formed following the abuse or childhood trauma to be a protector. By being hypervigilant and critical, the inner critic was often trying to keep the person from further danger or pain. However, in adulthood, the inner critic is no longer a protector but becomes a saboteur, undermining self-confidence and blocking acts of self-assertion or trust in moving forward in healthy ways in life. The inner critic, which was once a protector, is now hindering the formation and expression of the true self.

If this is the pattern that you are caught in and it is the source of many of your negative thoughts, then it can be helpful to identify this inner critic. Learn its voice and realize what phrases, thoughts, or judgments that it tends to make and how it sabotages you. Let your witness self recognize when the inner critic is active and then bring it into your heart, and thank it for its past efforts to protect you, but explain why it now needs to retire from this duty. As you practice this, the voice of the inner critic will gradually diminish, and you will be more clear when your thoughts are coming from this part of yourself, and then you can learn how not to attach to them or identify with them.

It can also be helpful to do a fire ceremony. Honor the critic for its efforts to protect you in the past and then release it from this role. Write out the thoughts and criticisms that have come from this inner critic and release them to the fire. Write out more accurate statements about yourself that are honoring of your true self and your qualities and gifts and energize these with the energy of the fire. Keep these in your journal or place them on your altar and continue to review them and reflect on them to strengthen your inner clarity and connection to your true self. (Remember if you do not have access to a fire, you can also use a candle to do this releasing ceremony.)

Research by the Heartmath Institute[9] has shown that we are healthiest when our brains attune to our hearts and not our hearts to our brains. Our emotional as well as physical health comes from being in balance and in harmony. When you are caught in negative thoughts, your mind becomes

---

[9] "Scientific Foundation of the HeartMath System," HeartMath Institute, accessed December 7, 2019, www.heartmath.org/science

embroiled in turmoil, and this in turn stresses your heart and throws your nervous system out of balance. These negative thoughts are not only from the ego-mind but are also usually from the left-brain. When stressed or anxious, our left-brains often go into overdrive seeking to solve the problem or re-establish some sense of control. This can lead to perseverative thinking, obsessive-compulsive thoughts or behaviors, and thought loops. Instead of increasing a sense of empowerment or control, this pattern actually leads to increasing anxiety and feelings of helplessness or overwhelm.

When you realize that you are caught in this pattern, take a time out. Get off this "thought train" and distract yourself or divert your attention to some other activity to give yourself some space from these negative or anxious thoughts. Then, meditate or tune into your heart. Go outside and connect with Mother Earth. Allow yourself to release these thoughts to the Earth. Call in the healing energy of the Earth and of the cosmos and place your hands over your heart and attune to the rhythm of your heart. Breathe in and out slowly, quieting your mind and tuning into your heart. Imagine your heart beating in rhythm with the heartbeat of Mother Earth. Keep doing this until you feel a sense of inner quiet and calm. Doing this will help your nervous system to calm down and allow your mind to begin to attune to your heart. You will begin to feel more in balance and in harmony within yourself and in relationship with the Earth and cosmos.

Working with affirmations
KRISTINA: Our thoughts and our words can have a powerful impact on ourselves and others. Words are energy that have their own vibrational resonance. Words come into form through different vibrational states that influence us through altering our vibrational currents. Positive words create coherent wavelengths that have the ability to foster healing, while negative words create dissonant waves that lead to imbalance and illness. We can use words to counter negative beliefs and thoughts. One way to do this is to take time for ourselves and open to inner stillness. Create safety or sacred space, and let yourself go deeply within. Allow yourself to meet and face your wounds and the associated feelings, core beliefs, or negative thoughts that

you have about yourself. As you open to the wound, welcome it in, and while holding it, repeat a countering or healing affirmation, such as:

> *I am worthy.*
> *I am enough. What I have is enough. What I do is enough.*
> *I am lovable and ready to receive love.*
> *I fully accept and love myself, with all my faults, limitations, and weaknesses.*
> *I don't have to be perfect to receive love.*

Find the words that best fit an affirmation that counters your false core beliefs or negative thoughts. If you are not able to fully believe what you are saying, say it anyway, and be willing and open to accept the affirmation, even if part of you is having difficulty trusting in it. As you hold the woundedness in your heart, keep saying the affirmation, with no agenda, just conveying unconditional love. Keep repeating the affirmation with the intention to heal the past. You can use your breath, taking in healing energy through the in-breath and releasing the woundedness with the out-breath. Try to stay with the exercise until you feel a shift, even if it is subtle. Follow this with an act of self-love as a way to confirm the affirmation.

It might also be helpful to put the affirmation that you are working with on a few post-its and stick them around where you can see them often. Putting a picture of yourself when you were a child (particularly at an age where the belief or negative thought began) with the affirmation you are using can help associate the new belief with the one from the past that is being healed.

Using intention and imagination to heal

Intention and imagination are sometimes not fully understood or valued for their importance and impact on healing past wounds and in helping to create the lives we want to be living. Through intention and your co-creative capacity, you align your desire with divine energies for an outcome that you believe is possible. When you hold an intention for a desired outcome, you first start with imagination. For example, you let yourself imagine what it would look like to be healed, whole, and complete. Can you remember a time when you were this way? Then, you move beyond just a mental image of what healing or wholeness would look like into feeling it with your whole being. What would it feel like? Who would you be without your woundedness? How would it be to feel whole? You see it, feel it, and with belief, bring it into being in the present moment as if your intention has already happened. The brain does not differentiate this imagined reality from tangible reality. By imagining the desired outcome and fully experiencing what the outcome would feel like, you have in essence rewired the brain to believe that this has already occurred. You are now in an energetic field to materialize what you have intentioned. (Consider the work of Gregg Braden and Joe Dispenza.)

As we open sacred space and set our intentions for healing, clearing, and creating, we focus in and direct energy in a way that allows us to be co-creative with higher vibrations and frequencies. We can literally heal, let go of the past, and step into our ideal life in a powerful and effective way through imagining and feeling ourselves as if we are already there. What is important as you do this is to hold the intention and imagined reality with feelings of gratitude, love, and openness. These emotions operate at a high level of vibration and help energize the intention and facilitate the manifestation of what you are creating in the present reality. Setting intentions and using this way of meditating can be a powerful way to healing. But it is important to realize that this does not negate the importance of doing the deeper emotional healing work and integration. Otherwise, it can become a form of spiritual bypass rather than a path to true healing.

Healing at the archetypal and spiritual levels

HEATHER: Healing involves gaining greater consciousness of the roots of our wounds and expanding our capacity to honor all that we feel and all of who we are. One profound way of facilitating, supporting, and integrating our healing process is through working with myths, archetypes, and ceremony. Myths have a long lineage that mainly arise from stories that have been told for thousands of years in various forms and in cultures around the world. Myths have a power to heal us and realign us with our deeper selves. While myths encode within them important information about natural law and the patterns of our consciousness and the Cosmos, they are primarily vehicles of wisdom, not factual knowledge. Myths communicate to us in more of a right-brained way and are not left-brained (linear or factual). We don't listen to myths or stories for their factual content. We hear and feel myths, and they live within us, healing us and reshaping us below our conscious minds. Myths speak to the emotional and intuitive aspects of ourselves. It is in the right-brain that we hold our repressed emotions and unresolved trauma memories, so through myths and stories we also find a portal for healing and transformation. This is also because myths teach us about archetypes. Archetypes are the energetic templates within us that remind us of who we are and of our relationship to nature and to the Cosmos. Archetypes are to the psyche what DNA is to our physical form. Archetypes are the living patterns from which all of our consciousness and thoughts and feelings arise. Myths therefore are a medicine for the psyche and a balm for the soul. Myths help us to heal, to come back into balance and harmony, and remind us of our soul selves and our connection with all that is.

Working with ceremony, myth, and archetypes helps you to hold your pain and healing journey in a larger context. The trauma that we each experience is unique, and yet, when we know that others have undergone similar journeys, we feel less alone in our process. Working at the archetypal and spiritual levels also helps us to realize that there is a deeper meaning in our experiences and even in our trauma. Our lives have meaning and purpose, and we can grow and evolve emotionally and spiritually through facing our feelings and experiences.

As we saw earlier in the book, the ancient Sumerian myth of Inanna is a powerful template for our experiences of descent and return that are intrinsic to the process of reclaiming the split-off, traumatized parts of ourselves in order to heal. This story guides us in knowing the importance of having support in our healing process and in understanding the phases of healing and transformation. It reminds us that healing is a journey into the darkness of our pain and wounds, but then it guides us to return to the light of day and the present moment in which we are then able to reclaim our wholeness and become more conscious, integrated, and empowered. Using stories, myths, and archetypes as models or maps can give us comfort, support, and guidance as we walk our own paths of healing and transformation.

A template for many successful films is the archetypal hero's journey as described by Joseph Campbell in his analysis of the themes of many myths and stories from around the world. We see this in films such as the *Star Wars* and *Lord of the Rings* series. It is also key in the Harry Potter books and films. Films such as *The Color Purple* and *Sophie's Choice* help us to understand and cope with cultural and collective trauma. Movies such as *Sybil* and *The Prince of Tides* explore early childhood trauma and its effects. And we find these archetypal themes in ancient myths and stories from cultures around the world. Through myths, stories, films, plays, and songs, we find that our own experiences are echoed, felt, expressed, and held in a larger context.

Symbols, rituals, and ceremonies are powerful vehicles for helping us to heal and become more whole through working at a level beneath the conscious mind. And through mindfulness meditation, prayer, or inner dialoguing with our soul selves and spiritual guides, we are able to commune with God, with Spirit, and with our own inner wisdom to feel held and to gain awareness about the meaning of our experiences and ways to heal.

Here are some examples of how to increase your consciousness and work your healing process at the archetypal and spiritual levels:

Working with archetypal myths
Here is an example of a powerful ancient myth that can support you in your process of reclaiming the lost parts of yourself and know that you are held and guided in this healing journey by the Divine and by your spirit guides and helpers:

Isis, the Great Mother and Healer—a myth from ancient Egypt (from over 5000 years ago)
Isis and Osiris were wise and benevolent leaders of ancient Egypt. Under their wisdom and care, the land and people thrived. They loved each other deeply and modeled and taught the importance of living in right relationship with each other, with the land, the water, and the energies of the cosmos. They taught about the meaning of aligning with Spirit and with inner stillness and with integrating mind, body, and spirit. However, Seth, Osiris' brother, was jealous of Osiris and wanted his royal position for his own personal power and gain. He harbored his envy and hatred for years. Finally, with the help of some co-conspirators, he built a beautiful box and tricked his

brother into getting into it. He then tossed the box into the currents of the Nile River, trapping his brother and condemning him to a slow and agonizing death.

Isis was bereft and combed the land looking for where the box might land in the river, so that she could retrieve the body of her beloved husband. She traveled the surrounding countryside, searching endlessly, until she finally found the box lodged into the side of a tree. She lovingly brought Osiris back to their home and revived him long enough to make love with him and be impregnated with their son, Horus. She then carefully prepared Osiris for a proper burial. Seth, enraged with this course of events, managed to steal the body and cut his brother into pieces, scattering the parts of him across the land. Again, Isis in her grief and in her love searched and searched—through the grasslands, along the river, through the trees and rocks until she found all but one of the lost pieces of her beloved Osiris. She reshaped him and healed him with her love. She then fashioned a new piece to replace the one that could not be found to make him whole again. She then held him and guided him through the transition to the other realms where he became the benevolent lord of the underworld. Together then, they held and reigned over the realms of life and death. Their souls and love were invincible and could not be destroyed.

This is a powerful story that teaches us that you can undergo trauma and yet heal and become whole again. It does not minimize the pain and grief associated with trauma or the ways in which it takes us through a death/rebirth. But it guides us to see that this can be a passage for healing and for transformation. When you are feeling lost and alone and as if the fragmented parts of yourself have been scattered across the land, remember this story and know that Isis is with you. She is truly the archetype of the Great and loving Mother who never abandons you but is always there for you. She may be with you in the compassion and care of those who love you and are supporting you. And even when you feel most desolate and abandoned, she is there for you as the divine Mother who knows who you are, who loves you and will search endlessly to locate and retrieve the lost parts of you to reweave you and make you whole again. You are not alone. You are held and heard and loved. When you are in a dark night of the soul, go out at night and gaze at the stars. The brightest star in the sky is Sirius, and it is the star that is associated with Isis. She is there. She is watching you and bringing her light to you as a beacon of love and hope in your darkest moments.

Working with myths and archetypal stories reminds us that we are part of the oneness of all that is and held by the creative, wise, and loving consciousness that permeates the cosmos and surrounds us here on Earth. As we deepen in our relationship with these energies that hold us and give us a context of meaning and purpose, we are able to feel supported and empowered in our healing journeys.

Astrology
HEATHER: Another modality for gaining more awareness about ourselves and the meaning of our experiences is through astrology. As a psychologist working with trauma, it has been profoundly helpful to me and my clients to incorporate astrology as part of the process of gaining consciousness and healing. I now understand why Carl Jung also felt this was a critical aspect of his therapeutic work. Astrology is our oldest known art and science. Astrology shows the patterns of the stars and planets in the sky at any given time. Like our current understanding with quantum physics, astrology holds the ancient wisdom that everything is energy, and everything is interconnected. The patterns of the stars and planets do not determine or cause events on the Earth but rather give us a mirror, a reflection of the patterns that we experience here. "As above, so below." In looking at the energies of your birth chart, you gain awareness of some of the core themes in your life. The configurations in the chart also give you guidance as to how to best work with these issues and how to bring all of the facets of yourself into consciousness. The chart also shows how you are in a profound, personal, and unique process of growth, healing, and evolution through your life, and how to discern the deeper meaning of your experiences and your soul's intentions or purpose in this lifetime.

Working with your soul self
HEATHER: A powerful form of inner dialoguing is to be in conversation with your soul self. This can be helpful in aligning with your true self as well as deepening the healing of your young parts. It is also an effective way to gain guidance when you are in times of inner conflict or feeling blocked in your healing process. Your soul self carries the wisdom of who you are in your wholeness and can give you guidance about next steps or provide a perspective

on the journey that you are in when you feel like the healing process is too hard and long.

Spiritual guidance

HEATHER: When we honor the spiritual level of reality, we remember that we are spiritual beings having a human experience. When you are working through your trauma and on a path of healing, it is important to know that you are held and supported in that process by love, wisdom, grace, and a spiritual consciousness beyond the human realm. Spirituality is not the same as religion. Spirituality does not involve institutional structures, doctrines, belief systems, or traditional practices as espoused by different religious traditions. As former Catholic priest Matthew Fox describes it, all religions are like wells in that, if we dig deeply enough, they bring us to the underlying river of consciousness and spirituality that nurtures us all. Another way to understand this is to think of the energy of the Sun as symbolic of the love, wisdom, and grace of the cosmos that is here to support, nurture, and sustain all of us. We may experience the sunlight in its different colors as it is reflected through a prism or lens of our historical or cultural context. So you may see the light of our Sun through your prism as blue, while where I grew up, it was perceived as green. Others would perceive it as yellow or orange or red. But all are manifestations of the light that is there for all of us. Spirituality is not about describing the light or prescribing how you should understand or honor the light. To be spiritual is to seek to be in relationship with the light of consciousness and with cosmic love and wisdom in whatever way is right for you.

Shamanic journeying and healing

HEATHER: One approach to this relationship with cosmic consciousness and to spirituality is the shamanic path. Shamanism is at the root of all spiritual and religious traditions around the world. It is the understanding that everything is energy and part of the oneness of the cosmos. From the shamanic perspective, when we are in balance and in right relationship with all life around us, we are in harmony and healthy on all levels. If we are experiencing illness or emotional distress, we need to come back into balance. In realizing that everything is energy, we need to acknowledge that we are more than our bodies and psyches. We are energy beings and ultimately, beings of light. We are sensitive to and influenced by the energies within us and around us. When we experience trauma or abuse, this creates heavy energy and turbulence or ruptures in our energy bodies as well as manifesting in imbalances and fragmentation emotionally and injuries physically. By rebalancing the chakras (our energy bodies) and clearing energy blocks, we help ourselves heal on all levels. Through shamanic "soul retrieval," the fragmented and lost parts of the self can be reclaimed and brought back into integration, supporting healing and wholeness.

Spirituality and shamanism also hold the awareness that we are able to open our consciousness to attune to wisdom and guidance that is available to us from other realms. We are not separate from Source or from the consciousness of all of the life forms which surround us. Through shamanic journeying (a form of deep meditation), we are able to gain wisdom from our spirit guides and be supported in our healing process. Using a rapid drum beat to shift the brain wave state from beta to alpha to theta, shamanic journeying involves calming the mind and opening to an altered state of consciousness that allows us to access guidance from other realms and our own inner knowing. Shamans were also able to identify healing herbs and medicinal plants, not through trial and error, but through going into these altered states of consciousness and communing with the spirits of the plants and their own spirit guides.

HEATHER: I have used shamanic journeying in my own life, in my work with individual clients and in my work with sacred circles, to access guidance and gain support for healing and for spiritual growth. In these shamanic journeys, you also are able to connect with spirit or animal guides who are with you to support you, help you heal, and give you practical guidance about next steps. It is also a powerful way to tune into and gain insight and guidance from your soul self.

Finding your soul song

HEATHER: A profound shamanic healing practice employed by many indigenous people is the practice of finding the person's soul song in order to sing them back into balance and wholeness. In that we are all energy beings vibrating at certain frequencies, you can think of trauma as throwing our energy or vibration into imbalance from being in a harmonic state to a disharmonic state, much like a piano that is out of tune. Your soul song is the unique harmonic or sound of your soul when it is in harmony and balance. This is your energetic signature. As you tune into this song and sing it, you are reminding your energy field and all of the parts of you how to be back in a healthy, balanced, and whole state. You can discover this soul song through meditation or a shamanic journey.

During a dark and stormy time in my life, I spontaneously began to sing a wordless chant one day while getting ready for work. As I sung this simple repetitive song, it felt as if my whole being began to vibrate. It carried the resonance of coming home to my true self. I began to sing this song when I was stressed or depressed. It filled me with a sense of hope and a profound feeling of being held in the love and compassion of the cosmos. I could feel how it helped my body and emotions to calm down and become more in balance. This was my soul song, and it was profoundly healing to sing it and feel a sense of dropping beneath the storminess of my life into the deeper harmonic vibration of my soul self, and it helped me to remember that I am one strand of music in the harmonic symphony of the cosmos.

Spiritual guidance through prayer, meditation, divination, and synchronicities

There are many other ways to connect with the Divine, to your soul self, and to your spirit guides and helpers. Find whatever path is right for you. Just as we each experience the colors of sunlight in different ways, there are different names for Spirit or Consciousness. Find ways to build that relationship and be in communication and communion with the love and wisdom of the Universe. For some, you may gain that connection and guidance through prayer. For others, that wisdom, insight, and love are experienced in deep states of meditation. It may also be found through divination, such as seeking guidance through using a Tarot deck or through using a pendulum or muscle testing. It can also be as simple as listening and paying attention to synchronicities, honoring that all of our experiences hold meaning and carry messages for us to help us on our paths.

HEATHER: This type of synchronicity for me came around the time I heard the spiritual call to leave Los Angeles, and I was going through a very difficult time in my life as I was dismantling every aspect of my life, closing down my clinical practice and preparing to sell my home. While I trusted the guidance that I had received, and it resonated with my inner knowing, there were times that I was filled with fear and confusion, wondering if I was making the right choice. When I felt overcome with anxiety, I would walk out into the garden behind my house. Almost every time that I did this and was feeling stressed, alone, and overwhelmed, a beautiful female hummingbird would come and hover literally inches in front of my face. Her appearance moved me to tears of joy and relief. I always felt that she was bringing me comfort and telling me that I was being guided and supported in this process of transition and transformation. She visited me again and again across the months as I was preparing to leave. And on the final day, as I was saying good-bye to my house and garden, she again hovered in front of me and then flew off towards the east, as if guiding me on my way to the east coast. I only learned years later in my shamanic training that for some indigenous cultures, the meaning of the hummingbird is that she is the one who helps us to follow the path of our destiny with courage and with joy.

Spirit guides, animals, and plant allies to help us heal
HEATHER: That experience with the hummingbird was a reminder to me that we are not alone in our healing journeys. Many of us have had people who were companions helping us along the way. Others of us may have felt let down by the people we turned to for support. It is important to know that human beings are not our only resource. We also have guides, healers, and allies all around us—in this earthly realm and beyond. I believe that we are deeply connected to the natural world around us. If we allow ourselves to open and to be in conscious relationship with the plants and animals around us, they can be profound guides and healers for us. In my herbal training, it often baffled me that so many plants that we, in western cultures, label as "weeds" are actually healing plants. I have also witnessed across the years how the herbs or healing plants that people need for their own healing often "magically" show up in their lawns or gardens. I had a friend who had sleep difficulties, and that spring, multiple valerian plants (an herbal plant that helps with insomnia) showed up in her garden. After my mother's death, my garden suddenly was overflowing with motherwort. Motherwort is an herb that can soothe the heart and calm anxiety. In my relationship with motherwort across

the years, it has always signified the mothering energy of the Earth, helping us to be grounded and feel nurtured and supported. It felt to me that the plant was coming to me to comfort my heart and to remind me that although I had lost my human mother, I was still held in the love and nurturance of Mother Earth. This was profoundly moving and healing to me.

Plants are powerful healers and are able to work on many levels. Plants can be used in teas or herbal tinctures for their physical healing properties. They can also be used in flower essences or in shamanic healing to work on a more energetic level. If you take time to sit with a plant, you can tune into its unique meaning and medicine for you. It is ultimately all about being in relationship with the plant and opening to what its gifts are for you. The way that you can do this is by taking time to meditate with the plant. Thank the plant for being with you. Then, let yourself begin to develop a relationship with the plant. Take in how it presents itself visually. Notice its texture, scent, and taste. Let yourself take time to get to know the plant in its uniqueness. Then, meditate and ask the plant to give you a message or to guide you in knowing what its medicine is for you. It may be coming to you to heal you physically, or it may be working with you on more of an emotional or energetic level. Let your intuition and attunement to the plant guide you. Then thank the plant for its gifts and its presence in your life.

One profound experience that I had years ago was with the plant red bee balm. During the time of my herbal training, I was struggling in my life with my inner conflicts about expressing myself or letting myself be visible due to painful experiences in my past. I had worked on these issues in my therapy over the years but still felt blocked. Part of our herbal training was to sit with a plant and meditate and tune into its healing gifts. I chose to spend time with red bee balm. I observed its beautiful color and the freedom with which it allowed its blossoms to open wide to the world. As I watched the flowers, I could see how hummingbirds and bees were strongly drawn to these exuberant red blossoms. The plant seemed to emanate the fire of creativity and freedom. I honored the plant for its gifts and made a bee balm flower essence. As I used this flower essence over the next several weeks, my fears about expressing myself, speaking out, or letting myself be visible melted away. The energy and gifts of this plant had a profound healing and life-changing effect on me. To this day, I can call on the energy of this plant or take a few drops of the flower essence and feel supported and held in this healing energy.

I have also had many healing encounters with animals. Taking time in nature is profoundly healing in and of itself, but you can also ask for guidance before going for a walk in the woods or in a natural environment. Ask for healing or for a message, and then watch what birds or animals show up in a synchronistic way. Tune into them and allow your intuition to guide you as to what their messages are for you. It is a daily practice for me to take a meditative walk in the woods near my home. At one point, during a very difficult time in my life when I was alone, depressed, and even at times suicidal, as I went out to walk, an owl appeared to me for several days in a row. Prior to this, I had walked for months in these woods and had never seen an owl. On the first day of these encounters, I rounded a bend in the trail in the woods, and there was an owl perched on a branch just a few feet above me, staring at me. The next day, I returned from a late morning walk, and to my astonishment, I found an owl on the ground in my backyard, just standing there, looking at me. The next day, an owl flew right over my right shoulder as I walked in the woods. These experiences were so unusual and synchronistic that I knew that I was being given a message. For me, owls symbolize profound transformation and death/rebirth as well as the gift of seeing in times of darkness. I felt that these owls were guiding me to trust that I was on a journey of transformation and showing me that I was being supported and held through that process. These encounters with the owls were a gift, and it showed me that I was being held in the love and wisdom of the Cosmos, and that the life forms around me were helping me to keep walking through the dark time and were letting me know that there was a deeper purpose and meaning in what I was going through even though I could not fully see it.

Using ceremony to heal
HEATHER: Too often in our modern western culture, we see time and the process of change as linear, moving forward step by step in a sequential manner. We also tend to overvalue doing and devalue the importance of reflection, stillness, and simply being. Indigenous cultures (as well as ancient cultures) view time and the process of transformation as cyclical and spiral (similar to the movements of the Earth, planets, Sun, Moon, and stars).

They also understand that healing happens in the "in-between" times, in the liminal place of not knowing, of uncertainty and of non-action. These cultures understand the importance of rites of passage and of using ceremony to honor the in-between time, for healing and transformation. When we are going through a profound time of change, we are letting go of an old way of being. We need to honor the liminal time in which we are no longer bound to the identity or patterns of the past but are not yet sure of what new forms we are moving into. This transitional time is a profound time of healing and transformation. It parallels the process of a caterpillar transmuting into a butterfly. The caterpillar first dissolves and is in the chrysalis (in-between) state before morphing into the butterfly. In a similar way, we need to dissolve our former sense of self as we heal and change. As we transform from one state of being to another, the process can feel disjointed and chaotic, but this is a necessary element of breaking down old forms and structures in order to create something new.

Working with ceremony is a powerful way to honor this transformational process and supports healing and the integration of a new sense of self. The power in ceremony comes from working at levels beneath our conscious mind, as it weaves together body, mind, heart, and spirit in the healing process. Ceremonies are found in all religious and spiritual traditions. To use them in your healing process, they need not be based on or tied to any religious structure or belief system but can be created by you to be an expression of your own process. Ceremonies also hold significance as they connect us to the transformational energies of the fundamental elements, such as earth, air, fire, and water, and the Cosmos. They can also connect us to our spirit guides, to powers larger than ourselves, and to transpersonal or universal energies.

Fire ceremony

Fire is known throughout time and across cultures as an element and energy for healing, releasing, and transformation. Doing a fire ceremony can help you to feel supported in your process, as you release to the flame what no longer serves you and energize with the fire what you are wanting to create and bring into your life.

To do a fire ceremony, build a fire in a fire pit or in your fireplace. You can even do this ceremony with a candle if you do not have a way to build a larger fire. In some form, such as calling in the four directions or saying a prayer, honor that you are entering into sacred space to hold you in this process. Take time to meditate and focus on your intentions for the fire ceremony. Take a piece of paper and write on it what you are wanting to release with this ceremony and what you want to draw in or energize in your life. You can also do this by taking a stick and blowing into one end what you want to release and blowing into the other end what you want to energize.

When you are ready, gift the fire with your paper or prayer stick. Watch as the fire transforms your paper or stick and allows your intentions or prayers to be released to the air and to the realm of Spirit or to the Divine. Then, after you feel the release is complete, imagine bringing the flame into your heart, so that the fire and energy of the Divine can heal you. You can set intentions or put into the fire your writing or stick symbolizing what you would like to energize in yourself and manifest in your life. When you are done, thank the fire and your spirit guides or allies for supporting you in this healing ceremony and open and release the sacred space that has been established for this ceremony by honoring the directions or by saying a closing prayer with words of gratitude. It is particularly powerful to do this ceremony with others in that it heightens the energy of the ceremony and provides a way of witnessing and supporting each other in integrating what has been released and what has been healed and energized.

Water ceremony
Water is a powerful element and force for healing, releasing, and cleansing. You can do a water ceremony by a river, pond, lake, or ocean. You can also do it by taking a bath or shower. When using a bath, it makes the ceremony more powerful to open sacred space by using sage, diffusing an essential oil, or lighting a candle, as you call in the directions or say a prayer. Set your intention for the ceremony. For example, it might be to release heavy energies related to your trauma. Using water, you can set the intention to cleanse your body and psyche of past painful experiences and of negative feelings and beliefs. You might want to add essential oils, rose water, or flower petals to the bath as a

way to honor yourself and the process. You can also add Epsom salt, sea salt, or baking soda to the bath, and cover all your chakras with the salt water. This allows the body to detox both physically and emotionally. Soak in the bath and feel yourself release what is needed to be healed, letting the water cleanse you as it washes over your body.

There is an ancient Greek story that the goddess Aphrodite would once a year take a ritual bath to cleanse herself of all past relationships and sexual experiences and to reclaim her body as her own, starting anew. This is a wonderful model for doing a cleansing ceremonial bath to clear away the imprint of past sexual and physical abuse. As you wash each part of yourself, give gratitude for what the body part has done for you, all that it has held and endured, and for how it has supported you. Use the bath as a way of honoring, letting go, and reclaiming your body as your own. You are coming back to your true self and moving forward with the freedom that allows you to make choices that are honoring of yourself and your body.

Another way to do a water ceremony is to use an object that is symbolic of something that you want to release. You might want to write words on it or add flowers and then release it into a body of water such as a lake, river, or ocean. Use something natural or biodegradable. For example, you can take a stone and blow into it what you want to release. Again, open sacred space for the ceremony and clearly set your intention. Then, throw your stone or object into the water, releasing what you are letting go of. Put your hand in the water and touch the water to your forehead or your heart, and honor and give thanks for the healing and cleansing energy of the water that is supporting you in your healing process.

You can also use water as a way to help support and manifest what you are trying to grow and bring more fully into your life. You can fill a glass jar with water and set it on a window sill so that it can catch the moonlight. Set an intention at the time of the new moon as to what you would like to energize or bring into your life. As the moon grows across the next few weeks, its light will help energize the water and your intention. When the moon is full, do a simple ceremony to thank the moon, and then drink the water, as a way to symbolize taking in your intention as it has grown and been infused with the moon's loving and healing energy.

Cord-cutting ceremony

This is a powerful ceremony to liberate yourself from addiction, dysfunctional dynamics in a relationship, destructive patterns, or relationships that need to be let go of. This ceremony supports you in releasing the energetic ties or "cords" that bind you in an unhealthy way to a pattern or particular person. You may do this ceremony once and feel that you have cleared the cords that need to be released. However, if you are working with a more ongoing pattern or long-term relationship, you may need to do this ceremony over a period of time. It can be powerful to begin this ceremony at the time of the new moon and continue it once a day through the full lunar cycle. Listen to your intuition and trust your experience with the process to know and feel when the releasing is complete.

Here is a possible way to do this ceremony:

- Call in the four directions or say a prayer and open sacred space.
- Face each of the four directions beginning with the east.
- Using your hand to make a cutting motion in front of you, name out loud the cords that you are cutting and releasing.
- Continue this with each of the other directions (south, west, and north)
- Then face the east and, using your hands, visualize and draw in to yourself what you want to energize in your life and feel these energies filling you in a nurturing and supportive way.
- Continue to do this with each of the other directions.
- Thank the directions and your spirit guides and open sacred space.

Spiritual connection

All of these ways that we have discussed are about coming into balance energetically and remembering our profound connection with Spirit or with the Divine. When we practice these ways of coming into harmony and of connecting with Spirit, we come back into balance and heal naturally by aligning to our soul self and to the power of Source, of divine love. Then, we are also able to tap into our deep intuitive wisdom and truth. In this space, deep healing and transformation takes place as we fold our woundedness into our pure essence. As you drop into the gap between your thoughts and words, you are in the flow of pure consciousness, your life force, and creative energy. Here is where you can merge your will with divine will and co-create a higher state of consciousness and manifestation. As you move through the healing process, you have more life force and joy available to you to create and manifest your unique gifts. Cosmic and divine energies are flowing through you to support you in being in the fullness of who you are and to be a vessel of pure love and light. As you align with stillness, you allow these higher energies to guide you through your healing process and into your creativity and life purpose.

Kristina
2000
Oh, Divine

Do you dwell above the starlit sky?
Or deep down in the ocean blue?
I think you are everywhere ...
In each blade of grass, in every moonbeam.

I see your eyes as I look into a child's eyes.
I feel your warmth as I hold another's hand.

And still, when the loneliness creeps in, I feel you forsake me ...

I try to feel you once again ...
Oh, Divine, do you remember me?
Do you yearn to be one with me as I do with you?

I search again and find you ... inside the flowers of the meadow.
Within the birth of each new babe.
You are the arms that hold,
And the face of those that show compassion.
Looking with my heart, I find you there and everywhere.

Healing and redefining your connection with Spirit or with the Divine
KRISTINA: After coming out of abuse or out of a religious context that no longer fits for us, we often have to find a new way to be in relationship with Spirit or divine source. We may experience feelings of betrayal, isolation, and confusion about God, Spirit, or our sense of the Divine, as we sort through our past and the trauma that we experienced. I have found that the mind doesn't have all the answers and can often not make sense about the terrible things that happen on this planet. However, when I tune into my heart for guidance or understanding, I am met with feelings of peace and an inner knowing that everything has a purpose, even if I do not have the answers. Having hope has kept me seeking throughout the years for something more than myself to help guide me through the healing process. I have had profound experiences when I have reached out, surrendered, and allowed a higher source to intervene and help heal me.

Ultimately, I feel the healing process and its time frame are being held by this divine cosmic force, but it was vital that I also chose to be a part of it. One of the greatest ways to open to higher help is to ask for it. When we ask, grace begins to enter our lives. It often speaks back to us through our intuition and hearts. Here we find our truth, to lead us to the next steps and be our healing guide. I found that when I asked the Divine why my healing was taking so long, the answer came from my heart space, "You are learning in this process. You are spiritually maturing. And you will better be able to help others." Even though I didn't like the answer, it came from a solid place and from my deeper knowing, so I began to trust it.

More and more, the connection with my heart began to build as I turned my life over to the Divine. As my heart connection grew, so did my relationship with God or Source. I was re-taught by my inner knowing what *my* truth was about the Divine, and more importantly, what wasn't my truth but rather had been taught to me by someone or something outside of myself. I needed to come back into alignment with what my heart had been telling me was my truth all along. I began to understand that Source was never separate and something outside of me, because ultimately it is in me. I was then able to let go of trying to control my life. Instead, I simply showed up and tried to learn everything I could from what I was experiencing. Opening to the Divine, asking for grace to flow through me, is a more natural way of being that has allowed Spirit to flow through my life, in my meditation practice, healing sessions, and inner work. And this also facilitates finding, opening, healing, and releasing all that is no longer needed in my life. I ask to be made new again, to return to how I was designed to be—whole, balanced, and magnificent.

When I pray, I come from my heart space, where there are no rules for how to be with the Divine, and everything my heart is communicating is acceptable. When I am in my heart, I am aligned, and I am one with the Divine or God. My will becomes one with Divine will for me and others. In this space, I feel as if my prayer has already been answered, and I give gratitude for all that is. Here, I pull in all the hurt and woundedness into love and honor it by saying, "Thank you, thank you, thank you. And so it is done, blessed be."

Kristina's daily prayer:

Oh Divine
Let me be your eyes that I might see what you see,
Your ears, that I might hear what you hear,
Your mouth, that I might speak what you would speak.
Let me be your hands and feet, that I might do what you would do.
Let me be your heart, that I might love how you love.
Wash over me with your grace, again and again and again.
Let nothing remain but you.

HEATHER: I have felt a profound connection to Spirit since my birth. At first, my relationship with the Divine was shaped by growing up in a conservative Evangelical Christian home. Later, I explored and redefined my beliefs and understanding of spirituality through my own experience and relationship with my inner knowing and with Spirit. When we realize that everything has consciousness and that the energy of the Divine is in all that is, then we remember that we carry the Divine within us. If we open to that connection, we come into alignment with our soul self, the part of us that is eternal and has been with us throughout our lifetimes. That soul self is connected with the Spirit that is in all of life and beyond all that is. It is as if our soul self is a drop of that vast ocean of Spirit. When we connect with and align with our soul self, we remember the truth of who we are and that this lifetime is a journey of growth in love, wisdom, and consciousness. Everything has a meaning and a purpose. But we also have free will and can stray from alignment with our deeper self and cause harm to ourselves or to others. But if we take time to tune into that stillness within, then we can be guided by the wisdom of our soul self that speaks to us through our hearts, intuition, inner knowing, and synchronicities and that connects us to the divine or to cosmic consciousness.

Heather's daily prayer:

I honor the Sun and, through the Sun, align with Source, with Divine love and light and wisdom. May I fulfill my purpose in this lifetime and be a vehicle of love and light and healing in this world.

The nature of evil and how to open to spiritual healing

KRISTINA: We are currently living in extreme states of separation on this planet. Some hold the belief that evil doesn't exist, and that God or love is all that is true, and everything else is illusion. That might be so in an ultimate cosmic way. But I have experienced people and situations that have felt so dark, that I could not detect even a trace of light in them and could only sense a never-ending chasm of separation between us. Consciousness runs through all sentient beings, but when we choose to move into darkness, the less we are able to hold the light and the more we separate from divine or Source energy.

Being emotionally or spiritually wounded can make us feel as though we are separated from the light or from the Divine, and this can lead to destructive dynamics with others. These actions can be harmful and yet are coming from woundedness, not evil intent. Perhaps evil is the conscious choice to live in separation from the light and from the Divine. Evil may be the result of the ego choosing to remain in separation and purposely working to generate negative emotions in others (such as fear, anger, helplessness, and hopelessness) for personal power and gain. Evil does not arise out of a wounded psyche but out of a conscious intention to deny or destroy the energy of light and love in others and in the world.

Unless we wake up to this truth that severe separation is occurring on the Earth plane, we will stay asleep and numb to the destruction that is going on around us. We have to become conscious enough to see the gross discrepancies of light and dark and choose to no longer be tolerant of people, leaders, structures, and institutions that are separate from Divine light. Otherwise, we ourselves are victims of these powers as we participate in agendas that are not for our good, but that keep us trapped in fear and ignorance.

HEATHER: As we allow ourselves to heal and realize that we are not separate from each other and from Spirit, then we are no longer controlled by fear. We wake up and are no longer controlled by the trauma from our past or by the trauma in our collective consciousness. We break free from being captive to the influences of social media or the efforts of those in power to control our minds and behavior. This allows us to raise our consciousness and become agents for healing and change—in our own lives and in interactions with others. The more of us that heal and awaken in this way, the more we can support healing at a collective level.

Kristina
2012

> *The wounds of this planet are too much for me. Is it too much for God? I want to believe that I can help change things on this planet. Who am I to do such great things—God things? Could I be like God? To love like God? Everything feels so far beyond us, and yet everything is inside of us. We are healing, healing, healing, by grace and the flow of God's love, moving in us, through us, through you and me, until we are all surrounded and consumed in God's light and love. Then, we heal, and truly love. Then, the wars and hunger and hurting will come to an end.*
>
> *When I was little, I was separate. I was a girl, separate from a boy. A daughter, separate from a mother. My white skin was separate from your dark skin. And then, abuse happened to me, and I began to internally separate. This one holds the anger; that one holds the pain. Another holds the memory. Now, I have grown much wiser and have a different knowing. Now, I am going about doing many God things. I am becoming one with me ... and one with you. Free to be open. To be love. To be one.*

As we experience abuse and being hurt in relationships, we tend to close down our hearts to protect ourselves. As we heal, we learn to open back up again. We do this because love is who we are, and when we shut down from our truth and authenticity, we close ourselves off from our true nature, which is a permanent, non-transient state of stillness, peace, joy, and love. Love can heal all wounds, grief, anger, regret, unworthiness, and lack of forgiveness towards ourselves and others. Love is the ultimate ointment used to heal the wounded self. We do not need to find the perfect healer or lover to give us the love that we long for. The key is to open and remember our true essence, and the Source of all that is. Unconditional love is the highest vibration of all emotions. When we meet denser lower vibrational feelings like fear, shame, despair, and hatred with love, then our wounds transmute, heal, and release.

Coming from an abusive past, we may feel we are not worthy of love, but we see that this is not true when we discover that we are not separate from love. All we need is a willingness to let love in and allow it to hold our woundedness. As we experience pure love, we come home to our wholeness. No matter what we have done, or what has been done to us, there is a place inside that can never be touched, tainted, desecrated, or altered. It stands as it has from the beginning, pure and whole. In the space of stillness, we can go inward and ask for grace to lead the way, to show the path that has been forgotten, back to the center of who we are. Without the mask of what we are not, we are led back to our true selves as love. When we remember our divine nature, we are then able to radiate this truth outward, and like the breath, it returns and comes back to us. We breathe in love, we breathe out love.

CHAPTER 7

Integration - Coming to Center

In your walking meditation with the medicine wheel, you are now ready to move into the center. Giving thanks for the profound journey that you have been on, you complete the circuit around the ARCH medicine wheel, returning to the stone in the south. With gratitude and holding the deepening sense of wholeness within you, you turn and walk into the center. Here, you honor the integration of all of the aspects of yourself and the phases of your healing journey. You feel your profound connection to the Earth and sky and energies of divine love and cosmic consciousness that are within you and are able to hold all that is. Take time here at the center to breathe in and out and deeply honor your soul self, your journey in this lifetime, and your interconnectedness to the energies of the directions, to Source and to all of life.

In this section of the ARCH model, we will explore ways that you can deepen your integration process and movement into wholeness and into joy. An ongoing part of the healing journey is the process of integrating your sense of self with your expanded awareness, while also developing healthier patterns in your life. There are many aspects and layers to this integration process, which like healing, is not linear. The journey is likely to have many detours and setbacks along the way, but as you witness your progress and allow yourself to track your changes, you are able to see the ways that you are transforming and becoming more and more true to your unique, real, and whole self.

Integrating the parts work

HEATHER: Over time, as the internal dialogue with the parts of yourself becomes more and more natural and fluent, you no longer need to set aside daily or consistent time for this process. You are likely to find yourself more spontaneously tuning in and recognizing the voices of different parts of yourself as they come up in your daily life. You begin to see yourself as a multiplicity of parts and honor your complexity. As you honor these different parts of yourself and give them all a voice, you begin to feel more and more integrated and whole. The parts are no longer separate entities but increasingly feel like aspects or facets of the complexity and wholeness of who you are.

It can be profound to do this process in conjunction with walking the medicine wheel. As you circle the perimeter and then walk into the center of the medicine wheel, you feel your connection with the Earth and sky and all of life and your connection with all of the parts of yourself. Imagine these different aspects of yourself as if they are standing around the rim of the medicine wheel. Honor the wholeness of who you are and allow all the parts of you to come into connection with each other as you hold all of yourself in love and greater consciousness.

Developing new beliefs and healthy patterns

The healing process is not only about letting go of unhealthy patterns and distorted beliefs about yourself, but it is also about integrating new, more healthy beliefs and behaviors in your life. As you become more conscious of some of the ways in the past that you have reinforced your wounds through your thoughts and actions, you can now choose to replace these old patterns with new, more empowering and life-affirming beliefs and ways of being. At first, it is helpful to journal and record your progress in implementing these new thoughts and behaviors until they become an integral way of being and no longer need to be worked in an intentional and disciplined manner.

Developing new coping mechanisms

HEATHER: Here are some further ways to support your healing and shift out of old coping mechanisms:

Healing the Fight Response: When this has been your primary coping mechanism in the face of trauma, you tend to respond to stress or conflicts with anger. When triggered, you are apt to be reactive, angry, and at times hurtful or aggressive. This energy of "fighting" may manifest verbal or physically. You may lash out at the other who has hurt you with criticism or anger, or you may act out in a destructive manner. As you bring the memories and feelings from your trauma into awareness and heal, this old pattern may still get triggered at times since it was your familiar way of coping. When associated with complex PTSD and early trauma, this coping style is often associated with avoidant behavior in relationships due to insecure attachment. Engaging in a fight response often leads to ruptures in relationships or avoidance of intimacy and difficulties with trusting others. In childhood, the fighting response was a way to try to survive and avoid further abuse, but it can become in adulthood a barrier to trust and intimacy.

Remember that beneath the protective "fight" response are feelings of vulnerability and of not being safe. To begin to shift this pattern, when you find yourself triggered and reacting in anger or aggression, take a time out. Allow yourself to tune into what triggered you and how this event or experience resonated with your early trauma. Give yourself time to tune into the feelings beneath the anger, particularly the feelings of vulnerability, pain, helplessness, sadness, or despair. This allows you to hold these deeper feelings with compassion and take action to honor what you need in the moment. Do you need to take time to journal or allow these deeper feelings to feel held and heard? Do you need to share with the person that triggered you that this activated your past trauma and communicate what you need to feel supported in the moment? Let yourself formulate a plan of action that is not about pushing your feelings or the other person away but is about active self-care and an honoring of your needs and emotions. This then allows you to feel more empowered and open, with the capacity to directly address the conflict or stress in the moment in an effective way rather than in a reactive way. You can then begin to let go of this old way of coping that is now blocking you rather than protecting you, and you can gradually begin to feel the safety of being in true relationship and developing the ability to trust and open to intimacy.

Healing the Flight Response: When this has been your primary coping strategy in the face of trauma, your tendency will be to avoid conflict and stressful situations. You may try to numb out pain or stressful feelings through addictions or distractions. In relationships, you may tend to feel anxious and withdraw or dissociate in stressful or more intimate or intense interactions. Underlying this pattern of coping is a sense of helplessness and of feeling powerless. In relationships, this also can manifest in alternating between anxious attachment and avoidance. When you are triggered and feel the impulse to flee, breathe in deeply and remind yourself that you are safe now. Take a moment and reflect on what ways you can act to feel more empowered in the moment rather than withdrawing or avoiding the interaction. Allow yourself to take the steps to say what you are feeling or to actively address what you need in the moment. Consciously move forward in the interaction. Rather than just reacting or withdrawing, state what you are feeling and allow yourself to risk being assertive even if this means engaging in conflict. Let yourself begin to see that you have options as to ways that you can feel empowered and assertive in the moment rather than feeling overwhelmed and powerless. Let yourself be discerning about who you can be in relationship with and who feels safe to you, and then allow yourself to take risks to deepen in your trust and to be more open in your communication and capacity for intimacy.

If taking any of these active steps feels too overwhelming, then take time alone to journal about your feelings and hold space for the overwhelming sense of fear, vulnerability, and of not feeling safe. Send compassion to these frightened parts of yourself and actively do some act of self-care. When you feel centered again, make a plan for how to work through the conflict in a safe and structured way. This allows you to begin to move out of a pattern of numbing or of flight into more engaged healing and intimate relationships.

Healing the Freeze Response: If in your trauma, you were helpless in protecting yourself and felt overwhelmed and terrified, you may have coped by going into a freeze response. This is a process of shutting down your feelings and body sensations in order to survive, much like a frightened animal who will go into paralysis to avoid being killed by a predator. To heal this, it is important to develop a strong enough witness self so that you can begin to sense when you are getting triggered and going into a freeze state. Then, you can actively take steps to remind yourself that you are safe in the present moment. You might take a walk, dance, move, or shake your body to release the feelings of paralysis. It is also helpful to visualize warm, healing light coming from Mother Earth up through your feet and from the cosmos through the top of your head, filling you with love and safety.

If you know that the freeze response is your primary coping mechanism, when in a calm state, write down how you experience being in the freeze state and ways that help you to "thaw" out and feel safe again. Some ways to release the freeze state may be through taking a hot bath, calling a friend, or doing physical exercise. Referring to a list of options can be a useful guide when you feel numb, incapacitated, unmotivated, hopeless, or helpless, so that you will begin to recognize what feels most healing and supportive to you at such times. Keep this list in a special place so that you can find it easily when needed. Then, if you are triggered by a flashback or trauma memory or current interaction that instigates a freeze response before your witness self can intervene, go to the list and engage in one of the self-care activities and remind all parts that you are safe now. It is safe to come out of hiding, to melt the terror and return to your true essence and present life.

Healing the Fawning Response: The fawning way of coping is often more complex in that it is less of a reactive protective response and tends to become more of a personality style. This response is related to early complex PTSD and a lack of secure attachment with one or both parents. The fawning response involves developing ways of being in relationship that feel protective of the self. Often, if you have had an emotionally abusive father, you may learn to submit to those in authority in an effort to avoid conflict and abuse. If you had a volatile or narcissistic mother, you may strive to accommodate, take care of, and, at an unconscious level, try to heal your mother in hopes that you can finally get the love and support that you need. This can become an ongoing personality style of submitting to or accommodating others or becoming a compulsive caretaker, constantly putting aside your own feelings and needs to defer to or take care of the other person. Interestingly, many people with this coping response become therapists or healers. Sadly, the professional identity and validation for being a caretaker can block the much-needed personal healing and growth of the therapist.

If you are a therapist or healer and sense that you have some of this style of coping, be careful about keeping clear boundaries with your clients and maintaining a balanced schedule for yourself so that you don't end up spending all of your time and emotional energy in this professional caretaking mode. Honor your needs for your own healing and be very discerning in your personal relationships so that you are not continuing, albeit informally, to still be in a therapeutic dynamic with others. When this is your primary coping style, it is important to honor the gifts of empathy, perceptiveness, and attunement that you have for others, but also to discern when your caretaking behavior is coming from your trauma and underlying fear of loss or rupture in relationship rather than from genuine caring and compassion.

It is important to understand the difference between true love and "fawning." Fawning is ultimately fear-based and is an effort to avoid conflict or abuse. It is at work and is expressed when you accommodate another, put their needs first, and shut down your true feelings and needs in order to avoid disagreement or conflict. True love means taking the risk to stand in alignment with the truth of who you are and to honor your feelings and needs, not in a reactive way but in a centered way. Then, your acts of compassion and love for another come from a clear place and from the heart rather than from a defensive effort to avoid trauma or pain.

For those with this fawning coping style, it is important to take time alone to allow space to tune into your own feelings and needs. Allow yourself to develop a witness self that can begin to discern when you are abandoning yourself and suppressing your feelings and needs in relationship. Tune into the body sensations and emotional undercurrents that may accompany this fawning response. Do you feel tense inside in these moments? Does your stomach hurt? Do you feel an undercurrent of frustration or resentment? As you can begin to identify these warning signals, you can become more conscious of when you are slipping into this coping mechanism. In these moments, hold yourself with compassion and don't become critical of yourself. Then, take time to be alone and to tune into what you were feeling or needing that was suppressed when you were in caretaking or submissive mode. Take action to name and in some way honor those feelings and needs. Actively do some form of self-care. Then, if possible, return to the relationship and share what happened and take the risk to express your true feelings and needs in the relationship. Be discerning in your relationships in that you are a prime magnet for those who are emotionally needy or dependent and who are seeking to be in this type of out-of-balance, caretaking dynamic. Be willing to distance from or end these out-of-balance relationships and allow yourself to seek out more mutual relationships in which it is safe to be vulnerable and express your feelings and needs.

Remember that letting go of any of these old patterns of coping and allowing the deeper feelings to surface, to be heard and held and healed, takes time and is not a simple or linear process. Be compassionate with yourself when the familiar coping response is triggered. Often, it can feel as if you take two steps forward in the healing process and then one step backwards. And, at times, it can feel like one tiny step forward followed by a huge tumultuous stumble and fall backwards. It takes time for all of your young parts to feel safe with the new patterns and often when you make a shift, there is an initial internal backlash. Hold this also with compassion and allow yourself to continue to practice the new ways of being. All of this, including the setbacks and moments of self-sabotage, is part of the healing journey.

Kristina
2008

I desperately longed to be noticed, mainly by my parents more than by anyone else. It was their attention and love that I yearned for and at some primal level ached for. As a child, I began to think that it was something that I wasn't doing or wasn't doing well enough that was the reason for their neglect and oversight. I believed that if I could just change me, I would gain their approval and love. And so I began to live a life that I felt would earn me the right to their love. I worked hard at the act of being the perfect daughter. But after years of effort and role playing, I realized my strategy wasn't working. It had failed, and so had I. All the work to gain my parents' love was in vain.

And so the mask that had become my identity slowly began to crack. And beneath the surface ran a river of sadness, deep and devastating sadness, all the way down through my bones. And my heart began to melt because of the sadness, and I tried to hold my heart and stop the sadness. But the river of sadness ran through my fingers. And I thought, "How do I stop all this sadness, before I lose my heart as it becomes one with this unstoppable current of sadness?"

And I began to understand that I had no control over the flow of my emotions and of my soul. I realized that my feelings must breathe and move with their own natural rhythm as they are intertwined with the essence of my being. And my wings that were so perfectly constructed behind my mask crumbled to ashes. And I withdrew into my cocoon to prepare for my rebirth. No mask. No artificial wings. Just me in my raw, vulnerable nakedness. My deepest feelings release and wash over me, cleansing all my wounds. And I slowly return to my natural state, my true Self. And the day finally comes to break open from my chrysalis state, rebirthing myself from the ashes. For the first time, I feel alive and free. My wings, made perfect through divine grace, stretch out far and wide, lifting me high in my authenticity, taking me far beyond anything I believed possible.

HEATHER: In the therapy process, these times of being with a client—in this intense raw pain, sadness, terror, and vulnerability as the old defenses and coping mechanisms are released and there is an opening to healing and transformation—are profound and delicate moments. I can sense and feel and see in the eyes of my client the fear of the young traumatized parts as well as the sense of awe for the true self that is starting to be birthed. This is not a time for words or for problem solving or advice giving. In these moments, what is most needed is safety, compassion, and empathic attunement. These are also the moments of silent communion, soul to soul, gazing into each other's eyes as this step of courage is taken that feels like walking off the cliff into an abyss. Words cannot truly touch this place of raw vulnerability. As a therapist and person who has also lived this journey, my heart breaks open, and I hold a sense of presence and love for the other as they enter into the sacredness of this process and into the mystery of healing and transformation.

Integrating feelings and memories

HEATHER: As you work through your past trauma, you are able to begin to integrate your memories and emotions in a more tempered and neutral manner. Instead of getting triggered by unexpected events and feeling re-traumatized, you now know your inner terrain more fully and have more consciousness of the experiences in your life that may be re-triggering for you. This allows you to be in better control of your choices and more aware of how you want to approach situations or relationships that may evoke some of the memories or feelings related to past trauma. In opening up and reclaiming the memories and feelings that were once repressed or split off, you know them now and are able to hold them in a conscious way as part of you and not feel afraid of them.

As you integrate the feelings related to your past wounds, you are able to hold them and honor them and let them rise up and flow through you. You become increasingly aware that they are part of you, but not all of you, and that as you embrace them and hold them with compassion, they can no longer terrorize or control you. You are able to witness them and work with them from a more centered place within yourself. You also are able to feel stronger and more secure in yourself as you shift the trauma memories from the right (more emotional) brain to the left (more analytical) brain in a way that allows you to remember these past painful experiences in a more calm, neutral, and stable way. The past becomes background instead of foreground in your life, as you are able to naturally be in the present moment.

Grief and letting go

In the end, just three things matter: How well we have lived, how well we have loved, and how well we have learned to let go. —Jack Kornfield

KRISTINA: Part of the integration process is honoring your grief about the losses and the pain of the trauma that you have experienced. As you work through the intensity of the abuse, you are able to feel more compassion and sadness for what the young and vulnerable parts of you had to go through. As you allow yourself to grieve, you can let go of being mired in the story of what happened and let go of an identification of yourself as a victim. You now are able to own your process and feel empowered in shaping and creating an authentic sense of yourself. And you can see both the scars and the strengths that have emerged from the trauma and your healing journey.

Always remember that grief is a process and may take years. What is healing is to eventually come to a place of acceptance and honoring of all of the feelings associated with the grief and loss.

Grief is not only about what happened, it is also about what didn't happen, the loss of possibilities. It is coming to accept that what you might have longed for will never happen, the loss of dreams and hopes that will never come true. When I finally came to the knowledge that my parents were never going to show up for me in the ways that I needed them to, I stopped waiting and wishing, and instead dropped into the pain I had been avoiding. I was finally able to grieve that I was never going to experience having loving, available parents. This opened me up to all the feelings around this wound, and the healing process then had the potential to be worked through. As we fully grieve, we come into our wholeness and are ready to let go of the past.

Kristina
2011
Free

Holding on tight to the past,
I am ...
Hollow,
Flat.

No movement inside.

It stops time ...
Suspends living.

Frantically looking for a fix …
Searching, searching, searching …
To make the pain go away.

Nothing works.
Waiting, waiting, waiting …
For the Universe to shift me,
Change me, and
Make the agony disappear.

Waiting, waiting, waiting, waiting,
For a correction of circumstances.
That would alter me,
Heal me,
Make me whole.

The loss,
The waiting,
The sadness …
The stagnant place inside.

At last, I gather in the pieces …
One by one.
Accepting.
Surrendering.
I am healing me. Making myself whole again.

The issue of forgiveness

KRISTINA: As part of the healing process, it is important to honor your anger at those who have hurt you and all of your feelings about the wounding and betrayal. As you allow space for this, you can gradually let go of the energy and emotions that keep you bound to the trauma and to those who have hurt or abused you. You now are able to release the ties to your abusers and see them in their complexity and woundedness. You have set yourself free from feeling as if your life is controlled or diminished by their power or abuse. You reclaim your life, your body, and your emotions as your own.

You may or may not come to a place of feeling forgiveness for those who have hurt you; this process should never be forced or seen as a prerequisite to fully heal. Ultimately, it is vital to realize that the act of forgiveness is not about releasing others from their accountability for their actions or for the consequences of the abuse. Rather, the act of forgiveness is a choice to set yourself free from being bound to those who have hurt you. Forgiveness is your gift to yourself. To fully heal, you need to set yourself free.

Kristina
2011

When I first started my work on the road to healing and reclaiming the lost parts of myself, I would quickly "forgive," so that I could avoid the pain and anger inside. It was an act of my mind but far from a process of my heart. It was easy to use this as a way to bypass the deeper undercurrents of emotion, because what is left to work on after you forgive? The problem was that I was still broken and miserable inside. I had to become more conscious of honoring where I was really at and to allow time and space for the expression and release of the hard feelings. And then, the "forgiveness" started to become more natural, and something that I didn't feel I needed to do. It became more about allowing the healing to flow through me and letting it all just go.

I think a better word for me than "forgive" is "release." To forgive seems like something God should be doing, not me. I don't know or understand the rules of mercy and judgment, but what I do know is that I want to release my past and everything tied to the pain of it. That feels more right to me—to just be responsible to release and let go of the pain, disappointment, and grief. To loosen the grip of it all, and let it sift through the fingers of my open hands. The process is not to forget or disregard or accept the injustices but to change my relationship to them. I am no longer the keeper, judge, or enforcer. I am now free to choose to let go, and trust that God will handle the judgment, so that I can move on with more space and energy to fill my life with joy and love.

KRISTINA: I believe that not choosing forgiveness means, at some level, choosing to stay caught in the suffering. What are you willing to drop and let go of to be free? Are you able to let go of needing to be right, needing justice, revenge, or to stay entrenched in the anger? Are you willing to release judgment and blame, so that you can move out of endlessly cycling through the pain of the past? When I began to see that all the judgment and blame that I had put on those who abused me was coming back as a judgment on myself, I realized I held the key to freedom. The key was letting go, and it opened the door to unconditional love for myself.

Kristina
2011

I started to be able to forgive my parents when I saw the same behaviors in myself. Of course, for years I was able to get away with just pointing the finger at them, creating more separation from them as the pain kept mounting. But, at some point along the road, I saw my own reflection in all of my projecting.

Was I actually neglectful and abusive? For so many years, I had identified with just being the victim, having no conscious thoughts about being the abuser as well, until I started to unwind my thoughts, even just for a bit, to see more clearly my own behavior. The trick that my mind kept telling me was that my behavior didn't look the same or wasn't to the same extent as what was done to me.

I had to face the times when I neglected my own children, and sometimes let them down when they most needed me. I had to acknowledge and take responsibility for the times that I failed them. What I saw in myself might not have been the physical or sexual abuse that happened to me, but I had to admit the times that my anger was misdirected at them, the moments of reactivity and impatience.

I also had to face the ways I abused and neglected myself, when I put other people first and let my own needs fall low on the list. I had to own the abuse on my body when I failed to take care of it properly and make it a priority and love myself. I also needed to consider my soul self and the ways that I had been ignoring that inner guidance. Do I put myself in environments that are loving and peaceful, or do I override what my heart is telling me? If I dismiss myself, then I am guilty of behaving just like those who neglected and abused me.

Forgiving is realizing that we are often doing the best we can under the circumstances we are in as we make choices in the moment. There are still consequences, and people need to be held accountable, but we no longer feel the need to judge and be the critic of everyone's behavior. We are better able to let go of judgment, when we realize that our job is to pay attention to our own behavior and take responsibility for how we act and relate to others. This allows us to be humble, when we see that we are all ultimately imperfect in life. We then become more open and accepting and are able to let go of the past and grow in consciousness.

It was very difficult for me to realize all of the times that I had distanced myself from others, because of a story that I had created about them or the situation. The truth is that we are more similar than we are different. Once I realized this, I had the capacity to feel compassion for myself and for those who had neglected and abused me. It is like something in my heart opened up, and my mind and heart finally had a chance to meet, connect, and commune together.

It is beautiful to come to this deeper understanding of connectedness, knowing we are all doing our part in this larger unfolding. Realizing that the behavior that I was trying to forgive in someone else was the very behavior I was needing to acknowledge and forgive in myself, helped me to turn inward and stay focused on changing the only thing I could—myself. And then the act of letting go of everything that I held onto as pain became more effortless, like dropping a leaf into a gentle stream and watching it float away in complete peace, surrendering to the current and flow. That is how it feels to forgive.

The more I release the anger, bitterness, resentment, and pain, the more space I have for all the good that was hiding underneath. Beneath the experience of neglect, I was now able to remember how my mother baked me a birthday cake from scratch every year. On that day, every year, I knew that I was thought of, and there was love. It was a message that I was special, even if it was hidden down beneath the layers of negatively charged memories. Now that I have distance from being consumed in the pain, I can allow myself to remember that there was also good in my childhood. I remember the care packages in college, being supported at my sporting events, and having warm food on the table and clothes on my back. Grace was there all along.

KRISTINA: Another aspect of forgiveness was the realization that every moment had meaning for me. From the seemingly insignificant moments to the extreme abuse, each one was given as a chance for me to awaken to my true self. Within each moment, I was able to choose movement towards wholeness. There is an overarching grace that governs and directs each experience as an opportunity to come home to the true self.

Through the trauma of my sexual abuse, my understanding of myself was constricted, and I came to believe that I was only my broken body, emotions, and thoughts. As I healed, my consciousness was able to expand to include experiencing other states of being, such as stillness or pure consciousness. I was then able to hold the wholeness of who I was. Now I am able to hold each moment as a gift, because I experience the outer world mirroring back to me the state of my inner world. And I ask, "Is there something that is still needing to be embraced, healed, forgiven, and set free? Can I see peace, love, and joy reflected back to me?" This is the work of waking up to what is true and whole within me.

Kristina
2010

When I was four, I was pinned down, held against my will by a man that was more than four times my size. This was too traumatic to remember until I was an adult, when it came back exploding through the dark of night as flashbacks, in which my current life began to fall apart. Tiny hands and frame, I was so small then. And no one was there to protect me, take care of me, and say NO for me. Instead, they just let him come and take me and rape me. The physical pain couldn't touch the deeper pain of my soul. I was forgotten and left alone. And I should forgive this?! Should I say, "The man who abused me was taken over by evil," or "he did what he knew to do," or "he was a victim himself?"

Today, in my mind, I stand across from him. And I look into his eyes. What do I see? Is the hate and evil still there? What does the soul look like inside this shriveled-up old man? Is there regret? Does he remember me and what he did to me? Does he remember that he ripped me apart and left me for dead, with no regard? Maybe I would yell and scream at him, tell him what he really did to me, and what it felt like inside my skin. Maybe I would try to kill him, now that he is old, and I am stronger than he is. Maybe that wouldn't help me or him. This time, it will be about me. And maybe it wouldn't matter what I saw in his eyes or his heart. I would look him in the eyes and say, "I give this back to you. Every moment of the horror. It is yours, and I no longer will hold it for you. I choose to fill myself with the love that you tried to rob from me, fill my soul up with so much love, there's no more room for hate. I release you and all that you did to me."

Is this forgiveness? I don't know. Maybe it is more than this and goes beyond releasing without hate or vengeance. Standing in a safe and neutral place, I let divine love seep in and go down deep, and it soothes the hate I feel for him. I open to wonder about this man, his soul's evolution, his healing, God's grace. I begin to question, "What made him do these things, to become filled with darkness?" Maybe one day, I will stand across from him and see what God sees, say what God would say, and love as God would love. I hope that one day I can. Then, will I know that I have forgiven him?

I want to make a grave and put all my memories inside of it. I want to get them out of my heart and into something else and put them all to rest. I want to pile dirt high on top of that grave and cry until there are no more tears, and I have emptied out all the pain of the past. I want to put my fingers deep down into the earth and plant seeds that will grow into a beautiful garden, where I will stand tall and move out into my brilliant life.

Developing more consciousness and a stronger sense of Self

As you integrate your healing process, you expand and deepen your awareness and grow stronger in your sense of yourself. You no longer feel as if you are living life behind glass or living in a reactive or defensive way; rather, you are able to act and live consciously from a centered, empowered, and creative place.

Imagine yourself as a house. Before you worked through your trauma and what was unconscious from your past, it was as if you lived in a house that was haunted, and you stayed in a few familiar rooms that felt safe, avoiding the rooms with locked doors that were hiding the unknown from you and a dark basement that terrified you. Now you have opened the doors and explored the depths of the basement. The house is now filled with light, the doors are all open and unlocked, and you have cleaned and redecorated the rooms, no longer clinging to objects from the past that do not fit with who you are in the present. You now feel at home in yourself, lighter and more free.

Living with gratitude

KRISTINA: As your body tries to heal the pain of the past, it is common for our focus to narrow and get stuck in negative emotions and memories that are coming up with strong force. It can be difficult to find any grace or peace in the present, when we are so bombarded with pain, sadness, and grief. But if we are able to be in the moment and widen our lens, we have more ability to also see the good around us—to feel the Earth being cleansed after a rain shower or soft sheets against our skin, or to see the way the sun brings light into a room. These types of experiences can be soothing and healing as gratitude begins to move through us.

It is also important to train your mind to recall the good from your past. These gems of light are the pieces of the past that are just as valuable and important as the agonizing ones. There were memories I needed to recall that brought me into more of the wholeness of my life experience, that touched me with joy, and kept me feeling warm and alive. It was nature that brought me peace when I ran to escape the pain of my home. It was a third-grade teacher who laughed at my jokes and a basketball coach who found talent in me, opening up the feeling that I was good at something. A home-cooked meal on Sunday afternoons was another reminder that life was not all bad. The many incidents that brought me joy, peace, comfort, and hope, whether large or small, helped me to remember that life held space for goodness, even in the midst of despair. These are the times that I honor and remember and try to hold space for the mystery of life and the process of healing. I remember that my childhood was not all good or all bad, but that it was a makeup of millions and millions of experiences, interactions, and incidents that made me who I am today.

HEATHER: As you heal and integrate the changes in your life, you open more easily and fully to a sense of gratitude. Your experiences begin to have more context and meaning for you, and you begin to realize the ways in which you are deeper, wiser, and more loving as you have worked through your trauma and have come into a new and more empowered and conscious sense of yourself. You no longer see yourself as a victim of fate or of another's abuse but now as the author of your own life. In trusting your healing process, you don't need to prove the validity of your experience to anyone. You can honor that trauma memories are encoded in feelings and are often not remembered in a linear or detailed manner. What matters is that you have heard and held the parts of yourself that have shown you what they are able to reveal, so that you can heal and recover and reclaim your full self.

KRISTINA: When we are centered in gratitude, we are aware of the constant stream of grace that is in each present moment, even in times of crisis. As we acknowledge this flow, we are better able to hold the wholeness of our experience, and not fall into despair, hopelessness, and depression. We can meet the trauma, and hold the beauty, love, and perfection of the moment. When we focus our attention on what we are grateful for, instead of what we are lacking or what we would like to be different, we are able to let go of suffering and enter a more peaceful space. This gives way for an effortless movement to life and how we experience living it.

Kristina
2004

Some of the things I am grateful for that I developed from being abused:

I learned at a young age to survive under the most extreme conditions, so I know how to function through very strenuous circumstances. I can overcome a difficult challenge or put it in a box until I can manage it, and then I can walk on and still cope in the world and not fall apart. I learned how to be strong, how to be self-reliant, and how to pull myself together with my own will. My intuition was refined as well as my inner sense of danger, and I learned how to feel what was beneath surface appearances. I searched to know God and be in deep relationship with divine energy at a very young age. My soul expanded and grew exponentially as my wisdom deepened with rich complexity. I ultimately found my true self, inner stillness, and the divine consciousness inside of me.

Measuring progress

KRISTINA: As you work through the healing process, it is valuable to record and measure your progress. This not only gives you a sense of hope when the journey might otherwise feel endless or overwhelming; it also gives you landmarks along the way to know that change is really happening for you. You can measure the progress of changes in daily habits or patterns like the reduction of self-destructive behaviors or more consistent self-care. You may also wish to monitor your progress with larger goals such as increased self-esteem, self-assertion, or your ability to be more vulnerable and open in relationships. Allow yourself to track your progress and the healing changes in your life in whatever ways work best for you. Every small amount of progress and healing is extremely meaningful and important. Taking time to acknowledge what has been healed and what progress has been made is a significant piece of your healing journey.

Kristina
2012

Today, I went for a run. I used to be a solid runner, but it's been years since I have been able to get myself to put my running shoes on again. Like most things in life, I have stood by watching from the sidelines. Nothing physically has held me back; I guess that's what has been so frustrating. There was never anything that was physically wrong that stopped me. I was a natural runner before the memories came. I never thought twice about getting up before dawn and hitting the streets. Like most things in my early twenties, I took this for granted. When I needed time to think or wanted to lose a few pounds, I'd lace up my shoes and hit the trails. At one point, I became dedicated and thought seriously about running a marathon, and I was close to being able to complete one. That is when I felt as light as air, and it seemed my feet just skimmed the surface of the pavement.

When the trauma memories came, so too came the pain, confusion, and disorientation in myself and how I related to my life. I began to rely on running more than ever before, trying desperately to run away from my pain and from myself. I ran in the pouring rain. I ran when the streets were covered in snow. I ran when I was sick, lonely, frantic, frustrated, and exhausted. I couldn't stop running. I thought that it was saving me. But really, it was just keeping me from me. Fragmented and disconnected from myself, it became my escape. It was my biggest distraction, my addiction. I ran and ran and ran.

And then the depression came. Something that I could not outrun. It started to come on slowly at first, then through a number of losses, it became full blown. It stripped me down to nothing. It took my freedom, dreams, ambition, drive, and everything that I could muster to create and control. It left me helpless, debilitated, and paralyzed at times.

I stopped running ... and living. On my good days, I was barely functioning. With the little effort and energy that I had, I would use it to fight against my life, trying to make it different, to make me different. I was fighting for the part of me that I had always known. The fun, optimistic, driven, smart, outgoing self was fading, dying really, and I was fighting to get her back. Resisting the change and the loss, I could not tolerate saying good-bye to the self that I had created and known. I could not see the process as being a metamorphosis. I could only see that what I had spent years wanting, working towards, and creating into existence was slipping effortlessly away.

That was eight years ago; today I stand a lot closer to wholeness. Having crawled, walked, and at times groveled toward relief and healing, I am emerging through the process of change. Needing to surrender to my circumstances, moment by moment, I sometimes allow myself to fall into the pain of losing childhood dreams and ideals. The release allows room for the new to unfold, and for the true authentic me to come into being. Change is the constant. We are on a continual path of life, death, and rebirth.

It is just how they say it is, how life has its seasons, and each season has its own time frame. Even if change cannot be seen or felt, movement is taking place. Change and healing are happening. The hard part is allowing myself to exist in a way that fits the season that I'm in. I don't help myself when I pretend to be in a different season. I have come to accept what is and let go of the rest. I am allowing myself to just be in a way that feels most authentic to me. If it is a season of pain, I draw into myself for more love and self-care, knowing that each season offers me a gift, each bearing its own kind of fruit. The season of depression leads my soul towards maturity and refinement, telling me it is time to listen, to gather all the parts of myself together, to deepen and heal.

Emptying out all the clutter and extra baggage, I refine myself down to my true essence. In this pure form, I am open to the unique gifts that I am meant to bring into the world. Each step, each tiny little step, leading itself to the next right step. And that is how I move with grace through each season. I never completed my dream of running a marathon, and the season of my youth is long over. This book was being created in its place, a new and different dream that had a life of its own and demanded to be nourished, cultivated, and birthed. Maybe that is how it was meant to be all along.

Living in the mystery

You can never cross the ocean until you have the courage to lose sight of the shore.
—Andre Gide

HEATHER: At a critical point in my own healing journey, I stepped out of my life as I had known it and felt as if I was stepping off a cliff into the void. I knew that the ways that I had defined myself and had been living my life no longer worked for me, but I had no sense of what I was moving towards. To be in the void, this time of not knowing, can be frightening, confusing, and sometimes even overwhelming. I remember during this period often waking up in the middle of the night flooded with anxiety. There were moments in the process when I also felt as if I had been abandoned by Spirit or by God. I had thought that if I had the courage to let go of the past and step into the abyss, either I would learn to fly or angels would come and carry me and take me to the promised land and a new way of being. Instead, I felt like I was in an endless free-fall.

Eventually, I landed—bruised, but intact. However, for years I wandered lost in the wilderness of transition, still in the mist of mystery with no sense of the destination. Without a map and with no guides, I had to rely on my intuition and trust what seemed to be the next right step, while never knowing if I was walking in circles or was actually headed towards some new land. It was like being at sea, lost in the fog, without a map, and in a rudderless boat with no compass.

It was a profound time for me of learning to trust in the process even when flooded with fear and doubt. I had to cling to the faith that, while I had no clue where I was headed, I was being held in a larger current in the ocean that was carrying me to where I was meant to go. I also had to come to the awareness that the process is truly about the journey and not about the destination. When I finally let go of the expectations on myself and my illusion that life is a linear journey, I began to more fully trust that I was indeed being held in the cosmic energies of love and wisdom that are beyond my comprehension.

As I finally surrendered to those currents, I began to honor the beauty of the journey, let go of my ego, and feel my oneness with the elements and energies that were all around me. As I released my longing for the destination and my absorption in my own angst, the fog began to lift, and I saw my new self reflected back by the calm waters of the sea. One of the most important lessons that I learned from this profound time of transition in my life was that the deepest healing and transformation happens when we are in the liminal times, the times in between the old forms and new ways of being. This time of mystery is critical to the healing process, even though we often wish that we could bypass it and move immediately from the old identity to the new, more evolved one. The caterpillar truly has to honor the time in the chrysalis before emerging as the butterfly.

As you heal and integrate your process, you are able to be more open to ambiguity, uncertainty, and the mystery of life. You realize that you may never fully understand all of the events of your life's journey or the reasons for your trauma, but you feel your increasing ability to not be mired in the past and to be able to choose how those experiences will shape you rather than feeling controlled or constricted by them. As you feel more comfortable in your own skin and more aware of the layers and levels of your feelings, you are also more open to uncertainty and to the aspects of your trauma that you don't (and may never) fully remember. You are able to honor and trust your feelings and let them guide you in your healing journey. You are also able to honor the truth of what you do know and allow the rest to remain in the gray of the unknown.

KRISTINA: Living in the mystery or in the gray zone can be difficult when coming from trauma or during times of crisis. Life seems to be filled with extremes during these times. Our thoughts and behaviors are often experienced as swinging from one end of the spectrum to the other with little rest in the middle. When we are living in the "not knowing," we can feel out of control, and life can seem threatening. When we are feeling the discomfort of ambiguity, it is helpful to try not to react out of an urge for safety. In other words, it becomes important to resist making decisions aimed at alleviating the discomfort of the mystery.

Being in the gray zone is a time for reflection, a quieting of the mind, for slow movements, and for caring for the soul. When I am in the mystery, and

I feel the impulse to act, I draw inward first. I gather up all the pieces of me that I can and hold them close. I give myself the powerful message that everything will be okay, that I am safe now, and that I will keep myself safe through the uncertainty. I remind myself that this time is different than the past. This seems to help settle down the anxieties inside and to bring a sense of peace and an awareness that time without action might be wiser than trying to jump in to fix or change things. Giving myself the space to be still and take care of my needs first actually helps me in making healthier and more whole choices. I often find that a lot of healing and growth has been done in this process before the decisions are ever made. It then has the potential to support the process of the deeper relationship that I am developing with myself.

Kristina
2013

I used to believe that there was some magical finish line, that an ultimate goal would be achieved, and that there would be a definite time in space when I would "arrive" at complete peace and joy, fully healed. I think for years I kept this idea floating around in my head to give myself hope, a lifeline to keep sane. But as time has gone by, I have continued to drop the illusion that there is some point of arrival, and I better understand that healing, loving, and creating are born out of each present moment. I discovered that growth usually happens slowly, without fanfare and is often messy. We tend to be unaware of inner movement and of our exchanges with grace and with divine help and intervention.

My life path and purpose weren't something that I instantly knew and jumped into. Just by living and breathing, I was exactly where I needed to be, in each and every moment. Life's gift is about learning, growing, and remembering, and it is in the everyday process of being alive that we fulfill our destinies. Once I realized that I wouldn't be crossing a magical finish line where life would effortlessly fall into place the way I wanted it to, I started to think about what I wanted my life to look like. I opened up to life being in a more organic flow, which allowed me to dream without fear or limits. I stopped trying to be something that I wasn't and began to discover the uniqueness of who I was.

I started to write, do art, and whatever made me feel good. And sometimes, that meant just staying in bed until noon! I had no agenda other than to keep following joy and trusting the grace that was always there to continue to hold me and guide me.

It mattered less what it looked like and how I did or didn't fit into the world around me and was more about honoring where I was within myself. There is no time frame for healing and discovering who we are, and how to honor our own unique creativity and divinity. Sometimes the veil becomes a little thinner, and we feel more connected to the divine energies around us. But mostly it is in the unmoving stillness inside where we find our deepest connection and healing.

Even if the relief that I seek comes slowly or doesn't last long, I continue to surrender to the greater wisdom of my being and the Divine as my soul continues to purge and purify. Life, death, and re-birth are all in one sacred cycle. Emotionally naked, drawn into myself, I release the dark, heavy wounds of the past, letting them move out of my body, and replace the void with clean, healing, light energy. This is a process of death and rebirth and re-creation of new energy and life force. Day by day, moment by moment, the healing happens. Sometimes it is big and powerful, and at other times quiet and subtle. But it is always with the knowledge that I am getting better and progress is being made, even if I can't see it. There is an ultimate destiny for me, and in this moment, I am exactly where I need to be and am deeply grateful for the gift of life.

Gifts of the healing journey

Emotional discomfort, when accepted, rises, crests and falls in a series of waves. Each wave washes a part of us away and deposits treasures we never imagined. Out goes naivete, in comes wisdom; out goes anger, in comes discernment; out goes despair, in comes kindness. No one would call it easy, but the rhythm of emotional pain that we learn to tolerate is natural, constructive and expansive ... The pain leaves you healthier than it found you.
—Martha Beck

Kristina
2006
Inner Sea Cave

The power of the ocean attacking zones of weakness in coastal cliffs,
Creating … sea caves.
Where light grows dim with each step that is taken until you reach the innermost chamber.

Air freezes still. And time stops.

Darkness, thick as molasses, chokes the life from all feeling
Leaving numbness inside
Where echoes mock hollow sounds
Making you believe there is no life inside this frame of old pirate bones.

Only the brave will face their fate and enter the unknown darkness of the cave.

Easy as the entry may be at low tide,
Beware—the power of waves and swell will be amplified in the cave's interior.

A tale of old: How grace smiled down on a fortunate soul.
Just when the weary explorer was about to turn back, thinking this to be just an empty, hopeless, void-of-feeling cave,
he sees a glimmer of light reflected from his lantern,
renewing his hope that life still exists even in the deepest place of the cave.

At last, it has been found.
In all its glorious array,
The treasure of the heart.

Raging red rubies
Dancing diamonds
Solemn sapphires

Gracefully green emeralds
Glittery gold pieces

Formed by a weakness,
Made strong by a process.

Never was it empty.
Created to be a sacred holding site,
For secret feelings, waiting to be found.

KRISTINA: As I moved through healing of my past, I gathered up the gifts I had found and developed along the way. At times during the process, it was hard to hold onto the good and to all that I was reclaiming, but it helped me to take note of the wisdom and deeper knowing that were growing inside of me. It is important to hold onto the good, as well as working the pain of the past, while we try to be in the present moment.

These are some of the gifts and lessons that I came to know through my healing process:

- I learned to listen to my heart and allow it to guide me.
- I came to realize that the Divine never left me.
- I now know that I deserve everything good.
- I can stand whole, even through the healing process.
- There is a place inside of me that can never be touched, that remains sacred, pure, and unmoving, no matter what has been done to me.
- Dreams really do come true.
- Miracles happen.
- I can always find within myself deep peace and unconditional love.
- I am worthy, just because I am.
- I never caused the abuse.
- I now realize that the prize is in the process, not in arriving somewhere. Life is about the journey of growing, learning, understanding, gaining insight and wisdom.

- I learned to listen to every aspect of myself and honor each part inside of me.
- Each step leads to the next, right step. You don't have to figure it all out at once, just the next best step.
- Listen, honor, and take action—this is living your life path.
- I am my best parent, partner, lover, and friend. I have the ability to love and know myself like no one else can.
- I learned to have gratitude for every aspect of myself and my life, to honor and embrace it all.
- I learned to be patient. As long as I am living consciously, everything is exactly as it needs to be, and I am exactly where I need to be for growth and healing.
- There is no growth or healing when I am coming from a place of fear, neediness, attachment, or anger. I must come from a place of love, acceptance and grace.
- I learned that to receive love from others, I must first connect with divine love and then love myself.
- I learned to stop wanting someone else's path and to step into my own life and say, "YES ... I AM HERE." I am the one I have been waiting for.

Kristina
2009
Who Am I?

Who am I?
Who am I?
To deserve such nice things. To be gifted.

Who am I to feel worthy?
Me?
Me?

Do you know who I am?
Full of shame and pain ...
And changing.

What becomes of me then? When the transformation is complete—and I stand whole.
Healed.

And what of my potential then?
Endless. Full of possibilities.

"A light set on a hill"
And then what?

What will they see?
Me?
Me?

Brilliant light.
Light
Light
Brilliant me.

Free ... free ... free ... to be me.

HEATHER: At times, the healing journey can feel endless and filled with pain and confusion, but as you continue on the path and strengthen your witness self and connection with your soul self, you begin to see the process from a higher perspective and begin to realize the gifts and profound lessons of this journey. The process of healing never ends. It is a lifelong, ongoing process of healing, growth, integration, and evolution. It is a spiral path and not a linear journey. There is no beginning and no ending. We are all on a journey to grow in love and wisdom and, through healing, we deepen and open to increasing levels of consciousness and wholeness. We become less identified with our personal stories and the content of our lives and more aware of the journey and of how we are each a part of the evolution of the Earth and cosmos. As we heal, we are more open to living in joy and living from the heart. As we become more heart centered, our minds are entrained to the energy of our hearts, allowing us to no longer be controlled by constricting beliefs from the past or our fears about the future. We are more able to live in the present moment and to be in the mystery of all that is.

We are no longer defined by the past or caught in a fixed identification of who we think we are. Our sense of identity becomes more fluid, and we are more open to a changing sense of ourselves and are able to engage with others without judgment, seeing them more clearly and honoring them in their complexity. We move beyond polarization and the dualities of the self and others, good and bad. We see ourselves and others in true interconnectedness and in the ways that we mirror and complement each other.

As you integrate your healing journey, you find that your compassion and love for yourself deepens. You relate to yourself with less judgment and feel more self-confident. As you become more accepting of yourself, you are also able to open more fully to receiving love and respect from others and giving love and respect in return. You are also more able to feel and know the love of Spirit and feel held in the love and wisdom of the cosmos. You are able to deepen in your awareness that you and all of us on this planet are ultimately beings of love and light, and that we all go through times of darkness and trauma as we live on this Earth plane. It is our choice whether to be blocked and maimed by those experiences or to claim the wisdom and deepening that come from facing and healing those wounds.

As we heal and let go of the patterns that we have relied on in the past to cope and to feel safe or in control, we experience more ease in life and live more from our intuition and in alignment with the energies of the Divine, of cosmic consciousness, rather than from fear or from external expectations or cultural conventions. We are open to express our true selves and to celebrate our uniqueness and to honor that in others. We remember that we are all spiritual beings on a human journey, and we no longer live in a paradigm of survival, competition, or of striving for control. Life is a process of deepening and becoming more whole, and death is now seen as a threshold, not as an ending. And we remember that we are part of infinity. In healing and moving into wholeness, we expand our sense of self beyond an identity limited to the stories of our lives, our egos, and our sense of separation. As we heal and step into our fullness and our unique gifts, our goal is not to create our own individual realities to please our egos or achieve our greatest fantasies. We now realize that we are part of the consciousness and creativity of the Earth and the cosmos and can live in celebration of and in service to all that is.

Opening to joy

HEATHER: As we heal and integrate our process, we are able to open more fully to joy. Joy is different from happiness, which is more dependent on the circumstances and events in our lives. Joy, like peace, comes from a deeper awareness of our being infinite spirits having a human experience and being able to take in and honor the fullness of life. This spiritual experience of joy is not reliant on circumstances but is a way of being. Joy is the understanding that we are carried by currents of consciousness beyond our comprehension and that everything is held in love. This allows us to then open to the full spectrum of our feelings with all of their colors.

There are days where the sadness of the past rises up within me, and I feel an undercurrent of depression. In the past, I would either try to resist or override this or get mired in it. Now, I just let it be. I hold myself with compassion and realize that this is a familiar feeling. Instead of trying to push it away, I welcome it and allow it to visit, like an old friend. I know that beneath this undercurrent is the deeper ocean of joy and acceptance that holds all of these surface currents and weather changes. I know that the depression will pass just as do the moments of happiness, frustration, anger, or delight. All are part of the winds and weather of the sea, but my true home is in the quiet stillness that is deep beneath the surface.

CHAPTER 8

Conclusion

Moving beyond the individual Self: Healing the collective and the Earth

> "We often think of peace as the absence of war, that if powerful countries would reduce their weapon arsenals, we could have peace. But if we look deeply into the weapons, we see our own minds—our own prejudices, fears and ignorance. Even if we transport all the bombs to the moon, the roots of war and the roots of bombs are still there, in our hearts and minds, and sooner or later we will make new bombs. To work for peace is to uproot war from ourselves and from the hearts of men and women."
> —Thich Nhat Hahn

Kristina
Journal 2018

Dear One,

Look down at the beautiful blue planet. They call that Earth. That is where you have chosen to go. There will come a time when you are there, that you will forget that you are a part of Me, and that you are there to be an experience.

"What do you mean?" said the one to the other. "How could I possibly forget who I am?"

There are many distractions on Earth, and many experiences that will make you feel you are separate from Me. But there will also come another time, when you have been the experience enough, and you are ready to come home to your true Self. You will have to let the illusions go that you are having an experience, and see that you are the experience. There will be times when you forget and feel very angry at the experience you are having there. But then that will also be an experience. And you will move on from judging the experience to just be the experience.

Long after you have felt abused and also hurt others. After you have hated enough and loved enough. Let fear consume you and been full of hope. Full of rage and full of compassion. You will be tired of feeling pulled around, in and out of experiences, avoiding them, and judging them. And you will finally surrender and just be the experience. This will help you to drop all your suffering on this planet. When you are sad, be sad. Hurt, in pain, wounded, do not resist being that. Healed, joyful, full of light, be that too.

You will seek to know who you truly are ... and your intention to find this will lead you back to your pure essence, the part of the experience that doesn't change, but stays the same. When you hold it all as who you are, you are in your complete wholeness, and it will make the experience on Earth feel like heaven. Because you are heaven. Rest in the experience, whatever it is, it will always bring you home to your heart.

HEATHER: When we have not worked through our trauma or the pain from the past, we tend to act out of these wounds in our interactions with others. Unresolved trauma is often passed down in families from one generation to the next. And when we carry deep wounds that are buried within, we often project our anger, blame, and pain onto others and act out of this woundedness. We stay caught in one or more of the roles in the relational triad associated with abuse—victim, perpetrator, or rescuer. The unresolved trauma then gets perpetuated in feelings, thoughts, and patterns of behavior with others. Individual trauma then becomes seeded in the collective consciousness and in the dynamics in our societies, and then countries around the world mirror this trauma signature. Our world is currently in a time of intense turbulence, and our planet is threatened by the destructive effects of our human exploitation of her resources. We are all acting out our individual and collective trauma.

It is important to remember that the trauma that we experience collectively in wars, violence, sexual abuse, human trafficking, or misuse of power, as well as in cataclysmic Earth changes or crises, are encoded in our cellular memories. If we do not heal these wounds, individually and collectively, we will act them out in destructive ways in interactions with each other. It is only as we heal individually that we are able to also heal collectively. It is only as we face and work through these wounds that we also can reduce the violence in the world and stop the abuse of the Earth. In healing ourselves, we are able to emanate healing energy to others and into the collective consciousness. We cannot generate world peace if we are not at peace in our own hearts. We cannot co-create a new world based on love and respect if we are in inner conflict and still caught in the trauma of the past. We cannot "love our neighbor as we love ourselves," if we have not healed and learned how to hold ourselves with love and compassion.

Loving others does not mean accommodating or sacrificing our own needs; that is actually a way to reinforce our early wounds that leave us feeling exploited and resentful. True love is about the capacity to see ourselves and the other in our wholeness and to mirror this back to others. True love means having clear boundaries and calling out the best in others and refusing to participate in traumatizing or hurtful patterns in a relationship. As we engage with others in this way, we create a more loving energy field and environment around us. In this way, we are emanating and seeding this love and wisdom into the collective consciousness and supporting our world in healing and moving into a more conscious way of being. In a similar way, we cannot support the healing of the Earth if we are caught in fear or anger or despair. In loving the Earth and being in right relationship with her, our actions will reflect that love, gratitude, and reverence, and we will stop harming or exploiting our Earth. We will truly be supporting the Earth in her transition and in her healing if we are in a loving relationship with her and see the ways in which she is whole and a beautiful expression of the love and creativity of the Cosmos. Then, we can mirror back to her wholeness and co-create with her a new Earth and a new consciousness.

To heal is ultimately to live in balance and harmony. Everything is conscious and has its own vibration. As we come back into balance and alignment, we remember our song that is part of the symphony of the cosmos. Then, we live in a way that is in harmony rather than being discordant. We tune into and honor the rhythms and music around us and find our place in this cosmic dance. Healing is ultimately about coming back into balance and living in right relationship with all that is—with ourselves, each other, with the Earth and sky. As we heal, we are able to remember that we are all beings of light. As we honor the light within us, we can also celebrate the light of all around us. We realize that our world is like a prism, and the energy of the light and love of the Cosmos manifests in us like the colors of the rainbow. Rather than fearing the differences between us, we are then able to honor our diversity and remember that we are all part of the rainbow of light and love. Then, together, we will heal, align with Source, and live in wholeness and oneness with all that is.

CONCLUSION

*There will come a day when people of all races, colors, and creeds
will put aside their differences. They will come together in love, joining hands in
unification, to heal the Earth and all Her children.
They will move over the Earth like a great Whirling Rainbow,
bringing peace, understanding, and healing everywhere they go.
Many creatures thought to be extinct or mythical will resurface at this time;
the great trees that perished will return almost overnight.
All living things will flourish, drawing sustenance from the breast of
our Mother, the Earth.
The great spiritual Teachers who walked the Earth
and taught the basics of the truths of the Whirling Rainbow Prophecy
will return and walk amongst us once more,
sharing their power and understanding with all.
We will learn how to see and hear in a sacred manner.
Men and women will be equals in the way Creator intended them to be;
all children will be safe anywhere they want to go.
Elders will be respected and valued for their contributions to life.
Their wisdom will be sought out.
The whole Human race will be called The People
and there will be no more war, sickness, or hunger forever.*

—Navajo-Hopi Prophecy of the Whirling Rainbow

Appendix

Meditation practices

Meditation to align with your center, the Earth and Sky and Source

Sit comfortably in a chair or stand. Tune into your body and feel your feet firmly on the ground. Begin to breathe in and out slowly and deeply. Imagine energetic roots going from your feet down into the Earth. As you breathe out, allow any stress, tension, or distracting thoughts to flow down through your body, through your feet and into the Earth. With your in-breath, take in your connection to Mother Earth and her grounding, loving energy. Let the energy of the Earth fill you and flow through you. Continue to breathe in and out in this way until you begin to feel your body relax. Then draw that energy from the Earth up into your body, filling you and energizing you. Put your hands on your heart and feel that nurturance and love of Mother Earth filling your heart.

Now visualize your crown chakra, or the top of your head, opening to the energy of the sky. With your in-breath, bring in the healing energy of the Sun and the wisdom of the stars. Draw this energy into your body, allowing it to flow through every cell in your body. Feel the light clearing you and healing you. Continue to breathe in and out, feeling this energy of the Sun, Moon, and stars filling you with light and love and wisdom. Now visualize the energy of the Earth merging with the energy of the sky at your heart. Breathe in and out slowly and deeply, feeling this healing energy of the Earth and sky filling your heart. Feel your deep alignment with the Earth and with the sky and with your heart.

Now, as you are centered in your heart, draw in all of your emotions, and all aspects of yourself into your heart. Honor the full range of all of your experiences as they present in the moment. Hold the wholeness of who you are in your heart. Continue to breathe in and out slowly, honoring all that you have learned and all the ways that you have evolved through the times of pain and of joy in your life. Breathe in and honor all of those experiences and allow them to feel held in the loving, healing energies of the Earth and the sky that are flowing through and surrounding your heart.

Now, continuing to keep part of your focus on your heart, begin to also feel and sense the energy field around your body. Feel that spaciousness around you and gradually allow yourself to begin to feel your energy field expanding further and further out. Expand more and more until you feel the connection between your heart and the crystal core at the center of the Earth. Then allow yourself to feel your energy expand out to the brilliant healing light of the Sun. Continue to feel your energy expanding further and further out to merge with the heart of the Cosmos. Feel your heart pulsing with the rhythms of the Earth and Cosmos as you breathe in and out deeply. Allow yourself to simultaneously hold that awareness of your heart and your earthly experiences with the expansiveness of your energy merging with the Cosmos. You are in this body and you are one with all that is. Breathe in and out, holding the sense of mystery and wonder as you honor yourself and your oneness with the Cosmos.

Then, gradually, when you are ready, bring your full awareness back to your body. Gently draw in your energy, breathing in and out as you return your focus to your heart and your body and the present moment. Then give thanks, and open your eyes.

Meditation to de-stress and align with stillness

This meditation will guide you through a process of observing the flame as a way to let go of stress and align with stillness. Once you have the idea, you no longer need to read it through, just be with the flame.

Meditation with a candle: To begin, light a candle and then start by closing your eyes and making sure that you are in a comfortable position. Take note of how your body feels. Take a deep breath in, and as you exhale, notice where your body feels the most tense. Focus on these areas as you take in another breath. Allow the tension to flow out and away from you as you breathe out. As you inhale, notice how raised or how tight your shoulders are. And then, with the exhale, let your shoulders relax down a little further, feeling the tension release out of the muscles, and allow yourself to settle down into a more comfortable position.

Continue to breathe in and out slowly and deeply as you open your eyes with a soft gaze and observe the flame of the candle. As you sit peacefully, keep your attention on the flame, and notice the gentle flickers of light that are coming off the flame. Watch the dancing light from the candle. Feel yourself relaxing as you watch the beautiful patterns made by the light of the candle. Observe the color of the flame, how the orange glow becomes brighter as it grows towards the tip of the flame. Do you see any blue hues in the flame? As you watch the flame, does the size or shape change? Allow yourself to feel more deeply into the gentle flickering of the flame. Observe how the wax slowly melts around the flame. Imagine that the warm flame gently melts away the stress and tension you have been holding in your body. As the candle burns, feel the tension easing and the relaxation flowing through your body. Notice the wax becoming softer. Feel your body also becoming softer.

Notice again the soft flame at the top of the candle. See how it flickers slightly in response to your breath as you gently exhale. Watch how the flame shifts as you breathe. Now turn your attention back to the wax of the candle. The softening wax is melting, turning to liquid. It is warm and flowing, free from tension. See the wax of the candle melting, and feel the way your tension is melting away. As wax continues to melt over time, it will slowly overflow, and pour down the side of the candle, drop by drop. Feel all the stress you are holding onto drip away with each drop of wax from the candle. The soft flame of relaxation warms you from the inside, melting away all the tension. Watch the wax melting, and let yourself feel the same effects on the tension in your body; as the tightness melts, you feel more fluid and relaxed.

As you watch the flame, continue to merge deeper and deeper with the glowing light. Feel this light moving into you and through you, filling you with a soft warm light, and with a sense of hope and peace. Feel how deeply you are becoming aligned to the stillness inside. Try to hold this alignment and sense of peace for a few minutes. Pull in from the flame healing light and love, and then release to the flame all you are wanting to let go of. Then when you feel ready, thank the flame, the energy of heat and light, that can also represent the Divine. Take a deep breath and exhale through your mouth, blowing out the candle flame.

Meditations for moving through depression

This is an exercise that will help you access and energize what is beneath or beyond all the layers of depression and feeling—a pure state of consciousness, peace, joy, lightness of being. Begin by connecting to the depression, heaviness, or lack of motivation that you feel. You can even move more into any feelings or sensations that might be around the depression. See if you can visualize what you are feeling as a mass that has qualities or structure to it. It could take form as a heavy blanket, a stone on the chest, or like mud that is covering the body. The point is to be able to connect with it in a way that you can work with it. Now, using your imagination, see if you can physically move it. If it is a blanket, can you remove it? If it is a stone, can you push it off your chest? If it feels like mud, can you wash it off your body? If you can't get a visual image, that is fine. See if you can imagine removing the heavy energy like you would shovel snow off the driveway or rake leaves off the lawn. When you feel you have removed enough of the heavy dense energy with your imagination, see if there are other layers underneath that also need to be cleaned off. Do this until you feel the heaviness has lifted, and you can sense into what might be under or beyond the depression and feelings. (If using your imagination to clear the heaviness doesn't work, then with your intention, simply tell yourself to take your attention to what is under the heaviness.)

Now that you are with what is under the depression, sense into what it is. If it is an emotion, thought, memory, or sensation, allow yourself to just be with it. Is there healing that can be done here? What does it need? How can you best take care of it? After you feel you have worked with what is just underneath the depression, see if there are more layers that are coming up to be healed. Continue to be with what arises, and send healing love and light into these deeper layers. At some point, as the layers heal and release, you should be able to be in the space and energy of pure consciousness, peace, contentment, lightness of being. You want to stay in this state of stillness for as long as you can, because as you keep your attention here, you are building this energy inside of you.

Stand with your feet spread shoulder-width apart and with your arms down at your sides. If you need to sit or lie down, that is all right too; make this meditation your own. Close your eyes and envision a brilliant column of light coming down from above you. Let it gently descend down through your head, neck, shoulders, chest, organs, pelvic area, legs, and finally out through your feet. The light's energy vibrates through you and breaks up all the heavy dark energy. As it moves down through your body, it cleanses and begins to release all of the depression and pain from your muscles, cells, tissues, blood, and bones, replacing the inner emptiness with light and soothing energy. Then, envision the Earth's energy, coming up through the soles of your feet and into your body, helping to gently find and pull back down any dark dense energy, again through the soles of your feet. Breathe slowly and deeply, as the dark energy is moving down and being replaced by light healing energy from above. When you feel the process is complete, thank Mother Earth and the healing light or cosmic energy for their assistance and love. Sometimes you might want to go outside and be in nature, to connect more fully with the flow of love and pure consciousness that is around you as well as within you.

Working with Sacred Circles

Being in a Sacred Circle

HEATHER: Being in a sacred circle is a profound and transformative experience. It gives us the opportunity to "hear each other into speech"[10] and to find and speak our own deepest truths. It is a practice that has existed for thousands of years in every culture. The circle process involves deepening our connections with each other and with the spirit in each of us and with the Spirit of the circle that is beyond the sum of our individual identities. Being in a sacred circle is about tuning into each others' words, emotions, and energies as well as attuning to the Spirit of the circle that has brought us together and guides us in our process.

Here are a few guidelines that can help in this process:

Council format – One of the main components of the council format is that it gives people an opportunity to share from their hearts. From this openness comes a weaving together of stories, of experiences, of personalities, which all combine to create a group or circle synergy. The sum of the whole is exponentially greater than its parts.

How it works: We sit in circle, and a talking stick or talking piece is passed (or you might use an egg-shaped stone, representing the potential and the totality of each individual and of the Circle as a whole). When an individual has the egg, or talking piece, they have the undivided attention of the Circle. They should not be interrupted, unless the group facilitators feel a need to do so—for instance, to call for a break, to resolve an issue or question, etc. An exception would be if you did not hear what a person said, you may ask them to speak up or to repeat what they said. When holding the talking object, your task is to speak from the heart, to discern what is important to share with the Circle, and to practice brevity.

As listeners, our task is to open our hearts and to listen as fully as we can without judgment to the individual who is holding the egg or talking object.

---

[10] Morton, Nelle. *The Journey is Home*. Boston: Beacon Press, 1985.

We listen with our hearts and try to feel what the person is sharing. We try, as a person who is waiting to share, to not rehearse what we will say when it is our turn to hold the object. Doing so takes us out of the moment and away from truly being with an open heart with the one who is sharing. We cultivate trust that Spirit will guide us in sharing what is sacred to us, in sharing what needs to be brought to the Circle, and that the rest will stay behind. We learn to search for what it is that the Circle needs from us—what bit of wisdom is percolating up from our depths that must be shared, what treasure is coming to the surface from the depths of our souls, that will be of benefit to the Circle. It is important to speak from our own hearts, and if we are compelled to respond to what another has shared earlier, to do so from what was touched in us, not as a way of commenting on or evaluating another's sharing.

Confidentiality – It is extremely important for the safety and integrity of the Circle to keep confidential all that is shared within the Circle. Also, it is important not to talk about what has been shared within the circle outside of the circle—even with others in the circle. With friends and loved ones, it is fine to share your own process but not the experiences or disclosures of others.

Watching for our own projections – In a circle, we learn about ourselves as we are mirrored by others, both in how we are seen and affirmed by others and in how we can become aware of split-off parts of ourselves as we experience them in others. Watch for ways you may be activated or triggered by others. Learn to work with these experiences as a way to deepen your own self-awareness rather than polarizing or projecting those aspects of yourself on the other and then distancing or reacting to that person.

Dealing with conflict – Many of us are afraid of conflict and anger. Yet, to be whole, we need to honor our full range of emotions. In a circle, when you feel anger or conflict, acknowledge it in yourself. Look to see what issues are getting activated for you and what you can learn from this experience. Then, in dealing with the other person, share your feelings with respect, openness, and a willingness to hear the other's feelings and perspectives. Use "I" statements and avoid placing blame or focusing on the other person's behavior. Take responsibility for your own part in the conflict. Also, it is important to realize that we cannot control or change others, only ourselves.

Take responsibility for your own process – Being in a circle is a shared experience, and yet we each are responsible for our own process, feelings, experiences, and actions in this journey together.

Honoring the shared journey and the growth of the Circle – Being in a circle means deepening in relationships with others and also honoring the circle as an entity that is more than our collective identities and relationships. When difficulties arise in a circle, it is an opportunity for the circle as a whole to grow and to deepen. Certain circle members may bring forward characteristics or dynamics so that, as a circle, we can more fully integrate these aspects. Rather than seeing those individuals or dynamics as a problem, we can use them as challenges for deepening our process as a circle. Growth in a circle means learning to continually expand our capacity to hold each others' differentness and the range of emotions and experiences in our midst.

Listening to the silence – Being in a circle is an opportunity to find our unique voices and also to listen to the depth of wisdom in the silence between the words. It is also important to attune to the rhythms and energy of the circle, to what is unsaid as well as what is spoken. It is also useful to engage in meditation and shamanic practices that assist us in being in an altered state of consciousness and attuning to the voice of Spirit within us and between us.

Giving and Receiving – For many of us, it is easier to give to others than to care for ourselves or to receive from others. It is important to allow ourselves to be deeply nurtured and to honor the gifts from others and to keep this in balance with our caring for others.

Developing the witness self – As we grow in consciousness and self-awareness, we can utilize the witness self to observe our emotions and behaviors rather than being mired in our experiences. We soon learn to let go of our stories and our identification with the details of our lives and honor the soul-self that is beyond time and space and that can guide us in our growth and purpose in this lifetime.

Having fun – As we develop our witness self, we realize that many things that often distress us are not that important in the larger scheme of life. The more that we are able to laugh at ourselves and with each other, the more our circle will deepen in closeness and in enjoyment of each other.

Be in the mystery – Being in a circle is a mysterious dance of intimacy and distance, times of growth and rest, light and dark, sorrow and joy.... The journey within a Sacred Circle will often surprise us and challenge us, and it will be filled with magic, wonder, and mystery—if we are open to the moment and how the process unfolds.

The practice of sitting in a Sacred Circle is very ancient. It is a gift that many people never experience. From being in a Sacred Circle, we emerge transformed, with a deepened sense of self, of the others in the Circle, and of the Spirit which lives within the Circle. The energy of a Sacred Circle, like a stone tossed into a pond, ripples out with love and healing energy, affecting all who are in our lives.

About the Authors

KRISTINA LEA has a Bachelor of Science in Psychology with a focus on early development and a minor in Sociology from Texas A&M University. She worked for many years as a postpartum doula and lactation consultant with women after delivery, with an emphasis on high risk infants and in helping new mothers with postpartum depression. Kristina is trained in the healing modalities of Usui Shiki Ryoho system of Reiki, shamanic practices, Biofield Tuning, Zero Balancing, and Chinese Energetic Medicine. She also teaches and leads groups in meditation and mindfulness. Her work focuses on helping people to heal from trauma and to integrate their lives on all levels: physical, emotional, mental and spiritual.

Kristina can be reached through her website: www.open2truefreedom.com.

HEATHER ENSWORTH Ph.D. is a clinical psychologist with over 30 years of clinical experience with an emphasis on trauma work. In addition, she has years of experience in neuropsychological evaluation as well as in the supervision and training of therapists and in teaching psychology at the graduate level. Heather has spent years studying ancient and indigenous healing traditions and other forms of holistic healing. She is also an internationally known astrologer.

In addition, Heather has a background in cultural anthropology with a focus on ritual and symbolism and has a Masters degree in theology. She has facilitated earth-based and women's spirituality programs for over 25 years. Heather strongly believes that to truly heal ourselves and support the healing of the Earth, we need to be in right relationship — with ourselves, with each other, with the Earth, with the Cosmos, and with all of life.

Heather is the author of *Finding Our Center: Wisdom from the Stars and Planets in Times of Change*, IUniverse, Inc, New York, NY, 2009 and *Higher Vibrational Living: Through Astrology, Essential Oils and Chinese Medicine*, Body-Feedback for Health, Madison, WI, 2018. She also has many videos on her youtube channel.

Heather can be reached through her website:

www.risingmoonhealingcenter.com.